SMART MONEY

Using Educational Resources to
Accomplish Ambitious Learning Goals

SMART MONEY

Using Educational Resources to Accomplish Ambitious Learning Goals

JACOB E. ADAMS, JR.

Editor

Harvard Education Press

Cambridge, Massachusetts

Library of Congress Control Number 2009942797

Paperback ISBN 978-1-934742-59-4
Library Edition ISBN 978-1-934742-60-0

Published by Harvard Education Press,
an imprint of the Harvard Education Publishing Group

Harvard Education Press
8 Story Street
Cambridge, MA 02138

Cover Design: Nancy Goulet

The typefaces used in this book are Sabon for text and Clarendon for display.

Contents

Acknowledgments

The research and convening that led to this book were supported by the School Finance Redesign Project at the University of Washington's Center on Reinventing Public Education through funding by the Bill & Melinda Gates Foundation, Grant No. 29252. A portion of the work for chapter 11 also was supported by The Spencer Foundation, Grant No. 200900171. The views expressed in these pages are those of the authors and are not intended to represent the project, center, university, or foundations.

I owe special thanks to Christopher Cross, Christopher Edley, Jr., James Guthrie, Paul Hill, Michael Kirst, Goodwin Liu, Susanna Loeb, David Monk, Allan Odden, and Joanne Weiss, my colleagues on the National Working Group on Funding Student Learning, who navigated cross currents of perspective and experience to find a common landfall.

A number of individuals shaped the School Finance Redesign Project (SFRP) in meaningful ways, and it gives me real pleasure to acknowledge their contributions. John Bransford, Robert Durante, Paul Gazzero, Michael Goetz, Eric Hanushek, Julia Koppich, Lorraine McDonnell, Lawrence Picus, Lori Rhodes, Diana Sharp, and Jason Willis braved commissions and produced papers that challenged and broadened the working group's thinking.

Melissa Bowen, Mike Foote, Scott Joftus, Charles Kerchner, and Lynn Olsen provided fresh perspectives at critical moments that helped the working group move toward a coherent and useful conclusion.

Heather Barney, Melissa Bowen, Richard Brandon, Tricia Davis, Michael DeArmond, Scott DeBurgomaster, Kate Destler, Shelley De Wys, Stephen Frank, Dan Goldhaber, Kacey Guin, Janet Hansen, Gina Ikemoto, Albert Liu, Julie Marsh, Allison Demeritt, Anthony Milanowski, Karen Hawley Miles, Allan Odden, Dan Player, and Marguerite Roza conducted the studies and wrote the reports that gave SFRP its empirical legs. And Julie Angeley, Deb Britt, and Lydia Rainy skillfully produced and disseminated the reports.

Tom Vander Ark, Stefanie Sanford, David Ferrero, Shari Ranis, and Melissa Chabran at the Bill & Melinda Gates Foundation saw the need for this work, tracked its developments, and created connections to other initiatives that made it immediately practical to groups struggling with resource challenges.

All those named above—and none more than me—owe a debt of gratitude to Shelley De Wys, whose tireless and effective work kept this enterprise on track.

Thank you, one and all. It was a pleasure working with you and learning from you.

As the School Finance Redesign Project developed, it became increasingly clear that the promise of using educational resources to accomplish ambitious learning goals depends on new directions in education finance policy and practice. If this book plays a role in that transformation, it will have accomplished its purpose.

—*Jacob E. Adams, Jr., Claremont Graduate University*

Smart Money and America's Schools

Jacob E. Adams, Jr.

W hat would it take for America's schools to accomplish the ambitious learning goals that state and federal governments now demand? The answer depends, in part, on the scale of the challenge.

THE STUDENT PERFORMANCE CHALLENGE

For more than a quarter-century U.S. schools have been striving for better results and falling short. The new language of expectation has all students achieving at "proficient" levels or performing "at standards." Both terms signal student competence over challenging academic content and its application to real-world situations. At face value, this goal seems commonsensical. After all, student learning matters—to the students themselves and to the communities that rise and fall on their participation and productivity. The problem is that American students do not come close to this level of learning.

Results from the National Assessment of Educational Progress, the self-styled "nation's report card," show that 33 percent of fourth graders, 31 percent of eighth graders, and 35 percent of twelfth graders achieve at or above the proficient level on tests of reading.[1] In mathematics, 39 percent of fourth graders, 34 percent of eighth graders, and 23 percent of twelfth graders score at or above this level. Among the states, Massachusetts students score the highest, with 49 percent of fourth graders and 43 percent of eighth graders performing at or above proficient in reading, and 57 percent of fourth graders and 51 percent of eighth graders reaching this performance level in mathematics. The District of Columbia defines the bottom of the performance range, with 14 percent of fourth graders and 12 percent of eighth graders achieving at or above the proficient mark in reading, and 17 percent of fourth graders and 11 percent of eighth graders reaching this mark in mathematics.

The numbers may seem tedious, but they make the point. Only about one-third of U.S. students perform at a level that authorities define as competent. Even the best-performing state sees only half, or a bit more, of its students perform at this level of accomplishment.

The performance picture gets bleaker if three other considerations make it into the mix. First, the trend in student performance is essentially flat. During the twenty years between 1990 and 2009, fourth graders improved their reading scores by 4 points and eighth graders by 3 points, while twelfth graders dropped 6 points, all on a 500-point scale. The same flat-growth pattern holds in the percentage of students scoring at or above proficient in reading, with fourth graders advancing only 4 percentage points and eighth graders only 2 points during this same period. Mathematics results were better. Here fourth graders improved 27 points and eighth graders 20 points.[2] And both groups more than doubled their percentage scoring at or above proficiency, with fourth graders jumping from 13 to 39 percent, and eighth graders improving from 15 to 34 percent. Yet even accounting for these math results, the overall twenty-year student performance record is discouraging.

Second, student performance data show a persistent achievement gap between white and nonwhite students. That is, white students outscored their black and Hispanic counterparts in reading by 27 and 26 points, respectively, in fourth grade; by 27 and 25 points, respectively, in eighth grade; and by 26 and 21 points, respectively, in twelfth grade. These gaps have narrowed since the early 1990s at the fourth- and eighth-grade levels, but only by 1 and 5 points, respectively; and they have widened for high school seniors by 2 and 3 points, respectively.

Third, the rigor of performance standards varies from state to state. Simply put, some state standards are high but others are low, with passing scores ranging from the 6th to the 77th percentile on an independent scale.[3] This variation led analysts to observe that two-thirds of U.S. students attend class in states that have middling to low expectations for what students should know and be able to do, labeling these differences the "proficiency illusion" and arguing that "Mr. and Mrs. Smith know that little Susie is 'proficient.' What they don't know is that 'proficient' doesn't mean much."[4] Even so, according to the same analysis, eight states have lowered their standards by making their tests easier. A more recent U.S. Department of Education study confirmed these differences.[5] From a national perspective, cross-state variations in learning standards render student results difficult to interpret, and thus less meaningful in terms of gauging public education's success.

Of course, there is another dimension to student performance. Analysts have identified schools and school systems that have "doubled student performance" or cases in which low-income and minority students have successfully completed their academic programs ready for the next step.[6] Each year thousands of students graduate from high school and matriculate at the nation's colleges and universities or secure productive work. These are worthy accomplishments. The problem, again, is that these individual and small-group successes belie the system-level results that shape America's challenge regarding student performance. All told, U.S. elementary and secondary schools have made incremental gains and a few places have made big leaps forward, but, by and large, student performance still falls far short of expectations.

REFORMING SCHOOLS WITHOUT IMPROVING RESULTS

It is not that America's schools fall short for lack of trying. Taking shape in California's electoral and legislative politics of the early 1980s and then motivated nationwide by a report from the National Commission on Excellence in Education, changes began to enter the education landscape.[7] In no time, elected officials, judges, policy entrepreneurs, educators, and voters turned U.S. schools into a veritable laboratory of education reform. Along these lines, so-called intensification strategies worked from the top down, raising graduation requirements, adding time to school days and years, and boosting homework. Restructuring strategies worked from the bottom up, adopting site-based management, crafting comprehensive school reforms, and distributing leadership more widely.[8] Privatization strategies worked from the outside in, introducing school choice, charters, contracting, and vouchers into an otherwise bureaucratic environment. In the litigious arena of education finance, equity claimants attempted to equalize the distribution of resources, and hence educational opportunity, while adequacy proponents sought to infuse public schools with sufficient resources so that *equal* opportunity also meant *meaningful* opportunity.[9]

Still more reforms surfaced. Coalescing in the 1990s, the standards movement clarified learning goals, and accountability initiatives linked state expectations to schoolwork. Designers of systemic school reform sought greater policy coherence by aligning learning goals, curriculum, professional development, and assessment, ensuring that education's essential elements all pushed in one direction.

At the more granular level of classrooms, teacher quality strategies introduced skill tests for beginning teachers, differentiated teacher compensation, and assessed the "value added" by each teacher to student outcomes.[10] Some reforms even overran the boundaries of K–12 itself, promoting early learning and school-linked service initiatives that pegged student success, respectively, to the running start that preschool provides or to the social and emotional support available through health and social services.

Behind every reform one finds a theory that (1) uniquely explains why low student performance persists and (2) shapes a policy remedy to fit that explanation. The list of rationales has grown to include low effort, ineffective school structures, social and economic pathologies, unequal or insufficient resources, and calcified bureaucracy. It includes ambiguous goals, unaccountable work, misaligned policies, lack of school readiness, ineffective teaching, and more. Policy remedies have ranged from silver bullet solutions like California's class size reduction initiative to whole-system change such as Kentucky's omnibus education reform.[11]

Three decades of theorizing, policy making, and searching for positive effects have altered the education landscape. Reforms have changed policies at all levels of government, defining goals, creating standards, developing tests, increasing regulations, and so on. Reforms have introduced new institutional structures, adding school site councils, charter schools, family resource centers, and accountable relationships. In turn, new policies and institutional arrangements have shifted authority over education's goals and work from local educators and interest groups to state policy makers, business leaders, mayors, and parents.[12]

In these ways and others, the landscape looks different in 2010 from what it looked like in 1980, but the difference is not without cost. One analyst described this degree of change as "shock and overload."[13] Another observer diagnosed the nation's proclivity for reforming "again, again, and again."[14] Bluegrass State educators captured reform's turmoil, effort, and uncertainty in the metaphor "rebuilding the airplane while flying it."[15] What's missing from this new landscape are improvements in student learning that match public expectations and that, after a survey of all the commotion, would make a "tough but worth it" judgment more satisfying.

The Legacy of School Reform

Modest results notwithstanding, three developments from this reform era shape the context in which future educational improvements must be won. The first development deals with policy theory. Standards-based reform, encompassing performance accountability, has become the standout survivor of the education reform experiments. It now constitutes the predominant school improvement approach in the United States. All states and the federal government base their main school improvement activities on some version of this theory, stimulating like-minded efforts in every school and district in the country.

That said, the ascendance of standards and accountability has not fully displaced competing theories nor their policy and practice progeny. Many locations maintain a diversified approach to the issue, even if other elements in the reform portfolio are minor by comparison. But standards and accountability set the tone: it is now all about the results students achieve.

The second development affects education governance. Education reforms centralized authority. State courts and legislatures, for instance, laid greater claim to public education during the 1980–2010 period, affirming the state's central role and finding new constitutional obligations in state education clauses, dictating what students should know and should be able to do, assuming a larger share of education funding, and controlling local resource decisions through greater use of tax policies and targeted spending programs.

Similarly, the federal government extended its reach into the nation's schools through the No Child Left Behind Act (NCLB), in effect using the standards and accountability platform to craft a new federal role in education.[16] The assumption of centralized responsibility brings with it an even greater press for centralized solutions, just as it creates new electoral dependencies between state officials and education-oriented interests.[17]

The third development relates to learning ambitions themselves. Importantly, public aspirations changed, ratcheting upward, first, to a definition of excellence that had each student performing "at the boundary of individual ability."[18] Then it rose again to a federal legislative commitment to "leave no child behind," the latter promising all students "at standards" by 2014. The difference between each student's individual best and all students at standards changes the very definition of educational success.

Let us be clear: state and federal policy now demands that all students, regardless of race, language, economic status, or disability, must achieve a level of success in core academic subjects that has never before been broadly accomplished. This goal changes the public and professional commitments needed to get the job done, just as it removes opportunities to excuse failure based on pernicious interpretations of "individual best."

Ambitious Learning Goals Signal an Institutional Transition

New, ambitious learning goals surely put U.S. schools in the midst of a critical transition. No longer merely erecting buildings, opening schoolhouse doors, or "delivering" programs and instruction, public schools now must educate all students so that they meet mandated standards.

The track record of the past twenty or so years indicates that schools do not know how to accomplish the task. Neither did NASA, in 1962, know how to achieve President Kennedy's seminal commitment to land a man on the moon by the end of the decade and return him safely to Earth. But the agency's administrators, engineers, and astronauts, in concert with their elected benefactors and public supporters, accepted the challenge and went about marshaling the technical, economic, and political capacities to accomplish the job. Surely, public schools can do the same. President Kennedy's words almost could be expropriated for the purpose: "We meet in an hour of change and challenge, in a decade of hope and fear, in an age of both knowledge and ignorance . . . We choose to [educate all children to standards] . . . because that goal will serve to organize and measure the best of our energies and skills, because that challenge is one that we are willing to accept, one we are unwilling to postpone, and one which we intend to win."[19]

Transitions can be disconcerting. One day schools were doing fine. Then elected officials upped the ante, and suddenly schools were failing or at least far behind the target. Also disquieting, transitions may require a retooling of institutional capacity, a search for the technologies, resources, and support that match the goal.[20] Public schools now find themselves in this position. That is, the magnitude and novelty of the ambition—never before this high, never before broadly achieved—allow some latitude in interpreting the status of student performance in 2010, but they likely necessitate new ways of approaching the work, new technologies, or other nonincremental fixes.

Whatever the right approach, transitions do not diminish the urgency, alter the challenge, nor excuse the gap between success and failure. To all those responsible for change, transitions should signal the need to work the problem in all its technical, economic, and political dimensions and to judge success and failure in those terms.

The Stakes of Success and Failure

Where does this picture of student performance and education reform leave the United States? In 1983, the new excellence-oriented education debate was all about mediocre student performance and international economic competition. Twenty-seven years later—after two full generations of students have transited K–12—the continuing education debate is about mediocre student performance and international economic competition. The competitors have changed, with China and India replacing West Germany and Japan as the economic bugaboos. Cold war geopolitics have given way to a "hot, flat, and crowded" world.[21] Economies have boomed and busted. Throughout, U.S. schools seemed animated by an increasing sense of urgency but an incommensurate ability to respond.

Fundamental to this sense of urgency is the seemingly uniform assumption that poor educational performance puts economic and civic life at risk. Describing education as "the most important domestic issue of the 21st century," national commentator Jonathan Alter went on to argue that "if we don't tuck in our shirts and pay attention to educating the workforce of the future, we're going to flunk as a nation. The days when we could write off millions of young people and expect to survive economically are over."[22]

This sentiment has been brewing for some time. In the run-up to the millennium, academic and governmental analysts touted a twenty-first-century workplace that would demand highly educated and trained workers, workers who could adapt as jobs change and who could increase their productivity to stay competitive in a global marketplace.[23] From this vantage, problematic levels of academic performance put students at risk of leaving school lacking the knowledge and skills they need to succeed in a rapidly changing and increasingly demanding environment.

More recent analyses do nothing to allay fears of this likelihood. A 2009 report from the Public Policy Institute of California, for example, demonstrated an impending skills gap in which California's economy would demand more skilled workers than the state could provide. According to the report, that skills gap portended a less-productive economy, lower personal incomes, reduced tax revenue, and more dependence on social services.[24] Similarly, weak academic preparation makes it increasingly difficult for adults to enjoy or participate effectively in a civic life that forges equal opportunities, unifies diverse populations, enjoys the rights and effects the responsibilities of citizenship, and improves social conditions.[25]

In fact, in the context of legal challenges to state education finance systems, state courts have defined a constitutional obligation to produce learning outcomes that bolster economic and civic participation. In *Rose v. Council for Better Education, Inc.*, for instance, the Kentucky Supreme Court defined an "adequate education" in terms of seven qualities.

(i) [S]ufficient oral and written communication skills to enable students to function in a complex and rapidly changing civilization; (ii) sufficient knowledge of economic, social, and political systems to enable students to make informed choices; (iii) sufficient understanding of governmental processes to enable students to understand issues that affect his or her community, state, and nation; (iv) sufficient self-knowledge and knowledge or his or her mental and physical wellness; (v) sufficient grounding in the arts to enable each student to appreciate his or her cultural and historical heritage; (vi) sufficient training or preparation for advanced training in either academic or vocational fields to enable each child to choose and pursue life work intelligently; and (vii) sufficient levels of academic or vocational skills to enable public school students to compete favorably with their counterparts in surrounding states, in academics or in the job market.[26]

Notice that all these qualities address levels of knowledge and skill that allow students to act competently in life's various dimensions.

Similarly, in *Campaign for Fiscal Equity v. State of New York*, the New York Court of Appeals anchored its definition of a "sound basic education" in the most fundamental of civic duties: voting and serving on juries.[27] Think about that. Given the scope and complexity of modern-day electoral choices and legal actions, an education that provides individuals with the literacy, calculating, and verbal skills to effectively vote in elections and serve on juries constitutes a reasonably high standard of academic and analytic achievement. In turn, the consequence of not performing at this level likely diminishes the efficacy of public decision making.

The notion that education is a solution to broader economic and civic challenges is as old as the republic, and the connection between learning and economic and civic capacity remains plausible.[28] As skill requirements for jobs increase, as the complexities of civic life grow, it is not surprising that learning goals also will rise, keeping pace with the new demands. That is why the constant across these emerging standards, judicial and legislative perspectives, and cascading reforms is the demand that public schools turn out students who perform at proficient levels. In the demanding context of the twenty-first century, educational programs must support state standards and students must demonstrate their mastery of content. Yesterday's input- and process-oriented educational expectations have given way to measures of what students know and are able to do. Such ambition brings this discussion full circle to student performance.

Educating only one-third of U.S. students to meet standards, making only painstaking progress toward that goal, experiencing persistent achievement gaps, and calling different levels of achievement by the same name define the performance challenge that confronts U.S. schools. Educating *all* students to meet standards begins by acknowledging the magnitude of this challenge and by anticipating policy and professional responses on this scale. Knowing what other reformers have attempted, and why, helps shape these responses, helps answer another part of the question, What would it take? It takes more than earlier initiatives have been able to accomplish.

In a context of rising ambitions, decades-long effort, and mediocre results, are continued change and uncertainty worth the effort? It depends. If student learning is important to economic and civic life, if learning standards are meaningful in relation to that life, and if legislative policies fairly represent public ambitions and commitments, then poor student performance is a problem worth solving. If public schools are an institution in transition, then the continued search for new technical, economic, and political capacity is an effort worth maintaining. Once the nation is resolved to the task, the question remains: how do elected officials and educators accomplish it? A smart-money perspective on these matters provides a novel approach to the predicament.

SMART MONEY AND AMERICA'S SCHOOLS

What is "smart money"? And how does it advance the search for greater student learning? In everyday language, smart money is a bet or investment made by individuals whose experience or information helps them discern advantages and reap high returns. In this book, particularly, smart money is a metaphor, a figure of speech that represents a simple, powerful idea: using educational resources to accomplish ambitious learning goals.

As an analytical perspective or investment strategy, smart money has the potential to upend conventional finance practices, changing the way elected officials and educators distribute, use, and account for educational resources. To the extent that smart money manages this disruption, it will do so by redefining the context of resource decision making, enabling a fresh and critical look at the finance systems that governments operate today.

A Commitment to Student Learning

Smart money redefines the resource context, first, by taking seriously the new public commitment to educate all students to meet standards. Gaining momentum and practical meaning since the mid-1980s, this commitment is evident in state-adopted content and performance standards that define what students should know and should be able to do.[29] It is evident in federal law that seeks "to close the achievement gap . . . so that no child will be left behind."[30] And, at this writing, it is evident in the Common Core State Standards Initiative of the National Governors Association and the Council of Chief State School Officers.[31] The latter addresses college- and career-readiness content and skills that developers describe as research- and evidence-based, internationally benchmarked, and aligned with college and work expectations. Smart money embraces the policy and practice implications of this commitment, as the following pages elaborate.

As you have seen, the commitment is ambitious, aspiring to educate all students to a level of academic success that has never been broadly achieved. Such ambitions make the task challenging but no less real. Public commitments either marshal effort and anticipate benefits, or they signify social ideals. Unless there is widespread acknowledgment that state and federal standards play a merely symbolic role in elementary and secondary education—an argument that schools on the receiving end of accountability would spurn—then the public can fairly expect elected officials, educators, and others to accomplish these ends.

The test of commitment becomes particularly tangible when elected officials and educators use the smart-money focus on learning to deflect competing claims that advocates would impose on schools. In short, if student learning matters, then the public interest in that learning must trump the private interests of adults who make narrower demands on the system. This balance may be hard to strike, given the dispersed authority, competition for resources, bargaining and coalition formation, responsiveness to constituent demands, individual agendas, and other governance dynamics that shape the context of schooling and its outcomes.[32] Yet these dynamics must be checked so that elected officials and educators can use available resources to accomplish the public goals that benefit communities broadly. Smart money can be a tool to deflect competing claims or a metric to signal movement off course, even when the move is intentional.

A New Stewardship of Results

Smart money redefines the resource context in a second way by crafting a new stewardship for educational resources. *Using* resources *to accomplish* ambitious learning goals construes resources as an instrument of student learning, a cause of the results schools achieve. Much of this book explains how this can happen. For now it is enough to note that this instrumental perspective takes elected officials and educators far afield from the issues of program fidelity (spending in required categories) and compliance accountability that drive many resource decisions. Running the shop while minding the money is a different kind of stewardship from one that expects results. In this regard, too, the fiduciary role of balancing revenues and expenditures, assessing school district fiscal conditions, and managing accounts, although always important, also must expand to include academic results and the resource uses that support them. A stewardship of results makes elected officials and educators responsible for outcomes, and not only opportunities.

Those results are the kicker. Americans spend more than $500 billion annually on elementary and secondary schools, making K–12 education the largest expenditure in state budgets.[33] This scale matches the public's long regard for education as the most important function of state and local government.[34] A return on this investment seems reasonable, particularly in hindsight, as conventional resource decisions seem, from this new vantage, perhaps not so smart.

Spending on elementary and secondary schools keeps going up. Between 1990 and 2005, inflation-adjusted expenditures increased 29 percent, to almost $11,000 per pupil, and this during a period when student performance remained essentially flat.[35] Conventional modes of funding school improvement—such as across-the-board salary increases, class size reduction, and targeted spending programs—have resulted in greater costs without corresponding gains in performance. High spenders and low spenders alike get good and bad results. Accordingly, a stewardship of results reasonably might ask whether or how conventional practices support greater student learning. And if not these practices, which ones?

A Broader View of Resources

Smart money redefines the resource context in a third way by broadening the view of resources that bear on the problem. Here *resources* encompass the funds governments allocate to education. They also encompass the teachers, time, books, buses, and other things those funds buy, what the New York Court of Appeals called the "instrumentalities of learning."[36] And they encompass the conditions that give those instrumentalities meaning: a teacher's motivation and skill, the knowledge a principal calls on in making resource decisions, the discretion to act on that knowledge, information that reveals instructional or learning problems, and so on.

These conditions affect the way the instrumentalities are employed, determining their practical effect on student learning. Therefore, they are just as much a resource as people, time, or money, and just as much the result of resource decision making as class sizes, bell schedules, or teacher salaries.

A New Resource System

Smart money alters the resource context in a final way by redefining the finance system that shapes schools and learning. It does this by breaking down conventional barriers between finance systems and resource allocation strategies. *Finance systems* are focused on policy design (taxing, distributing funds between levels of government, equalizing spending capacity, budgeting), whereas *resource allocation strategies* are focused on professional knowledge and implementation (connecting resources to learning—or not).

This division collapses in a smart-money context because smart money recognizes that policy designs enable or constrain professional knowledge and implementation options. Thus, policy designs circumscribe the resource decisions that educators can or will make.

This interdependence is evident in a negative sense, for instance, in the categorical funding, collective bargaining, and accounting mechanisms that motivate educators to make resource decisions they know will diminish the coherence of instructional programs, but they do it nevertheless to satisfy federal or state funding rules or to respond rationally to perverse incentives.[37] The only way to address system effects like this is to recognize the impediments, remove false or outdated distinctions among a system's parts, and retool the connections so that resources can become better instruments of learning. The result would be a resource system better able to bridge the divide between policy and practice.

Smart Money's Different Perspective

These things together—a serious commitment to educate all students to meet standards, a stewardship of results, a broader view of resources that bear on the problem, and a resource system that productively integrates policy and practice—answer another part of the question, What would it take? It takes a perspective that opens new opportunities to assesses the fit between learning goals and resource practices and to act accordingly, even if unconventionally.

Consider the implications. If the commitment to accomplish ambitious learning goals is serious, then those goals become the touchstone for resource decision making, top to bottom, and a shield against competing claims. If resources are an instrument of student learning, then resource decisions must be made strategically and explicitly with reference to that learning, with the recognition, all the while, that decision makers can act strategically only insofar as they know how to make that connection. If resources encompass funds, the things they buy, and the conditions that give them meaning, then the test of good decision making is the effect of those decisions on instruction, instructional supports, or learning. Anything short of these direct effects misses the point. If states were to better integrate the resource roles of policy and practice, then policy makers and practitioners together could more effectively figure out how much to spend, who gets what, how resources are used, and which outcomes to track, all with regard to ambitious learning goals.

These implications and the possibilities they represent challenge the conflicting commitments and claims, compliance orientation, formula-driven allocations, and compartmentalized responsibilities that typify education finance. The chapters that follow elaborate the difficulties and explore alternatives. Before I introduce those arguments, however, there is one final smart-money facet worth considering, one arrived at by grappling again with the question, What would it take?—this time from the vantage of doing the work that ambitious learning goals demand.

The Burden of Reforms That Work

Education reforms that would educate all students to meet standards carry an unusual burden. They must embody ideas and marshal resources that can accomplish a novel and ambitious goal, that succeed where nearly thirty years' worth of effort have not, and that navigate a transition of undetermined degree in public education's core technology. The burden increases when the uncertainties of large-scale change, the coincidence of change and experimentation, the need for new knowledge and skills, and the probable retooling of roles and responsibilities are factored in. If one wraps all this in the need to satisfy a persistent civic and economic urgency and in the recognition that results matter to notions of fairness or social justice, the task begins to take shape.

Few education reforms of the 1980–2010 period have even approximated this degree of change. Single-purpose initiatives, such as raising graduation requirements, reducing class size, or equalizing resources, are more typical of education policy making and reform. Even performance accountability or comprehensive school reforms, which arguably entail more moving parts, represent smaller-scale ambitions. Small-scale policy making involves relatively smaller technical, economic, and political demands and uncertainties, and that leads to smaller-scale effects, real and valuable though they may be.

Education reforms that would accomplish ambitious learning goals push in the other direction. Even reduced to its simplest conceptual elements, educating all students to meet standards will cause elected officials and educators to wrestle anew with the knotty—but ultimately tractable—issues of policy and practice that often stand in the way of accomplishing public goals.

In the public domain, accomplishing anything is the result of policy making and implementation. Ambitious learning goals are no exception. Working within the confines of political and economic feasibility, policy makers set goals and commit resources, and often they specify how those goals will be pursued, first establishing general strategies—for example, standard setting or class size reduction—and then focusing and enabling implementers' efforts through mandates, incentives, or other policy tools.[38] In turn, working within legislative guidelines and regulatory structures, teachers, principals, or other implementers then marshal resources, do the work, and account for the results. The practical effect of their activity depends on the efficacy of policy ideas and implementation efforts as well as the fit among policy, practice, and the contexts in which the work takes place.

From an implementer's point of view, a number of factors can cause results to lag expectations. For instance, people may not agree on the goals. Disagreement can be evident in heavily compromised or closely contested legislative decisions; in classroom, school, or district determinations that policy goals are not important or cannot be achieved; and in competing community demands that pull teachers, principals, and others in different directions. Disagreement in any form can diminish the direction, persistence, or vigor of implementers' actions or put them in the position of dividing limited resources among competing claims.[39]

Even if goals are widely supported, the underlying policy strategies may be flawed.[40] Recall the policy theories that have explained poor student performance to date and have shaped reform's remedies. Although often out of sight, these theories have much to do with a reform's success. At one point in the mid-1980s, for instance, education reformers attributed poor student performance to too little instructional time. As a result, they lengthened the school day and year.[41] Student performance stayed flat, however, because the explanation was short-sighted—that is, the theory was wrong—and no amount or quality of implementation will mitigate a problem if its "solution" does not fit.

Alternatively, a policy theory may be sound, but the legislative or regulatory design that puts it into play, that guides implementers' actions, may be defective or incomplete. For example, if an accountability system failed to focus students' and educators' behavior on state standards because it omitted meaningful rewards or sanctions, or if an instructional strategy worked in suburban schools but not in inner cities, then even good implementation of these initiatives would not produce the desired effects. In such cases, flawed policies can waste effort and resources or can limit results to a few settings.

What's more, implementation technologies—the tools and practices that give knowledge its practical effect—may not be up to the task. Imagine NASA engineers in the early 1960s staring at a commercial aircraft, wondering, "How will we get that thing to the moon?" Even the Redstone rocket that launched Alan Shepard into space was incapable of a moon shot. Public education's technology comprises classroom instruction, age grouping, bell schedules, and other attributes of the "grammar of schooling."[42] Education finance has its technology, too, found in funding and staffing formulas, targeted spending programs, the single salary schedule, collective bargaining agreements, fund accounting, and the like. In the context of ambitious learning goals, these technologies should explicitly support student learning. If they do not, then new ways of doing business would make sense. The persistence of old-school technologies shortchanges knowledge, signals the need to know more, or bespeaks an intransigence that impedes implementation progress.

Beyond the technical, implementers themselves may not rise to the occasion. Implementation depends fundamentally on willing participants—the students, teachers, principals, school district leaders, elected officials, and others whose combined efforts determine the results students achieve. With much riding on individual effort, individual-level motivation becomes a vital part of the implementation story. Misalignment between implementers' personal goals and public goals can diminish any student's or teacher's willingness to do new things or to do old things differently.[43]

Sometimes even highly motivated implementers are not sure about the right things to do. Professional knowledge and skills may not match a novel task or may not extend to new or best practices. One's training may be geared to older goals, conditions, or technologies. Implementation requires up-to-date professional knowledge and the ability to apply it usefully across settings. Outdated knowledge or skills can tilt even the most highly motivated implementation efforts toward the futile.

At the other end of the spectrum, the resource systems in which these matters play out may fail to support implementation. In some ways, system failure is the hidden danger, because systems themselves are hard to see. Most implementation behavior is compartmentalized: distributing resources from state to local agencies, assigning teachers to schools, managing categorical funds, finding extra-help strategies for struggling students, negotiating a labor agreement, complying with regulatory mandates, instructing "in my classroom." Compartmentalization limits implementers' views of the larger work. It encourages them to ask, Did we use the money as directed? Did only eligible students receive the services? Did we protect our interests in the contract? Did we account for our actions as required?

This kind of thinking supports standard operating procedures or "the way we do things." As a result, compartmentalization fails to recognize all those ways in which a system's components fit and function together. It misses the system's aggregate effects, whether good or ill, and this means that it misses the need to fine-tune or replace any of the parts. In contrast, reforms that work emerge from a supporting system that is intentional, that aligns goals with operations, that adapts practices to implementation needs, and that accounts for results in terms of core goals and the means used to accomplish them. In other words, implementation success comes from a system that supports "the right things to do."

All told, reforms that work do so because of clear and aligned goals, sound policy theory, and a design that works across settings or can be adapted to fit.[44] Successful reforms also have adequate resources, certain technology, motivated and capable implementers, and a system that supports implementation. In a smart-money sense, as you will see, system "supports" deliver resources transparently and fairly, induce productive behavior, build capacity, expand knowledge, develop needed technologies, and account for results in meaningful ways, and the system integrates these things so that their aggregate contributions move student performance toward the proficiencies that define public expectations.

System integration is easy to see in an automobile. When any one part breaks—the battery dies, the fuel runs out, a tire goes flat—the car goes nowhere because its parts are tightly integrated and mutually dependent. It takes a system, so to speak, to get a car down the road. Public education could work similarly, but because its parts are not as tightly integrated, not as mutually dependent, schools can chug along regardless of missing or misaligned parts.[45] It then takes a longer view to see that schools have not made as much progress as their constant effort might imply. In this sense, the burden on policy entrepreneurs, elected officials, educators, and others who would educate all students to meet standards is to design educational systems whose parts are productively integrated and mutually dependent in a way that accomplishes greater student learning. As the recommendations in chapter 1 indicate, smart-money investments in education include indicators, supports, and other mechanisms that also make educational systems potentially as robust as they are effective.

Absent this integration, education reforms have failed to educate all students to meet standards because their scale has been too small, or their underlying ideas too flawed, or their designs never realized in practice. Whether the barriers have been technical, economic, or political, reformers have yet to work through the whole set of knotty problems that influences success on an ambitious scale, have never integrated policy and practice to this degree.

Some education reforms have been more prescient or promising than others. Teacher quality initiatives and performance accountability—if governments could develop it more fairly and reliably—are examples. But even the more complex reforms such as accountability, systemic school reform, or adequacy have not gone far enough in integrating the relevant components. An educational system needs components that work, that work together, and that press toward the public's central goal: all students educated to meet standards. The more ambitious the goal, the more salient the system to its accomplishment. That system is the only vantage, the only unit of analysis, that is able to see and assess all the parts separately and together.

In the quest for better student results, policy makers nationwide have established ambitious learning goals, have committed resources, and have outlined general reform strategies. From this point on, finance systems dictate how those resources are distributed, how they are used, and which outcomes are tracked. Finance systems thus imbue resources with a measure of fairness, productivity, and accountability, with the particular measure achieved in any state determining whether that state's resources support or impede education's progress. Unfortunately, the way they do these things no longer matches the results states expect from schools.

THE CENTRAL ARGUMENT

The central argument of this book is that states will never educate all students to high standards unless they first fix the finance systems that support America's schools. This book does not contend that fixing finance systems alone will close the gap between public expectations and student performance. It does, however, demonstrate that the way these systems manage the nation's sizable investment in elementary and secondary education actually impedes educators' ability to accomplish ambitious learning goals. It also demonstrates that smart money's treatment of resources and resource decision making offers new purchase on a broader range of factors that influence student performance. Thus, fixing finance systems is a necessary, even fundamental, step toward accomplishing the nation's learning goals.

At this point in the argument, the centrality of finance systems to the smart-money perspective should be no surprise; that education finance systems themselves impede higher student performance, that they are part of the problem rather than the solution, however, is new.

Exactly how these systems are problematic for ambitious student learning will become clear. But in the sense that they constrain better student results, these systems confront the same transition as does public education generally: shifting from conventional to novel work. For finance systems, specifically, this transition means no longer merely enabling programs, equalizing spending capacity, or funding specific priorities but rather using resources to accomplish ambitious learning goals. And, again, as with public education generally, this transition questions whether conventional perspectives and practices can get the job done. The following chapters argue, no, that the connection between resources and learning is growing weaker, not stronger, and that finance reform is fundamental to greater accomplishments.

If education finance systems are problematic, then those systems must be redesigned. Recent reforms provide proof enough that greater student learning will not result from adjustments to funding formulas, from new programs, or from single-issue legislation—the usual fixes. Accomplishing ambitious learning goals begins with elected officials, educators, and others stepping back from the current mix of finance structures, tools, and practices to ask a fundamental question: how can educational resources support the nation's ambitions for student learning? *Smart Money* provides this more fundamental analysis and presents perspectives and recommendations that begin to answer the question.

All told, smart money advances the U.S. search for greater student learning because the idea of using resources to accomplish ambitious learning goals is powerful enough to organize the educational system that would produce these results. Its treatment of resources and resource decision making reaches deeper into the core processes of schooling and its support and thus marries resources with educational program and instructional issues in ways that other approaches either have not attempted or have not achieved. This concept is more demanding in terms of crafting a system of components that fit together and fit the task. It is more demanding, again, in terms of marshaling the technical, economic, and political resources needed to put these components into play. But smart money is more powerful, too, in creating opportunities for elected officials and educators to see problems and solutions differently, to unknot the issues of policy and practice that often stand in the way of success, and to find plausible next steps that can be developed, tested, and used to get better results.

For the moment, hold aside calculations of political feasibility—calculations that color conventional notions of what is possible. The book's last chapters address these issues, including ways those calculations can change. At this point it is important only to understand problems that are worth solving and to think systematically about responses that make sense.

These matters are important to schools and governing authorities alike, whether they are striving for better results, grappling with economic recession, or demonstrating political and organizational accountability. These issues are important, too, given the extent to which resource questions continue to shape discussions about policy and practice at national, state, and local levels and to influence legislative, judicial, and administrative decision making.[46] But these matters will not be resolved satisfactorily until elected officials, educators, and others begin to recognize and remove system impediments that break or cloud the connections between resources and student learning and to replace them with structures, tools, and practices better suited to the work of educating all students to meet standards.

These matters are important, but they also are problematic. Policy makers and practitioners lack good ideas about how to use resources to accomplish ambitious learning goals. A legislative working group and a gubernatorial commission in Washington State, for instance, each set out specifically to make the connection between resources and learning; they discovered no solutions and instead recommended marginal changes in funding formulas.[47] Similarly, a school principal told researchers that he knew how to use money "accurately"—that is, according to his budget and spending rules—but that there was nothing in place to help him use resources "effectively."[48] He is not alone in this regard. High salience, high stakes, and limited information create an urgent need for original analyses and new ways of thinking and acting regarding the distribution, use, and accounting of educational resources and their connection to student learning.

EVIDENCE FOR THE ARGUMENT

This book grew out of the deliberations of the National Working Group on Funding Student Learning and the research of the School Finance Redesign Project (SFRP) at the University of Washington's Center on Reinventing Public Education (I served as principal investigator of SFRP and chair of the working group).[49] Working group members—representing various academic fields; federal, state, and local government experience; legislative, executive, and judicial roles; and Democratic and Republican affiliations—convened seven times from January 2006 to July 2007 and continued to confer through other means until the publication of the final report in October 2008.[50] This diverse group agreed on a set of problems and recommendations, revisited in chapter 1, that underlie education finance reform.

To assist in their deliberations, working group members commissioned analyses, drafted working papers, contributed their expertise, and drew lessons from SFRP research. That research encompassed issues of intergovernmental and within-district resource allocation, school and district resource practices and spending choices, teacher labor markets and compensation, collective bargaining, incentive structures, and cost estimates. It captured the perspectives of teachers and principals, school board members and central office administrators, and state-level elected officials and staff. It included the development of two tools: one to guide strategic resource decision making locally, and another to simulate the consequences of state-level resource decisions.[51] The chapters in this book represent a combination of revised working group background papers and new analyses. *Smart Money* adds value by bringing these ideas together, elaborating issues that appeared in the working group report, and nesting the collection in a fresh and coherent argument that is not accessible through any paper alone.

Smart Money enters an arena of high standards but low performance, rising expenditures but growing inefficiencies, policy ambitions but structural roadblocks, performance pressure but gaps in professional training. It is unique in its systemwide assessment of problems and solutions, its integration of resources and learning, its partnership of policy and practice, and its present and future orientation. Its ambition is to contribute to an emerging public and professional conversation about why and how resources can be used effectively to support the nation's ambitious learning goals.

READING THIS BOOK

Smart Money is organized in five parts, each representing a pillar of the overall argument. Part I introduces the central resource challenge associated with ambitious learning goals: making smart-money investments in public education. In chapter 1, I make the case that conventional finance systems fail to support the nation's ambitious learning goals. This reality should come as no surprise, I argue, given that finance systems were never designed for this purpose, they are not operated to accomplish it, nor are they accountable for it. In short, current education finance systems miss the connection between resources and student learning, and in this context, smart-money failures are inevitable. Game over—or not, depending on the choices that elected officials and educators make. What are their options?

Putting the smart-money logic to work, chapter 1 maps a route between resources and student learning, making connections among the actors, resource choices, and system conditions that support education's new ambitions. The result is a candidate theory of resource allocation that explains not only how educational resources can be used to accomplish ambitious learning goals but also the contingencies that make this outcome more or less probable. Drawing on this model, I then contrast the conventional finance systems—the ones governments operate currently—with the learning-oriented resource systems that public expectations now demand. I end by outlining changes in policy and practice that will better enable federal, state, and local authorities to make smart-money investments in U.S. schools—and to expect a return. In short, this chapter establishes the resource problem and possible solution that subsequent contributions elaborate.

Part II delves deeper into a central obstacle blocking effective resource use: the one-size-fits-all inflexibility of targeted spending programs and traditional collective bargaining agreements. Christopher Cross and Marguerite Roza launch this discussion in chapter 2, demonstrating how the federal government's targeted spending programs prevent resources from being used effectively. These programs became problematic early on when a few local misappropriations led to the imposition of spending regulations and audit requirements meant to ensure compliance with program intent. Thus began what Cross and Roza dub "policy making based upon the worst-case scenario." The ensuing system of compliance-oriented account structures, record keeping, and staffing policies created a mentality that spending compliance was more important than student learning. To this day, these structures confuse who is responsible for student achievement, fragment instructional programs, prevent adoption of coordinated funding strategies that work in the best interests of students, and distort the underlying funding system. These finance structures became so much a part of the intergovernmental resource picture that the federal government's later efforts to integrate services at the school level fell far short of expectations. In effect, forty years of federal, state, and local interplay have created resource structures that prevent educators from addressing the poverty-based challenges that prompted federal intervention in the first place.

In chapter 3 Julia Koppich examines resource allocation through the lens of collective bargaining agreements, demonstrating how traditional contracts prevent the bulk of school district resources from effectively supporting student learning. Organizing her analysis around four questions— what resources get allocated through the contract? What mechanisms are used to allocate them? What assumptions support those allocations? And in what ways do contracts link resources with student learning?—Koppich shows how the "wages, hours, and working conditions" focus of traditional contracts makes adversaries of union and management, treats all teachers alike, limits access to professional development, and blocks teacher evaluation. These same traditional contracts focus on teachers' rights rather than teaching, allow little flexibility in practice, and make no reference to student learning.

These two chapters contrast the resource inflexibilities of targeted spending and collective bargaining with alternatives that bring resources and student learning closer together. For Cross and Roza, targeted spending programs become a counterpoint to student-based funding that follows every child. For Koppich, traditional labor agreements give way to "reform-oriented" labor–management partnerships that assume joint responsibility for student learning. As Koppich concludes, reform contracts protect high-quality teaching as fervently as they protect teachers' rights. Given these differences, the policy question, she explains, is not so much a choice between collective bargaining and no collective bargaining but rather is about the kind of collective bargaining that states and school districts choose to embrace.

Part III turns the argument away from resource impediments toward the finance frameworks, decisions, and costs that integrate resources with student learning. In chapter 4, Joanne Weiss introduces the notion of continuous instructional improvement, a strategic framework that anchors classroom, school, and district goal setting and resource decision making in a cycle of teaching, assessment, analysis, and adaptation. Continuous improvement describes a process through which teachers adapt instruction to the needs of their students and, by learning from experience, also improve their own practice. When implemented well, Weiss contends, the continuous improvement cycle represents a thoughtfully constructed academic system whose components interlock smoothly, in stark contrast to the "fractured and fragmented" instructional practices that now typify many schools and districts.

According to Weiss, continuous improvement asks much of educators, requires visionary and stable leadership, and demands courage to stay on track. Its data-based decision making and deep collaboration on teaching and learning challenge long-standing professional cultures and thus introduce uncertainty. That said, continuous improvement provides a mechanism to transform schools and districts into the consistently learning-oriented systems that ambitious goals demand. It cannot do this alone, but it does anchor the transformation. Accordingly, Weiss concludes, the only smart choice is that governments and school systems organize to deliver continuous improvement.

In chapter 5, Karen Hawley Miles shows that greater student learning depends importantly on strategic resource decisions. What exactly does *strategic* mean in the context of student learning? Miles makes four claims. First, a strategic school clearly defines an instructional model. Second, it makes resource choices that use people, time, and money in ways that implement that model. Key among these choices: boosting teaching quality, student instructional time, and individual student attention. Third, strategic schools make resource trade-offs, moving resources from one use to another, to support their most important instructional strategies. Finally, strategic schools constantly assess their instructional models and resource choices and trade-offs, adapting them as needed to accomplish their learning goals.

In effect, strategic decision making gives direction and practical meaning to the "align resources" component of continuous improvement. Miles goes on to discuss roles that school districts must play to support strategic schools. She ends by anticipating how strategic resource decision making will transform the way schools and districts do business, all of which promises improvements in student learning.

In chapter 6, Allan Odden, Michael Goetz, and Lawrence Picus merge effective resource strategies with costs, estimating the price tag of a strategically resourced school district. Their analysis contributes to an emerging line of work that estimates the cost of an "adequate" education, one that allows school districts to deploy the programs and strategies that enable all students to perform up to standards. This analysis moves the adequacy issue ahead by demonstrating that the national average expenditure per pupil comes close to funding adequacy, a much smaller number than many assume to be the case. Odden, Goetz, and Picus reach this conclusion after reviewing various approaches to adequacy, highlighting programs and strategies associated with the evidence-based model, costing out these core recommendations using a prototypical school district and national average salary and benefit data, and comparing these costs to the national average expenditure per pupil. The finding that the national average expenditure per pupil comes close to funding adequacy raises questions for the authors about a federal role in education finance, ways to promote more-productive use of resources in states that spend more than this amount, and a research agenda that could hasten this transition.

Part IV acknowledges that public education as a field knows more now than ever before about effective resource use and can do a better job of taking advantage of that knowledge, but also that no one can now answer core educational and resource questions in ways that hold up across settings or remain fixed over time. Accordingly, these three chapters explore ways to expand knowledge about resources and to experiment with new methods that promise better links between resources and student learning.

In chapter 7, James Guthrie and Paul Hill make the case for an aggressive research and development agenda, including strengthened charter schools or other thoroughgoing market mechanisms to test a wide array of instructional and resource strategies. Why the need? The authors express dismay by what they see as resource decision making based on politics and inertia and not evidence, and they ask why states cannot make better connections between education spending and its outcomes. Short of this goal, they contend, schools make instructional and resource decisions in a context of uncertainty, relying on political bargaining, judicial processes, expert opinion, performance incentives, and competition as substitutes for evidence. For Guthrie and Hill, ambitious learning goals now make these practices unacceptable and the lack of answers to fundamental educational methods and resource questions intolerable. A research and development enterprise would push the boundaries of knowledge outward, and charter schools or other market mechanisms would provide places for new programs to take hold while allowing money, people, and students to flow from lower- to higher-performing schools. Both mechanisms will help states learn more about what works, under what conditions, for whom, and at what cost, allowing school systems to know more tomorrow than they do today.

In chapter 8, David Monk takes advantage of this research and development potential to examine several departures from conventional finance thinking about the way governments educate U.S. youth. Although it is easy to observe discontent with current methods for financing and organizing schools, Monk asserts, the public also has become accustomed to the existing system, faults and all. Sizable bureaucracies have developed at local, state, and federal levels to administer the system, and these bureaucracies are adept at protecting themselves.

In this context, Monk proposes five ideas that fundamentally alter the ways states organize and finance public schools: differential add-ons and variable pricing for noncore services (such as an extra fee for instrumental music in elementary school) substituting technology for more-expensive human resources rapid-response capabilities that move extra resources to schools extraordinary needs that not appear until after the school year underway differentiated teacher roles that match assignments to teacher skills; and creating laboratory schools that, like teaching hospitals, link research and practice while providing close attention to the field's most challenging problems. In each case, Monk examines ways the idea might be implemented and its implications for equity, efficiency, and choice. He closes by imagining what a finance system would look like if all five ideas were adopted simultaneously. Along the way he stimulates entirely new thinking about ways to conceive of effective resource use.

In chapter 9, Michael Kirst and Lori Rhodes question the premise of mainline finance frameworks that have long shaped education resource policies. They argue that equity, adequacy, and choice fail to incorporate two complementary and potentially powerful funding strategies. The first approach links education finance to the nuts and bolts of standards-based reform. To realize the potential of that reform, Kirst and Rhodes maintain, finance policies and practices must reflect the full array of standards-based components and costs, supporting the changes in teaching and learning that this improvement strategy represents. So far, no state has attempted this level of resource allocation.

The second strategy pushes the educational resource discussion out the school door and into the economic and social settings of surrounding communities, effectively bridging education with community-based resources for children and youth. The community–school link is effected by the co-location of services, putting youth development, family support, health and social services, and the like in or near schools. Kirst and Rhodes demonstrate how the resulting "community schools" bring new resources into play and engage and motivate students by fostering social, emotional, and physical growth as well as academic skills. The authors introduce these finance frameworks, examine their benefits, and identify their elements and operations. The outside-school perspective raises the important question of whether education reform that supports ambitious learning goals depends on a combination of inside- and outside-school approaches—encompassing economic and social policies that have a direct impact on children and families—and not only changes aimed solely at classrooms.

Part V grapples directly with the transition from conventional to learning-oriented resource systems. Lorraine McDonnell initiates this discussion in chapter 10. Drawing on political science theory and prominent cases of education reform, McDonnell engages in "grounded speculation" about what it takes to create the political conditions that allow major alterations in education finance policy. Her starting point is the confluence of ideas, institutions, and interests that determine public policy outcomes, along with the critical role played by policy entrepreneurs and issue networks in challenging existing policy and institutional arrangements. Although the political conditions for change are relatively straightforward, she argues, they are not always sufficient. The required conditions include generic lessons regarding an engaging and feasible idea framed as a solution to a pressing problem, skilled policy entrepreneurs willing to invest resources in advancing that idea, interests dissatisfied with the status quo and able to overcome opposition, multiple points of access to decision making, administrative arrangements vulnerable to change, and sufficient time for agenda setting and change processes to work; these conditions still need to be adapted to each state's particular policy and political context before anyone can understand how genuine opportunities for agenda setting and policy enactment may arise.

I extend this argument in chapter 11, exploring the choices, role-based implementation needs, and political challenges posed by the recommendations for change outlined in chapter 1. Because such systems necessitate large-scale change, redefine resource roles and responsibilities, and upend conventional practices, their emergence poses greater hurdles than those associated with single-issue legislation. The question then becomes how to make those challenges more manageable, their particular demands more feasible. Chapter 11 proposes next steps regarding the selection of reform sites; the development of new structures, tools, and practices; the sequencing of reform components; the logic of stepwise changes; and the emergence of a performance culture that fuels the system's learning orientation.

I end by staking out smart-money resource systems as a matter of individual choice, a we-are-going-to-the-moon attitude. All difficulties aside, the determination to establish structures, tools, and practices that use resources to accomplish ambitious learning goals must be made by elected officials, educators, and others who would educate all students to meet standards. Little progress can be made without that assent.

PART I

Making Smart-Money Investments in Public Education

1

Ambitious Learning Goals Require a New Approach to Educational Resources

Jacob E. Adams, Jr.

Where is the smart money in public education? Three developments, all of which require close connections between resources and student learning, set the stage for an answer. These developments include the rise of ambitious learning goals and the nation's inability, so far, to achieve them; the shift from equity to adequacy in education law and the contentious policy debates it has spurred about how much money is enough; and the emerging demand for effective spending in government generally and in public education particularly.

NEW DEMANDS, NEW OPPORTUNITIES

The primary policy focus of elementary and secondary education targets ambitious student learning in core academic subjects. States have been developing this agenda since the mid-1980s, eventually establishing content and performance standards and accountability structures, the latter to track results and encourage better outcomes. The federal government joined the effort in 2002 with the No Child Left Behind Act (NCLB).[1] Touting "all students at standards," these initiatives require two things: that students achieve a level of academic success in core subjects that has never before been accomplished, and that school systems achieve this goal with all students, regardless of race, language, economic status, or disability.

Greater achievement in core subjects and performance accountability by student subgroups are widely viewed as instrumental to accomplishing a larger social purpose: ensuring that U.S. students—all of them—graduate from high school ready for citizenship, college or technical school, and the challenges of an increasingly global economy.[2] This book's introduction examines these ambitions in terms of the nation's student performance challenge. It notes that this focus on results marks a critical transition in public education, raises questions about the capacity of conventional technologies to accomplish the job, and stakes education's success and failure on its ability to address the demanding economic and civic challenges of the twenty-first century. At first a concern primarily of governors and legislatures, student learning soon fell, as well, under the purview of the states' judiciaries.

In a parallel development to standards-based reform, high courts in about 30 percent of the states have defined a new constitutional obligation to fund public education adequately. Adequacy derives from education clauses in state constitutions.[3] Plaintiffs have used these clauses to argue that student learning was fundamental to a state's educational responsibilities and that higher levels of funding would allow students to reach proficient levels of performance. Thus, following this line of argument, in the context of standards-based reform, adequacy provides a means for states to discharge their constitutional duties. Starting in the late 1980s, this new theory regarding adequate spending marked a turning point in judicial assessments of education finance.[4] The Alabama high court eloquently justified the transition when it noted that states could offer plaintiffs *"equal* educational opportunity but still offer them virtually no opportunity at all."[5] Because courts have served as the primary stimulus for changes in education finance, this new orientation is noteworthy.

The shift from equity to adequacy has wrought two principal consequences. It has refocused judicial attention from resource inputs to academic outcomes, and it has signaled the need to integrate educational funding and programs.[6] Before adequacy, educational funding and school improvement operated, essentially, as parallel concerns. That is, states satisfied judicial attention to resource equity and equal educational opportunity simply by allocating resources differently across school districts, compensating low-wealth districts for revenues they could not raise locally. Once a more equitable distribution was effected, the remedy was complete.

That remedy has been consequential for state–local relations, finance policy, funding formulas, local tax efforts, and school district resources and hence for educational opportunity.[7] But equity remedies have not required improved student learning. In contrast, the notion of adequacy is based on the expectation that some level of funding will be sufficient for students to achieve standards. Thus, the adequacy remedy directly anticipates better student performance, and it implies the search for resource uses that accomplish better performance.[8]

As standards-based reform and adequacy gained momentum, state and national leaders and policy entrepreneurs stepped up calls for more-effective spending in the public sector. Signaling the importance of the new link between resources and results, the federal Government Performance and Results Act of 1993 proposed that the federal government be held accountable for program outcomes.[9] Similarly, in 2002 the chief executive officer of the Council for Excellence in Government reported to the House of Representatives on recommendations to improve governmental results and to better justify the resources spent to produce them.[10] Washington governor Chris Gregoire later echoed this orientation when she announced her willingness to invest additional resources in elementary and secondary schools once she saw that the resources already committed were well spent.[11]

This demand for effective spending added a new dimension to education policy debates and leadership challenges. Elected officials began to question how well education spending was aligned with state academic ambitions and how officials might alter funding mechanisms to better support those ambitions. But with no ready frameworks or examples to address such questions, early discussions devolved into a focus on conventional changes in funding formulas or new investments in high-need areas, such as math and science education or remedial assistance for students facing high-stakes tests.[12] For principals and school superintendents working under the press of state and federal accountability mandates, the problem was more practical: searching for ways to spend available resources more effectively but doing so with conventional frameworks, tools, and training that did not match the task.

Why do changes in educational goals, legal reasoning, and government spending heighten attention to the use of education resources? In short, it is because these changes demand better academic results and because they link resource use to its accomplishment. Legislation in California made this point explicitly when it sought "the best use of available resources so that the vast majority of pupils may meet academic performance standards established by the state."[13] When performance matters, resources become instrumental to student learning.

In broader terms, the rise of ambitious learning goals calls for adequate funding, and demands for effective spending represent a new era in U.S. public education. For the first time, arguably, the policy system, top to bottom, is focused primarily on student learning rather than infrastructure development, school and district consolidation, national defense, access of student groups to schooling, or resource distribution to address funding inequities. This performance focus aligns federal, state, and local educational agendas. It aligns legislative, executive, and judicial agendas, and it aligns policy with parents' and educators' interests in student success.

The convergence of federal, state, and local agendas around student learning creates an unusual opportunity to effect conditions that make resources better instruments of student learning. Taking advantage of the opportunity, however, requires attention to a new question: how can elected officials and educators use educational resources to accomplish ambitious learning goals? That question now stands as central to student success.

Developments in learning standards, judicial reasoning, and effective spending create new opportunities but also challenges. At the moment, educational ambitions outstrip the field's accomplishments, and judicial expectations overestimate the ability of the social sciences to respond reliably while social scientists themselves debate ways to estimate costs and foster performance.[14] And new demands for effective spending make problematic the question about which practices can get the job done.

Moreover, these same developments challenge the underpinnings of education finance (see table 1-1). The policy problem has shifted from wealth disparity to low student performance, and this means that the central policy goal has likewise shifted from equalizing spending capacity to educating all students to meet standards. The relevant legal theory has changed from equal protection to adequacy, and the remedy has evolved from resource distribution to academic results.

In this new context, the resource target moves from school districts to students. Funding demands change from what is available to what is needed, and finance policies themselves, formerly addressed separately from educational programs and school improvement, now must be integrated with the core activities of teaching and learning.

However, that is not all. These developments also alter the focus of resource decision making from formulas and standard operating procedures to strategic investments and trade-offs. Similarly, expectations for resource management shift from accurate spending in budgeted categories—in other words, program fidelity—to effective spending that promotes student learning, something the following discussion addresses in terms of continuous improvement. Finally, long-standing input- and compliance-focused accountability structures must give way to a concern for student learning. All told, these developments alter the entire terrain of finance policy and

TABLE 1-1 How ambitious learning goals, judicial adequacy, and effective spending requirements change resource expectations

System attribute	Conventional expectations	New expectations
Policy problem	Wealth disparity	Low student performance
Policy goal	Equalize spending capacity	All students at standards
Legal theory	Equal protection	Adequacy
Remedy	Resource distribution	Academic results
Resource target	School districts	Students
Funding standard	What's available	What's needed
Link between resources and educational programs	Separate	Integrated
Resource decision making	Formulas, standard operating procedures	Strategic investments and trade-offs
Resource management	Accurate spending (program fidelity)	Effective spending (continuous improvement)
Accountable outcome	Compliance	Student learning

practice, thus providing ample reason to question the ability of conventional resource structures, tools, and practices to accomplish ambitious learning goals.

FINANCE SYSTEMS AND STUDENT LEARNING

In some ways, education finance systems are remarkable. In support of U.S. elementary and secondary schools, these systems are used to oversee the annual expenditure of more than $500 billion. Raised from various taxes, these monies are disbursed by local (44 percent), state (47 percent), and federal (9 percent) agencies to more than 14,000 school districts and 100,000 schools. Finance systems fund 49 million students, compensate 4 million teachers, and construct and operate facilities that house them all.[15] They enable general educational programs, but they also fund the particular challenges of student poverty, language acquisition, migration, and disability. They support instruction up close, paying for things like materials, professional development, and extra help for students while also funding large-scale initiatives, such as standards-based reform and class size reduction.

Anchored by state government, this edifice is operated by 1.5 million administrators, 100,000 school board members, 50 sets of state legislators and chief state school officers, members of Congress, and the leadership of the U.S. Department of Education. These public officials have used education finance to address problems as diverse as the distribution of educational opportunity and school maintenance, child nutrition and vocational training, and preschool and the economic impact of military bases on community coffers.

By design, education finance systems manage a portfolio of responsibilities and address salient and successive public purposes. These purposes have included, for instance, building schools, enabling programs, and expanding opportunity; addressing basic differences in student need, demonstrating resource comparability, and improving equity; and promoting fiduciary responsibility and accommodating intergovernmental priorities. In pursuit of these goals, elected officials and educators have employed familiar tools (intergovernmental grants, foundation programs) and have adopted new ones when needed (guaranteed tax bases, targeted spending, fund accounting, and so on). On an enormous scale and amid broad responsibilities and complex governance, finance systems provide fundamental stability to the education enterprise and yet adapt to changing circumstances. No doubt, they have done these things more and less well.

If finance systems have accomplished these things, how can they fail to support ambitious learning goals? The answer lies in the mismatch between new education ambitions and long-established values and operations. Part of the problem is that finance systems have been developed piecemeal over decades as local, state, and federal officials separately recognized and addressed problems and as they adapted to a growing thicket of program interactions. This record indicates how education finance can be intentional at the program level but not at the system level, where one would expect to see all the parts cohere, pushing in one direction. Even regarding programs, finance arrangements do a better job of linking problems and resources (what elected officials invest) and not resources and academic accomplishments (how investments promote results).

In this context, one would not expect to find a close connection between education resources and student learning, and that is what the evidence demonstrates. In fact, the closest thing now to an overarching finance system strategy would be fiduciary responsibility in a context of compliance accountability, and neither of those values inherently promotes student learning. A results orientation would refocus attention away from resources as general support and toward the ways resources are allocated and used to support student learning. Thus, the ways resources can be used to accomplish ambitious learning goals increasingly must frame resource discussions for both policy and practice. Four questions guide those discussions: do elected officials invest enough money? Do elected officials and educators distribute it fairly? Do they use it effectively? Do they account for it meaningfully?

Sufficient Funding

Elected officials and educators need to know what level of funding is required to accomplish ambitious learning goals—what level is adequate, in the parlance of emerging legal contests. If funding is to be instrumental to student outcomes, then it must support the things that produce those outcomes—teachers, time, materials, tutoring, or what have you. Once an adequate amount is determined, then states must possess the fiscal capacity, along with the political will, to raise it. If any one of these three conditions—knowledge, capacity, will—is absent, then the right level of investment cannot be guaranteed. Funding could be too little, too great, or just right only by chance.

In fact, continuing uncertainty about the level of funding needed to educate all students to meet standards works against a closer alignment of resources and learning goals. No school or district has yet achieved standards across all student subgroups, so there has been no demonstration of a requisite level of funding in any one setting, much less settings with various characteristics and educational challenges. In the absence of such knowledge, funding levels are negotiated and changed incrementally based on available resources, conflicting values, and competing demands. In a representative democracy that process is not wrong, but neither is it adequate.

As with funding levels in general, the empirical basis is weak for determining how much additional funding is needed to address student needs related to poverty, language acquisition, or disability. Thus, there is little empirical support for determining the additional funding increments, or *weights,* used in funding formulas.[16] Estimates of need as well as actual weights vary across states.

Analysts have begun to address the "how much?" question, but their initial estimates have been rudimentary, based on current schooling arrangements, business-as-usual professional perspectives, or a nascent research base. These methods also produce different estimates in the same states, lacking the certainty that states desire.[17] Like all early technologies, these costing-out techniques themselves have become the source of growing debate.[18] In chapter 6, Allan Odden, Michael Goetz, and Lawrence Picus address these issues directly.

Educators' perspectives on funding also vary. When asked whether their funding was sufficient to get students to standards, superintendents and principals responded: yes, no, and I don't know.[19] Their answers illustrate that school leaders lack a reliable framework to help them make such judgments.

Fair Distribution

Learning requires support for students' educational needs. Clearly, students come to school with varying experiences and abilities. Some are disadvantaged by poverty, poor nutrition, neighborhood violence, or other social ills. Yet all must reach standards. Providing extra help for some students means differing costs across the system. Moreover, needs-based aid must reach the students it intends to serve. If it does not, then funding inequities will persist, even if hidden, students and teachers will be shortchanged, and finance systems will operate inefficiently.

In fact, states have worked on interdistrict equity for decades, but their policy successes have been limited.[20] Analysts also have recognized that inequities exist among schools within the same district, drawing fresh attention to the question of funding disparities.[21] Similarly, there is no interstate equity policy. Only the federal government can address such a problem, and it has not acted on this issue.[22]

Needs-based aid can be problematic as well. The formula that distributes federal Title I funds, for example, in part exacerbates the very inequity it purports to address.[23] Moreover, federal, state, and local resource distributions that fund schools, programs, or staff rather than students, as well as conflicting agendas across levels of government, impede needs-based aid from reaching its target.[24] At the district level, too, resource distributions that do not rely on per-pupil formulas, and lower-level staff discretion over resource deployment, promote inequitable distribution of resources among schools.[25]

Effective Use

At base, using education resources to accomplish ambitious learning goals means that educators must translate resources into results. Given variation in student needs and teacher skills, the nuts-and-bolts resource adaptations that make money matter will vary across classrooms, schools, and districts; these adaptations also will vary over time as elected officials, educators, and researchers learn more about using resources to accomplish ambitious goals. Thus, different locations may be using resources differently to get the results they desire, and that variation will be productive. For educators, then, having the incentives and the capacity to make those judgments is central to using resources effectively.

In fact, incentives are often disconnected from learning or even work against it. State and federal accountability policies that are focused on schools and districts, for example, have captured educators' attention, directing their efforts to adequate yearly progress and similar accountability waypoints. But few, if any, incentives reinforce ambitious accomplishments at the individual level.[26] Staff compensation is disconnected from student results, and local school systems resist individual-level incentives based on student performance.[27] Even if they embrace the notion of incentives, school leaders have few tools to induce different behavior.[28]

At the school and district levels, particularly, incentives work against learning goals. Programs funded on the basis of student enrollment, for instance, induce educators to overidentify students with problems or to keep them enrolled longer than necessary. Categorical spending rules and auditing requirements inspire educators to spend in prescribed ways, regardless of the fit with educational needs or the consequences for student learning.[29]

And the politics of collective bargaining encourage superintendents to seek new funding in categorical form, even though, by their own admission, those programs diminish the coherence of instruction. They prefer it, nevertheless, just to keep general-purpose resources off the bargaining table.[30] Forsaking incentives and operating perverse incentives prevent more-effective uses of education resources.

Even motivated educators often lack the knowledge they need to manage resources effectively.[31] Having never been trained to use resources to accomplish student learning, educators report that they have no strategic or management framework to direct their efforts.[32] Recall the principal mentioned in the introduction. He said he knows how to spend money accurately, according to his budget, but not how to spend it effectively. Not surprisingly, then, educators frequently do not understand the effect of trade-offs among different spending decisions.[33] As a result, resource allocations often end up misaligned with educational intent.[34] An across-the-board mentality prevails.[35]

Where educators have developed new resource capacities, they frequently lack the discretion to match resources with needs. Categorical program rules and collective bargaining agreements restrict the range of local decision making, limiting local leaders' ability to hire, deploy, and replace staff;

allocate time and materials; organize schedules; remove underperforming teachers; or coordinate educational offerings. Categorical funding as well as collective bargaining agreements apply a one-size-fits-all solution to schools facing different challenges and levels of resources, while at the same time confronting staff with bureaucratic complexity and inflexibility. What is more, school staff members funded by categorical programs often report to, and take their direction from, school district central offices rather than the principals they work for, confusing who works for whom and which needs will influence practice.[36]

As states fund a greater share of total education costs and make wider use of categorical programs, local decision making may become further separated from learning needs.[37] Weak incentives, low capacity, limited discretion, and instructional incoherence are not strategies for accomplishing ambitious learning goals. In chapters 2 and 3, Christopher Cross and Marguerite Roza, and Julia Koppich, respectively, continue the discussion of these impediments.

Meaningful Accountability

To help accomplish ambitious learning goals, financial accountability must provide information directly about student learning and about the resources used to accomplish it. They also must operate as an incentive, encouraging greater learning. These informational and motivational roles require enough transparency and detail for observers to match resource decisions with student leaning and to assign responsibility to the persons who make those decisions. Conventional practices that have the effect of hiding resource transactions, providing accounts that reveal nothing of importance, or holding the wrong parties accountable only strip accountability of its role in democratic government and its utility in accomplishing ambitious learning goals.

In fact, conventional accountability arrangements fall short on all these fronts. Three problems stand out. First, funding systems are complex and opaque. Their many levels, various mechanisms, and multiple sources of control make it hard to tell what is going on or whom to hold accountable. Amid this complexity, educators sometimes do not know where their resources end up, and the connection between resources and students is easily lost at the district level, where administrators translate funding into programs, services, and staff.[38] Few people understand complex staffing formulas, second- and third-tier decision making hides actual resource deployments and their consequences, and funding restrictions are not easily discernible or evenly applied.[39]

Second, the compliance orientation of accountability—focusing on spending in correct categories rather than understanding what the spending accomplishes—structures accounts and draws attention away from student learning. When learning matters, such accounts mean little. Thus, compliance accountability runs counter to school accountability for results. It is focused on the wrong thing. Similarly, accounting practices focused on general and special-purpose funds, broad functions such as administration and instruction, and objects such as salaries and books, and on the account codes that define these categories in practice, reveal little of substance about the use of resources to support student learning.

Third, accountability is misapplied. Schools are held accountable for results even though federal, state, and central office agents dictate how their resources can be used. As a result, schools are held accountable for results they did not control, and federal and state policy makers and agency personnel escape accountability for their contributions to student learning.

Missing Connections

In short, conventional finance systems do not operate as one would expect when student learning matters. Their structures, tools, and practices work against the alignment of resources and student learning, against the adaptation of resources to those needs, and against accountability that matters. These gaps define a missed opportunity in U.S. public education. Finance systems contribute resources, enable programs, employ staff, and address numerous problems, but the way they do it—establishing funding levels based on convention rather than need, addressing equity in one place while ignoring it in others, spending resources with little regard for results, tolerating accountability that is off target—precludes system connections that matter for student learning. Using resources to accomplish ambitious learning goals requires better connections. The question now is how to secure them.

A FRAMEWORK FOR LINKING RESOURCES WITH STUDENT LEARNING

If conventional structures, tools, and practices miss the connection between educational resources and student learning, then the main resource responsibility for policy and practice is to establish those connections, enabling decision makers at all levels to use the resources they have to accomplish the ends they seek. Only in finance systems whose parts together support ambitious learning goals can policy and practice bring resources fully to bear on the nation's student performance challenge, and only in this way can finance systems gain a greater measure of fairness, productivity, and accountability. Funding levels, formula adjustments, and new programs notwithstanding, continued reliance on values and practices that served other purposes leaves elected officials and educators floundering in zones of wishful thinking regarding the utility of resource conventions to accomplish novel goals.[40] Simply put, resource mechanisms not aligned with student learning can never satisfy the nation's ambitions for education.

Importantly, this constraint, to a degree, does not preclude educators from managing resources more effectively right now. Principals, superintendents, and others have varying degrees of discretion to make resource choices and trade-offs regarding curriculum, teacher quality, student time, and other resources that affect learning. Attention to these issues can improve resource management and student learning, and they should be pursued. Karen Hawley Miles (chapter 5) elaborates these opportunities.

But those choices and trade-offs cannot surmount resource impediments ingrained in finance systems, artifacts of eras that focused independently on problems of misappropriation, arbitrary management, inequity, poverty, and the like. In a system now organized by ambitious learning goals, those solutions stand at odds with each other and with education's new challenge. To secure connections between resources and learning that better serve contemporary goals, those barriers must be removed and new mechanisms developed and deployed—not an easy task. Moving beyond convention is difficult when convention defines one's world and when it represents the steady state of affairs for both policy and practice.

The remainder of this chapter explores specific ways to connect resources with student learning. It first introduces a framework (see figure 1-1) that describes the people, settings, decisions, and contingencies that influence resource allocation. The framework also identifies the connections among them that explain how resources promote (or fail to promote) learning. Like all frameworks, this one illustrates those underlying structures that support a larger purpose or enterprise—in this case, the complexities and nuances of education policy and practice, the very things that will measure the framework's practical strength and utility. The final section in this chapter recommends changes in policy and practice that would enable elected officials and educators to use resources more productively to accomplish ambitious learning goals.

The framework's basic insight is that using resources to accomplish ambitious learning goals depends on three things: explicit pathways that connect resources and learning, strategic decisions that match resources with

FIGURE 1-1 A framework for linking resources with student learning

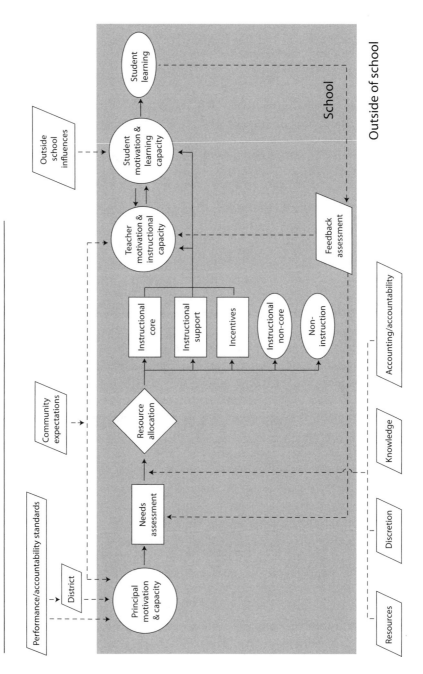

needs, and conditions inside and outside schools that enable and encourage decision makers to act strategically and hence productively. The framework rationalizes these contingencies in several ways.

Decision Arenas

First, resource decisions occur in two settings: schools and the policy, organizational, and community contexts in which schools operate. In school settings, principals make resource decisions that support one of three outcomes: student learning in the instructional core; student learning in subjects outside the core (instructional noncore); and results not related to student learning (noninstruction) that instead support ancillary functions like maintenance and procurement or satisfy constituent demands, pet projects, staff requests, and the like.

For these purposes, in the framework "principal" represents the school-level decision authority, whether that authority resides in an individual, a school site council, or another collaborative arrangement. Similarly, "instructional core" represents the academic content and performance standards that define ambitious learning goals. That content may be as narrow or as expansive as states or national standard-setting bodies choose to make it. The breadth of this core is important in defining public ambitions and well-educated persons, but it is not important in terms of the framework's operation. The key here is simply to distinguish public ambitions from other purposes.

Decisions that allocate resources to noncore and noninstructional purposes do not support ambitious learning goals, as the term is used here. The goals they support may be worthy in other contexts; nevertheless, in this framework they represent a disconnect between resources and the student learning that defines policy, and hence public, ambitions.

Allocating resources across these three outcomes is a choice that decision makers must confront and justify. Being mindful of these choices, investing new resources in the core, improving practices or making tradeoffs that free existing resources to support the core, keeping budget cuts away from the core, and denying resource claims that compete with the core—all these practices connect resources and learning explicitly.[41]

Strategic Decisions

Second, decisions that allocate resources to the instructional core address the learning encompassed by public ambitions, but simply moving resources in the right direction will not guarantee results that matter. Those results depend on strategic connections, too. In this sense, "strategic" encompasses resource decisions, plans, or investments that distinguish more-effective from less-effective uses and match those more-effective uses with the demonstrated instructional and learning needs in classrooms and schools. Those more-effective uses target, for example, teacher quality, student time and attention, formative assessment, extra-help strategies for struggling students, professional collaboration, and the use of expertise.[42]

These are no mean factors. Schools and districts that have improved student learning make regular use of them.[43] In part III, Joanne Weiss, Karen Hawley Miles, and Allan Odden and colleagues examine these factors in depth. These strategies represent plausible ways to connect resources with learning. At the same time, the field continues to learn more about what works, where, and at what cost. Thus, resource strategies that are "best practice" today may evolve in the face of future lessons. Regardless of those changes, the continuing need to match resources with classroom conditions affirms a contingent approach to resource decision making. Beyond some basic level, standard solutions cannot productively serve varying needs.

Resource Contingencies Inside Schools

Third, the ability to act strategically is itself contingent on conditions inside and outside schools. Inside schools, the most important of these regard the motivation and capacity of teachers to teach, students to learn, and principals to resolve resource issues.

The salience of these conditions stems from a convergence of findings across academic fields. For instance, research on the development of competence indicates that learning is a function of an individual's motivation and capacity operating in an environment that provides information, materials, support, and opportunities to practice.[44] These concepts appear again in implementation research, which views learning and change as functions of an individual's will and skill operating in a context of external pressure and support.[45] "Will and skill" and "motivation and capacity" refer to the same factors.

Research on learning policies themselves argues that effective policies promote teacher and student capacity via training and materials.[46] And lessons from the learning sciences describe how motivation and capacity shape learner-, knowledge-, assessment-, and community-centered learning environments, even sketching ways that the "how people learn" framework can inform resource allocation.[47]

Confirming the centrality of these concepts to education generally, the National Research Council's strategic education research plan identified motivation and capacity as two of the four core interests in education research.[48] And similarly confirming their utility to resource issues, the

National Research Council's committee on education finance shaped its recommendations, in part, around the use of incentives and capacity-building investments to "make money matter."[49]

Clearly, motivation and capacity are central to human behavior. They are equally central to teaching, learning, and resource decision making, because they dictate the effort that teachers, students, and principals will devote to their respective responsibilities and the capabilities they will bring to these tasks.[50] That is, people are motivated by their own goals, the things they want to accomplish. The more those goals are aligned with ambitious learning goals, the more individuals will endeavor to accomplish the latter. Accordingly, the more teachers' personal goals for their students are aligned with the ambitious learning goals defined by policy, the more teachers will endeavor to accomplish those externally imposed goals. In contrast, the less teachers' personal goals are aligned with ambitious policy goals, the less teachers will seek to accomplish those externally imposed goals.

People also are motivated by their sense of capability: whether they think they can accomplish their goals. And they are further motivated by a sense that their peers, families, professional colleagues, and other reference groups will support their efforts, affording them opportunities to succeed. Teachers and students influence each other in this way, too. Once people are engaged, their knowledge and skills, whether generic or task specific, dictate how much they are likely to accomplish.

Motivation and capacity, thus, are reinforcing: the more capable a person is, generally or in a particular context, the more willing that person is to take on a novel task; the more motivated, the more he will search for additional knowledge and skill. However, neither motivation nor capacity is fixed. They change in response to knowledge and experience. And they both can develop after people become involved in a task, a change process, or another activity. In other words, motivation can follow experience; it need not lead it.[51]

The framework shown in figure 1-1 addresses teacher, student, and principal motivation and capacity in several ways. Inside schools, it shows how they mediate, and thus explicitly link, resources and student learning, directly influencing principals' resource decisions, teachers' instruction, and students' performance. The framework also indicates that principals', teachers', and students' motivation and capacity constitute strategic targets. For instance, using resources to increase teacher and student motivation and providing instructional support—coaching, professional development, tutoring, and the like—that boosts teacher and student capacity both further the accomplishment of ambitious learning goals.

The framework further shows how specific allocations of incentives, support, and other resources depend on the recurring assessment of instructional and learning needs, what Joanne Weiss refers to in chapter 4 as the cycle of continuous improvement. Those assessments happen in classrooms and schools, as teachers and principals review results and adapt their behavior to fit changing circumstances.

Resource Contingencies Outside Schools

The framework also identifies contingencies outside schools that equally influence teacher, student, and principal motivation and capacity. Policy, school district, and community expectations, for instance, all create demands for school and student performance that principals must mediate. Community expectations reach teachers directly through parents, just as families, peer groups, and work commitments influence students.[52]

These outside expectations can reinforce or work against ambitious learning goals. If the latter, the willingness, persistence, and enthusiasm of teachers, students, and principals to accomplish those goals may be diminished. In such cases, principals will find themselves in the position of complying with competing demands and thus diverting resources from student learning; or rejecting those demands, thereby fomenting ill will among school constituents. Because neither option is desirable, principals will be left searching for ways to mitigate the competing demands, to reduce their salience, or to address them while still protecting core goals and resources. These same competing demands also may inspire principals to search for incentives that fit their school culture and are powerful enough to trump those demands.

Resource decisions are contingent, again, on outside school conditions controlled by elected officials. Imagine principals who are motivated by ambitious learning goals and who understand the needs of their faculties and students. Their ability to respond effectively to those needs still depends on their access to adequate resources, on their discretion to deploy those resources strategically, and on their knowledge about effective resource strategies and practices. Furthermore, their willingness to deploy resources effectively cannot be diminished by financial accounting or accountability requirements that introduce competing demands.

For instance, suppose that accounting practices or accountability structures conflict with the coherence of instructional programs or the effective use of resources—for example, that categorical program rules inspire pull-out services.[53] In that case, principals will face an unfortunate choice: serve the mandates that diminish student learning, or privilege the learning at the risk of sanctions. A rational decision maker would choose the path that avoids the harshest penalty. In connecting resources with learning, finance systems need to align rational choices with more-effective choices, encouraging principals and others to privilege student learning.

Altering these conditions to answer results-oriented expectations means tackling the most ingrained impediments in conventional resource arrangements: restoring the connection between funding and students, a connection that gets lost in programs, services, and staffing arrangements; retooling funding formulas that exacerbate inequities; removing incentives that elevate program interests over student learning; shifting resource discretion toward schools to better match resources and needs; refocusing accountability from compliance to student learning. In short, the framework's explicit, strategic, and contingent connections represent new possibilities but new challenges as well.

The Framework and Smart Money

What does this framework accomplish? It maps connections between resources and student learning, and it differentiates inside-school (practice) and outside-school (policy) responsibilities in securing those connections. It encourages principals and other decision makers to use their knowledge and discretion to promote and protect ambitious learning goals and to support those goals by implementing resource strategies grounded in knowledge of classroom needs and effective use of resources. Then it goes further, identifying contingencies that strengthen or distract attention from the core and from attempts to connect resources with learning across the core.

In other words, the framework answers the question, Where is the smart money in connecting educational resources with student learning? According to the framework, the smart money is on student learning in the core and on strategic investments in the technology, incentives, and support that drive teaching and learning. The smart money also is on the cycle of continuous improvement that assesses needs, allocates resources, enables work, and tracks results. And because that cycle and the adaptations it spawns are important, the smart money also is on the data systems and decision-making capacities that make sense of student results and fine-tune the resources and practices needed to accomplish more.

Finally, the smart money is on the resources, discretion, knowledge, and accountability that allow schools to act strategically, including the management of expectations that encourage or discourage attention to the learning that defines public expectations.

At another level, the framework replaces conflicting goals, compliance orientation, formula allocations, compartmentalized responsibilities, and one-size-fits-all approaches that characterize resource conventions. Instead, the framework illustrates the learning goal, results orientation, strategic allocations, integrated responsibilities, and contingent approach that smart money introduces. Thus the framework explains how resources can bear more fully on the student performance challenge in terms of system integration: connecting the parts to accomplish ambitious learning goals.

If conventional structures, tools, and practices miss the connection between resources and student learning, and thus the opportunity to promote better outcomes, then securing those connections depends on changes in policy and practice that give the framework a practical purchase in schools, boardrooms, and legislatures.

NEW STRUCTURES, TOOLS, AND PRACTICES

Smart Money is the outgrowth of the National Working Group on Funding Student Learning, the capstone initiative of the School Finance Redesign Project (SFRP) at the University of Washington's Center on Reinventing Public Education. The book's chapters include a combination of working group background papers and new contributions; together, they elaborate the group's considerations and provide a fresh perspective on the work as a whole.

Whether prepared as fodder for the working group or for this volume, each chapter represents the perspective of its authors. Eight of the fifteen authors who appear in these pages served on the working group (Jacob Adams, chair, Christopher Cross, James Guthrie, Paul Hill, Michael Kirst, David Monk, Allan Odden, and Joanne Weiss); the other seven contributed commissioned papers or conducted original research for SFRP, all of which seeded the working group's deliberations and helped it toward a set of findings, conclusions, and recommendations. Accordingly, those recommendations represent one place in this book where individual perspectives converge.

The purpose of this section is not to duplicate the working group's report but to sketch its recommendations, highlight key conclusions, and link recommendations to succeeding chapters where authors explore the arguments in more depth.[54] These arguments led the working group to its judgment that using resources to accomplish ambitious learning goals requires changes in policy and practice, changes that, in the working group's terms, would "fund student learning." The working group report and this book discuss this goal similarly in terms of securing needed connections between resources and student learning.

The working group set out to craft a vision of learning-oriented education finance and to determine what it takes to get there. To accomplish that task, its members addressed four questions.

1. What is wrong with education finance systems today when measured against the goal of student learning?
2. What design principles better link resources with student learning?
3. What funding mechanisms are consistent with those principles?
4. What conditions are necessary to implement these practices?

In a foreword to the report, I argued that "by identifying problems, recognizing core principles, matching funding mechanisms to goals, and defining the context in which money can matter, the Working Group was able to identify opportunities that today's school finance systems miss and to show how public funds can be used more effectively toward achieving results the public now expects."[55]

Those questions productively structured the working group's deliberations and enabled it to fulfill its purpose. They apply equally to *Smart Money*, and they offer the same utility to elected officials, educators, and others who are seeking ways to connect educational resources with ambitious learning goals and who desire a greater measure of fairness, productivity, and accountability for their resource systems. For the working group, those connections came in the form of new resource structures, tools, and practices that require adaptation on the part of elected officials and educators.

Manage Resources for Continuous Improvement

The working group built its recommendations on the need to integrate resources with instruction, improvement plans and activities, and accounts, and the cycle of continuous improvement provided a school-based process to effect that integration. The concept of *continuous improvement* positions teachers, principals, and superintendents to improve teaching and learning continuously through a cycle of goal setting, resource allocation, instruction, assessment, analysis, and adaptation. Accordingly, the working group recommended that educators adopt continuous improvement as the core resource strategy for schools and districts (see table 1-2).

Although the concept is not new, it provides a mechanism that allows explicit and strategic links between resources and student learning. As the working group argued,

> Continuous improvement is . . . a fundamentally different institutional process for managing educational resources. It shifts the resource focus

TABLE 1-2 How educators can support continuous improvement

Requirement	Action
Adopt continuous improvement as the core resource strategy for schools and districts.	Set clear goals and align resources with those goals.
	Engage students effectively with good teaching and high-quality curriculum.
	Gather performance information that tracks academic progress.
	Analyze performance information to assess strengths and weaknesses of teaching and learning.
	Develop action plans and adapt resources to build on strengths, address weaknesses, and propel the cycle forward.
Move resources from less-effective to more-effective uses.	Begin with a first approximation of effective resource deployment.
	Make resource trade-offs that support core instructional goals and needs.

Source: National Working Group on Funding Student Learning, *Funding Student Learning: How to Align Education Resources with Student Learning Goals* (Seattle: University of Washington, Center on Reinventing Public Education, School Finance Redesign Project, 2008).

from districts to students and moves resource accountability beyond compliance to student learning. It promotes learning directly by blending resources and resource adaptations with high-quality information about teaching practices and student results, knowledge about what to do with the information, and flexibility to act accordingly. As an institutional process, therefore, continuous improvement illustrates how resource and instructional decisions can be integrated, thus how resources can support student learning. Importantly, too, continuous improvement provides transparent feedback on whether and how resources influenced student learning.[56]

An earlier section introduces the logic of continuous improvement as part of the framework for linking resources with student learning. Joanne Weiss elaborates these issues in chapter 4.

An essential component of the continuous improvement cycle requires educators to align resources with instructional and learning needs and to do so repeatedly to fit changing circumstances. The working group clarified that responsibility in recommending that educators move resources from less-effective to more-effective uses, arguing that they could accomplish this by deploying "first approximation" resource strategies and by making resource trade-offs that support core instructional goals and needs (see table 1-2). That so-called first approximation represents the current state of practice and research knowledge regarding the use of resources.

> For local educators launching a continuous improvement process, seeking confirmation of existing resource plans, or revising plans that came up short, this "first approximation" of effective resource deployment represents a plausible way to begin aligning resources and student learning goals. It harnesses what the field knows now, but it is not a prescription or solution to the system design problems identified earlier. It addresses the problem that resources often are not effectively aligned with learning goals or instructional needs, and it signals that steps can be taken immediately, within existing finance arrangements, to get better results.[57]

In chapters 5 and 6, Karen Hawley Miles and Allan Odden and colleagues, respectively, explore strategic resource decisions associated with these choices and trade-offs, describe first-approximation activities in depth, and explain how to merge costs with effective resource strategies.

Enable and Support Continuous Improvement

Educators, however, cannot launch productive continuous improvement processes on their own—that is, not processes that reflect the cycle's full potential. That potential depends on elected officials' creating conditions that enable and support educators' work (see table 1-3). According to the working group, "absent this support . . . standards, accountability, and resources can lose their purchase on student learning. The policy challenge here is to remove the structures, rules, or practices that prevent educators from using resources effectively."[58]

The working group also argued that elected officials and policy-level administrators could create conditions that support continuous improvement by fulfilling four requirements (see table 1-3): delivering resources transparently and flexibly, focusing and enabling educators' work, expanding resource knowledge and experimenting with new methods, and redesigning resource accounting and accountability.

> Delivering resources transparently and flexibly, by itself, can remove many of the impediments associated with conventional finance systems. Transparent funding maintains the connection between resources and students so that it is easy to see who gets what and how resources are used to promote learning. Flexible funding gives teachers, principals, and superintendents the freedom to align resources with instructional goals and to adapt resources to student, classroom, or school circumstances.[59]

TABLE 1-3 How elected officials and departments of education can support continuous improvement

Requirement	Action
Deliver resources transparently and flexibly.	Attach federal, state, and local funding to students.
	Deposit student-based funding in school-linked accounts that operate on the basis of real-dollar budgeting.
Focus and enable educators' work.	Develop performance incentives for adults and students.
	Create and support data systems that link information about student learning, finance, and human resources.
	Develop educators' abilities to align and adapt resources effectively.
	Explore reform-oriented collective bargaining.
Expand resource knowledge, and experiment with new methods.	Fund research and development on continuous improvement.
	Strengthen charter laws or create other mechanisms to allow outside-the-box experiments on resource and school options.
	Continue to investigate how much money it takes to educate all students to meet standards.
	Expand the R&D agenda to link education with the broader array of resources available to children and youth.
Redesign resource accounting and accountability.	Revise government accounting and financial reporting standards and practices to reflect outcome principles and measures.
	Define resource responsibilities and structure contingencies on jobs, schools, and funding.

Source: National Working Group on Funding Student Learning, *Funding Student Learning: How to Align Education Resources with Student Learning Goals* (Seattle: University of Washington, Center on Reinventing Public Education, School Finance Redesign Project, 2008).

The working group made the case to create flexible funding by converting federal, state, and local general and categorical dollars (except funding designated to educate students with severe disabilities) into student-based funding that supports basic and special needs; adjusting these amounts for regional cost differences; and depositing the funds into school-linked accounts. A school's budget then would account for the actual salaries of its teachers, rather than using districtwide salary averages, and for the direct costs of services used by its students. The school-linked accounts maintain the connection between funding and students but hold open the option that resource decisions can be made by principals or superintendents, the latter in the context of districtwide instructional and improvement strategies. In chapter 2, Christopher Cross and Marguerite Roza discuss the impediments that give rise to this recommendation.

The working group's case for focusing and enabling educators' work, and thus enhancing their motivation and capacity to accomplish ambitious learning goals, rested on four actions: developing performance incentives for adults and students; creating and supporting data systems that link student learning, finance, and human resource information; developing educators' abilities to align and adapt resources effectively; and exploring reform-oriented collective bargaining. This chapter has established the importance, to student learning, of incentives and individual-level capacity. The working group reinforced these notions, arguing that "in a context of new learning goals, incentives can reorient work toward the content and performance standards that define success. In a context of never-before-achieved goals, incentives can encourage persistence and boost effort. In a context of uncertainty about how to accomplish such goals, incentives can lead to innovation and new evidence about what works and how much it costs."[60]

In concert with incentives and capacity-building investments, performance information derived from data systems directly fuels the continuous improvement process, and reform-oriented collective bargaining opens opportunities for labor and management to assume joint responsibility for student learning. Part of the reform involved in these new agreements includes, for example, implementing differentiated teacher roles and compensation, fitting teacher assignments to classroom needs, and permitting new forms of professional development and evaluation. Joanne Weiss and Julia Koppich take up these arguments in chapters 4 and 3, respectively.

The working group's recommendation to expand resource knowledge and to experiment with new methods acknowledges the need to move beyond first approximations of effective resource use by creating and testing new ideas, developing new tools and methods, and incorporating these developments into the continuous improvement process.

> In the absence of experiments and other investigations to discover what works, under what conditions, for whom, and at what cost, no one reasonably can expect to learn important resource lessons, such as how much to spend, how to use resources effectively, how to focus behavior, how to support teaching and learning, or how to account for resources and results . . . A research and development investment further protects states, educators, and families from unnecessary and unfair system upheaval.[61]

The working group recommended accomplishing this goal by funding research and development on continuous improvement, strengthening charter schools or creating other experimental mechanisms, continuing to investigate how much money it takes to educate all students to meet standards, and expanding research and development efforts to link education with the broader array of resources available to children and youth. James Guthrie and Paul Hill (chapter 7), David Monk (chapter 8), and Michael Kirst and Lori Rhodes (chapter 9) examine these possibilities.

The working group's final recommendation regarded redesigning resource accounting and accountability. The intention was to replace conventional fiduciary- and compliance-oriented structures with mechanisms whose central purpose is to encourage and promote the effective use of resources to accomplish ambitious learning goals. Such systems would require financial tracking tools that integrate resource, instruction, and student performance information for schools and districts, "promoting the system's outcomes, not just tallying its funding."[62]

To accomplish this transition, the working group called on officials to revise governmental accounting and financial reporting standards and practices to reflect outcome principles and measures and then to define resource responsibilities and structure contingencies on jobs, schools, and funding. Together, these two actions acknowledge the dual roles of accountability in providing information and operating as an incentive, the latter by assigning consequences for good and bad behavior. Both roles are required, the working group concluded, so that accountability is reoriented from compliance to student performance and to provide a fair basis to hold educators and schools accountable for student learning.

The working group's recommendations embody principles, funding mechanisms, and conditions that remove impediments to effective resource use, align resources with student learning, and create mechanisms that allow elected officials and educators to expand resource knowledge and to experiment with new methods. The recommendations give practical meaning to the framework for linking resources and student performance, and they provide an equally practical perspective on the question, Where is the smart money in connecting educational resources to student learning?

The following chapters explore these actions and their consequences in depth. Then the general argument turns to the challenges and choices involved in building a smart-money resource system.

PART II

Removing Impediments to Effective Use of Resources

2

How Federal Categorical Funding Prevents the Effective Use of Resources

Christopher T. Cross and Marguerite Roza

Observers of school finance and education policy in the United States often comment that because the federal government contributes only 7 to 9 percent of total K–12 funding, its presence is minimal. That is far from reality. In fact, by the ways in which it allocates funds, regulates states and school districts, and holds them accountable, and by the very existence of its numerous *categorical* spending programs—those restricted-purpose or targeted resources that often shape how money is allocated and students are served—it is clear that the federal government has played a significant role in shaping public education finance.

Despite having a profound impact on resource allocation at the school district level, federal grants have not made great progress in solving the problems that prompted them. Poverty continues to be the most defining characteristic of student performance, despite the forty-year-old federal Title I program, which still has at its core the goal of reducing the achievement gaps experienced by low-income students.

Clearly, responsibility for these failings should not land only on the federal government. States and school districts, too, have tried to tackle these challenges, with only sporadic triumphs at best. As this chapter demonstrates, success has been limited by the interplay of well-intentioned federal, state, and local entities. As in any large bureaucratic system—in which actions and reactions at one level exist largely in response to actions and reactions at other levels—education policies have had more to do with federal, state, and local entities responding to each other than with their attempts to address educational problems in schools and districts. The result is that four decades of federal policy making has structured resource allocation systems that now act as barriers to addressing the very problems that prompted federal involvement in the first place.

FEDERAL POWER VIA COMPLIANCE

Federal aid to public schools is relatively new. Before passage of the Elementary and Secondary Education Act of 1965 (ESEA), almost the only federal money going to public schools went to school districts where there was a substantial federal presence; this usually meant that real property owned by the federal government was not on the local tax rolls.[1] Hence, *impact aid* was developed as a substitute for lost local tax revenue.[2] Impact aid came without strings, and hence school districts could use it in the same way that they used their own locally generated revenues. Because only a small percentage of school districts received this aid, and because none of it went through state agencies, few school districts and none of the states had much experience with federal funding before 1965.

ESEA changed all that. Created as part of President Lyndon Johnson's War on Poverty, ESEA was aimed at alleviating the effects of poverty on children's education. Once the law was signed, most of the nation's school districts came within the federal orbit.

In those early days, most school districts honored the spirit of the law by providing services that supported the education of poor children, but a few made headlines by paying for a superintendent's car or building a swimming pool. Inevitably, those few worst-case examples set the stage for the imposition of audit requirements and new regulations. These developments soon created the mentality that documenting compliance was more important than demonstrating educational outcomes. Thus began the era of policy making based upon the worst-case scenario.

Tinkering with Compliance

Almost from the start, government auditors and outside watchdogs were vigilant in holding schools and districts accountable for the use of federal funds, but they seldom held them accountable for student learning. Educational results were more complicated, and adequate measures were not available. The Department of Health, Education, and Welfare (HEW) Audit Agency (the Department of Education was not created until 1980) issued fifty-five reports on Title I from March 1967 through February 1971, and the General Accounting Office (GAO, now Government Accountability

Office) issued a score of its own. In June 1972, GAO reported that twenty-four of the HEW Audit Agency findings, totaling $37 million in questionable spending, were still unresolved, some of them for two to four years.[3]

In its own reports, GAO cited state after state for violating restrictions on the use of funds. In March 1970, West Virginia was cited for three school districts that charged $300,000 in salaries to Title I for staff to build a cafeteria, even though the staff also performed other duties, and for purchasing $40,000 in equipment without identifying a need for it.[4]

In Ohio, GAO found that the state had approved the Cleveland Public School District's use of Title I funds for central kitchen facilities and for operating a summer arts program in which only twenty of sixty-nine students were Title I eligible. It also found that Cincinnati had charged Title I with accrued sick leave for Title I employees but had made no corresponding charge from its own funds for non-Title I staff.[5]

At the heart of many complaints were accusations that school districts were using Title I funds to offset inequities in the distribution of state and local funds, even though districts did not track spending by schools. At this point, the federal government's response was to impose regulations that specified exactly how school districts could prove that state and local funds in Title I schools provided services that were comparable to those available in non-Title I schools. The law eventually was modified so that school districts could document comparability by demonstrating only the presence of a salary schedule, a staffing policy, and an even distribution of supply costs.[6] One clear implication of such requirements was the federal endorsement of a districtwide salary schedule based largely on experience. In addition, as should have been predicted, confusion ensued concerning the way instructional aides were to be used in comparability counts demonstrating equal staffing.[7] Once again, federal actions reacted to local practice more than they advanced the original intent of federal grants.

In these and other cases, GAO noted that state education agencies had not provided adequate guidance and had approved expenditures that clearly were not appropriate. All the states were urged to improve their management of federal program funds.

Ensuring School District Compliance

The GAO reports had the natural effect of causing states and school districts to become compliance oriented. States recognized that their role in ensuring the continued flow of federal funds was to avoid compliance violations. Thus, states instituted policies that prioritized compliance-oriented record keeping. They mandated that school districts account for all resources, including nonfederal funds, by using accounting systems that detailed spending by categories deemed relevant to federal compliance, namely, federal account codes such as fund, function, and object.[8] Many states then implemented accounting systems—manuals and, later, software—and reporting schemes structured to reflect these compliance categories.

With these new state fiscal requirements, school districts grew proficient in the latest procedures and became more compliant in managing funds from federal grants separately and independently from all other resources. Fiscal staff became experts in fund accounting and turned over federal resources directly to school district departments that were created specifically to manage these grants. Grant administration became a job classification, as some district employees grew proficient in judging which functions and objects were and were not allowed for each federal allocation.

Inequities in Federal Formulas

What's more, the allocation of federal funds often is based, at least in part, on a state's average per-pupil spending, and almost every program guarantees a minimum amount per state.

As documented by U.S. Department of Education budget tables, the resulting federal funding is extremely variable, and often it does not work in the best interests of the lowest-income students. For example, in the 2003–2004 school year, Wyoming, with fewer than 10,000 poor children, received $2,957 per child, but Arizona, with 213,000 poor children, received $881 per child. The different allocations are based on the fact that Wyoming's state spending is about 50 percent more per pupil than Arizona's, and the fact that each state is guaranteed a certain minimum level of funding. Therefore, Wyoming is a major beneficiary, as are Vermont and North Dakota. Conversely, states with growing populations, especially of poor children— such as Arkansas, Utah, Nevada, and Arizona—receive far less funding per student.[9]

This funding approach means that Wyoming, with 0.1 percent low-income students, gets 0.3 percent of Title I funds, whereas Arizona, with 2.5 percent low-income students, receives 1.7 percent of Title I funds. Formulas that allocate funds strictly on the basis of student enrollment are more fair, even though there is usually a two- to three-year lag in such data.

CATEGORICAL PROGRAMS PROLIFERATE

As noted, when Title I was first created as a part of the Elementary and Secondary Education Act of 1965, there were almost no federal programs that served regular public schools. By the time of ESEA's first reauthorization, the march for additional new programs had begun. Bilingual education was one of the early entries and, in one form or another, has been funded ever since. Others came in time—metric education, Javits gifted and talented, women's educational equity, civic education, and arts education—each with its own sponsor, some with appropriations, and all with organized constituencies determined to fight for their existence. In fact, the 2006 *Catalog of Federal Domestic Assistance* programs listed seventy-six educational programs, some of which are for colleges and universities.[10]

The existence of these programs often has meant the creation of little empires, especially at the state agency level but frequently also in school districts. Chief state school officers have found that because staff in their agencies are paid with federal funds, those staff may feel more beholden to their federal counterparts than to their own state leaders. Although that relationship can insulate federal programs from political interference at the state level, it also prevents the development of coordinated funding strategies that work in the best interests of children.

One of the earliest studies examining the impact of multiple school programs was done in 1981 by Jackie Kimbrough and Paul Hill at the RAND Corporation. In this landmark study, which certainly influenced later congressional actions, Kimbrough and Hill found that in some schools children were pulled out of class so frequently that the primary teacher had the total class only one and a half hours daily, and was unable to implement the state-mandated curriculum. In districts with migrant Hispanic populations, students were often involved in four or five pullouts daily. The researchers further noted that by fifth grade, the students had received no instruction in science or social studies.[11]

Kimbrough and Hill also found that administrative burdens were great, often resulting in reduced teaching time, and that schools used categorical funds intended for one group of students to provide services for another group. School districts carried out such "cross-subsidization" of funds by assigning students who were guaranteed services in an unfunded program to receive services in a funded program, and by diverting administrative and teaching staff from one program to another. In their recommendations, Kimbrough and Hill favored making it easier for programs to work together.

Even with these cautions, categorical programs continued to proliferate. However, beginning in the months following President Ronald Reagan's inauguration, Congress passed the Education Consolidation and Improvement Act (ECIA).[12] That law actually eliminated a number of categorical programs, such as metric education, and few new ones were enacted during the Reagan years, largely because education budgets were either cut or held flat and members of Congress were generally reluctant to have new programs enacted at the potential expense of existing ones, such as Title I, that enjoyed widespread support.

By the end of Reagan's second term, pressures again had begun to mount, and soon more new federal categorical programs were enacted.

DISRUPTION BY CONGRESSIONAL EARMARKS

More recently, a new and troublesome budgetary phenomenon has emerged as a serious disruption in creating a rational system of education finance. From the time ESEA became law in 1965 until the mid-1990s, federal funds flowed to state and local programs entirely through the mechanisms established in law: distribution formulas, competitive grant programs based on regulations, and, in the case of competitive programs, review processes that rewarded the best ideas or assisted those with the greatest need.

Starting in the 1990s, congressional *earmarks,* or set-asides, began to emerge in legislative bills funding educational programs. At first, only a few programs or institutions benefited, but by 2005 the number of set-asides in the bills appropriating funds for the U.S. Department of Education numbered in the hundreds and accounted for more than $700 million.

A quick glance at a list of identified recipients shows the nature and extent of the problem. A program in a Kansas high school, for example, received $149,000 for equipment and technology, a school district in Wisconsin received $249,000 for afterschool programs, a New Mexico school district got $99,000 to support teacher excellence, and a Florida district got $124,000 for a family literacy program.[13]

There have been hundreds of these examples. Earmarks now circumvent school finance mechanisms, with little transparency on how these funds affect spending among schools. They are granted on the basis of political favor rather than merit and are based neither on demonstrated need nor on competition. Complaints have led to a temporary moratorium on earmarks in the education budget, but new rules may allow them to resume.

STATE CATEGORICAL PROGRAMS

The categorical funding action did not stop at the federal level. In recent decades, the state share of education spending has grown substantially, up from 36 percent in 1960 to 51 percent four decades later.[14] Many states have structured a portion of these new funds using the same strategies employed by the federal government, with state lawmakers creating new programs rather than providing general aid, as had been their historic role. New earmarked funds come with prescriptions for functions, student types, services, and programs.

At this writing, Wisconsin has 34 of its own categorical programs, each with a separate revenue code.[15] South Carolina has 74.[16] California has 124.[17] In fact, California has created so many special programs that in the 2006–2007 budget, it was estimated that categorical programs would account for almost one-third of state spending, covering everything from school food programs to counselors to art and music education—almost 6 percent of the total education budget.[18]

States have been able to layer on a great many categorical programs, in part, because of the budgeting and accounting systems that were created in response to federal funding streams. Districts knew how to handle these restricted allocations because of their experience with federal rules. In the end, these new allocations have magnified the effects of the federal grants by adding restrictions on spending, further fragmenting local programs.

The Problem of Categorical Restrictions

Some of the concerns raised by Kimbrough and Hill persist. A 2004 study by Thomas Timar of the University of California, Davis, demonstrated that 24 of the state's 124 separate categorical programs accounted for 88 percent of the funding.[19] This distribution means that while 24 programs divide $11.4 billion, the remaining $1.6 billion is divided among 100 other programs, for an average of $16 million per program divided among almost 5 million school-age children and 1,000 school districts. The math is staggering and the fragmentation makes no educational sense, but it does feed the egos and political reputations of elected leaders, a major issue in a state with strict term limits and few opportunities for legislators to make their mark.

In his excellent analysis, Timar also noted that these categorical programs are regressive and distort the underlying state education finance system. "School finance in California," he wrote, "has shifted from a demand-driven to a supply-side system of funding . . . based *not on the real cost of providing education services* in any given district. Categorical funding should be tied to a system of planning and accountability . . . based on needs assessments, planning and evaluation."[20]

Other analyses have highlighted an array of built-in problems that comes with categorical allocations. Evidence from various locales has shown one or more of the following.

- Burdensome paperwork and other compliance activities take a toll.
- Resources are disconnected from school strategy and inhibit spending coherence.
- A one-size-fits-all approach creates inefficiencies.
- Accountability for categorical programs runs counter to school-based accountability systems.

Each categorical program has its own paperwork to justify school district eligibility and documenting expenditures. As a 1996 RAND study demonstrated, districts with more categorical funding allocate a disproportionate amount to administrative functions linked to those programs.[21] Similarly, California's bipartisan Agency on California State Government Organization and Economy noted that "teams of district personnel to fill out the paperwork are matched by teams of state workers to check it. In addition, most school districts of any size spend money on consultants for advice on how to maximize funding or pass audits."[22]

The huge cost of this red tape and paper pushing could only be guessed: "While no one the Commission talked to could estimate the cost on all sides, most agreed it was in the multi-millions of dollars statewide."[23] One consequence, however, was clear. As a leader in one large Wisconsin school district noted, the primary qualification for new grant administrator hires is "knowledge of compliance." The trade-off, she acknowledged, was that these candidates knew little about how best to use resources to address student needs.[24]

Various reports have cited the role of categorical funding in fragmenting local instructional programs. If local programs lack a strategy for integrating categorical and basic educational resources, then process requirements in the categorical programs, rather than the needs of students, shape local responses. For example, Georgia allocated a "graduation coach" to every high school. The new full-time position was tasked with addressing dropout rates by working directly with the students most at risk of dropping out.[25] Although the use of graduation coaches represents one distinct approach to truancy prevention, small schools, magnet schools, and redesigned schools offer alternative approaches. For those using an alternative approach, the imposition of a graduation coach may amount only to interference. And for the few schools that are not battling a dropout problem, the dedicated resources for graduation coaches represent an inefficient use of funds.

A report on categorical programs in South Carolina demonstrated that if a school district wanted to use restricted funding to support an innovative new school, the district could cobble together funds from twenty-five programs earmarked for alternative schools, junior scholars, youth in government, homework centers, and other programs or services.[26] For districts working toward building teacher knowledge and skills, there are fifteen state categorical funds that can be combined for these purposes.

In another state, a high-performing Catholic elementary school entitled to $7,000 in Title I funds does not take them. As the school's vice principal for academic affairs explained, "The federal regulations that come with the funds make them not worth it for us. The prescriptions specify what the money can and can't be used for, and how we account for it makes the funds a poor fit for our overall program."[27] Clearly, schools like this one—whose students rank in the 90th percentile on standardized tests—have figured out what works for their students, and for them Title I regulations are an interference.

Creating separate programs for specific student needs even creates confusion about who is responsible for improving student achievement. A large portion of the personnel paid through categorical grants reports to central departments and not to the schools in which they work.

Effects of Changes in Federal Rules

As states and school districts grew proficient in the separate management of federal funds, the federal government changed directions, promoting greater integration of resources. In the late 1980s, Congress began to permit schoolwide Title I programs. It took this action in part to respond to the rigidity of the earlier regulations, and in part in recognition that poverty was becoming more concentrated; in schools having large majorities of Title I-eligible children, often it was too difficult to separate Title I children and services from the general school population. At first these schoolwide programs were allowed only in schools having more than 75 percent of low-income students, but by the time of the ESEA reauthorization in 2002—that is, No Child Left Behind (NCLB)—schools with as few as 40 percent low-income children were permitted schoolwide projects.

In 1994, Congress approved Ed-Flex, a six-state experiment under the Goals 2000: Educate America Act.[28] The new program granted states the power to waive federal statutory and regulatory provisions governing federal allocations, provided that states waived similar provisions of their own. In 2005–2006, ten states participated in this program.

In October 1994, with the enactment of the Improving America's Schools Act, Congress granted states and school districts more flexibility in combining federal education funds with other resources.[29] Congress had hoped that federal funds, including Title I funds used in schoolwide programs, would be combined with state and local funds to upgrade entire educational programs in eligible schools.

More recently, Congress initiated NCLB's teacher quality funds (Title II), which delivers funds with almost no strings attached. The federal government asked that school districts use their best judgment about how to achieve NCLB's goals with regard to increasing teacher quality and distributing funds across schools of high and low poverty.

These provisions represented a new direction for the federal government, in that funds were to be used more flexibly at school sites to offer more-comprehensive programs for all students. The federal government, it seemed, was looking for innovation at school sites and trusted that decisions made locally regarding how best to serve students would result in better programs.

How Old Barriers Prevent Progress

Unfortunately, the compliance mentality and audit lessons of the previous thirty-plus years had become so ingrained in the fabric of state agencies that Congress's new direction was having only a minimal effect on school districts.

Twelve years after its inception, Ed-Flex had not exactly taken off. Of the ten states covered, four of them granted no new waivers to school districts in 2005–2006.[30] Although state officials noted that they enjoyed the option of granting waivers, they pointed to existing constraints as the reason the program was not used more.

Similar results have plagued federal efforts to encourage school districts to combine funds for schoolwide projects. Here, too, constraints imposed by states and habits developed from past behaviors were cited as the main culprits. A March 2000 Office of Inspector General (OIG) report found that of fifteen states reviewed by the OIG, ten did not allow school districts to combine all their funds for schoolwide projects, and six of the fifteen did not permit any combining of funds.

For most states, the barriers ran deep. As one state reported, its account structure dictated separation of resources, first by fund, then activity, and then program. Resources were separated twice before being coded as a schoolwide program. The state account structure, created as an accountability measure to ensure compliance with earlier federal programs, now stands in the way of consolidation.[31]

With little progress on consolidating funds, the federal government pushed states again. In January 2002, NCLB mandated that states modify or eliminate state fiscal and accounting barriers to consolidating funds in schoolwide programs, a mandate that was largely ignored.[32] In 2004, the Department of Education published a notice in the *Federal Register* to remind states of their duty to encourage schools to consolidate funds.[33]

Despite these messages, an OIG report issued June 9, 2005, found that even a state like Illinois, which did not overtly prevent consolidation, offered no guidance on how to consolidate federal, state, and local funds, even though the practice was explicitly allowed in Title I and several other federal programs. As a result, not one of the fifteen school districts in Illinois visited by the OIG was doing any consolidation. Among comments received by the OIG, officials in four school districts stated their belief that it was necessary to separate funds to be consistent with audit or state requirements. Three school districts saw no reason to consolidate; five said that they had always done it that way and would not change.[34]

Part of the problem was that the nature of fiscal barriers varied from state to state. States and school districts needed help figuring out what exactly needed to be changed so that they could consolidate funds. In eleven states, the 2005 OIG report found no official accounting barriers, but it noted that state data systems and reporting requirements made it difficult to consolidate these funds. Some states recognized that they would need new fund or object codes for the consolidated funds. Of the states earnestly working toward helping schools consolidate, one noted that it was "prohibitively expensive" for schools to set up new accounting systems. Now that the federal government was interested in integration of services at the school level, that very integration was made nearly impossible by the fiscal systems built to satisfy earlier federal regulations.

Furthermore, regarding the federal priority of more evenly distributing teacher quality across schools, one of the key barriers is the existing teacher salary schedules in place in nearly every school district. These salary schedules, it turns out, are part of the fabric not only of district and state structures but also of federal law through Title I comparability requirements.

Ironically, efforts to provide extra services and support to poor children that started with the 1965 law, especially those in heavily impacted schools, have, over time, worked against the interests of these same children. As the state of the art in serving targeted children has improved—moving, for example, from pullout programs to regular classroom instruction—the same compliance mentality that was created by rules and regulations to prevent the wrongful use of Title I funds now operates against the interests of those same children, who would be better served by the provision of comprehensive services.

THE DILEMMA OF CATEGORICAL PROGRAMS

Despite the complaints associated with categorical programs, the problems that motivated this form of funding persist, and the structures now in place to support them cannot be dismantled easily. These problems include the need to bring additional funds to districts that have unique student populations; the need to counter local forces that push for disproportionate funding for wealthier, less-needy schools; and the desire of lawmakers to encourage experimentation, fund pilot efforts, or encourage innovation.

Funding Districts with Unique Populations

Some school districts have a handful of severely handicapped students or great concentrations of poverty or limited English proficiency, making the accomplishment of student performance goals not only more difficult but also more expensive. Many categorical grants are intended to offset district costs associated with increased services for these students.

Countering Advocates for Wealthier Schools

In different ways, parents, teachers, and communities can work the system to the benefit of less needy students. Parents with means tend to be organized and vocal in advocating for resources. Experienced senior teachers often migrate to schools having fewer impoverished students, resulting in higher rates of teacher turnover and the assignment of less-experienced teachers in the highest-need schools. As researchers Heather Rose, Jon Sonstelie, and Ray Reinhard indicated, a larger share of California's unrestricted resources lands in low-poverty elementary schools (see table 2-1).[35]

In interviews with superintendents, researchers found that even though these officials supported reducing the number of categorical grants, they did not support the next step of releasing more unrestricted funds. They worried that local political pressures would "make it difficult for districts to allocate more resources to schools with high concentrations of struggling students."[36]

In fact, investigation of new federal allocations indicated that this concern is well founded; flexible federal allocations disproportionately can benefit wealthier schools. In one Pennsylvania district, officials allocated newly awarded flexible federal Title II teacher quality funds exclusively to wealthier schools, deliberately offsetting the allocation of Title I funds that can be delivered only to high-poverty schools.[37]

It is worth noting, too, that when the federal government granted Title I schools increased flexibility through schoolwide programs, the services to

TABLE 2-1 Unrestricted spending per pupil in elementary schools in sampled California school districts

Category	Low poverty	High poverty
Unrestricted teacher expenditures	$2,570	$1,973
Teachers per 1,000 students	44.9	41.5
Average teacher salary	$57,242	$47,545
Unrestricted other expenditures	$1,839	$1,648
Total unrestricted	$4,409	$3,621

Source: Heather Rose, Jon Sonstelie, and Ray Reinhard, *School Resources and Academic Standards in California: Lessons from the Schoolhouse* (San Francisco: Public Policy Institute of California, 2006).

many Title I children actually were diluted. Earlier, four hundred eligible students in a six-hundred-student school might have received services, but now all six hundred were to benefit in some way.[38] And when one looks through the waivers granted by states through the federal Ed-Flex program, most of them served to relax the minimum poverty enrollment necessary for Title I eligibility, thereby allowing federal funds to be diluted across students in less-needy schools.[39]

Encouraging Experimentation, Pilot Efforts, and Innovation

Some lawmakers have argued that in the context of existing finance structures, schools are not likely to try new approaches to serving students. Thus, categorical grants are needed to jump-start innovation that can serve as a demonstration for others.

STUDENT-BASED FUNDING WITH FEWER STRINGS?

One solution is to consolidate categorical grants and to distribute funds on the basis of student need, avoiding prescriptions for how these funds can be used.[40] With requirements that funds be deployed to schools based on their mix of students, lawmakers could still counter local forces that push for a greater share of funds to be spent on schools having fewer needy students.

Of course, one may expect that efforts to allocate funds based on specific student needs may bring about another series of unintended consequences. For example, if schools, districts, and states receive extra funds for students having specific needs, what is the incentive to remedy that need, if doing so means that funds will be reduced? As observers have seen with the identification of children for special education under the Individuals with Disabilities Education Act (IDEA) or the identification of students as English language learners, it has become very hard for a child to lose that label, because doing so means less revenue for a school district. [41] Yet with the fiscal systems and habits now in place, allocating funds on the basis of students and ensuring that those funds reach their intended schools are things the system is not now set up to do. Again, in previous decades accounting systems were based on fund, function, and object, and not on school or student type.

As the experience of moving to schoolwide Title I projects and of encouraging the consolidation of federal programs has demonstrated, achieving change is quite difficult. A culture exists that is oriented to maintaining the separation of categorical programs, and this situation in turn encourages the identification of children by needs as defined by federal or state law.

Moreover, the federal government's own policies regarding earmarks have had the effect of working counter to the federal goals of fiscal transparency and augmented spending by student type. By delivering funds that are exempt from other compliance regulations, the federal government forces districts to compartmentalize funds and funding intent. Although Congress has adopted new rules that would allow earmarks to resume with more transparency, the effect of this funding mechanism remains highly suspect. As long as earmarks skirt established funding mechanisms, they will distort the purposes and practices of education funding.

At the next reauthorization of the Elementary and Secondary Education Act, some groups are contemplating recommendations that would further work around, and thus accommodate, the perverse fiscal system now in place. These recommendations advocate such things as modifying Title I to require that school districts monitor total teacher salary differences instead of comparable per-pupil spending. Additionally, one of the most politically difficult changes in the reauthorization will be a move away from state average per-pupil expenditures as a major factor in determining state allocations.

It is clear that virtually any action will have unintended consequences. Although every attempt should be made to anticipate these issues, it is essential that Congress recognize this fact, authorize studies that explore how laws are implemented, and then act when presented with evidence.

3

Allocating Resources Through Traditional Versus Reform-Oriented Collective Bargaining Agreements

Julia E. Koppich

Given their importance in education policy, teacher unions and their measurable impact have drawn surprisingly little research attention. Researchers know anecdotally that many teachers, administrators, and policy makers are interested in change, but they know little about the depth or breadth of that interest. Perhaps more important, even though collectively bargained contracts have substantial resource implications, these allocations are rarely tracked or evaluated.

The combination of No Child Left Behind and state accountability systems has shone a bright light on student achievement and, collaterally, on teacher unions and their work.[1] Reports have asserted, for example, that unions, and the contracts they negotiate on behalf of teachers, handicap schools, needlessly constrain administrators, and disadvantage students.[2]

Field work for the School Finance Redesign Project (SFRP) surfaced these same themes in often-repeated comments by school administrators.

- The contract won't let me hire whom I want.
- The contract forces me to take teachers I don't want.
- There are too many procedures I have to follow exactly.
- I can't reward really good teachers.
- I can't ask teachers to do anything outside the contract.
- It's too hard (or too time-consuming or too cumbersome) to get rid of bad teachers.
- The contract is too inflexible to . . . [*fill in the blank*].

These allegations are neither uncommon nor atypical. They mirror common complaints and reflect conventional wisdom about teacher contracts.

Taken together, these comments signal what is perhaps the main criticism of teacher contracts: that they constrain management's prerogatives. To many school and district administrators, this "fact" is unsettling, confining, and inappropriate. As a high-level administrator in a large urban school district remarked, when asked what most vexes principals about contracts, "Principals are uncomfortable with the intricacies of due process."[3]

A key purpose of collective bargaining is to create procedures and due process to rationalize what is still an exquisitely bureaucratic educational system. But the choice in labor–management relations is not between unfettered management determination, on one hand, and a collectively bargained contract, on the other. Even in the absence of collective bargaining, statute and policy affect this relationship, applying brakes to management action.[4] The real choice is between a union–management contract that is mutually acceptable to teachers and administrators and some other mechanism that renders policy decisions with which all parties are bound to live.

For school districts in thirty-seven states and the District of Columbia, collective bargaining is the preferred choice. In these jurisdictions, negotiated contracts shape a significant percentage of school district budgets as well as operational procedures.[5] This chapter explores resource allocation through the lens of these contracts. It focuses on four central issues:

- What resources get allocated through the collectively bargained contract?
- What mechanisms are used to allocate them?
- What assumptions underlie these allocations?
- In what ways do contracts link resource allocation with student learning?

Data for the study discussed here were derived from an examination of teacher contracts in diverse school districts (see table 3-1). The collection of these data represents a purposeful sample—one that illustrates the relationship between resource allocation and teacher collective bargaining in traditional and reform contracts—and not one that generalizes about this relationship across all bargaining agreements.

The nine numbered districts in table 3-1 were part of an SFRP study that promised the districts anonymity as a condition of their participation.[6] Five of these districts are in states that have teacher collective bargaining laws; four are in states with no teacher collective bargaining. An

TABLE 3-1   Location, type, and representation of selected school districts

District	Location	Type	Representation
District 1	Midwest	Urban	NEA
District 2	West	Urban	NEA
District 3	West	Suburban	NEA
District 4	Midwest	Urban	AFT
District 5	Midwest	Urban	AFT
District 6	South	Urban	No collective bargaining
District 7	South	Urban	No collective bargaining
District 8	South	Urban	No collective bargaining
District 9	South	Urban	No collective bargaining
Columbus	Midwest	Urban	NEA
Denver[a]	West	Urban	NEA
Minneapolis	Midwest	Urban	AFT
Montgomery County	Mid-Atlantic	Suburban	NEA
Toledo	Midwest	Urban	AFT
Rochester	Northeast	Urban	AFT

a. Colorado actually has no collective bargaining law for teachers. Nevertheless, as a result of history and tradition, unions and school districts in the state do negotiate contracts.

additional six school districts and their contracts, named in table 3-1, also were examined.[7] In addition to their geographic diversity, teachers in six of these school districts are represented by the National Education Association (NEA); those in the remaining five districts are represented by the American Federation of Teachers (AFT). Of particular interest here, contracts in the named districts are among the most prominent examples of collaborative, or reform-oriented, bargaining, which provides a novel counterpoint to traditional practices.

TRADITIONAL AND REFORM BARGAINING

Collective bargaining reflects an evolutionary process. Shaped by experience, the exigencies of changing times, and shifting policy preferences, two types of bargaining, and two types of contracts, have emerged: traditional and reform. Table 3-2 displays the differences between these types.

TABLE 3-2   Characteristics of traditional and reform bargaining

Bargaining characteristic	Traditional (industrial) bargaining	Reform (professional) bargaining
Labor–management relationships	Separation of labor and management	Blurred labor–management distinctions
Style of negotiations	Adversarial	Collaborative
Bargaining type	Positional	Interest-based
Scope of negotiations	Limited	Expanded
Focus of protection	Individual interests	Teachers and teaching

As table 3-2 illustrates, *traditional* bargaining emphasizes the separation of labor and management, with strict lines of demarcation between teaching and management. *Reform* bargaining blurs this distinction, as unions and management recognize the interconnectedness of their work.

In traditional bargaining, labor and management are separated because unions and school districts are assumed to have different and often conflicting interests. Thus, the bargaining unit—the employees covered by a negotiated agreement—is defined as a *community of interest*. In this arrangement, teachers are workers who follow orders and who, if they are unhappy with the orders, follow them anyway and file a grievance. Management's job is to determine what teachers do and to oversee how they do it.

Reform bargaining turns labor and management separation on its head, making it a kind of policy fiction. In this context, unions and management form a professional partnership in which they foster mutual goals while acknowledging and attempting to reconcile continuing differences.

Traditional bargaining is adversarial. Unions and management engage in an ongoing jousting tournament to see who can gain the upper hand as negotiations are played out as a zero sum game. Labor relations operate as permanently contested terrain; an "us versus them" mentality permeates the relationship. The National Labor Relations Act discouraged labor–management cooperation as a way of warding off company unions.[8] Teacher collective bargaining laws contain no such admonition, but adversarial labor–management relations remain a borrowed consequence of industrial-style unionism.[9]

Reform bargaining tends to be collaborative, with unions and management emphasizing the collective aspect of their work and assuming joint custody of reform.[10] The functional slogan of collaborative bargaining, sometimes called *win-win* or *interest-based* bargaining, is, "Hard on the problem, not hard on each other."[11] To be sure, collaborative bargaining does not imply that unions and management always agree; they do not. But collaborative bargaining enables the parties to reach accord by recognizing their mutual interests and finding common ground.

Sometimes the contract itself is clear about the process used to reach the agreement. For example, the contract in table 3-1's District 1 (a traditional agreement) describes a conventional, formal negotiating process involving the exchange of proposals and counterproposals, with no mention of mutual interests. Language describing negotiation meetings and reporting of progress also is stark and formal: "Meetings between the negotiating team of the [union] and the Board shall be scheduled for a mutually convenient time within 15 days after the request for a meeting . . . Interim reports of progress may be made to the [union] by its representatives and to the Board by the superintendent and his/her designee; however, each party shall be restricted to reporting to its own organization." Clearly there are "sides" here, and little stated evidence of mutuality or collaboration.

District 2's contract, on the other hand (a reform-oriented agreement), states, "This agreement commits [the union and district] to building a collaborative partnership" and describes how students and student learning are at the center of the agreement. Although this agreement spells out salaries and conditions of work, the foundation on which the contract is built is a joint union–management interest in the fundamental business of the enterprise: student achievement.

The Montgomery County (Maryland) Public Schools (MCPS) and Montgomery County Education Association (MCEA) have perhaps the most expressive self-definition of their contract. The parties refer to their agreement specifically as "a compact for collaboration."

> This negotiated agreement was created using an interest-based bargaining process between the Montgomery County Public Schools and the Montgomery County Education Association. It is much more than a contract that describes the wages, hours, and working conditions of the unit members covered by it . . . MCPS is committed to creating organizational structures and processes that solidify the collaborative relationship between MCPS and the . . . MCEA so that parties will work together to do what is best for students.

Yet another difference between traditional and reform bargaining is found in the scope of negotiations. Collective bargaining laws specify those items that are mandatory, permissible, and prohibited subjects of bargaining. Delineating the scope of negotiations—what can be bargained, what must be bargained, and what is barred from bargaining—represents an effort to balance employees' interests in negotiating working conditions with the impact of an issue on managerial prerogatives and public policy.[12] Traditional contracts maintain a limited scope of bargaining, typically staying within the commonly understood meaning of the conventional negotiations triumvirate of wages, hours, and working conditions.

Traditional agreements reinforce a basic assumption of collective bargaining: that the system restricts teachers' issues to the conditions of work, and management maintains control over the conduct and content of that work. In traditional (or industrial) bargaining, in other words, unions represent employees' economic and day-to-day work concerns; management, acting for the school board, is responsible for making education policy.

Reform contracts, in contrast, operating under the same collective bargaining laws as traditional agreements, illustrate the remarkable elasticity of the legal scope of negotiations. These agreements shape much education policy by broadening the definition of negotiable items to include topics such as new forms of teachers' professional development and evaluation, alternatives to traditional teacher pay schemes, mentoring programs for novices, and the practice of linking contract provisions to districtwide efforts to improve student achievement.

Nevertheless, unions that seek to expand the contract portfolio face a potential legal dilemma. Under the industrial model, workers who exercise discretion and have a voice in decisions affecting the operation of the enterprise are not "employees"; they are managers and, as such, are not eligible for collective bargaining.[13] This theory derives from the 1980 U.S. Supreme Court decision in *NLRB v. Yeshiva University*.

In 1974 the unaffiliated faculty at New York's Yeshiva University petitioned the National Labor Relations Board (NLRB) for the right to represent the university's full-time faculty. University management claimed that faculty members were not employees but rather managers and supervisors and therefore were ineligible for collective bargaining, because their recommendations on matters of hiring and tenure were often accepted. The National Labor Relations Board sided with the faculty; the university appealed to the U.S. Supreme Court. In a 5-4 decision, the Supreme Court ruled in favor of the university.[14] Faculty were declared not eligible to negotiate a contract setting their wages, hours, and terms and conditions of employment. Although no state has applied the *Yeshiva* decision to a K–12 district, the decision has had something of a chilling effect on efforts at labor–management cooperation as well as on attempts to broaden teachers' involvement in educational decision making through collective bargaining.

Finally, traditional contracts are about protecting the interests of individual teachers—a statement, in effect, of teachers' accrued rights.[15] In this bargaining tradition, the contract is more about how teachers as solitary practitioners interact with the system that employs them than it is a collective professional compact about how the work of teaching gets done. As a result, many contracts are quite long and provide inclusive language for subgroups of teachers, from those in specialized fields to those with specialized assignments. Traditional bargaining thus reflects something of a conundrum: negotiations are handled collectively by the union, but contract provisions apply squarely to individuals and not to the larger profession to which its members belong.

Reform contracts take a somewhat different tack. Ensuring that individual teachers' rights are not abrogated remains an important union function. But beyond this, the contract is a vehicle for engaging teachers in thought about the ways in which their collective professional actions affect their public obligations as members of the teaching profession.[16] Reform bargaining, in other words, aims to protect teaching as well as teachers.

In sum, the differences between traditional and reform contracts can be substantial. In traditional bargaining, unions and management operate in separate spheres in a well-established hierarchy. The contract reflects the distinct places that unions and management occupy and the roles they assume. In reform agreements, mutual interests shape roles and responsibilities; they are no longer predictable by titles.

Agreement is reached in traditional negotiations after a period of adversarial and open dispute. Reform agreements tend to be achieved through a process that is collaborative and centered on mutual interests. Industrial contracts adhere to a narrow, traditional definition of wages, hours, and working conditions. Reform contracts expand the scope of negotiated items to include issues that fall into the realm of education policy. Traditional contracts protect the rights of individual teachers. Reform agreements are shaped largely by union–management concern for the welfare of the profession and the health of public education as an institution.

Collective bargaining is a dynamic process. Thus, the differences between traditional and reform contracts continue to evolve. The source of these differences may become clearer with an understanding of the historical underpinnings and central events in the short history of teacher collective bargaining.

ORIGINS AND EVOLUTION OF COLLECTIVE BARGAINING FOR TEACHERS

In 1935 President Franklin Roosevelt signed the National Labor Relations Act (NLRA) into law.[17] Enacted during heightened public support for organized labor in the period of the New Deal, the NLRA gave private sector employees, mostly working in the nation's factories, the right to "form, join, or assist labor organizations, to bargain collectively through representatives of their own choosing, and to engage in concerted activities for the purpose of collective bargaining or other mutual aid and protection."[18]

Teachers, as public sector employees, did not come under the provisions of the NLRA or gain the right to negotiate contracts with its passage. Teachers' terms and conditions of employment were set by a process called *meet and confer*. Sometimes this process was supported by statute, as in California, but often it was simply a matter of custom. In some places, it did not take place at all.

Meet and confer reflected quasi-negotiations, more akin to union advisory consultation with a school district. These sessions rarely resulted in written agreements and never in legally binding contracts. Teachers only half-jokingly referred to this process as "meet and defer" or "collective begging."

Under meet and confer, teachers were assumed to wield influence because their interests coincided with school district goals. In other words, teachers were powerful because they wanted what school districts wanted, and both were expected to express a selfless interest in "what's good for kids." Open displays of self-interest were frowned upon.[19]

This norm fostered a classically paternalistic system. Teachers were spoken for; they did not speak for themselves. Decisions of any importance, from salary to transfer and assignment to class size, were made by school boards and administrators. It was the duty of the institution to look after teachers' welfare. Administrators were to function as teachers' advocates, school boards as trustees of the common good.[20] Teacher organizations were seen as legitimate only as long as they recognized the ultimate authority of the administration and school board and did not challenge it publicly. When teachers' goals diverged from those of management and school boards, teachers were expected to defer and acquiesce.[21]

By the 1950s, industrial-style collective bargaining—the process, legitimized by the NLRA, in which employees elect a single organization to represent them for purposes of negotiating a legally binding contract with their employer—began to appeal to teachers. Private sector unions were winning substantial wage increases through collective bargaining. At the same time, wages of college-educated teachers were lagging substantially behind those of blue-collar factory workers. In addition, teachers were chafing under almost uniformly poor working conditions, including large class sizes, a plethora of assigned nonteaching duties, and multitudes of administrative directives.[22]

The bonds of meet and confer finally frayed irreparably with the social activism of the 1960s. Teachers came to see their interests as different from administrators' and began to seek an alternative means for dealing with their employers. They turned to industrial-style collective bargaining.[23]

A Turning Point

On April 12, 1962, twenty thousand New York City teachers, led by the AFT-affiliated United Federation of Teachers (UFT), walked out of their classrooms and onto the picket line. Newspapers called the strike leaders, including a young Albert Shanker, later head of the AFT, "hotheads." The city's other labor leaders refused to support the teachers. New York law made striking punishable by firing, and Max Ruben, president of the board of education, declared, "Teachers themselves have terminated their employment."

The strike lasted only one day. The *New York Times* editorialized in favor of higher teacher salaries. Governor Nelson Rockefeller offered money for the schools, and New York City teachers had a contract.[24]

The events in New York City precipitated a flood of state-level legislative activity. From the mid-1960s through the 1970s, states began to enact collective bargaining laws covering teachers.[25] Now thirty-seven states and the District of Columbia legally recognize teacher collective bargaining.[26] Unions rapidly organized teachers, and teaching became a highly unionized occupation. Whereas organized labor membership declined from 35 percent of the nation's work force in the 1950s to only 12.5 percent now, during this same period the AFT and NEA grew from a combined membership of 750,000 in 1960 to 4 million.[27] Together, these organizations—the nation's two major teacher unions—represent about 90 percent of the nation's public school teachers.[28]

The Rise of Industrial Unionism

Unions and collective bargaining first gained strength among teachers because school district officials were perceived to be arbitrary, punitive, and politically motivated.[29] The kind of bargaining teachers adopted, called *industrial bargaining* because of its antecedents in the nation's factories, gave teachers a voice through legally binding contracts that shaped the terms and conditions of their employment. As teachers adopted industrial-style bargaining, teacher unionism came to be identified by its hallmarks: separation of unions and management, adversarial labor–management relations, a limited scope of bargaining, and a focus on individual interests.

Teacher contracts developed in response to centralized educational decision making.[30] As power and authority accrued to school district headquarters, unions consolidated their efforts in master contracts to influence the terms and conditions of teachers' work.[31]

Early contracts served important, but often limited, purposes. They applied a districtwide template to teachers' employment conditions, codifying, often for the first time, the terms and conditions that shaped teachers' work lives. They introduced a modicum of fairness to the school system bureaucracy in the form of equitable, across-the-board treatment, uniform policies, and standardized procedures. And they protected teachers from arbitrary and capricious actions of their employers.[32]

A Shifting Scene

By the mid-1980s, circumstances had begun to shift; some school districts and their unions began a gradual process of reforming their contracts. The triggering event was the 1983 release of *A Nation At Risk*, the report of the National Commission on Excellence in Education.[33] This report riveted the nation's attention to the public schools, calling for fundamental reform in a system that, the commission argued persuasively, was shortchanging the nation's students and jeopardizing the U.S. economy.

At the AFT convention in Los Angeles that year, the national union's president, Albert Shanker (the "hothead" of the 1962 New York City strike), stunned delegates when he announced, "In a period of great turmoil and sweeping changes, those organizations and individuals who are mired in what seems to the public to be petty interests are going to be swept away in the larger movement. Those . . . who are willing and able to participate, to compromise, and to talk will not be swept away. On the contrary, they will shape the direction of all the reforms and changes that are about to be made."[34]

Teachers had expected Shanker to excoriate *A Nation At Risk* as yet another example of unwarranted "teacher bashing." Instead, he publicly acknowledged problems with the educational system, said the system needed to change, and asserted that teachers and their unions needed to be part of the solution. Shanker called for better, more comprehensive systems of teacher evaluation, advocated standards for students and teachers, supported the testing of beginning teachers, raised the prospect of differentiated pay, and called for rigorous accountability systems. In short, he called not only for fundamental changes in public education but also for a new form of unionism based on teacher professionalism.

The NEA for some years resisted reform, just as it had previously resisted collective bargaining. In February 1997, the organization's new president, Bob Chase, spoke to the National Press Club in Washington, D.C. In a speech titled "It's Not Your Mother's NEA," Chase acknowledged the NEA as a traditional, narrowly focused union, inadequate to the needs of contemporary education. He called for higher academic standards, less bureaucracy, schools better connected to parents and communities, and contract bargaining focused on school and teacher quality.[35]

By the late 1990s, both of the national teacher unions had come to recognize that, with education reform, the stakes had changed for students as well as teachers. School districts were faced with increasing calls for tougher academic standards and better student learning results. Some unions began to publicly acknowledge that they, too, had an organizational stake in how well or poorly students in their districts fared. This recognition gave rise in a handful of districts to a new kind of contract development, called reform (or professional) bargaining, that was different in both form and substance from traditional industrial-style bargaining.

RESOURCE ALLOCATION THROUGH THE LENS OF THE CONTRACT

Table 3-3 displays bargaining and contract types for the school districts and collective bargaining agreements that are the subject of this chapter. Three of the numbered districts (1, 3, and 4) have traditional collective bargaining agreements; two (2 and 5) are reform oriented. As the table illustrates, the form of negotiations and type of contract are not predictable by the organization (AFT or NEA) that represents the teachers in a given district.

The remaining four numbered districts (6, 7, 8, and 9, not shown on table 3-3) are located in nonbargaining states that have no collective bargaining laws for teachers and no teacher contracts. Nevertheless, in each of these districts, there is a dominant teachers' organization that participates to some degree in shaping teaching conditions and the allocation of scarce fiscal resources. Most teacher contracts are quite long, often running to more than one hundred pages. And in many of these contracts, regulations and procedures are spelled out in excruciating detail.

TABLE 3-3   Union representation, bargaining form, and contract type of selected school districts

District	Union	Form of bargaining	Type of contract
District 1	NEA	Adversarial	Traditional
District 2	NEA	Collaborative	Reform
District 3	NEA	Collaborative	Traditional[a]
District 4	AFT	Adversarial	Traditional
District 5	AFT	Collaborative	Reform
Columbus	NEA	Collaborative	Reform
Denver	NEA	Collaborative	Reform
Minneapolis	AFT	Collaborative	Reform
Montgomery County	NEA	Collaborative	Reform
Toledo	AFT	Collaborative	Reform
Rochester	AFT	Collaborative	Reform

a. Although union and management members in District 3 say they use collaborative bargaining, the content of the contract itself is traditional. Collaboration alone does not signify reform. An expanded range of topics, many of them student-oriented, does.

It would be easy to assert that every contract provision has resource implications. In a sense, this is true. Every part of the agreement requires, at a minimum, administrative staff time to implement. Thus, every provision incurs costs, however modest. Yet for purposes of this discussion, the focus is on those negotiated items that are likely to have substantial monetary implications, as displayed in table 3-4.

As table 3-4 shows, there is a great deal of overlap in the types of major provisions that have fiscal implications, and they are contained in traditional as well as reform contracts. However, knowing that an item is in a contract is different from knowing what that provision holds. All contracts, for example, contain provisions on salaries and transfers. Yet the differences in these provisions between traditional and reform agreements can be substantial.

On other issues, such as workday or leaves of absence, the differences between reform and traditional contracts tend to be slight. Table 3-5 shows the likelihood of differences between certain contract provisions in traditional and reform contracts.

In the area of benefits, for example, all contracts provide for employee health-care coverage. Traditional as well as reform contracts specify the

TABLE 3-4 Major monetary items allocated through the contract

Item	Districts	Type of contract
Salaries	All[a]	Traditional and reform
Benefits	All	Traditional and reform
Workday, work year	All	Traditional and reform
Leaves of absence	All	Traditional and reform
Nonteaching duties	All	Traditional and reform
Class size	Most[b]	Traditional and reform
Transfer, assignment	All	Traditional and reform
Professional development	All	Traditional and reform
Evaluation	All	Traditional and reform
Tenure	All	Traditional and reform
Dispute resolution	All	Traditional and reform
Layoff, dismissal	All	Traditional and reform
Career development	District 5, Toledo, Minneapolis, Rochester	Reform
Improving student achievement	Denver, Minneapolis, Montgomery County	Reform

a. "All" in this context refers to all of the contracts reviewed for this chapter. However, for the topics indicated, "all" could apply to all contracts more generally.

b. Most contracts contain provisions on class size, but not all do. The Minneapolis contract, for example, does not refer to class size goals or limits. Montgomery County does not have a provision on class size per se but does reference staffing allocations being based on each year's budget numbers.

health-care plans from which teachers can select, the employees' share of the cost, and whether and under what circumstances dependent coverage is available. In addition to health care, school districts typically shoulder the primary costs of prescription drug, dental, vision care, and long-term disability plans, as well as professional liability insurance, workers' compensation for on-the-job injuries, and retirement.[36]

Another area in which it is difficult to find substantial differences between traditional and reform contracts is in the outline of the workday and work year. All contracts spell out the salaried work year and workday. Agreements limit the number of workdays, including teaching days and noninstructional days, and describe the hour boundaries of the salaried teacher workday.

TABLE 3-5 Differences in traditional and reform contract provisions

Provision	Differences likely	Differences rare
Salaries	√	
Benefits		√
Workday, work year		√
Leaves of absence		√
Nonteaching duties		√
Class size		√
Transfer, assignment	√	
Professional development	√	
Evaluation	√	
Dispute resolution		√
Tenure, layoffs, dismissal		√
Career development	√	
Improving student achievement	√	

Salaried is the operative word here. Contracts typically specify a six- or seven-hour workday. The Columbus contract, for example, states, "The regular work day for all full-time teachers shall normally be 7 1/2 hours." However, this refers to the number of hours teachers are required to be on-site. Work done at home—additional planning, grading papers, and the like—is not part of this calculation.[37]

All the contracts reviewed for this chapter contain provisions for leaves of absence. Few differences can be found between traditional and reform agreements in this regard. Some leaves are paid, costing the district money; others are unpaid, ostensibly saving money if the absent teacher is replaced by a substitute and only the substitute's salary is paid.

Among the leaves most commonly found in the contracts examined here are sick leave (typically ten days per year), bereavement and child care leave, and leaves for military service and jury duty.[38] All the contracts in this set (except that of District 5) offer partially paid sabbatical leaves, usually after a minimum of seven years of service.[39]

These agreements also provide paid leave for the union president to conduct union business. For unions and management, this provision acknowledges that running a union is a full-time job requiring more than part-time attention.

Contracts typically limit the noninstructional duties to which teachers can be assigned, such as bus or yard duty and hall patrol. The contract in District 3, which is fairly typical, states that teachers are not required to supervise the cafeteria, collect money from students, supervise halls or bus loading at the secondary level, or supervise study halls. Such nonteaching duty provisions are an effort to ensure both that nonclassroom duties are spread evenly among the faculty and that teachers are not overburdened with responsibilities that reduce the time they spend in their classrooms.

Most contracts contain provisions on class size or pupil-to-teacher ratios. Some, such as District 4's, require payment to the teacher when class sizes exceed these limits: "The class size limit in elementary schools shall be 25, except by express written consent of the teacher. If the administration cannot meet that limit in one or more classrooms . . . one or more of the following options will be utilized: (1) reassignment of students; (2) add an additional classroom teacher; (3) pay the affected teacher $5.00 per day for each student above 25."

District 3's agreement includes class size limits, but for every student above the limit, a teacher must be allocated fifty-five minutes of daily paraprofessional time or a half-hour of release time. Class size provisions acknowledge the significance of limiting class size as both a teacher working condition and a student learning condition and reinforce the importance for unions as well as management of adhering to their negotiated agreement. These provisions also provide a bit of give for a situation that may not have a quick or easy resolution.

The contract in District 5 contains class size limits, but it has a unique way of resolving overages. In this district, a joint union–management Teacher Allocation Committee is given money and paraprofessional time at the beginning of each year. When a teacher alleges an overage, the committee has the authority to resolve the matter (by increasing salary or adding support time) or to let it stand as is. The committee's decision is final.

Procedural Issues

As table 3-5 indicates, differences between traditional and reform contracts are rarely found in the language of four significant, potentially expensive procedural areas: dispute resolution, tenure, dismissal, and layoff. Moreover, even though tenure, dismissal for cause, and layoff often are described in contracts, the procedures for each of these, as well as legally permissible reasons for layoff and dismissal, typically are specified in state law separate from the collective bargaining statute.[40]

Nevertheless, in practice, traditional contracts handle these matters somewhat differently from reform contracts. All contracts, for example, include a mechanism for resolving alleged violations of the agreement—called a *grievance procedure*—with progressive levels of hearings: school, district, (sometimes) school board, and, finally, advisory or binding arbitration, in which a neutral third party renders a decision. Under traditional negotiating arrangements, nearly all problems become formal written grievances. Teachers working under reform contracts, on the other hand, tend to file fewer grievances, because the parties employ informal mechanisms, such as regular meetings between union and district officials, to resolve disputes before they reach the formal grievance stage.

In most districts, earning tenure is a pro forma process involving periodic and often brief classroom reviews by a principal over two to three years.[41] Classroom support often is minimal, and nearly everyone achieves tenure. As described later in this chapter, many reform contracts substitute a process of *peer assistance and review* (PAR) for probationary teachers and underperforming tenured teachers. The main purpose of PAR is to improve teaching, but the result of this process is that fewer (poor) teachers make it to tenure, and more underperforming tenured teachers are dismissed.

Minneapolis has negotiated a unique tenure procedure. As a result of an agreement between the Minneapolis Public Schools and the Minneapolis Federation of Teachers, probationary teachers undergo a structured three-year process of professional development and peer and administrator review while they assemble a professional portfolio of accomplishments. At the conclusion of the three years, the probationers appear before a panel of teachers and administrators to make a case for tenure. Not everyone earns tenure in Minneapolis.

Finally, under traditional bargaining scenarios, layoff and dismissal for cause are lengthy, often cumbersome processes. In reform bargaining arrangements, these matters are sometimes handled in a more streamlined way without violating teachers' right to due process.

As a result either of contract language or state law, high-stakes decisions on matters of tenure, layoff, and dismissal—often called matters of *employment security*—typically are enmeshed in procedural obligations. The goal is to ensure that issues related to maintenance of employment are dealt with as fairly as possible. Traditional contracts rely on well-established, often cumbersome procedures in these areas. Reform contracts often find ways to protect due process without paralyzing the system.

Examining Significant Contract Differences

In a number of resource-significant areas, substantial differences are evident between traditional and reform contracts. These include salary setting, transfers, professional development, evaluation, career development, and improving student achievement.

Setting Salaries

In many contracts (including Districts 1, 2, and 4), salaries are constructed on a single salary schedule.[42] Teachers advance in pay on the basis of years of experience and education units accrued beyond the bachelor's degree. The contract specifies rates of pay for each step and column of the schedule, as well as extra salary earned for added responsibilities. Increasingly, single salary schedules also include pay boosts for teachers who earn certification through the National Board for Professional Teaching Standards (NBPTS).[43]

The single salary schedule has been widely criticized as providing neither encouragement nor incentive for teachers to upgrade their professional skills or to willingly assume challenging assignments. Increasingly, reform contracts are diverging from this traditional salary construct.

Table 3-6 displays the contracts reviewed for this chapter and indicates whether salaries are constructed on a single salary schedule or an alternative arrangement. As the table indicates, a number of school districts with reform contracts are adopting various forms of differentiated pay. For example, teachers in District 3 who have more than fifteen years in the district or twenty years in the profession can apply for Career Teacher assignment. This designation, which provides an extra $1,700 per year, is based on the recognition that "experienced teachers provide extra value, expertise, and professionalism to the school program."[44]

District 5 has a career ladder on which teachers advance in pay as they accrue experience and responsibility and earn favorable teaching evaluations. The top rung of the ladder is lead-teacher status, for which teachers earn added compensation by serving as peer evaluators, curriculum specialists, and university clinical faculty. The contract makes clear the purpose of the career ladder: "The [union] and the Board are both committed to improving the profession of teaching. A profession offers opportunities for professional growth, involvement in decisionmaking, communication and collaboration, and increased responsibilities and accountability . . . The parties . . . view a career ladder as a way to give incentives to attract and keep quality teachers in the profession."

TABLE 3-6 Compensation arrangements in selected school district contracts

District	Single salary schedule	Differentiated compensation
District 1	√	
District 2	√	
District 3		√[a]
District 4	√	
District 5		√
Columbus		√
Denver		√
Minneapolis		√
Montgomery County	√	
Rochester		√
Toledo		√

a. The contract gives the impression that this school district has an alternative compensation arrangement. However, this district is in a state in which the finance formula has been converted to a statewide salary schedule. It is not entirely clear from reading the contract, therefore, whether salary alternatives represent true differentiated compensation or simply a way to circumvent the statewide salary schedule.

Columbus, Ohio, offers $1,500 for teachers who agree to be "assigned at the superintendent's discretion" to low-performing schools—this in an effort to ameliorate the problem, endemic in urban districts, of the most challenging schools being staffed by the least experienced, often least well qualified, teachers. This contract also provides for *gainsharing*, or bonus money to schools that meet established performance goals. In addition, Columbus has developed a voluntary Performance Advancement System, in which teachers who participate can earn $2,500 a year for each of two years—money that is renewable "based on student achievement and demonstrated accountability for student progress."

The differentiated pay plan that has received the most publicity was negotiated by the Denver Public Schools and the Denver Classroom Teachers Association. Under ProComp, as it is called, teachers have a number of options for advancing in salary: raising their students' test scores, receiving outstanding evaluations, demonstrating knowledge and skill, and teaching in hard-to-staff schools or subjects. In Denver, simply accruing units and years of service no longer results in higher pay.

Rochester's contract provides a $1,500 annual stipend to teachers who qualify for lead-teacher status and agree to transfer to low-performing schools, again in an attempt to balance the staffing of underresourced schools. At the time of this writing, Minneapolis was in the process of implementing a professional compensation plan that included elements of the Denver plan as well as the Milken Family Foundation's Teacher Advancement Program (TAP), which bases pay on multiple career paths, ongoing professional development, and performance-based accountability.

Yet another differentiated compensation plan is found in the contract between the Toledo Public Schools and the Toledo Federation of Teachers. The Toledo Review and Alternative Compensation System, or TRACS, is designed to attract and retain high-quality teachers, reward teachers who raise student achievement, and support and reward experienced teachers who choose difficult teaching assignments.

> The overriding goal of TRACS is to promote teacher quality while improving the academic performance of students. This goal will be achieved through integrated and focused objectives that include ongoing professional development targeted to specific student academic and school improvement needs; more effective teaching and learning; retaining the most accomplished teachers in the classroom by acknowledging and rewarding teaching excellence; maximizing the talents of recognized teachers by assigning additional responsibilities and leadership roles; and/or placing teachers in high needs schools and challenging teaching assignment.[45]

Critics allege that these new pay plans, by and large, are not truly differentiated compensation and reflect only slight deviations from conventional pay patterns. But, in fact, paying more for challenging assignments and subjects and making evaluation results and test scores part of the pay calculus represent substantial changes, well out of the traditional union-negotiated salary norm.

Transfer and Assignment

Transfer and assignment are significant provisions of all teacher contracts. This category contains three components: (1) voluntary transfer, (2) involuntary transfer, and (3) assignment. *Voluntary transfer* refers to a situation in which a teacher seeks a different school assignment. *Involuntary transfer* results from a required reduction in school staff, typically because of a drop in enrollment or loss of funding. *Assignment* refers to a teacher's in-school teaching assignment.

Conventional wisdom holds that all teacher transfers and assignments are governed by *seniority,* defined as a teacher's length of service in the district. Conventional wisdom, however, is not foolproof.

In Districts 1 and 4—both with traditional agreements—seniority is the main criterion for voluntary transfers, but the language of the agreements provides some wiggle room. District 1's contract, for example, states, "The variables to be weighed in consideration of transfer requests include, but are not limited to, specific professional competencies, experience . . . preferences, diversity, and seniority. Of this, seniority will be the most important consideration, except where other variable(s) require greater consideration." Circumstances in which "other variable(s) require greater consideration" are left unstated in the contract, subject to case-by-case analysis.

District 3 also has a traditional contract. However, here, voluntary transfers are not governed by seniority at all but by "qualifications, as per the posted job description."

Districts 2 and 5, both with reform contracts, use school interview teams composed of teachers and administrators to select volunteer transfer applicants. The language of District 5's contract is representative: "Teachers shall be considered for vacancies by school interview panels . . . The Board and the [union] agree that teachers and principals should have a greater role in selecting teachers to fill vacancies. Therefore, the parties agree that such decisions should be jointly made by the principal and teachers in that department, team, or level of the school."

District 2's contract does not mention seniority at all. Seniority applies in District 5 only if all other circumstances—training, experience, individual qualifications—are substantially equal and "the transfer is consistent with the racial balancing of the staff."[46]

Several of the comparison reform contracts—Columbus, Denver, and Rochester—have eliminated seniority for voluntary transfers and have substituted a procedure in which, as in Districts 2 and 5, school-based teams of teachers and administrators interview applicants and make selections based on fit with the available position.

Involuntary transfers in nearly all contracts continue to be governed primarily by seniority. Here, too, however, considerations of credentials and, often, racial balance come into play. The language in District 1's contract is illustrative: "The administration may displace professional staff members due to pupil enrollment, program reduction, or staff realignment. When a professional staff member is to be displaced, the administration shall consider the following: (a) racial balance, (b) system seniority, (c) areas of certification." From the union perspective, some reliance on seniority represents an effort to reduce arbitrariness or personal favoritism from the decision about who stays and who leaves a school when a reduction in staff is required.

Although it is often assumed that teachers hold sway over in-school assignments, almost all contracts give principals the right to make these decisions. The language of District 3's contract is fairly typical: "Assignment is based on qualifications and [should] take into account the interests and aspirations of the employees." Principals may be obliged to solicit teachers' preferences, but the final decision about assignment remains with the administration.

In sum, traditional contracts maintain an often substantial reliance on seniority for purposes of voluntary transfers, but reform contracts rarely do. Most often, they engage a school-based team of teachers and administrators to select a candidate for a job based on fit with the available position.

Building Teachers' Professional Capacity

How do contracts address the issue of building teachers' professional skills? Four provisions, found in a number of reform contracts, deal with this issue: new teacher induction, professional development, evaluation, and career development.

New Teacher Induction

Providing induction (mentoring) for new teachers is increasingly part of negotiated (reform) contracts. District 2, for instance, provides a mentor for every new teacher. Some school district–union partnerships, such as those in Minneapolis and Montgomery County, jointly run orientation and induction sessions for new teachers. These meetings are not mentioned in the contract but are contained in extracontract agreements.[47] In these agreements, the union assumes an obligation to help induct novices into the profession of teaching.

Professional Development

All contracts contain a reference to professional development or continuing education for teachers. Historically, school districts have favored large-group, limited-session presentations or workshops as most efficient. Yet the research on professional development clearly states that the most effective professional development is school based and is related to teachers' professional assignments.

Traditional contracts often try to limit required professional development, based on teachers' consistent views that training rarely improves professional skills. This assessment of professional development, however, is changing based on the demands of standards-based education. The contract in District 1, otherwise among the most traditional, places professional development in a section on professional accountability and requires that each teacher participate in at least twenty hours of professional development per year, although it does not specifically define the nature of the professional development provided.

District 2's contract refers to an Educator Academy, still in the developmental stage at the time of negotiations, to take care of teachers' long-term professional development needs. That contract establishes a joint union–management steering committee "for professional development led by the Chief Academic Officer and the [union] president. The steering committee's primary role is insuring professional development to support sustainable progress in raising student achievement."

In District 5, wide-ranging professional development has long been provided through a local academy funded by a corporate sponsor. The union and management in this district, in cooperation with a local university, also have implemented professional practice schools to provide on-the-job training for novices.

The Minneapolis contract focuses extensively on professional development, with support for teachers attempting to earn National Board certification as well as a comprehensive process that requires teachers to prepare annual individual, as well as school team-based, professional development plans focused on increasing student achievement. The contract further defines what the union and district mean by professional development and what purpose it is designed to serve.

> Professional development is the process by which teachers individually and jointly enhance and update their knowledge of standards, curriculum, and content, and improve their instructional skills and strategies. Effective and continuous professional development extends the knowledge base and repertoire of practices and skills necessary [for] all students [to] acquire the highest quality of education. Successful professional development is focused on student learning and achievement.

Denver's contract is similarly clear about the purpose of professional development: "Professional development will focus on building teacher quality to increase student progress and growth." The same is true of the Columbus contract: "Professional development will focus on building teacher quality to increase student progress/growth."

Montgomery County has one of the most extensive contract focuses on professional development. A staff development teacher, whose sole job is facilitating professional growth linked to a school's school improvement plan, is assigned to each school to work with the teachers there. As that contract states, "To be effective with a diverse and challenged student population, teachers need a significant repertoire of skills, strategies, and practices derived from research about teaching and student learning, and the knowledge to match these skills to student instructional needs."

Professional development is beginning to occupy a prominent place in many teacher contracts. Increasingly, especially in reform-oriented agreements, professional development acknowledges an important link between enhancing teachers' professional skills and improving student learning.

Evaluation

Evaluation is a negotiable item under most state collective bargaining laws. The contract typically specifies how frequently evaluation will occur, who is responsible for conducting it, what procedure is to be used, and whether or not a teacher can grieve the results.[48]

Evaluations in districts having traditional contracts tend to be conducted by administrators, on average once every two years (every year for probationary teachers). Standards for evaluation are negotiated district by district. But teacher evaluations have long been criticized as pro forma, only modestly based on standards of good practice, and only slightly related to improving teaching or learning.[49] With increased accountability pressures, changes in evaluation are becoming increasingly evident.

For instance, District 2's contract provides for an intervention program for underperforming experienced teachers: "Evaluations of certificated employees will include the contractually mandated criteria *as well as student achievement* [emphasis added]." For teachers who receive satisfactory reviews, development and implementation of a professional growth plan can be substituted for the usual evaluation sequence.

In District 3, evaluation is based on criteria and standards detailed in the contract. These include knowledge of subject matter, instructional skills, professional preparation and scholarship, classroom management, handling of student discipline and attendance problems, continuous efforts toward improvement, and professional responsibility.

District 5, as well as Toledo, Rochester, Minneapolis, Montgomery County, and Columbus, has adopted a standards-based process of peer assistance and review to evaluate probationary teachers and tenured teachers in trouble. PAR uses experienced teachers called *consulting teachers,* jointly selected by the district and the union, to provide intensive support and subsequently to evaluate these teachers' professional practice. Consulting teachers' reviews and recommendations are submitted to a joint union–management PAR committee that makes recommendations to the superintendent and school board for final decision. Reviews of PAR programs point to this system as rigorous and effective, combining individual support and professional development with performance review.[50]

PAR also reflects the difficulty of change for unions as well as management, along with the challenge of reform unionism. Although the districts named earlier in this section have used PAR programs for more than a decade, these efforts, in which unions and school districts share responsibility for the evaluation of teachers' professional practice, still are not the norm. Teachers often are reluctant to evaluate their colleagues ("That's management's job"), and principals are not eager to relinquish what they view as their turf. Peer review challenges one of the key tenets of industrial unionism: separation of labor and management. Neither side finds it easy to change, and both, at least initially, resist.

Experience shows, however, that after about a year with peer review, teachers and administrators become enthusiasts. Teachers view the support they receive as crucial, and administrators come to recognize that peer reviewers provide their colleagues with far more intensive and targeted assistance than principals can. Nevertheless, birth pangs can be severe and must be carefully handled by unions and management if the process is to succeed.

Career Development

Teaching is famously an unstaged career in which practitioners historically have had few opportunities to move beyond day-to-day classroom teaching routines without leaving teaching for administration.[51] Although most traditional contracts do not directly address teachers' career development, a number of reform contracts do. The District 5 career ladder and Toledo's TRACS, previously described, fall into this category. These systems make it possible for teachers to advance in pay and to differentiate their professional responsibilities as they accrue knowledge and experience.

The Rochester contract also describes a Career in Teaching program, in which teachers advance from intern to resident to professional to lead-teacher status on the basis of their evaluations. Under the program, which is governed by a joint union–management committee, lead teachers must agree to accept any school assignment as well as serve as mentors and professional development providers.

Under some reform agreements, then, unions and management together have begun to professionalize teaching by differentiating roles and tasks. Taking on differentiated responsibilities no longer requires teachers to leave classroom teaching for administration.

Improving Student Achievement

To what extent do contracts specifically address issues of student achievement? It can be argued that improving teaching skills falls into this category, given research-based findings on the link between teacher quality and student learning.[52] But do contracts specifically link teaching and student achievement?

Traditional contracts, by and large, do not. They concern themselves mainly with teachers' economic and day-to-day work issues. In contrast, reform contracts are direct and specific about teachers' and unions' roles in influencing student achievement. This is one of the main issues that distinguishes traditional from reform contracts. That said, this chapter does not claim that a direct link exists between reform contracts and measurable gains in student achievement. That is not the purpose of this chapter, nor were data collected to make that judgment. What this chapter's data do suggest is that reform-oriented contracts reflect a clear understanding of teachers' responsibility for improving student learning.

The contract in District 2, for example, in a provision titled "Partnership for Closing the Achievement Gap," states, "We commit to ensuring that all students are provided the support they need to meet . . . standards . . . We are committed to changing the odds for student success and creating a culture of success. We are focused on closing the achievement gap." The Montgomery County contract contains a specific provision on "Shared Responsibility for Student Achievement and Student Improvement" in which the union and district acknowledge their mutual obligation and responsibility for consistently increasing student achievement results.

Much of the Minneapolis contract focuses on strategies for effective instruction: what it means, along with detailed criteria and standards for getting there. This agreement includes a section on "teacher professional ethics" and describes teachers' responsibilities to students, families, communities, and colleagues. And the "Fresh Start" provision deals with how management and the union together will reconstitute chronically low-performing schools.

The Rochester contract also focuses on teachers' responsibility for student performance. This agreement includes a section on "Group Accountability" that states, in part, the following.

> The Rochester City School District and Rochester Teachers Association recognize that schools or groups of educators within schools are the essential unit of accountability and that student achievement is the essential indicator of progress. Annual assessment of progress is linked to school

improvement results. Logical consequences [including the possibility of assigning an intervention team] must exist for schools that are unable to demonstrate progress toward agreed upon standards.

To be sure, the provisions described in this section focus primarily on administrator–teacher collaboration and mutual responsibility. Because these sections reiterate the earlier described joint custody for reform, they typically are not specific about desired achievement goals nor the specific strategies to reach them. Nevertheless, acknowledging in the bilateral agreement the mutual obligation to raise student achievement represents a substantial expansion of the traditional scope of collective bargaining.

JOINT LABOR–MANAGEMENT COMMITTEES

Joint labor–management committees provide a vehicle for unions and school districts to discuss topics of mutual interest that may not lend themselves to readily negotiable contract provisions. Table 3-7 lists the joint union–management committees named in the contracts examined for this chapter.[53] The types of joint committees often signal the nature of the union's involvement in school district policy and operational decisions.

As table 3-7 indicates, District 1's traditional contract refers to a District–Association Collaborative Budget Committee. This committee's mandate is to "review the district budget, identify unfunded needs for the current year, and make recommendations to the superintendent." District 3's contract cites a joint curriculum advisory committee whose responsibility is to "review curriculum recommendations and provide input into the implementation process." Neither of these provisions suggests that the union is involved in actual decision making in the joint committee areas; rather, the union plays an advisory role.

District 4, under a traditional contract, nevertheless has a number of joint committees on important topics: school climate, teacher recruitment, class size, and academic intervention for underperforming schools. From the contract language, these appear to be advisory only.

The contract in District 2 refers to a joint professional development steering committee whose "primary role is insuring professional development support [for] sustainable progress in raising student achievement." District 5's contract includes a number of joint committees: on evaluation, educational improvement (through a collaborative labor–management Education Initiatives Panel), professional development, and teacher recruitment. These committees call for joint union–management decision making.

TABLE 3-7 Types of joint union–management committees in selected school districts

Committee	District 1	District 2	District 3	District 4	District 5	Denver	Minneapolis	Montgomery Co.	Rochester	Toledo
Budget	√									
Curriculum			√							
School climate				√		√				
Class size				√	√					
Teacher retirement				√	√					
Professional development		√			√					
Academic intervention				√	√		√		√	
Evaluation				√	√		√	√	√	√
Shared leadership, union–management collaboration, school level	√		√	√	√		√	√	√	

Rochester has a unique joint committee: the Living Contract Committee. Rochester's contract does not expire; the union and school district work continuously to resolve problems and to deal with new issues as they arise. And in Montgomery County, the joint Labor-Management Collaboration Committee meets regularly to resolve issues before they mushroom into problems. These committees create venues for collaborative decision making on whatever issues arise, whenever they arise. They are not subject specific.

Many contracts also provide for school-level committees, typically structured around shared teacher–administrator leadership. District 1's contract provides for a school-based faculty council "to collaboratively resolve building issues." The contracts in Districts 3 and 4 provide for similar site arrangements.

District 5's agreement establishes instructional leadership teams at each school "so that the principal [and] teachers may share leadership and make decisions in the following areas: develop, review, and evaluate the instructional program; monitor and improve school operations and procedures that impact instruction; [and] develop and monitor the school budget."

The Minneapolis contract describes school-based committees devoted to "shared leadership for continuous improvement" and shared decision making linked to accountability for student results. Montgomery County has analogues to the district-level labor–management committee: school-based labor–management committees. And Rochester has school-based committees with a broad portfolio "to continue to work on conditions conducive to accountability and success, including expansion of school-based shared decisionmaking to include greater discretion over factors and conditions that affect student learning: the school budget, instructional materials, strategies and assessments; staffing, curriculum, in-service [professional development], student discipline codes, instructional time and schedule, student group and class size."

A simple reading of the contract, of course, does not reveal the results of these committees. Nevertheless, knowing whether committees are advisory or imbued with decision-making authority tells much about the nature of the union–management relationship.

DEVIATING FROM THE CONTRACT

To what extent do contracts provide the opportunity to deviate from their provisions? Under what circumstances is this possible? Few contracts, traditional or reform, make provision for waivers. Those that make such provisions typically allow waivers only for a single school for a limited time (usually one year) on approval from both the union and the school district. The purpose is to resolve a school-specific issue or to implement a school-specific program.

In this study, only District 2, Columbus, and Rochester allow such deviations. District 2 permits contract waivers if schools seek to implement programs or strategies "tied to increasing academic achievement." In Columbus, a union–management Reform Panel can grant contract waivers "focus[ed] on improving teaching and learning."

Rochester has perhaps the most unique waiver provision. Under the Rochester contract, School Level Living Contract Committees, whose "purpose is to improve student achievement," are "authorized to enter into contractual agreements different from provisions contained in the central collective bargaining agreement." These waivers require a sign-off by the principal and the union's school representative. Waivers can encompass a wide range of issues, including the length of the professional day, teachers' responsibilities, parent–teacher conferences, teacher assignments, teaching conditions, teacher facilities, the length of the pupil day, and job sharing.

Waivers acknowledge that one size does not fit all; different schools may require different arrangements. But using waivers is an option that has not caught on in the contract world. Few unions (and few school districts) are willing to grant schools the kind of decision-making authority that waivers imply.

SUMMING UP: HOW TRADITIONAL AND REFORM CONTRACTS DISTRIBUTE RESOURCES

What does this description of traditional and reform contracts reveal about differences in methods of resource allocation? Table 3-8 summarizes the differences.

On balance, traditional contracts are negotiated using adversarial bargaining techniques. Reform contracts tend to use collaborative bargaining practices.

Traditional contracts treat all teachers alike. For example, these contracts rely substantially on the single salary schedule. Reform contracts recognize that teachers differ in skills, knowledge, and ability. Thus, reform contracts increasingly offer opportunities for differentiated compensation and roles. Traditional contracts tend to cling to seniority as the method of determining most voluntary transfers; reform contracts often eliminate it, replacing it with selection by a school-based team of teachers and administrators who look for the individual who best fits the school and assignment.

TABLE 3-8 Contract issues, assumptions, and related mechanisms

Contract issue	Assumptions and related mechanisms	
	Traditional contracts	*Reform contracts*
Union–Management relationship	Adversarial	Collaborative
Teacher differentiation	A teacher is a teacher is a teacher. • Standard single salary schedule • Transfer and assignment by seniority	Teachers have different interests and skills that need to be acknowledged. • Differentiated compensation • Differentiated roles • Job fit replaces seniority
Capacity building	Contract limits professional development. • Limited offerings • No career development • Pro forma evaluation	Contract emphasizes professional development. • Expansive, targeted offerings • Career ladders and differentiated teacher roles • Rigorous, standards-based evaluation
Contract flexibility	No waivers	Some waivers
Focus of protection	Individual teachers	Teaching profession
Student performance	Little reference to student performance	Explicit reference to student performance

Whereas traditional contracts view professional development as something to be delimited and restricted, reform contracts use professional development as a means of supporting teachers' professional growth related to improving student achievement, and the parties try to shape provisions to accomplish this purpose.

Evaluation also differs between traditional and reform contracts. In the former, professional evaluation most often is administrator driven, based on vague standards of practice, and little related to improving teaching or student learning. Reform contracts, on the other hand, often use a system of peer assistance and review—more rigorous and standards based—which combines professional development (helping teachers improve in areas where they are deficient) with summative performance reviews and the prospect of dismissal if efforts to improve are not successful. Traditional contracts seldom concern themselves with teacher career development. Reform agreements, on the other hand, view career development as an important mutual obligation of union and management.

Traditional contracts rarely use the words *student achievement,* much less embed it in the negotiated agreement as a joint labor–management responsibility. Reform contracts include improving student achievement as a key obligation of the agreement and of those who negotiate and are covered by it.

Traditional as well as reform contracts include school district and school-level labor–management committees. Traditional contracts tend to structure these committees on important but customary issues, such as school climate. Moreover, industrial contracts typically grant these committees only advisory authority. Joint committees in reform contracts tend to revolve around issues that are fundamental to teaching and educational systems: the provision of effective professional development, oversight of teacher evaluation systems, districtwide reform and improvement of student achievement, and shared union–management decision making. The products of these committees' deliberations often are joint labor–management decisions, and not only recommendations by the union to the administration.

Finally, the provisions of traditional contracts tend to be sacrosanct. Any violation, or perceived violation, becomes a formal, written grievance. Individual schools are not allowed to deviate from the negotiated agreement. Reform contracts are more likely to allow contract waivers that enable schools to make decisions attuned to their particular needs.

In sum, in traditional contracts, a teacher is a teacher is a teacher. Differentiation is eschewed. Reform contracts, in contrast, acknowledge that each teacher has unique skills and strengths and recognize these with money and authority. Traditional contracts are all about teachers' individual rights. Reform contracts are documents that speak both to teachers' individual interests and to the profession's public responsibility. In the reform context, unions promote and protect high-quality teaching as fervently as they protect teachers' rights.

CONTRACT PROVISIONS WITH LIMITED RESOURCE IMPLICATIONS

All contracts contain a number of important nonmonetary provisions.[54] These provisions, sometimes referred to as *rights clauses,* describe the obligations and rights granted under the contract. Although they do not have monetary implications, these provisions are essential elements of any bargained agreement, regardless of contract type.

All contracts, for instance, include a *recognition clause* acknowledging the union as the sole and exclusive representative of teachers in the district; a statement of the *duration* of the agreement (state law specifies the maximum length of the contract, typically three years); and a description of the *bargaining unit* (in other words, who is covered by the contract). Contracts include a statement of organizational rights—for example, granting the union access to the district's school mail system and the right to have an official, designated representative at each school.

Some contracts contain a specific management rights clause. The one found in the District 4 contract is typical: "Management retains the right to direct, supervise, evaluate, and hire employees; determine the overall methods . . . by which educational operations are to be conducted; and effectively manage the workforce." Whether stated or not, it is understood that whatever rights are not otherwise granted in the contract are retained by management.

Other common contract provisions with limited or no resource implications guarantee teachers' academic freedom, that is, the right to teach without undue influence; place restrictions on teacher personnel files—for example, requiring that only one file be retained on each teacher and that it be kept in a central location; and authorize deduction of union dues.[55]

Finally, contracts commonly include a *no strike* clause for the duration of the agreement; a provision for mid-contract negotiations on specified topics, called *reopeners;* and a *savings clause,* which holds that should any provision of the contract be declared illegal, the rest of the agreement remains in effect.

THE UNPREDICTABILITY OF BUDGETS

Determining how much money is allocated for negotiating purposes is not a straightforward matter. School districts may choose to set aside a certain percentage of their budgets to settle contracts, but this money, both its amount and its specific purpose, must, by the nature of the process, be somewhat fungible.

Moreover, school districts and their unions face a chronic problem. In the interest of labor peace, both sides typically seek longer rather than shorter contract periods. However, regardless of the source of school district funding, budgets are developed annually. School districts often have little certain knowledge about the state of their finances from year to year. Thus, for both parties, agreeing to multiyear contract provisions that carry fiscal implications is something of an exercise in educated guesswork. There is no easy solution for this dilemma.

NONBARGAINING STATES

Four of the study districts are in states that do not allow collective bargaining for teachers; thus, teachers and their school districts do not negotiate contracts. In these jurisdictions, resource allocation and teachers' terms and conditions of employment are shaped by state law and local school board policy. Teachers in these jurisdictions often belong to an affiliate of the NEA or AFT and might play an advisory role to the school board, but they hold no official decision-making authority.[56]

In one of these nonbargaining states, state law provides for consultation with teacher organizations of at least five hundred members. In this situation, state law specifies many of the kinds of agreements that typically are found in contracts. For instance, it authorizes a minimum of 180 days per year of instruction for students (187 days of service for teachers); limits class size in the early grades to twenty-two students; guarantees teachers a duty-free lunch period of at least thirty minutes; specifies guidelines for professional development; authorizes payroll dues deduction; provides grievance rights, including a kind of binding arbitration; specifies termination procedures; grants teachers preparation periods; and provides for a process of paperwork reduction.[57]

The provisions just described apply in Districts 7, 8, and 9. In District 7, consultation has resulted in an agreement on a $2,500 stipend for teachers holding a master's degree and $1,500 for teachers enrolled in a graduate program, as well as a union–management agreement to consider how to implement high school redesign and to conduct a study on improving teacher quality, with special attention to recruitment, retention, and incentive pay.

District 8 implemented value-added pay, but without agreement from the union.[58] This district also had a mentor program for new teachers (mentors earn about $3,000 per year) and provided signing bonuses for teachers in bilingual, mathematics, and special education.

District 6 is in a different nonbargaining state from Districts 7, 8, and 9. State law here addresses issues of maximum class size and maximum teaching load, provides planning time and a duty-free lunch period for teachers, gives teachers ten annual days of vacation time and at least five days to use as teacher work days, and establishes a statewide salary schedule.[59] District 6, which has a Teacher Advisory Committee that makes suggestions to the administration on various matters, has signing bonuses for teachers in mathematics, science, technology, foreign language, English as a second language, and special education; provides stipends to teachers holding master's degrees; and has instituted a pay-for-performance pilot in several schools. National Board certified teachers in this district receive a 12 percent pay boost as a result of state policy.

Thus, even in states that do not have collective bargaining, teachers and their organizations are involved in shaping significant education policy.

MAKING WAY FOR CHANGE

A 2006 report on collective bargaining asserted, "The job of union negotiators is to defend and advance the economic interests of their members. School [boards] are charged with representing the interests of the district and the taxpayer."[60] This sentiment reflects the conventional wisdom about bargaining, reinforced by decades of experience and traditional contracts. But reform contracts reveal a different possibility.

Reform contracts blur the distinctions between unions and management, acknowledging the collective aspect of their work. Such contracts place unions in the position of helping teachers assume their obligation to be active partners in the development and implementation of education policy, to tackle thorny issues of colleague competence and resource allocation, to come to terms with the definition of good teaching and issues of educational quality, and to assume their share of responsibility for student learning outcomes.[61] Reform contracts thus live at the intersection of individual interests and collective professional obligations.

Reform agreements engage a major challenge of industrial unionism. Industrial unionism allows teachers' organizations to respond to teachers' concerns about essential matters of wages, hours, and working conditions. But it fails to recognize teachers' expertise as professionals, their need and desire to exercise professional judgment in the performance of their duties, the interests they legitimately share with management, and the obligation to involve them in significant decisions about policies affecting their professional lives.[62] In short, industrial unionism circumscribes teaching, creating a chasm between teachers and administrators, and relegates unions to a backseat role in shaping the education policy that intimately affects the organization's members.[63]

Those who cling to industrial (traditional) unionism find themselves in the position of defending the status quo. But those who advocate change are in an equally difficult position. Thinking about what collective bargaining should be requires deciding what kind of teachers the nation wants.

Conservative critics favor a continuation of industrial-style work and workers, with tight managerial authority. They cast principals in the role of chief executive officer of the schools, with greatly increased authority to hire, fire, and assign teachers. In this vein, a teacher's job is largely to follow the rules and to employ judgment in decision making as little as possible.

Those who advocate for reform unionism see a different vision for teaching, with teachers organized along professional lines that recognize the work's inherent art and craft. Under this vision, teachers and administrators work cooperatively toward common goals and share the responsibilities of decision making.

Similarly, those who describe reform unionism as labor–management cooperation miss the bigger picture. Reform unionism is not simply about organizational civility. It is about endorsing a different kind of teaching, teaching that needs the support of a different kind of collective bargaining policy.

To be sure, reform unionism has not grown very much very fast. Although currently there is nothing to prevent more unions and school districts from adapting the examples of reform contracts to their own contexts, there also is little policy incentive for them to do so. Current collective bargaining laws shelter unions' and managements' traditional ways.

Unions that want to change have a difficult task. They must persuade longtime members that a new way of doing business does not mean abandoning traditional union values or issues, and at the same time they must convince newer members that the union is an important vehicle for educational improvement. This is not an easy sell, even in places where it is most consistent with reality.[64]

Despite obstacles created by current law and traditionalists on union as well as management sides, unions increasingly find themselves compelled to change. Research shows that newer teachers—those hired in the past decade or so—have different expectations of their union. Earlier generations of teachers preferred the isolation of the classroom, eschewed differentiated pay and staffing, and looked to the union to protect them in all work-related circumstances. By contrast, teachers newer to the profession welcome collaboration, support differentiated compensation and roles, and want the union to be the organization that both ensures them fair treatment and helps them become more accomplished professionals.[65] The first set of values is a good fit with traditional bargaining. The second is not.

A fundamental reordering of collective bargaining requires a new conception of the process and a shift in expectations. Policy must enable contracts that sanction labor–management cooperation; agreements that center on mutually determined, measurable student achievement goals; and an expansion of scope to include a broader swath of significant education policy.[66] Absent such a policy shift, educators are likely to find themselves continuing to wage old battles in a world that long ago left them behind.

PART III

Integrating Resources with Learning

Organizing School Systems for Continuous Improvement

Joanne Weiss

In many states, standards-based reform has laid the groundwork for a strong academic infrastructure that describes what students should know and be able to do at each grade level and in each subject. It is a difficult task, however, to embody these standards in rigorous academic programs that successfully prepare all students for college, careers, and citizenship.

Organizing an entire school system around high student achievement requires a thoughtful, systemic approach to teaching and learning, one in which standards, curriculum, formative and summative assessments, professional practices, and professional development are carefully designed and mutually reinforcing. Some schools and school systems are better at this than others. And although knowledge about high-performing exemplars continues to expand, the work they do is far from replicable or scalable, relying as it does on extraordinary leadership and effort. This chapter lays out a framework for the practices that need to be in place, the solutions and tools that need to be built, and the financial and human resources that need to be deployed in order to take continuous improvement and academic success to scale.

THE ECOSYSTEM FOR STUDENT LEARNING

In the past forty years, one would be hard put to find examples of federal education policies that broadly affected classrooms. Court-ordered desegregation rulings, faddish education trends, and state-level policies have had more influence on what and how teachers taught than almost anything coming out of Washington, D.C. During this time, the federal Elementary and Secondary Education Act (ESEA), first passed in 1965 and reauthorized periodically, has affected state education offices, which have had to administer block grant and categorical programs of increasing complexity and magnitude. [1] ESEA's effects also have trickled down to school district offices, mostly in the form of compliance regulations and reports. But in classrooms, federal laws often have been greeted with the same heads-down denial that welcomes new leadership in many school districts: "If we just keep doing what we're doing and wait them out, they'll go away."

This dynamic began to change with the 2002 reauthorization of ESEA: the No Child Left Behind Act (NCLB). [2] NCLB was enacted during a moment of growing outrage about educational achievement gaps and amid increasing recognition that global economic shifts were demanding a more educated work force than U.S. schools were delivering.

NCLB had its roots in a bipartisan movement toward standards and accountability that was spearheaded in the 1990s by a number of bellwether states and supported at the federal level by the Bill Clinton administration. This movement succeeded in creating a state-by-state framework for teaching and learning, consisting of standards that described what students should know (content standards) and should be able to do (performance standards) and statewide assessments tied to these standards that determined each student's level of proficiency. Because most states had standards in place since the mid- to late 1990s, there was an educational infrastructure in place on which the 2002 federal legislation could build. [3] Hence, when NCLB was taken up by Congress early in the millennium, it had a broad coalition of backers who had come together around this issue over the course of a decade.

Two key provisions of NCLB made it different from earlier federal education laws. First, it changed the Title I funding metrics from a focus on inputs to a focus on student outcomes. Second, it disaggregated these metrics by school, grade level, subject matter, and student subgroup, making transparent the results of what was happening inside classrooms. When the focus of legal compliance changed from reporting on inputs (such as number of students served, number of certified teachers, funds spent per pupil, and programs offered) to reporting on outcomes (for example, student achievement levels, value added by teachers, cost to achieve proficiency, and curricular effectiveness), then educational outcomes started to matter. And when these outcomes had to be reported separately for different subjects (mathematics, reading, science) and for different student populations (race/ethnicity, English language learners, special education, economically disadvantaged), then each student started to matter. One group's high performance could no longer be used to mask another group's lows.

Whatever one thinks about NCLB, it and the state-level standards and accountability movements have created momentum to improve academic outcomes for all students, especially those who traditionally have been underserved—momentum that the nation can and must harness. The intense pressure on each school to make adequate yearly progress—that is, to meet its academic improvement targets under NCLB—requires that virtually every teacher improve the academic performance of virtually every student.[4] For the first time, federal education policies were having widespread effects in U.S. classrooms.

Still, massive cultural shifts are needed if elected officials and educators are to remake education as a performance-driven system. That transformation will create high levels of uncertainty and discomfort across the education landscape, as processes are reengineered and ways of thinking are altered. These changes will deeply affect how schools manage their finances; how teachers and principals are prepared, hired, assigned, developed, evaluated, and compensated; and how students are taught.

Foremost among these changes, an emerging body of research shows persuasively that when teachers regularly use student performance data to inform and guide their instruction, student results improve.[5] It is fairly simple to explain the cycle of continuous instructional improvement, as this data-based framework is coming to be called, but it represents such a departure from the training and preparation teachers receive in school, and there are so few effective tools and systems to support it, that implementing it effectively is challenging. So why bother?

CONTINUOUS INSTRUCTIONAL IMPROVEMENT

Continuous instructional improvement is the process by which teachers adapt instruction to meet the differing needs of their students and, by learning from experience and evidence, also improve their own practice.[6] Great teachers always have made this kind of improvement instinctively, taking responsibility for the learning of each of their students and constantly following up to see how each is doing. With rising expectations for all students, the question now is how to bring the benefits of continuous improvement to all teachers and classrooms.

Student performance data lie at the heart of the continuous improvement cycle. As researchers Amanda Datnow, Vicki Park, and Priscilla Wohlstetter described it, "The endeavor to continuously improve instruction requires school systems to engage in a cycle whereby performance data are constantly gathered, shared, analyzed, and used to inform what is taught and how it is taught. Data are used to inform decisions at all levels and to ensure that system goals are accomplished through alignment of resources and effort."[7]

These data emphatically are not the mountains of useless information that every school system finds stuffed into binders, pouring out of filing cabinets, and cluttering computer hard drives—storage methods that render much of it inaccessible, unusable, and out of date. To be useful, continuous improvement data must be relevant, accurate, timely, and trusted as the basis for instructional decision making.

Using this approach, teachers can harness research practices that help them understand, for their group of students, what works and what doesn't; they make corrections and retest for understanding. In effect, this cycle turns teachers into researchers and innovators—people who try things, quickly assess whether they are working, make corrections as needed, and reassess. In the absence of scientific trials to validate which instructional strategies work for which students under what conditions, the continuous instructional improvement approach offers the most hopeful path to success.

Importantly, however, the cycle is pedagogically agnostic, deriving from a belief that there is no one best way to teach all students. Thus, continuous improvement can encompass multiple strategies for teaching and multiple methods for assessing learning. It assumes that these how-to instructional decisions are best left to the educators who know their craft and their students.

Performance data and the continuous instructional improvement practices they enable must find their way into school districts, schools, and classrooms if the U.S. educational system is to improve student learning. Although it is simple in concept, the cycle is difficult to implement well because high-quality information must exist, it must be accessible when needed, professionals must know what to do with the information, and they must do it. Figure 4-1 outlines these steps.

Step 1: Set Goals and Align Resources

This step represents the planning and preparation phase, the stage during which a coherent system of instruction must be articulated, designed, and developed. During this phase, school systems must specify, for each grade level and content area, what standards will be taught, when each standard should be mastered, and what instructional materials are available

FIGURE 4-1   The cycle of continuous instructional improvement

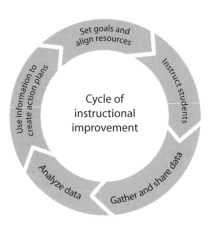

for teachers to use. It also is the time for creating high-quality benchmark assessments that can determine which standards students have mastered and which teachers and students need what types of support. Finally, it is the time for school system leaders to think deeply about how their talent pool of teachers, principals, instructional coaches, and others should be deployed to maximum effect.

In an ideal school system, the following activities occur before the start of each school year:

1. Goals and learning expectations are defined for the school system and for each school, classroom, and student. These goals should be realistic and grounded in data, and this means that student-level goals cannot be set until early diagnostic results are available and teachers have had a chance to analyze and "own" them.
2. A curriculum road map is developed that is aligned with the standards, is sequenced appropriately, and is paced carefully.
3. An instructional calendar for the year is set that correlates to the pacing guide and includes benchmark assessment administrations, professional development time for teachers and principals to collaborate on assessment analysis and action planning, reteaching time, and so on.
4. Benchmark assessments are developed that are aligned with the standards and that match the sequencing and pacing charts.
5. Talent—teachers, principals, and other instructional leaders—is deployed so that the neediest schools get the most effective educators.

Step 2: Instruct Students

This step encompasses the bulk of teachers' time. The cycle of instructional improvement has little to contribute during this step. The cycle focuses on what a high-performing system looks like, but it allows variation and flexibility in how the system gets its results. One school might use direct instruction, another might take a constructivist approach to teaching and learning, and a third might engage students in project-based learning. Regardless of the instructional philosophy of a school—and there should be a coherent philosophy—all schools must be able to assess what their students learn and make appropriate midcourse corrections when students are not learning.

The goal here, of course, is to teach high-quality content effectively the first time so that as few students as possible fail to master it. But what works for one student may not work for another. The most successful teachers have multiple instructional strategies in their quivers. They draw on a range of interventions depending on student needs, effectively employ "dipstick" assessments—informal questions integrated into a lesson—to gauge student understanding in the moment, and use this feedback to guide their instructional delivery.[8]

Schools must strike a delicate balance between allowing teachers freedom to make data-based tactical adjustments as they deliver curriculum to specific students, and ensuring that these day-to-day, class-by-class decisions are still integrated into a coherent, schoolwide teaching strategy. This clarity of teaching approach at the school level and proficiency in instructional delivery at the teacher level are rare, and professional development and teacher support systems must focus on building and expanding these key competencies.

Step 3: Gather and Share Data

The highest-performing school systems use all types of data to inform their understanding of student performance. They look at essays and research papers, presentations and exhibitions, homework and work sheets. They use in-class quizzes and systemwide benchmark assessments. All these kinds of data contribute to their judgment of what students know and can do.

Of these various forms of information, benchmark assessments appear to be among the most powerful instructional levers.[9] Benchmark assessments are standards-based tests given systemwide at approximately the same times during the year. Because of this consistency in administration, they allow comparison and collaboration across classrooms and schools.

When high-quality benchmark assessments are implemented effectively, they have several important uses. First, while there is still ample instructional time available, these assessments tell teachers which students are learning the material, which students need additional instruction or full-scale interventions to master key standards, and which standards need to be retaught to whole groups because the initial instructional approach was not effective. In addition, benchmark assessments enable deep collaboration among same-grade or same-subject teams of teachers to improve instructional quality. They also tell principals which teachers are struggling and need immediate support. They tell principals and school systems what kinds of general professional development teachers need— based on schoolwide or system-wide instructional weaknesses—and they highlight gaps and weaknesses in the system's curriculum materials.

High-quality benchmark assessments have several critical attributes. First, they are administered at intervals that balance the need to give teachers reasonable chunks of instructional time with the need for teachers to have current profiles of student performance. Every five to nine weeks appears about right. Second, they are administered before the end of these instructional periods, while there is still time for teachers to use the results in their reteaching.

Third, they are expertly developed to accurately and completely reflect and assess the standards defined by the school system. Assessment items therefore can vary dramatically from one school to another, depending on the instructional approach and philosophy followed by the school. One school, for example, might use multiple-choice items and carefully constructed distracters to assess understanding, and another might use portfolio exhibitions to judge learning. In all cases, assessments must, at the very least, address a state's required standards.

Fourth, for many students, benchmark assessments provide much-needed test-taking practice, especially if the benchmark assessments mimic a state's standardized tests in item format and content. Fifth, it also can help if benchmark assessments focus not only on the standards covered during the current instructional period but also sample standards covered earlier in the school year. This approach provides a way to understand students' learning decay rates and to trigger content reviews. Finally, these assessments affirm student progress and form a foundation for celebrating success.

Step 4: Analyze Data

Such benchmark assessments, even those of high quality, carry little benefit if the results are inaccurate, if they are delivered late or not at all, or if the presentation of the results is not easily understood. They also are of little use if teachers and principals file them away without analyzing the data and learning from the results. As a result, the fourth step in the cycle of continuous instructional improvement centers on analyzing student performance data and turning them into actionable information.

The best assessment reports eventually are delivered using technology-based tools, because truly exceptional analytic quality is beyond the scope of manual analysis and such reports do not assume that teachers are statisticians, expert at the art of data interpretation. With such tools, the display is the analysis; that is, the data's visual presentation is so clear and compelling that little analysis is required, and the instructional actions to be taken are evident.[10]

Current research suggests that interpreting student and class data is best done in collaborative groups composed of a combination of teachers, principals, and instructional coaches. Such collaboration has several advantages. In the beginning, data analysis is so new to most teachers that working in data teams is a useful way to extend the reach of expert coaches across the widest applicable group of teachers. In addition, when student work is being analyzed, it is critical to ensure that criteria and standards are consistently applied and that all teachers have similar high expectations for the quality of student work. To this end, groups must work together until consistent norms are established.

Moreover, data analysis is a creative task; there is rarely one "correct" answer. As with many ideation activities, the outcomes of a group conversation typically are superior to the results individuals might come up with on their own. In educational settings, in particular, group discussions help break down walls between classrooms and teachers, exposing expertise and making clear who can offer helpful advice or modeling. Finally, at the most basic level, scheduled collaboration ensures that time is actually set aside for analysis.

From these data discussions, action plans for classrooms can be developed as teachers answer questions such as, Which students mastered the key standards and which ones did not? How should I group my students for reteaching and enrichment activities? What new instructional strategies should I use for students who did not understand concepts the first time? Which teachers taught this well, and how did they do it? How could our time and resources across classrooms be reorganized to maximize student learning?

Step 5: Use Information to Create Action Plans

Finally, action plans must be developed and implemented. Most high-performing school systems employ formal action planning protocols: plans teachers use to document what their data analysis showed, how they intend to group students based on this analysis, and what instruction each group will receive. Such plans are vetted with principals, coaches, and other teachers on the team, and time is set aside to accommodate any reteaching needs.

Teachers might, for example, have one group do enrichment activities, another take additional practice, and a third tutor individual students who need extra help. The teacher down the hall might teach a lesson to an adjoining class if her results demonstrated that she has more-effective instructional techniques. Three teachers might dynamically group their students across classrooms by need and then each reteach a standard. Yet another teacher might run afterschool or lunchtime tutoring sessions to provide one-on-one help to struggling learners.

All this activity requires that teachers have time in their schedules to provide additional instruction when needed and the capacity to teach and reteach using various instructional strategies. Team teaching, beforeschool and afterschool classes, and other innovative approaches must be on the table. Finally, teachers and principals must be able to enlist not only students but also their parents or guardians in students' educational improvement, ensuring that everyone in a student's life knows what is expected and is committed to helping the student meet his academic goals.

Putting It All Together

What might a performance-driven classroom, organized for continuous improvement, look and feel like for a typical fifth-grade teacher? For six weeks, she teaches the standards identified in her school system's pacing guide. In the weeks preceding this period, she and other fifth-grade teachers worked together to develop unit plans for this content, sharing the lesson planning.

During the six weeks of instruction, as she teaches, her students periodically stop her by holding up their red cards to tell her, "Slow down, we're lost." Or they wave green cards to let her know, "We get it." She integrates all types of questions into her lessons and homework to ascertain what her students understand and which instructional nuances they've missed.

At the six-week mark, she gives them the systemwide benchmark assessment. That afternoon, she grades any free-response items that were on the test, such as short answer or essay questions, scans in all the answer sheets, and immediately prints her class's progress reports. Guided by the action planning sheet she fills in, she starts doing the analysis.

Sitting down the next day with her colleagues and their instructional coach to look at the data, she expresses dismay about the items her students missed, gets ideas from a colleague about how to teach a difficult skill, and shares an idea with him. That afternoon, she follows up by reteaching two things her class failed to master, tutoring a targeted group of students at recess, and tailoring her in-class "do nows" and homework to provide additional practice where needed. After three days of enrichment for the proficient students and reteaching for those who needed it, she is ready to move on to the next unit.

Of course, real classrooms are a lot messier than this scenario paints them, but there is no rocket science involved here. There is, however, an abiding belief that every student can and must learn and a determination to do what it takes to get every child to that point.

Creating a Coherent Academic System and Supportive Culture

When implemented well, the cycle of continuous instructional improvement represents a thoughtfully constructed academic system whose components interlock smoothly. However, when looking at data-driven decision making in schools, one typically sees a fractured and fragmented set of practices. Benchmark assessments do not always align with what teachers are covering, and so they yield useless data and waste instructional time. Seven-hundred-page textbooks are used as the curriculum and rushed through, page by page, by teachers who assume that this textbook—usually the superset of all states' standards—represents the scope and sequence they are responsible for covering in a year. Teachers spend so much time on their favorite curricular topics that they leave no time for other core content, so children move to the next grade underprepared. To overcome such fractures, educators and others must think about which pieces belong and how those pieces fit together as a system, because when instruction is not approached systemically, gaps open and students fall through.

In addition to the need for systemic thinking, continuous instructional improvement demands a significant cultural shift. A pervasive mind-set demands that "we get the testing over with," because testing is antithetical to, and gets in the way of, "real learning." In fact, planning, doing, and reflecting based on data all support real learning and professionalize teaching. Testing is an important part of the instructional cycle and has a clear place within it. Working to replace more teacher-centered notions of classrooms with student-centered, evidence-based continuous improvement practices is hard but critical work. As educators implement effective cycles of instructional improvement, and as teachers begin to see real student achievement gains in their classrooms, schools will have a strong foundation on which to build this new culture.

IMPLEMENTATION CHALLENGES

School systems that are implementing the cycle of continuous instructional improvement are doing so by brute force. They hire teams of teachers during summer vacations to write benchmark assessments. Filled with good intentions, these untrained professionals often turn out tests riddled with problems. Districts then employ statisticians at the central office who produce spreadsheets filled with data analysis, much of it centered on the prior year's standardized test results and thus instantly out of date. Self-appointed school champions spend hours working with colleagues to help them make sense of their data and, in doing so, risk burnout themselves. And local technologists cobble together software at the district's behest to meet specific and urgent needs, often producing code that cannot easily be enhanced, generalized, or scaled.

Until recently, without a clear vision of the instructional improvement cycle, educators and others could not build the right tools. Now the vision exists, but the dearth of tools remains. School systems need tools that allow teachers and school leaders to undertake continuous instructional improvement in robust, supportable, and sustainable ways. These systems must fund the purchase and implementation of these tools in school districts, schools, and classrooms and then develop the professional capacity to manage change, conduct professional development activities, and revamp teacher and administrator credentialing programs so that newcomers can enter school systems prepared for this new type of work.

Needed New Tools

To implement the continuous improvement cycle at scale, school systems need high-quality, robust, technology-based solutions that support a wide swath of critical school processes: curriculum-to-standards mapping and sequencing, test item banking, benchmark assessment delivery, data reporting and analysis, knowledge management for sharing effective practices, and action planning. All these tasks could be done most easily and effectively with technology mediation or assistance, but few high-quality tools exist, even though none requires a technology breakthrough; all are feasible today. Although the most likely creators of these tools are for-profit technology companies, thus far the private capital markets have not jumped in to fund these needs. Why not?

First, there are quality concerns. For understandable, bottom-line reasons, most large education companies—such as publishers—conform their products to the superset of state needs. This approach works—barely—in the textbook side of the business. However, in the testing arena this approach has led to a raft of low-quality formative assessments that are not properly targeted to the needs of individual states and school districts. For example, test items are not customized to the standards of specific states. Or items are designed to match a textbook but only to approximate a state's standards.

For standards-based instruction to work, the standards must be at the center of the system, curriculum must correlate to the standards, and test items must independently correlate to the standards. If curriculum only loosely correlates to standards and if test items correlate to curriculum materials, then the translation problem will quickly render the assessment data useless for formative purposes. Aggravating the problem, tests designed against one set of standards often are presented to teachers in the language of their own state's standards, masking and further muddying the question of what they really assess. If formative assessments do not test the right standards and do not report the results in the right ways, teachers make important instructional decisions using faulty information, and student achievement suffers.

Second, school systems are notoriously poor purchasers. They generally do not understand their needs well, have protracted and expensive sales cycles, rely on personal vendor relationships, and use underinformed, cross-functional committees to make key purchasing decisions. As a result, weak products often are adopted, allowing good ones no opportunity to rise to the top, as they would in other industries.

In this sector, the results are predictable. Because many developers of instructional management systems have no clear vision of instructional improvement, they develop software based on a checklist of the features and functions they believe schools want. Similarly, those defining the feature sets on behalf of schools have no clear vision of classroom needs, although they do understand their state and federal compliance or reporting requirements. The result is a raft of software systems developed not to address the instructional improvement needs of teachers and principals but to address state and federal accountability requirements. Compliance features trump instructional features, and when the software is rolled out to classrooms it becomes clear too late that the product makes teachers' lives harder. Teachers then do not use the system; and if no data go in, clearly no useful instructional information comes out.

Finally, venture capitalists, who in other industries seed innovation and enable early-stage start-up organizations to address new market needs, largely have turned away from investments in education. When it invested heavily in education throughout the 1990s, the venture capitalist community learned that there are not large returns on investments in education and, virtually to a firm, ceased investing in early-stage education start-ups (although limited capital has been invested in some later-stage companies). Without start-up capital, innovation simply cannot happen.

Seed funding must be provided in order for these desperately needed tools to be created. Thus, it falls to the nonprofit capital markets, including governments and foundations, to address this problem. It is critical for these groups to ensure that the right solutions are built, solutions that will enable school systems to implement continuous instructional improvement reliably and to make the adoption process easier and not harder.

Implementing Continuous Instructional Improvement

Once the tools are built, the field needs funds to equip school systems, schools, and classrooms with these solutions. Even more critical, it needs the professional development capacity—the trained, knowledgeable resources in schools and districts—to manage the change process and to implement a new set of data-driven instructional practices. Continuous instructional improvement both depends on and helps construct a different way for teachers to think about their craft. It turns a process that is internal and instinctive for the best teachers—"what worked today, and what didn't?"—into one that is external, explicit, and empirically grounded for all teachers. This transition has implications for the pre-service preparation of teachers, school culture, on-site change management, and ongoing professional development. All these elements must be built into a new core of school and district operations in order for predictable, continuous instructional improvement to occur.

However, unlike the creation of tools, which requires investment by external capital markets, school-level implementation costs may be folded into a school district's normal operating budget. After all, these activities represent the ongoing, everyday work of schools; they are not special programs to be bolted on to the existing day; they are the school day. So except for start-up costs, the implementation of data-driven instructional improvement practices can be woven into the fabric of existing budgets, perhaps even displacing costs that are less effective in addressing student learning.

CONCLUSION

This continuous improvement vision is not radical; it is being adopted in many of the highest-performing charter schools and urban school districts in the country, and it is working.[11] But implementing data-driven instructional improvement demands much of educators. It requires visionary and stable leadership at the school and district levels, it demands courage and stamina to stay on track and to ignore the myriad distractions that arise, and it takes efforts clearly above and beyond levels that are easily sustainable for teachers and principals in conventional, low-tech school settings. And because continuous instructional improvement represents a systemic approach to instruction, it demands concerted, carefully orchestrated activity all across school systems.

No matter how effective, it is impossible to scale an innovation that relies on such superhuman efforts. The implementation problem becomes more manageable, however, with the assistance of technology. Once school systems have effective technology-based tools to help manage, mediate, and make sense of instructional data, this continuous improvement approach will be scalable and replicable. It will not be easy. It will require a new type of preparation for teachers and leaders, new practices inside school systems, and new support and development infrastructures. But it can be done.

The promise and benefits of data-driven continuous instructional improvement go well beyond helping individual students in scattered classrooms. If these practices are implemented properly, and if technology is used intelligently as a repository for the right kinds of data, then the knowledge base in education will grow substantially. Researchers will have access to data-supported insights into the critical questions that hamstring education. They will learn more about which curriculum materials and instructional strategies work best in which settings, under what conditions, for what purposes, and with which learners. They will be better able to shed light on the quality of teacher and leader preparation, credentialing, and professional development programs, and they will have information to guide educational practices as educators restructure those programs to maximize their effectiveness. As educators and researchers increasingly understand how continuous improvement can promote greater student learning, governments and school systems must organize themselves to deliver it.

5

Making Strategic Resource Decisions

Karen Hawley Miles

With accelerated pressure to improve academic success for all children coming from the Obama administration and the federal No Child Left Behind Act (NCLB), many school and district leaders struggle with varying levels of resources—and in some cases, dramatically shrinking resources—to transform their student results.[1] Some policy makers and practitioners even argue that more money is needed before school systems can accomplish such ambitious learning goals. Yet research shows no consistent link between the level of education spending and student performance.[2] At the same time, research and common sense suggest that a strategic investment of educational resources can lead to dramatic improvements.[3]

Public school leaders face particular challenges in using resources strategically, because doing so demands hard choices and difficult long-range planning. Resource shifts usually affect jobs, and long-range plans can be swept away by a change in leadership, a drop in funding, or a shift in legislation. Moreover, many educational leaders do not have access to information that would help them understand the key drivers of district-level costs or the fundamental resource trade-offs that can be made among them.

The typical school district budget process works against innovation and the strategic consideration of resource choices and trade-offs. At budget time, district finance offices ask central departments and schools to submit changes to their budgets and staffing. When times are tough, they ask for across-the-board cuts in departments and schools, and they delay investment in innovations or improvement. Financial officers, and not educators, consider which priorities make sense, and there is rarely any effort to reconsider the fundamentals of school and district design that drive costs.

Relying as much on history and politics as policy considerations, such short-term, financially oriented processes lead to budget actions that appear sensible on the surface but in fact can reduce the resources that otherwise would be available to improve instruction or to create more-effective school models. The result is a striking sameness in the basic organization of schools and the spending patterns of school districts.[4]

These basic organizational patterns have stayed the same even as education budgets have steadily increased: students grouped into classes organized by age and subject, with struggling students pulled out for extra help; teachers working independently as sole providers of instruction, with their compensation based on a single salary schedule that accounts only for teaching experience and course credits beyond the bachelor's degree.[5]

The nation's educational goals are higher now than when these structures were created. Instead of sorting students and ensuring that they simply receive their course content, school systems in the twenty-first century increasingly are shaped by an economy that demands critical thinkers and adaptable workers.[6] Educators have new technologies for reaching these goals, including an advanced understanding of how students learn.[7] They also have better tools for diagnosing and measuring learning and a better understanding of how professionals collaborate most effectively.[8] Still, these advances have not improved schools nor the structures that support them to a degree that matches contemporary expectations.

Can resources play a role in achieving new, ambitious learning expectations? Of course they can. To transform school structures and student outcomes consistent with NCLB, school and district leaders need to (1) understand how high-performing schools use resources, (2) assess their own school and district resource use in light of this vision, (3) make resource choices and trade-offs consistent with it, and (4) build long-term success by shifting resources to more-effective practices and structures. In short, school and district transformations that result in better student performance depend importantly on a strategic approach to resource decision making.

In the first main section of this chapter, I provide a framework for describing strategic resource use at the school level and typical sources of resource misalignment. I then explore key resource decisions and trade-offs that school leaders might consider as they deploy their resources effectively to accomplish ambitious learning goals. In the second main section, I focus on critical ways in which district-level resources must be restructured to support high-performing schools at scale.

FIGURE 5-1   Creating strategic school designs

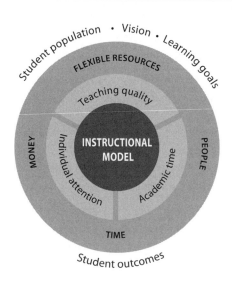

Source: Permission to reprint from Regis Anne Shields and Karen Hawley Miles, *Strategic Designs: Lessons from Leading Edge Small Urban High Schools* (Watertown, MA: Education Resource Strategies, 2008).

ORGANIZING SCHOOL RESOURCES STRATEGICALLY

What does it mean to make strategic resource decisions? At Education Resource Strategies (ERS), we have combed the research, conducted our own, and learned from experience how high-performing schools organize and use resources.[9] We have learned that despite differences in student demographics, instructional approaches, and funding levels, high-achieving schools share a common set of resource practices. They implement what we have come to call strategic designs, which have four characteristics (see figure 5-1).

First, strategic designs clearly define an instructional model that advances a school's vision for student learning. Regardless of the specific model schools adopt—and they can range from thematic, project-based, or interdisciplinary instructional strategies to traditional approaches—all strategic designs encompass content, delivery, programs of study, learning locales, and methods of assessment.

Second, strategic designs create a high-performing organizational structure that uses people, time, and money in research-proven ways that best implement a school's vision and instructional model. These structures focus school resources on student learning needs through something ERS calls the Big Three resource strategies:

- Big Three strategy 1: Organize to continuously improve teaching quality through hiring, team assignment, professional development, and collaborative planning time.
- Big Three strategy 2: Use student time strategically, linking it to student learning needs in core academic areas.
- Big Three strategy 3: Create targeted individual attention and personal learning environments for students.

The third characteristic of strategic designs is that they allow resource trade-offs and choices that support their most important instructional priorities, sometimes at the expense of traditional programs, staffing, and scheduling.

Finally, strategic designs assess and adapt school instructional models, structures, strategies, and resource trade-offs. That is, because school conditions do not remain static, schools must continually evaluate their circumstances and performance, adapting to changes in student needs, external conditions, and information about the effectiveness of their programs and practices.

In sum, strategic designs combine instructional models with strategic resource use and ongoing assessment and adjustment.

University Park Campus School

University Park Campus School in Worcester, Massachusetts, illustrates how a well-constructed strategic design can transform a school's instructional model into a powerful engine for student success. The school is district run, serving 230 students in grades 7–12. Some 70 percent of these students receive free and reduced-price lunch, 80 percent speak English as a second language, and most come into the school performing below grade-level expectations; University Park makes trade-offs that prioritize investment in the Big Three: teaching quality, time on core academics, and targeted individual attention for all students. These trade-offs result in graduation rates and proficiency levels far higher than state averages. How does the school put these resource strategies into play?

Teaching quality at University Park begins with a rigorous hiring process that finds teachers who fit the core academic and college preparatory focus of the school and who are certified to teach more than one subject, the latter a critical issue in a school of this size. Every spare dime pays for core teachers. In the typical Worcester high school, 60 percent of school instructors teach in the core academic subjects of English, math, science, history, and foreign language. At University Park, 94 percent of all teachers have core subjects as their main responsibility.

Through creative scheduling and staffing, University Park provides three times as much professional development time for teachers as do the Worcester public schools. Teacher teams meet weekly to review student progress and adjust instruction. They meet during release time created by school officials hiring part-time, noncore staff. In addition, teachers collaborate regarding student work and instruction during ninety minutes of curricular and departmental meeting time every other week. A local partnership with Clark University, through which both faculties mentor student teachers, provides additional opportunities for teachers to continuously improve their practice.

The school supports strategic use of student time by trading off student time in electives and devoting 75 percent of the standard student school day to core academics, with literacy teaching embedded throughout all subjects. This arrangement contrasts with the 60 percent of time spent on core subjects in a typical urban high school. Ninety-minute block scheduling in language arts and math in grades 7 and 8 provides essential academic support for incoming students, who often lag several years behind grade level.

University Park also extends the school day before and after school hours by providing extra academic support and enrichment. Because of contractual limits on the length of the student day, this time is voluntary for students and teachers, but core teachers plan how to use this time and create an expectation that most students will attend.

Individual attention begins at University Park with the use of multiple formative student assessments, which help teachers guide and adjust instruction throughout the year based on each student's needs. The school focuses first on ensuring student proficiency in English language arts (ELA) and math. Unlike traditional high schools, where smaller class sizes are more common in advanced and specialty subjects, University Park designs small class sizes and teaching loads in foundation years for core subjects. Teaching loads for ELA and math are forty-five or fewer in grades 7 and 8. In grade 9, class sizes in ELA remain relatively low, at seventeen, compared with the schoolwide average of twenty-one. Because the school offers few electives, core class sizes are small for all students and subjects. University Park targets instruction and ensures the development of relationships by keeping students and teachers together over multiple years—a practice known as looping—focusing on ELA and math.

Although there is no magic in these strategies, University Park makes resource use strategic by deliberately prioritizing core academics and teaching quality while sacrificing other "nice-to-haves." Of course, it would be wonderful to raise overall spending enough to add these things as well, but if choices must be made, research indicates that funding these strategic priorities first pays off. Furthermore, University Park has found creative ways to extend students' learning time and to diversify students' opportunities by using nontraditional and community resources.[10]

This conception of strategic school design suggests that the ideal use of educational resources depends on a school's instructional model, student and teacher needs, and funding levels. Thus, strategic resource use will vary by school or in a given school over time. It will change as student needs and teacher capacities evolve and the level of resources varies. However, strategic schools will be consistently deliberate in their use of resources; they will not merely accept the allocations that result from industrial-age staffing formulas, as most schools do. Even though specific targets for resource use depend on context, strategic schools look different from typical schools in ways that can be quantified.

In the remainder of this section, I look at each of the Big Three resource strategies, describe the common principles that high-performing schools follow, and compare resource use in typical versus strategic schools.[11] I then describe typical trade-offs faced by school leaders in these areas and provide tips for overcoming common barriers to making them.

Organizing for Continuous Improvement in Teaching Quality

Research confirms what parents intuitively understand: good teaching trumps all other factors in determining what and how much students learn.[12] Yet schools and districts consistently weight other factors more heavily. In particular, school districts reduce spending on professional development and time for teachers to work together while maintaining or even reducing class sizes. Allan Odden and colleagues reviewed a raft of research that compares the effects of raising teaching quality to reasonable reductions in class size. They found that effective teachers have five times as much effect on raising student performance as do typical reductions in class size.[13]

Equally important, a single teacher does not change the overall course of student performance, but a succession of effective teachers can accelerate and sustain academic achievement. How much? Researchers Steven Rivkin, Eric Hanushek, and John Kain showed that students who had an above-average teacher for three consecutive years outperformed their peers who experienced a below-average teacher during that same period by an entire grade level.[14] This finding demonstrates why educational leaders need to continuously improve teaching quality across entire schools.

If teaching quality is so important, how can schools promote it? Table 5-1 lists four basic principles for investing in teaching quality, shows how strategic schools implement these principles, and then contrasts these principles and strategic practices with practices in typical schools. As the table indicates, leaders in strategic schools view teaching as a collective enterprise that requires continuous management and investment. They hire and assign teachers to play specific roles in their schools and on school teams. They move teachers to new roles—grades, subjects, leadership responsibilities—that either give them opportunities to develop new skills or allow them to leverage exceptional skills and interests.

Leaders also ensure that teaching teams have time to work together as well as expert support to facilitate this common work, which involves the review of classroom practice and student needs in the context of data on student results. Depending on a school's capacity, this expert support can come from school-based teacher leaders or outside instructional coaches. Whether internal or external, instructional coaches bring subject matter expertise and effective coaching skills to schools. They need time to observe teachers and to work with them in their classrooms as well as during non-teaching time.

To promote high-quality teaching, strategic schools create planning time for teaching teams, and they pay for the time and expertise of those who support them. Creating weekly sixty-minute (or longer) blocks of planning time, plus regular time throughout the year for teaching teams to meet, may not require significantly more resources. Many school districts already have four to twelve days set aside for staff development.[15] Especially at the secondary level, many school districts already schedule teachers with two (of six or seven) periods free from instruction.

Scheduling common time for teachers, however, takes juggling and creativity. In some cases, schools need to pay stipends for afterschool time or hire additional teachers to cover planning time for core teachers. Others may create additional planning periods by raising class size by small numbers in some subjects. Schools with lower teaching capacity may need to hire outside coaches to facilitate the work of teacher teams; others, if they are lucky, may have assistant principals who can play this role. Higher-capacity schools may have teacher leaders who can assume this role, paying for this extra responsibility through stipends or release time.

TABLE 5-1   **Strategic investments in teaching quality**

Principles of high-performing schools	Typical school	Strategic school
Hire and assign teachers to leverage and build expertise of teaching teams.	• Distribution of teacher experience and expertise is unplanned. • The most expert teachers have the fewest preps, lowest teaching loads, and most accomplished students.	• Teachers are assigned and hired to fit school and team needs so that each team has strong leaders and balanced skill set. • The most expert teachers work with the most challenging students and support novice teachers to generate student results.
Ensure expert support for teaching teams to assess student learning and adjust instruction.	• Teachers use data individually without comparison or discussion with peers.	• All teaching teams have coaches or team leaders who have responsibility for facilitating team use of data to improve instruction and respond to student needs.
School schedules ensure that teaching teams that share common work have significant time together weekly.	• Teachers have forty-five-minute blocks of time, inconsistently used for common work.	• Teachers have ninety minutes or more weekly for teaching teams, with planned agendas and goals.
Implement systems that promote individual teacher growth through induction, career path, and compensation.	• Support for new teachers is limited. • Individual growth occurs through teacher-initiated university course work. • Effort to leverage the impact of the most effective teachers is limited.	• Investment is organized to support new teachers through paid mentors and reduced teaching loads. • Most effective teachers serve as team leaders, mentors, and curriculum developers.

School leaders often find money to invest in teaching quality by trading off lower-cost ways of providing noncore academic services or by raising class size. Like University Park, many schools have found that they can offer an array of nonacademic coursework through partnerships with other organizations or by using part-time, lower-cost providers. In addition, some schools have found lower-cost ways to accomplish noninstructional activities such as clerical support, monitoring, and custodial work by using outside providers and part-time staff.

When raising class size, school leaders might look first to nonacademic subjects or later grades. In secondary schools, some school leaders have freed up time for teacher collaboration by adding an extra instruction-free period and spreading these students throughout the remaining classes. For example, instead of teaching five classes of twenty students, teachers would teach four classes of twenty-five. Of course, this solution depends on the starting size of these classes and the needs of students. If class sizes already are twenty-eight, then raising them greater than thirty probably makes little sense.

Scheduling Student Time Strategically

Strategic schools are deliberate in their use of student time (see table 5-2). Research shows that extra time on task makes a difference, especially for students who are not meeting growth targets.[16] Some of the most successful reform models for low-performing students add time on task, especially in English and math.[17] Students in urban Massachusetts schools that have extended their school day by 30 percent are showing promising improvements.[18]

In addition to the amount of time, strategic schools think carefully about how they structure students' time. Some classroom activities work better in nonstandard time blocks. For example, science labs, class debates, and fieldwork require longer blocks, whereas opportunities for silent reading or learning computational math skills might work better in shorter blocks. Strategic schools often create schedules that vary time blocks throughout the day or even over a week.

The common thread here regards the deliberate use of time by prioritizing and changing schedules in response to student and instructional needs. Two major resource implications arise from extending time and prioritizing time in core subjects.

Analysis of spending patterns on extended learning programs indicates that the costs of adding time differ depending on the model selected and on the details of implementation. For instance, in one study the incremental cost of extending time ranged from $900 to $1,500 per pupil.[19] Costs vary based on who provides the extra time and how it is paid for. Experience demonstrates that costs do not rise proportionally with the increase in time. In other words, lengthening a school day by 30 percent adds much less than 30 percent to the operating budget. Marguerite Roza and Karen Hawley Miles estimated that, depending on the model, adding 30 percent more time raises costs by only 6–20 percent, for two reasons.[20] First, school-related nonteaching costs, such as facilities, transportation, and administration, do not automatically rise with additional instructional time, thereby creating cost efficiencies. Second, not all teachers participate in extended

TABLE 5-2   Strategic investments in student time

Principle	Typical school	Strategic school
Align school schedules with instructional model and student needs.	• Daily schedule is divided into six or seven equal-time blocks regardless of subject or lesson.	• The length of time blocks varies to match instructional needs. • Instructional minutes are carefully managed to prioritize academic subjects.
Maximize scheduled time on highest-priority subjects.	• Student day is 6.5 hours long. • Less than 50 percent of time is spent on core academics in secondary schools (60 percent in elementary school). • Time is allotted equally by subject in secondary schools, with about 35 percent spent on English language arts and math. • Significant time is spent in student passing, recess, and unstructured time.	• Schools maximize total instructional time by limiting passing time and other noninstructional time. • Student day may extend to include extra support or enrichment. • Students spend more time on ELA and math until they master foundation skills.
Vary time for individual students based on progress.	• All students have the same amount of time for each course and skill.	• Students who struggle are given sufficient opportunity to catch up with peers in core academic subjects, focusing on ELA and math. • Students who master material more quickly have the opportunity to explore new topics and skills.

time, and those who do, do so with different compensation and class-size arrangements.

At the secondary level, shifting the use of time means changing the composition of the teaching force. If schools require more courses or more time in core subjects, they need to add teachers in these subjects, especially when this practice is combined with lower teaching loads and class sizes in these same subjects. As they do this, many schools, especially smaller ones, may find that they no longer need full-time teachers for certain noncore or specialty subjects. Finding creative ways to offer these courses by offering online sources, forming partnerships with other schools, or hiring nontraditional teachers also can free up resources to invest in teaching quality.

In some school districts, union work rules based on short, fixed periods may present a barrier to flexible scheduling. For example, the Boston collective bargaining agreement stipulates that no teacher can teach more than 160 consecutive minutes without a break, regardless of that teacher's schedule for the rest of that day or other days. This stipulation would preclude schools from organizing instruction in, say, 90-minute blocks if teachers had to teach consecutive blocks. Such rules are especially counterproductive for teachers, because most longer-block models reduce teachers' overall load by half.[21] Many school leaders, nevertheless, have developed creative scheduling models through a collaborative process with teachers.[22]

Providing Individual Attention to Students

Strategic schools also target and design individual attention to fit student needs (see table 5-3). They prioritize subject areas in which individual attention is most important, and they think carefully about who provides that attention and when. Although perhaps the most widely used option, small class size constitutes only one strategy for getting students the expert assistance they need.

In fact, some schools create larger class sizes so that they can place specialists in classrooms to provide small-group support for certain subjects and lessons. The district of St. Paul, Minnesota, or example, achieved remarkable results with English language learners by assigning expert teachers to rotate through elementary classrooms during regularly scheduled time for English language arts instruction. These experts supported teachers and targeted student needs through tutoring, leading small-group instruction, and coteaching lessons.

Individual-attention strategies are made possible by the ongoing assessment of student learning, which provides the information needed by teachers to adjust instruction and to group students. Although many schools assess learning, fewer have systematic protocols and processes to ensure that students who do not meet expectations get immediate attention. Even in strategic schools having limited resources, core teachers can use this information to determine when they need to keep students after school, refer them to an academic center, or contact their parents.

There is, however, limited research on class size reduction, small-group instruction, tutoring, and reduction of student loads at the secondary level. As a result, school leaders need to consider not only how they deploy

TABLE 5-3 Strategic investments in individual student attention

Principles of high-performing schools	Typical school	Strategic school
Use ongoing assessment results to guide instruction, small-group, and individual support.	• Assessment results are not used to drive class composition, student grouping, or individual support.	• Assessment results inform individual attention and student grouping on a daily and weekly basis.
Assign small-group sizes and reduced teaching loads for targeted purposes.	• Regular education classes and teacher loads are roughly the same size regardless of grade or subject. • Students who need extra support are pulled out of class for special instruction in small groups. • Tutoring is provided by instructional aides who have limited education and expertise.	• Class sizes and teaching loads are reduced in high-priority areas such as early grades, reading, and math. • All students have opportunity for small-group instruction based on skills and progress. • Expert instructors come into classroom to provide tutoring and other support during flexible group time. • Individual support is systematically provided to at-risk students as soon as they begin to fall behind.

these strategies for increasing individual attention but also their costs and expected effects. The most popular strategy for providing individual attention to students is to reduce class size. Unfortunately, class size reduction is an expensive strategy, and not the most cost-effective strategy when compared with its results.

Thus, the cost of reducing class size should be weighed against other options. For example, to free 8 percent of school spending so that it can be invested in planning time for teachers or stipends for teacher leaders, most urban school districts would have to raise class size by about three students across the board.[23]

Although there is limited research on the effect of class size reduction in secondary schools, randomized studies at the elementary level have shown that smaller class sizes can improve results when they drop to relatively low levels—for example, from twenty-five to fifteen students—and that such reductions matter most for students in grades K–3 and for those who live in poverty.[24] Even for these students, the benefit of smaller class sizes is relatively small compared with other interventions, particularly one-on-one tutoring.[25] In fact, such findings suggest a wide range of benefits from individual tutoring, perhaps because there are many ways to implement a tutoring strategy. Tutoring that is tightly linked to curriculum and coordinated by core teachers has the greatest effect.[26]

In terms of resource trade-offs, a 40 percent drop in class size from twenty-five to fifteen students would increase average teacher salary costs by the same amount (because the other ten students must be taught by another teacher), resulting in a spending increase of about 25 percent, or about $1,250 per pupil, garnering only a small increase in student achievement. The comparative cost of tutoring or small-group instruction depends on which model is used, who provides the tutoring, how long students are tutored each week, and over what time period students are tutored.[27]

School leaders who are considering how to target individual attention face two primary sets of trade-offs: which subjects, grades, and students should have smaller classes, and whether to focus individual and small-group support on early intervention or later, after problems have been identified and student results lag far behind. It can be hard to prioritize some subjects and grades for small class sizes, because this action goes against school norms regarding equality. But a strategic middle school with limited resources might decide to reduce class size and teaching loads in sixth-grade English language arts to make sure that all students reach foundation levels of proficiency before moving to high school. Similarly, the strategic schools ERS studied chose to make academic classes systematically smaller than noncore classes.

Investing money in early intervention can pay big returns, especially if the early investment reduces the number of students who end up in special education, which is much more expensive. On average, school districts spend more than twice as much on students in special education as on other students. Emerging research indicates that providing early intervention to students at risk of special education referral leads to greater student success and lower school district costs.[28] These findings indicate that individualized attention for students who fall behind can be much less expensive in the long run than the alternatives.

SCHOOL DISTRICT RESOURCE DECISIONS
THAT SUPPORT STRATEGIC SCHOOLS

Effective school leaders can make many important resource decisions on their own, but school districts play a critical supporting role by creating a context that allows strategic resource decision making and by implement-

TABLE 5-4   School district resource decisions that support strategic schools

Big Three strategic school strategy	Typical district-level resource misalignment	Restructuring required
Organize to continuously improve teaching quality.	• New teachers and poorly performing teachers are distributed unevenly in schools within the district. • New teachers do not receive sufficient support or assignments that support success. • Teacher compensation systems reward experience and course work, not contribution to results. • Teacher work hours do not include sufficient time for collaboration.	• Create incentives to attract and retain highly effective teachers in hard-to-staff schools. • Invest to support new teachers in first three years. • Rethink compensation and career path to reward contribution to results. • Rework contract requirements to include significant collaborative planning time.
Use student time strategically.	• Insufficient time is provided in the school day.	• Rethink school hours to expand learning time.
Target individual attention.	• Staffing allocations based on class size do not vary by subject or grade. • Partnership with lower-cost, community-based providers of nonacademic instruction and support is limited.	• Target class size adjustments to most important subjects, challenged students, and grade levels. • Use nontraditional providers or outsource nonacademic instruction and support where cost-effective.

ing these strategies at scale. Table 5-4 highlights three resource practices that require district-level attention: organizing systems to support continuous improvement in teaching quality, reconsidering the total amount of student and teacher time, and rethinking the mix of providers for nonacademic instruction and other school services.

Investing to Build Teaching Quality

Hiring high-quality teachers who fit school needs is the first step in ensuring students' academic success. However, it is well documented that teacher expertise and experience are not evenly distributed across school districts, or even across schools within the same district. Moreover, most school districts do not give schools having concentrations of new or poorly performing teachers extra resources that could be used to support these teachers or to encourage expert teachers to join their faculties.[29] Cost estimates of effective new teacher induction programs range from $4,000 to $16,000 per teacher, and stipends for teaching in hard-to-staff schools range from $5,000 to 15 percent of teaching salaries.[30]

Once a school has high-potential teachers, it needs to organize time for collaboration, find ways to pay teacher leaders to facilitate the effective use of this time, and reward teachers who generate strong student learning. Although many school districts have created positions that offer expert teachers extra salary for serving as instructional coaches, fewer have modified traditional teacher compensation structures to link substantial increases in salary to results or increased leadership roles.

Substantially raising the salaries of high-performing teachers without ballooning school district budgets means that not all teachers can earn salaries at these levels and that schools might end up looking more like other twenty-first-century organizations, in which there are different ways to work at different levels of expertise with different levels of pay. The ERS District Resource Allocation Modeler (DREAM) tool allows users to calculate where they can find resources to raise some teacher salaries by altering class size in nonacademic subjects, lowering salaries for some categories of teachers, or saving on noninstructional activities.[31]

Increasing Learning Time for Students and Teachers

Although individual schools might find ad hoc ways to add learning time, many need system-level support to negotiate new contracts, operate on new districtwide calendars and bus schedules, and work through the trade-offs required by such decisions. As states begin to forecast tighter budgets, it is not likely that expanded learning time will be funded solely with new public funds. Schools and districts need to carefully define the goals of their extended time and then consider who will cover the additional learning time and how to structure compensation for the parties. As recent research has demonstrated, many schools and districts are finding ways to combine traditional providers with community-based partners to create enriching experiences for students.[32]

Rethinking Providers for Nonacademic and Other Services

As schools and districts search for ways to pay high-capacity teachers in core subjects and to expand the time spent in these subjects, it follows that they must increase spending dramatically or reduce spending in other areas. Typical schools use certified, full-time teachers for all subjects as well as full-time staff in other positions. Another option is to bring experts and other adults into schools in nontraditional ways—for example, using contract workers or part-time employees—or staggering schedules.

When severely constrained by budget challenges, charter schools and others are finding ways to provide high-quality instruction in noncore areas—music, art, computer science, physical education—by contracting with groups that specialize in these areas. Sometimes these groups can provide higher-quality services at more-convenient times. For example, Edwards Middle School in Boston contracts with Citizen Schools to provide after-school enrichment and to cover common planning time for teachers at the end of each school day. Citizen Schools provides a rich array of offerings to schools using a lower-cost mix of staff, including volunteers.

In schools where few students take advanced or specialty courses, maximizing spending on core courses may require sharing the advanced courses with other schools or using online resources or part-time expert teachers. Similarly, innovative schools are creating new roles in schools, giving staff the option to work flexible hours to meet student needs and dividing jobs to enable higher salaries for technology-oriented positions and lower salaries for jobs that require fewer skills. For example, to keep libraries open longer hours and to provide specialized assistance to teachers and students, a school might eliminate a full-time librarian position and hire a highly paid but part-time media or literacy specialist who directs the work of a combination of volunteers and lower-paid aides.

These kinds of solutions often require school district help in finding and screening talented individuals and providers to play these roles and in negotiating the union, budget, and human resource requirements they affect.

CONCLUSION

A school system with limited resources needs to continuously reconsider resource allocations, rethink opportunity costs, and make difficult choices about how best to use available resources. Reallocating funds away from accepted practices such as class size reduction (thereby raising class size) can be politically challenging and may require waivers from state regulations, but the resources involved are substantial and could support different, potentially more-effective resource choices, especially those that directly improve teaching quality, use student time strategically, and provide targeted individual attention to students.

Four resource shifts hold great potential for improving student performance: away from the quantity of staff and toward the quality of teachers and educational leaders; away from spending teacher time on remediation and toward early identification of learning challenges and early intervention to accelerate learning progress; away from teachers as isolated practitioners and toward teacher teams collaborating to improve and adapt instruction based on student performance data; and away from full-time teachers as the sole instructional delivery model and toward alternative, creative, and effective models, including the integration of community providers and learning technologies.

These shifts require schools and districts to approach their learning goals and resource decisions strategically. In doing so, they will find themselves truly transforming the way they do business. Strategic transformations—strategic designs—will break apart the traditional ways that schools and districts hire and assign teachers, use student and teacher time, focus their resources, and build a culture of high achievement and accountability, all of which promise improvements in student learning.

6

Merging Costs with Effective Resource Strategies

Allan R. Odden, Michael E. Goetz, and Lawrence O. Picus

Across the United States, debates rage about numerous issues in education finance.[1] Historically, the focus has been on inequities in per-pupil expenditures among school districts, both within and across states.[2] Another issue has been whether money matters—that is, whether higher-spending school districts provide students with an educational advantage or, conversely, whether lower-spending districts necessarily shortchange their students.[3] More recently, as both state standards-based education reform and the federal No Child Left Behind Act (NCLB) require high levels of student performance, the issue of whether schools have sufficient resources to meet these demands has assumed new importance.[4] Many educators claim that the federal government should fully fund NCLB and that state governments should hike funding to school districts.

The shift in education finance from equity to adequacy joins all these issues.[5] Adequacy requires states to provide each school and district with an "adequate" level of resources, one that would allow them to deploy the programs and strategies that all students need to achieve the state's performance standards.

Although adequacy is conceptually straightforward, various analytic approaches have been developed to calculate its cost.[6] These alternatives can result in widely varying expenditure estimates, and there is emerging debate—quite strong debate in many cases—about whether any of those approaches reflect good science.[7] Despite this contention, states and school districts are moving forward on the adequacy agenda. Many states are under court mandate to provide adequate levels of funding, and nearly all pending education finance lawsuits raise the adequacy argument.[8]

This chapter advances the adequacy issue by demonstrating that the national average expenditure per pupil comes very close to funding adequacy. We show what could be purchased with this amount if it were applied using the evidence-based approach to adequacy, and we explain how evidence-based resources have been linked to improvements in student performance.

The chapter makes this argument in five sections. The first section reviews the various approaches to adequacy. The second section discusses the programs and strategies recommended by the evidence-based approach and then summarizes research on schools that have doubled student performance using this strategy. Next, we identify the method used to cost out (estimate the cost of) the evidence-based model's core recommendations. The ensuing section analyzes the costs of these recommendations and compares the result to the national average expenditure per pupil. The final section broadens the discussion, draws conclusions, and suggests research for the future.

To foreshadow the findings, the analysis shows that, using national average student demographics and educator salary and benefit data, the cost of the evidence-based model is nearly covered by the national average expenditure per pupil.

APPROACHES TO ADEQUACY IN EDUCATION FINANCE

Starting in the mid-1980s, the focus of education finance shifted from equity to adequacy, as courts and legislatures began interpreting education clauses in state constitutions as requiring a level of funding that allows each school and district to achieve the state's educational performance standards. To determine that level of fiscal resources, states, nonprofit organizations, and plaintiffs began contracting with education finance experts.

These experts developed four methods to determine the cost of adequacy. These methods are known, respectively, as cost function, professional judgment, successful schools or districts, and evidence-based approaches.[9] Each has its unique advantages and limitations. Reviews of these approaches have been prepared by researchers Lori Taylor, Bruce Baker, and Arnold Vedlitz; James Guthrie and Richard Rothstein; and Allan Odden.[10]

Two of these approaches—the successful district approach and the cost function approach—estimate an adequate expenditure level per pupil and make adjustments for various pupil needs, but they do not indicate how those resources should be used. In contrast, the professional judgment and evidence-based approaches specify a set of programs and strategies for prototypical elementary, middle, and high schools, as well as resource configurations for school district central offices, operations and maintenance, and transportation, arguing that these recommendations reflect adequate resources.

The professional judgment approach uses panels of educators to recommend adequate programs and strategies, whereas the evidence-based approach uses research evidence and best practices to frame its recommendations. Although the evidence-based approach starts with a set of core recommendations, it also employs teams of state policy makers as well as educational leaders and practitioners to review the recommendations and to modify or otherwise tailor them to the unique conditions, cultures, desires, and requirements of their states. The resulting set of strategies and resource needs forms the basis of the cost estimates derived for schools and districts in that state.

THE EVIDENCE-BASED APPROACH AND ACHIEVEMENT GAINS

The evidence-based approach to adequacy has been used in Arkansas, Arizona, Kentucky, Washington, Wisconsin, and Wyoming, with varying levels of expenditure estimated to bring funding in each state to adequate levels.[11] Recommendations from the evidence-based approach have been used by the Arkansas and Wyoming legislatures to restructure their states' education finance systems.

Evidence-based adequacy studies identify school-level programs and educational strategies that research has shown to improve student learning. Although the rigor of the evidence supporting each strategy varies, this approach alone among the four costing-out techniques nevertheless includes recommendations that are supported by research or best practices. Although the evidence-based recommendations, individually or together, can be debated, this approach includes educational strategies that researchers and practitioners argue should be part of any high-performance school.[12] These strategies include the following.[13]

1. Full-day kindergarten.
2. Core class sizes of fifteen for grades K–3 and twenty-five for grades 4–12. Core is defined as a regular classroom teacher in elementary school, and teachers of mathematics, science, reading/English/writing, history, and world language in secondary school. With these ratios, class sizes average eighteen in elementary school and twenty-five in middle and high schools.

3. Specialist teachers to provide instruction in art, music, physical education, career technical education, and the like, and in numbers adequate to cover a six-period day in middle school, with teachers teaching for five periods, and ninety-minute block schedules in high school.
4. At least one period, usually an hour, of planning and preparation time each day for all teachers in elementary, middle, and high schools.
5. Pupil support staff, including guidance counselors (one full-time equivalent [FTE] position for every 250 students in middle and high schools), nurses, social workers, and family liaison personnel, the latter provided on the basis of one FTE position for every 100 at-risk students.[14]
6. A full-time librarian and principal in every prototypical school, two secretarial positions in the prototypical elementary (432 students) and middle (450 students) schools, three secretaries in the prototypical high school (600 students), and an additional library media technical person and, sometimes, an assistant principal in the prototypical high school.
7. An ambitious set of professional development resources, including one instructional coach for every 200 students (three FTE positions in a 600-student high school); at least ten pupil-free days for professional development, which usually means extending the school year for teachers by five days; and $100 per pupil for trainers and other expenses related to professional development.
8. Supervisory aides to cover recess, lunch, hall monitoring, and bus loading and unloading.
9. About $180 per pupil for instructional materials, formative assessments, and supplies; $250 per pupil for technology and equipment; and $250 per pupil for student activities (sports, clubs, and the like).
10. The sum of $25 per pupil to provide extra strategies for gifted and talented students.
11. A comprehensive range of extra-help strategies for students who need additional instructional assistance and extra time to achieve rigorous state proficiency standards, including the following.

   - Resources to provide one-to-one tutoring at the ratio of one FTE teacher tutor position for every 100 at-risk students.
   - Extended-day resources to provide an eight- to nine-week summer program, up to six hours per day, with academic help, at the ratio of one FTE position for every 30 at-risk students, assuming about 50 percent of at-risk students would participate.
   - Summer school resources to provide up to a six-hour-a-day, eight- to nine-week summer program and academic help for two-thirds of the

time, at the ratio of one FTE position for every 30 at-risk students, assuming about 50 percent of at-risk students would need such extra help and would attend the program.

- An additional one FTE teacher position for every 100 English language learners (ELLs), primarily to provide instruction in English as a second language. Most of these students also are at risk and thus trigger the first three extra-help resources.
- One FTE teacher for every 150 students to provide services for high-incidence but lower-cost students with disabilities (three positions at the prototypical elementary and middle schools and four positions at the prototypical high school), with an additional half-time aide per full-time special education staff member. The model also advocates full state funding of high-cost, special-needs students (assuming 2 percent of those with disabilities are in the high-cost category).

12. Substitute teacher resources at ten days for each teacher and instructional facilitator position.
13. Central office staff covering the superintendent's office, business office, curriculum and pupil support, technology personnel, and an operations and maintenance director (configured on a prototypical 3,500-student school district and then prorated depending on actual district size).
14. Food services in the model are assumed to be a self-supporting activity; where such services operate at a loss, the model recommends outsourcing the function to a private sector company whose core business is food services.

To show what these core recommendations mean in staff positions and budget, we applied them to prototypical elementary, middle, and high schools (see table 6-1). In actual use, however, the core recommendations are fit to the student numbers and demographics of each school in a state. Thus, schools that have more students than the prototypical schools would receive proportionately more resources; schools with fewer students would receive fewer resources, although several core resources—principal, secretary, librarian—often are retained for smaller schools to address the diseconomies of small schools. Similarly, schools with larger concentrations and numbers of at-risk students would be eligible for a greater level of resources.

To determine the costs of an adequate education, salary and benefit figures need to be attached to the staff positions. This process often entails analyses of what would constitute an adequate teacher salary and adequate benefits package.[15] The estimated costs of all the individual school-based

TABLE 6-1 **Adequate resources for prototypical elementary, middle, and high schools (evidence-based model)**

Resource element	Elementary schools	Middle schools	High schools
School characteristics			
School configuration	K–5	6–8	9–12
Prototypical school size	432	450	600
Class size	K–3: 15 4–5: 25	6–8: 25	9–12: 25
Full-day kindergarten	Yes	NA	NA
Number of teacher work days	190 teacher work days, so an increase of 5 days	190 teacher work days, so an increase of 5 days	190 teacher work days, so an increase of 5 days
Percent of students with disabilities	13.7%	13.7%	13.7%
Percent poverty (free and reduced lunch)	36.3%	36.3%	36.3%
Percent ELLs	10.6%	10.6%	10.6%
Personnel resources			
1. Core teachers	24	18	24
2. Specialist teachers	20% more, assuming a six-period day with each FTE teaching five periods: 4.8	20% more, assuming a six-period day with each FTE teaching five periods: 3.6	33% more, assuming a 90-minute block schedule with each FTE teaching three blocks a day: 8.0
3. Instructional facilitators or coaches (ratio of 1 for every 200 students)	2.2	2.25	3.0
4. Tutors for struggling students	1 for every 100 poverty students: 1.57	1 for every 100 poverty students: 1.63	1 for every 100 poverty students: 2.18
5. Teachers for ELL students	An additional 1.0 teachers for every 100 ELL students: 0.46	An additional 1.0 teachers for every 100 ELL students: 0.48	An additional 1.0 teachers for every 100 ELL students: 0.64
6. Extended day	1.31	1.36	1.74
7. Summer school	1.31	1.36	1.74
8. Students with mild disabilities	Additional 3 professional teacher positions and 0.5 aides for each special education teacher	Additional 3 professional teacher positions and 0.5 aides for each special education teacher	Additional 4 professional teacher positions and 0.5 aides for each special education teacher

continued on next page

Resource element	Elementary schools	Middle schools	High schools
9. Students with severe disabilities	100% state reimbursement minus federal funds	100% state reimbursement minus federal funds	100% state reimbursement minus federal funds
10. Resources for gifted and talented students	$25/student	$25/student	$25/student
11. Substitutes	10 days per FTE	10 days per FTE	10 days per FTE
12. Pupil support staff	1 for every 100 poverty students: 1.32	1 for every 100 poverty students plus 1.0 guidance per 250 students 3.18 total	1 for every 100 poverty students plus 1.0 guidance per 250 students 4.25 total
13. Supervisory aides	2.0	2.0	3.0
14. Librarians and media specialists	1.0	1.0	1.0 librarian and 1.0 library technician
15. Principal	1	1	1
16. School site secretary	1.0 secretary and 1.0 clerical	1.0 secretary and 1.0 clerical	1.0 secretary and 3.0 clerical

Dollar-per-pupil resources

Resource element	Elementary schools	Middle schools	High schools
17. Professional development	Included above: Instructional facilitators 10 summer days Additional: $100/pupil for other PD expenses: trainers, conferences, travel, etc.	Included above: Instructional facilitators 10 summer days Additional: $100/pupil for other PD expenses: trainers, conferences, travel, etc.	Included above: Instructional facilitators 10 summer days Additional: $100/pupil for other PD expenses: trainers, conferences, travel, etc.
18. Technology and equipment	$250/pupil	$250/pupil	$250/pupil
19. Instructional materials, including textbooks, formative assessments	$165/pupil	$165/pupil	$200/pupil
20. Student activities	$250/pupil	$250/pupil	$250/pupil

Other expenditures

Resource element	Elementary schools	Middle schools	High schools
22. Operations and maintenance	$890 per pupil	$890 per pupil	$890 per pupil
23. Transportation	$375 per pupil	$375 per pupil	$375 per pupil
24. Food services	Self-supporting	Self-supporting	Self-supporting

resources then are aggregated to the school district level, at which point central office and other district resources are added. District resources then are summed to determine the total cost for the state, which is the cost of adequacy for that state.

The cost of adequacy varies from state to state, mainly because of differences in personnel costs—specifically, the number of FTEs in the recommendations and the salary and benefit levels for each of these positions. Determining the number of staff positions and their corresponding compensation levels involves policy and political decisions specific to each state. The policy choices with the greatest fiscal effect include the salary and benefit levels identified as adequate, followed by the number of FTE positions needed to accommodate class size limits, instructional facilitators or coaches, certified teachers or tutors for struggling students, summer school, and extended-day programs.

As noted, the research evidence for each of the model's recommendations varies in strength. Variance is caused by the paucity of high-quality studies and the small number of randomized controlled studies in education research. Some strategies also have widely varying results in the sizes of effects, and these variations could be caused by implementation issues, the focus of the intervention (for example, whether a summer school program had an academic emphasis), or other causes. In addition, because the evidence-based approach relies on available research, alternative and lower-cost strategies may emerge in the future.

Nevertheless, the strategies included in the core evidence-based recommendations are those widely suggested by practitioners and researchers as strategies that work to boost student achievement. Moreover, these strategies will adequately address all the resource elements in Jacob Adams's framework for linking resources to student learning (see chapter 1), Diana Sharp and John Bransford's learner-centered classrooms, and Joanne Weiss's cycle of continuous instructional improvement (see chapter 4).[16] As with any emerging ideas, however, debate continues over whether these strategies are effective in dramatically improving student academic achievement.[17]

To expand the evidence regarding the efficacy of these strategies, particularly their combined effects, we and others have conducted case studies of schools and districts that have doubled student performance, as measured by state tests over a four- to seven-year period.[18] The cases encompass rural, suburban, and urban communities and small, medium, and large schools. They show that schools followed similar steps to achieve their results—steps that track closely with similar research on improving organizational performance in the private sector and education and that employ the kinds of resources described in the evidence-based model.[19] These common strategies and resource deployments included the following.

- Small class sizes (with a goal of fifteen) in grades K–3
- Extensive teacher professional development, including added days of training and the placement of instructional coaches in schools
- Extensive use of formative assessments to help tailor and focus instruction to the precise needs of each teacher's students
- Deployment of a series of extra-help strategies that usually include a combination of one-to-one tutoring, extended day, and academically oriented summer school programs
- Creation of a collaborative, professional school culture

More research is needed to test these findings. Such research would examine the individual strategies, their various combinations, and the schools and districts that have used them to improve student performance. That said, the present combination—of evidence, schools and districts that have used these resources to boost student learning, and policy maker and practitioner support—is sufficient to argue that, if provided and used well, the evidence-based strategies should produce dramatic improvements in student performance. As evidence accumulates, these strategies and resources can be recalibrated, but they provide a substantive and reasonable basis for moving forward.

Of course, in a finance context, a key question is, How much do these strategies cost? In many places, educators and policy makers have strongly supported the recommendations but have argued that the costs would be prohibitively high, perhaps as much as $15,000 per pupil. As the next section demonstrates, actual costs are considerably lower.

METHOD FOR COSTING OUT THE EVIDENCE-BASED MODEL

To determine the national average cost of an evidence-based approach to ensure education finance adequacy, we used a prototypical district consisting of four 432-student elementary schools, two 432-student middle schools, and two 576-student high schools. These school sizes yield a school district of 3,744 students, with about 108 students in each grade.[20] This district contains the national average percentages of low-income students (defined by free and reduced-priced lunch participation), English language learners, and special education students.[21]

We determined staff in each school by applying recommendations from the evidence-based model to the numbers and demographics of these proto-typical schools (presented earlier in table 6-1).[22] We applied national average salary data, as well as a defined group of benefits (see table 6-2), to the per-sonnel resources of the prototypical elementary, middle, and high schools, and then we added the school-based cost-per-pupil resources (instructional materials, technology, professional development, and the like). This calcu-lation produced a cost for general education at the school level of $5,851 per pupil.

For each school, we then allocated resources for extra-help strategies. For instance, students eligible for free and reduced-price lunch trigger resources for tutors, extended-day and summer school programs, and additional pupil support staff, all with appropriate substitute teacher days. ELL stu-dents trigger resources for ELL teachers and their substitute days, and spe-cial education students trigger teacher and aide resources using a census approach, as well as resources for high-cost special education students (stu-dents who need services above and beyond the staffing provided via the cen-sus approach).[23]

The cost for these high-cost students, who are estimated at 2 percent of all students with disabilities, was estimated from an analysis in Wisconsin; that analysis, reconfigured to national special education percentages, esti-mated that fully funding all high-cost students would require about $137 per regular student.[24] These extra-help resources, triggered by pupil charac-teristics as noted, total $1,601 per pupil over regular pupil costs (including $2,382 per low-income student, $653 per ELL student, $3,893 per low-cost, high-incidence special education student, and $50,000 per high-cost, low-incidence special education student).

Next, we added district-level resources to these school-level costs. These district resources included the costs of the central office, maintenance and operations, and transportation. Table 6-3 includes a central office staff-ing strategy for a school district of 3,500 students.[25] These central office resources total $678 per pupil and would provide slightly more total budget to the prototypical 3,744-student district than for the 3,500-student model in table 6-3. An additional $890 per pupil for maintenance and operations and $375 per pupil for transportation, which represent the average of 9.5 percent for maintenance and operations and 4.4 percent for transportation, bring total district-level resources to $1,943 per pupil.[26] One can determine similar expenditures for operations and maintenance by applying a set of standards for those functions.[27]

TABLE 6-2 Salary and benefit rates

Position	Salary	Benefits	Total compensation
School-Based			
Principal	$80,411	$20,986	$101,397
Teacher	$46,953	$15,583	$62,536
Librarian	$52,505	$16,480	$68,985
Media tech	$37,562	$14,066	$51,629
Counselors	$51,862	$16,376	$68,238
School secretary	$24,887	$12,019	$36,906
School clerical	$19,910	$11,215	$31,125
Supervisory aide	$15,915	$10,570	$26,485
Central office			
Superintendent	$116,244	$26,773	$143,017
Asst. superintendent	$99,771	$24,113	$123,884
Business manager	$78,154	$20,622	$98,776
Staff-personnel services	$80,568	$21,012	$101,580
Technology	$66,832	$18,793	$85,625
Other areas	$68,229	$19,019	$87,248
Secretary	$33,077	$13,342	$46,419
Accounting and payroll clerks	$34,829	$13,625	$48,454

Source: Salary information from Education Research Service, *National Survey of Salaries and Wages in Public Schools,* 2005–2006. Costs for instructional facilitators, coaches, psychologists, and OT/PT are estimated using "other professional staff" salaries. Principal salaries are based on an unweighted average of elementary, junior high/middle, and high school principal salaries. Media technician salary is 80 percent of teacher salary, and school clerical salary is 80 percent of secretary salary. Supervisory aide salary is based on 7.5 work hours for 185 school days. Benefits are 7.65 percent FICA/social security, 1 percent unemployment compensation, $8,000 health, and 7.5 percent retirement.

RESULTS

Table 6-4 presents the final results. General education resources for the schools totaled $5,847 per pupil. Resources for all the extra-help strategies—tutors, extended day, summer school, ELL, all categories and degrees of disabilities—totaled another $1,601 per pupil. District office resources, including central office, operations and maintenance, and transportation services, added $1,943 per pupil, for a total of $9,391 per pupil.

TABLE 6-3 Composition of a central office for a school district with 3,500 students

Superintendent's office
1 superintendent
1 assistant superintendent
2 secretaries

Curriculum and support office
1 director of pupil services
1 director of special education
1 psychologist
3 secretaries

Business office
1 business manager
1 human resource manager
1 secretary
1 payroll clerk
1 accounts payable clerk

Technology office
1 director of technology

Operations and maintenance office
1 director of maintenance/operations
1 secretary

Of course, this cost figure would vary among the fifty states because of differing demographics and differing average salary and benefit packages. We also know that states would make decisions that vary from the core evidence-based recommendations represented in table 6-1. Nevertheless, we are confident that this figure is a good estimate of what the combined evidence-based recommendations would cost on a national average basis. And we are confident that if such resources were provided, on average, to each school and district, and if they were price adjusted to ensure purchasing power parity across states and school districts, then schools would have resources sufficient to produce substantial improvements in student academic achievement, which is the ultimate objective of educational systems and of education finance adequacy.[28]

The final per-pupil cost of the evidence-based model, derived using national average student poverty, disability, and ELL rates and applying

TABLE 6-4 Per-pupil resource needs for evidence-based funding in a prototypical school district of 3,744 students

Resource	Personnel	Total cost	Per-Pupil cost
General education			
Teachers	180.5	$11,286,481	$3,015
Specialist teachers	42.1[a]	$2,631,911	$703
Instructional facilitators	18.7	$1,170,672	$313
Counselors	8.1	$550,269	$147
Librarians	7.8	$540,839	$144
Principal	8.0	$811,176	$217
School secretary	7.8	$289,345	$77
School clerical	11.7	$363,540	$97
Noninstructional aides	17.6	$466,133	$125
Media specialists	1.9	$99,127	$26
Gifted		$93,600	$25
Substitute teachers		$259,745	$69
Additional PD days		$423,254	$113
PD funds		$374,400	$100
Technology		$936,000	$250
Instructional materials		$658,080	$176
Student activities		$936,000	$250
Subtotal		$21,890,572	$5,847
Special-needs education			
Low-income	49.8	$3,237,353	$865
ELL	4.0	$248,183	$66
Special education teachers (census) and aides	38.2	$1,997,053	$533
High-cost special education		$512,928	$137
Subtotal		$5,995,516	$1,601
District resources			
Central office	19.3	$2,539,196	$678
Maintenance and operations		$3,332,160	$890
Transportation		$1,404,000	$375
Subtotal		$7,275,356	$1,943
Total evidence-based approach cost		$35,161,444	$9,391

a. Low-income, ELL, and special education teacher (census) resources include funding for substitute teachers to cover sick days for full-time staff as well as an additional five days for staff professional development. Personnel are displayed to the tenths, although actual decimal places are used in calculations.

national average data on the cost of personnel, is $9,391. We now compare that number to various estimates of national average expenditures per pupil in 2005–2006.

In January 2007, the federal government had not yet provided an estimate of per-pupil expenditures for the 2005–2006 school year, so we turned to the most recent estimate, which was published by the National Education Association in December 2006. The NEA estimated that 2005–2006 public school expenditures per pupil, including all revenues and operating functions, equaled $9,576 per average daily attendance (ADA) and $9,022 per enrolled pupil.[29] These expenditures comprised roughly 44 percent local, 49 percent state, and 7 percent federal revenues.

Applying national average salaries (table 6-3) to the evidence-based model, the cost produced by the model averaged $9,391 per pupil in 2005–2006, which included full funding for low-incidence, high-cost special education students at the rate of $137 per student (table 6-4). The NEA estimates included roughly $375 in food services expenditures. Because the evidence-based model assumes that food services are self-sufficient, we can subtract this $375 from the national ADA and enrollment estimates, and that brings these national figures to $9,201 and $8,647, respectively.

In short, using the evidence-based model, this analysis calculates that the national average adequate level of funding was 8.6 percent greater than the 2005–2006 average per-pupil expenditure using the enrollment count of pupils, and 2.1 percent greater than the national average per-pupil expenditure using the ADA count. These figures suggest that the national average expenditure per pupil is very close to providing an adequate level of resources.

DISCUSSION, CONCLUSIONS, AND FUTURE RESEARCH

Using the recommendations from the evidence-based approach, the central finding of this analysis is that, on average, the nation overall is close to providing an adequate level of education funding. This finding is both good and unexpected news. Most educators and policy makers would predict that the nation is far from adequately funding its schools. This analysis demonstrates that such a pessimistic conclusion is not warranted.

At the same time, there is no state that looks exactly like the national average. Some states spend considerably more than this estimate, and others, considerably less. Even those that spend close to the calculated figure might not be adequately funding their public school systems, either because they have a higher concentration of students who need extra help or because they provide relatively low salaries and benefits. Without specifically applying the recommendations of the evidence-based approach to each state, it would be inappropriate to say that these fiscal findings apply to any state.

That said, the conclusion still should cause federal, state, and local officials to consider the way they fund public school systems. If, on average, overall funding is adequate or nearly adequate, does it make sense that some states might be funding public schools at a level greater than—sometimes far greater than—adequacy, while others might be funding public schools at a level less than—sometimes far less than—adequacy? And if the finding that the country as a whole is close to adequately funding public schools is on the mark, what does that finding suggest for a federal role in education finance? To what degree does it make sense for the federal government to iron out funding inequities across states so that extant resources could be deployed in ways that bring most students in most schools to adequate funding levels? What would these strategies entail?

Furthermore, in schools and districts that are adequately funded but not using their resources as productively as possible or not getting the results they could get, what are the strategies for creating a sense of urgency and change? How can policy makers and others encourage schools and school systems to rethink their curricular, instructional, and organizational strategies and create more-powerful school visions? How can they help schools and school systems restructure and, in the process, reallocate their resources toward more-effective and more-productive approaches to student learning? What strategies could be used to scale up and fund all schools and districts, transforming them into educational organizations that produce higher levels of student achievement? Put differently, adequate funding is only one step in a series of steps required for schools to re-create themselves into the kinds of high-performance organizations envisioned by Adams's framework for linking resources to student learning.[30]

One approach is to focus on states that already provide adequate funding for their schools, create multiple strategies that effect a sense of urgency so that schools restructure themselves into more-effective organizations, and study these efforts so that a knowledge base can be created regarding the incentives and mechanisms that enable schools to use resources effectively. The lessons learned could be used in states that need to increase funding to an adequate level.

Simultaneously, the federal government could work with states to launch an ambitious research agenda, bolstering the knowledge that undergirds evidence-based strategies and related approaches that boost student learning. Such a research agenda should include the following:

- Use of other adequacy methods to determine how national education funding tracks with the cost estimates generated by those models.
- Randomized controlled trials to provide more evidence to show which class sizes produce the highest levels of achievement in elementary, middle, and high schools and to determine whether different class sizes are needed for mathematics, science, history, reading, and writing—the core subjects. Because class size is a prime determinant of school costs, these studies are critical in estimating the cost of adequately funding schools.
- More analysis of what constitutes adequate teacher salaries. This information is important in determining whether teacher salary increases, by themselves, could enhance the effectiveness of teachers by allowing school systems to recruit and retain a larger number of high-quality instructors. This research also would help determine the salary premiums that are needed to recruit and retain high-quality teachers in hard-to-staff positions, such as mathematics and science, and in urban, high-poverty, and low-performing schools. Because teacher salary is the second major determinant of school costs, these studies also are critical in establishing a more accurate estimate of adequate funding.
- Additional randomized controlled trials of each evidence-based strategy and various combinations—for example, class sizes of fifteen in only grades K–1 or other grade spans, small class sizes combined with one-to-one tutoring, and so on.
- Additional case studies of schools that are dramatically improving student achievement, identification of the strategies they use, and delineation of the resources and funding needed to support those strategies.
- Additional studies of the comprehensive use of computer technologies to support student achievement while reducing the personnel needs of schools and districts.

Undoubtedly, a research agenda could be even more ambitious. But this list would add greatly to the field's knowledge about what works and how best to create effective and efficient school systems—systems that produce the levels of student achievement that the country needs if it is to remain competitive in the emerging global economy and for each student to be successful in his or her adult life.

PART IV

Expanding Resource Knowledge and Experimenting with New Methods

7

Making Resource Decisions amid Technical Uncertainty

James W. Guthrie and Paul T. Hill

Americans want and need their schools to be more effective, and they have shown themselves willing to spend money in search of better performance. During the past half-century, annual per-pupil spending in the United States increased from $2,606 (1960) to $10,041 (2006) after controlling for inflation. In 2006, annual expenditures on public elementary and secondary education cost taxpayers approximately $529 billion, or about $54 per pupil per day.[1]

However, in recent decades spending has been decoupled from performance. Spending increases—even dramatic ones, as in the cases of court-mandated reform initiatives in New Jersey, Kansas City, and Kentucky—have produced little.[2] Student achievement improved slightly in the early- to mid-1990s but has remained stagnant ever since. Efforts to connect spending and performance by legislatively prescribing uses of funds thought to be effective also have not been consistently successful. Witness the billion-dollar effort in California to reduce the size of primary grade classes, even when classroom space and qualified teachers were insufficient to fulfill legislated hopes.[3]

Politics and inertia, and not evidence about what is productive, continue to drive spending. In the absence of clear connections between spending and outputs, legislators fund programs to satisfy interest groups and courts intervene to mandate equity. Much new spending (on, for example, special education) is not even rationalized on the grounds of effectiveness.

Why can't the United States draw better connections between spending on public education and its outcomes? This chapter attempts an answer, showing that the ways the United States funds and governs education make

159

it almost impossible to learn what works effectively and how much it should cost. It is possible to learn more about which educational practices work, under what conditions, for whom, and at what cost, but Americans have not put themselves in a position to obtain this evidence.

In education policy discourse one frequently encounters the statement, "We know how to educate all children effectively, we just lack the [fill in the blank: money, political will, moral commitment, and so on] to do it." It is easy to accept that more money, political will, and moral commitment would be nice to have, but the assertion that we know what to do does not hold water. No state or district has succeeded in a sustained, coherent, or reproducible manner in closing, or for that matter significantly narrowing, the achievement gap between advantaged and disadvantaged groups. Although some schools have done much better than others, the best that can be said is that they have narrowed the gap but have come nowhere near closing it. School designs like the Knowledge Is Power Program (KIPP), and the Catholic schools that KIPP resembles, have positive effects on student effort and persistence, and they give graduates a leg up on college admission.[4] But no school can claim that its graduates have all the skills and knowledge normally expected of children leaving middle-class schools.

At the level of targeted instructional programs, methods such as Success for All sometimes have measurable effects at the grade levels where they are applied, but they seldom last throughout a student's remaining years in middle and high school.[5] Similarly, rigorous summer programs can have positive effects on elementary students' learning in reading and mathematics, but, as Melissa Roderick's studies have shown, these gains are often lost in the subsequent school year.[6]

Educators and others know bits and pieces about how to make a small difference in the short term, but they do not know how to eliminate the differences in learning and in consequent life outcomes between economically advantaged and disadvantaged children, especially when economic disadvantage is combined with minority group status and central city residence.

Examples of at least partially successful programs, media stories, single-shot case studies, and anecdotes about poor and minority children who perform as well as the most advantaged students suggest that the field can do better.[7] But that is not the same thing as systematically knowing how to do better. Elected officials and educators are in the position of primitive physicians who know that some people recover from a disease that is usually fatal: they know that the disease is survivable, but they do not know by what mechanism.

The political left and right disagree about virtually everything important connected with public education, but there is emerging agreement on one proposition: if it is not working now, then elected officials and educators should try something different. The left, represented by Richard Rothstein, claims that new approaches to schooling are not likely to be effective without big changes in students' family lives and economic status.[8] The right—represented by voucher advocates and in company with charter school supporters on the left and right—claims that the educational opportunities now available to the poor and disadvantaged are substandard, and no one can ever know what education can accomplish until states try providing much better schools.[9]

Neither side can prove its case. Antipoverty programs have been as messy and inconsistent as school reform efforts, and their links to student learning are unproven. Efforts to transform students' schooling experience also have had inconsistent effects, and, as noted, the best have fallen far short of eliminating gaps in student performance.

Yet both sides have undeniable points in their favor. Chaotic families and neighborhoods surely interfere with children's learning, and programs to ameliorate these conditions or remove children from them make sense. KIPP and the Catholic schools might owe some of their success to the socially ameliorative facets of programs that immerse students in environments quite different from their neighborhoods and that model middle-class values and behavior.

On the school reformers' side there is undeniable evidence that poor and minority children routinely are assigned the least-experienced and lowest-paid teachers and attend the most turbulent and unfocused schools. Surely the purely educational facets of their experience could be improved to good effect.

Left and right could come together on the proposition that initiatives to improve outcomes for the poor and disadvantaged should combine school improvement with efforts to reduce the effects of poverty and family disruption. However, even if they could so agree, those who would improve outcomes would face a great deal of uncertainty about how to proceed.

The truth is that elected officials and educators do not know how to provide effective schools for the millions of poor and minority youngsters served by the nation's big-city school systems. Public education is not well designed for solving new and unfamiliar problems, such as how to educate a constantly changing and disadvantaged urban and rural population. It does not know how much it costs to do the job or how best to allocate resources effectively. The point of this chapter is to sketch a path for testing new and old practices and learning from the results.

WHY WE DON'T KNOW

Americans have been schooling young people of many backgrounds and abilities for nearly two hundred years; why don't their elected representatives and school professionals know for sure what works?

The question can be answered in two ways. First, the nation's methods of education work well enough to produce graduates needed by the professions, industries, small and large businesses, schools and universities, the military, and, at least until recently, scientific institutions. Under those circumstances the nation has not routinely found it imperative to ask whether states could educate everyone, even every middle-class student, well.[10]

Second, the nation's educational institutions are not constructed to support experimentation or continuous improvement. Although the United States now wants and needs to improve education for groups other than the elites who have been served satisfactorily, federal, state, and local entities do not have a systematic mechanism for doing it.

This chapter focuses on explaining and suggesting alternatives to the second answer. The first answer, though valuable as a historical explanation, does not apply well now. Americans are aware of harm done to millions of poor and minority students who are not educated well, and they are coming to fear that the nation is not producing enough students who have the scientific and mathematical skills that will be needed in the twenty-first century workplace.

Why do educational institutions overlook the need for continuous improvement and stifle efforts to optimize performance for all students? The basic answer is that the educational system is designed for stability and not adaptability, and so it cannot adopt the classic problem-solving approach that Americans pursue when they want to address a challenge, such as going to the moon or conquering cancer or AIDS. That approach—to go through several cycles of innovation, rejecting the least successful methods and investing further in the best—requires suppleness and adaptability. However, public education in the United States is shaped principally through politics, in which groups, particularly groups having narrow interests, contend for control of state legislation or school board policy.

In an environment that must serve many different needs, where children with new needs arrive on our shores every day, and where the nation persistently fails to provide effective schooling for the majority of low-income and minority students, the system's stability is a problem and not an asset. The existing system renders it difficult to distinguish the effective from the ineffective. Following is an illustrative list of impediments.

Allowing Only Micro-Scale Innovation

Teachers and principals constantly experiment with new ideas in their schools and classrooms. Although some of these experiments might be quirky or self-indulgent, others are probably smart and worth spreading.[11] However, there is no ready method for identifying these innovations, assessing their value, transmitting them to others, or combining several small ones into a broader innovation that might constitute a more productive way of teaching a whole course or grade level.

Teachers' isolation from one another and love of independence are two factors that retard the spread of innovation, but other sectors of the economy—for example, medicine—have overcome similar isolation. They do so by institutionalizing the search for new ideas, formally testing the most promising, and aggressively spreading information about them. The entire academic medical establishment exists for this purpose, as do the knowledge management mechanisms inside innovative companies such as 3M. No one has this innovation and dissemination assignment in public education. This is a crucial assignment, and later the chapter suggests where to lodge the responsibility.

Resisting Innovations That Trade Off Labor and Capital

The idea of education as a craft activity, with a teacher directly instructing a group of students, is firmly entrenched in law and policy. State laws controlling class size and teacher licensing ensure that the lion's share of spending will be on salaries, limiting the spending on new instructional materials and other resources. Teacher hiring and compensation generally consume spending increases. Purchases of technology are possible only at the margin, as add-ons to existing budgets.

As a result, even vendors of new instructional methods carefully avoid suggesting that fewer teachers could do the same work or that funds allocated to salaries could be deployed differently. These restrictions limit what can be spent on new ideas and ensure that innovations will be constrained financially and by teachers' work preferences.

Rewarding Unproductive Activities

Until recently, public schools were presumed permanent, regardless of how much their students learned. Standards-based reform initiatives, including the No Child Left Behind Act, have at least raised the possibility that unproductive schools would be sanctioned and productive ones rewarded.[12] However, few states or localities have determined how to do this. School districts have not created the databases on which such decisions can be made accurately, and they are still constrained by politics and tenure laws from making decisions based purely on performance. When it comes to particular programs, districts are similarly ill equipped to measure effectiveness (not to mention cost-effectiveness) or to act on performance data.[13] Although programs come and go and the stocks of schools in a locality change over time, transitions are caused more by funding availability and fashion than by judgments about effectiveness.

In public education, flows of people and money are not rapid but gradual, slowed by entitlements and habits; movement of funds is seldom driven by the search for higher performance. Tenure and licensing requirements ensure heavy spending on permanent staff, and collective bargaining agreements and unions' political dynamics facilitate the preferences of senior teachers and shape how funding is distributed within a district.[14] The school principals and within-school department heads who are most likely to seek more-effective uses of finances and people do not control funds, nor do they have much say about who works under them. Although states fund school districts on a per-pupil basis, the link between students and funds is broken at the district level, where money is allocated to programs and staff categories rather than to units whose productivity can be measured. Moreover, families in most districts have little say over which schools and programs their children will be assigned to; even when parents can choose, issues of income or racial balance and enrollment capacity often constrain movement.

Resisting Experimentation

Education historians routinely chronicle the faddish waves that wash across the landscape of U.S. schooling. Books such as David Tyack's *The One Best System,* David Tyack and Larry Cuban's *Tinkering Toward Utopia,* or Raymond Callahan's *The Cult of Efficiency* make clear that many of the fundamental activities and operating conditions characterizing our schools are a product of forceful advocacy but seldom are a result of systematic empirical research.[15]

One does not have to cite historic hoaxes such as phrenology, efforts to convert left-handed students to right-handed practices, or left–right brain instructional strategies to make the argument. Within the lifetime of many readers of this chapter, contemporary schools have been subjected to unproven, unproductive, unsustainable, costly, and sometimes harmful practices, such as classrooms without walls, school mathematics study group math, individually prescribed instruction, the sixty-five percent solution, self-esteem management, and small-school and school district consolidation.

In the early part of the twentieth century, during the Progressive Era, reformers strove mightily to insulate schools from the alleged evils of excessive partisan politics. School boards in big cities became appointed. Where elections were retained, school board positions were rendered nonpartisan and elections were held off cycle. Ironically, now, at the beginning of the twenty-first century, mayoral takeovers of public schools are seen by some observers as a panacea for solving urban school problems.[16]

In the same period, the number of U.S. school districts has been reduced from 127,000 to approximately 14,000. The main argument for this dramatic consolidation was that small schools were economically inefficient and denied students the full curricula provided by larger schools. In the 1960s, former Harvard president James Bryant Conant championed larger high schools, attributing the nation's low levels of academic achievement to diseconomies of scale.[17] Similarly, at the opening of the twenty-first century, the Bill & Melinda Gates Foundation launched a major national policy initiative to persuade school districts to reduce the size of high schools, rendering them smaller and more conducive to personal relationships that fostered learning.

Education policy and practice seemingly are trapped in a never-ending spiral, moving from one fad to another and then back. One hundred years ago, student homework was widely touted by some education theorists as being bad for students. Indeed, claims were made that homework was injurious to student health, known to trigger disease. As recently as fifty years ago, the school board of Santa Cruz, California, banned homework, preventing teachers from making homework assignments. Alfie Kohn and others have again raised the same flag.[18] Another recent book now asserts that homework contributes to childhood obesity.[19]

This vulnerability to fads persists because intellectual leaders of public education, including superintendents and researchers in central offices and schools of education, often resist the experimentation by which other fields sort out more-productive from less-productive methods. Educators generally resist the standardization of methods necessary to compare the productivity of one well-defined practice against another. To them, it is more important to respect the uniqueness of every student and teacher than to discipline practice even temporarily to allow rigorous tests.[20] Educators also resist random assignment to alternative treatments, a second requirement for experimentation, on grounds that they cannot assign a child to anything that might be risky.[21] Taken together, these positions limit what can be tried and what can be learned.

These impediments to the natural process whereby better methods win out over worse ones are deeply seated. They force evidence about effectiveness to the margins and resist major public policy initiatives and foundation investments. Any effort to remove them will have to be comprehensive and bold.

THE CONSEQUENCES OF NOT KNOWING

Elected officials and the public get little help from the research or practice communities in identifying or sorting advocacy pronouncements. Engineers, architects, physicians, pharmacists, and scores of other professionals, along with craft workers such as electricians, pilots, and plumbers, routinely are expected to adhere to high standards of research reliance and craft practice. Not to do so places them in substantial professional jeopardy and exposes them to charges of tort and product liability. For example, an engineering design for the replacement Tacoma Narrows Bridge (in Washington State) was subjected to careful technical review, and remedies for past aerodynamic and structural mistakes were incorporated amply into the modern design.

Education policy proposals seldom are subjected to the same intensity of technical review or held to rigorous standards of scientific evidence. Public officials cannot easily be expected to possess the scientific expertise to impose high standards on a specialized field. They must look to the professional field itself for the imposition of rigorous standards. Until recently, education has been insufficiently vigilant to police its own research and the proposals of advocates, and hence the vulnerability of education and education policy to fads.

The following is an illustrative list of unanswered—at least not yet scientifically addressed—but hugely consequential education policy issues.

- What is the nature of effective early childhood education? What long-term effect on academic achievement and other performance dimensions can it have? What are its relative costs and long-term benefits? And how much should be invested in its operation relative to other alternative reforms?

- What is an effective teacher? What training is necessary to prepare an effective teacher? And to promote effective teacher training and recruitment, what expectations should be defined in state credentialing mechanisms?
- What sustained professional development activities should teachers be supplied with or mandated to obtain? Who should pay for such activities?
- What is an effective class size, for what grade levels, and for what kinds of students? And what is the relative benefit of investing in this treatment compared to other possible investments?
- What is the optimum size of a school? What are the trade-offs between operational economies of scale and individual student engagement? To what degree does school size influence students' academic achievement? Does the school configuration or the size and condition of the physical facility itself matter?
- Are there any best or preferred practical means for instructing in mathematics, science, language arts, world languages, art, and so on?
- What is the role, if any, of instructional supplies and materials? Can technology be deployed to enhance instruction or to dilute the labor-intensive nature of U.S. public schooling?
- What are appropriate performance incentive systems? Should incentives be applied to individuals or to teams? Should incentives encompass administrators? By what means should student achievement or performance be gauged when incentive systems are designed?
- How can education accountability systems best be designed? What is an effective governance system? What are the consequences of unfettered or even structured parental choice? What data system can best serve education policy?

Taken together, these unresolved questions make it impossible to answer the underlying question that motivated this chapter: how much will it cost to educate all American children to high standards?

TOLERATING UNCERTAINTY

How, a reader reasonably might ask, can there be so little known regarding such important issues associated with formal education? Schooling has taken place for thousands of years, and yet the scientific base is slender. Moreover, the United States annually expends hundreds of billions of dollars on education. How can it not be subjected to careful scientific scrutiny?

Once the questions are posited, the answers are understandable. Medical science, something of a gold standard for rigorous applied professional research, has only a hundred-year history. It was not until the Flexner report in 1910 that the United States began to undertake health-related inquiries in a truly scientific manner.[22]

Education had its Flexner report analogue in 2002. It took the form of the Education Sciences Reform Act.[23] This landmark federal legislation created the Institute for Education Sciences (IES), which, in its short existence, has systematically established high standards for the funding, conduct, and judging of education research. These standards have had a disquieting effect. Much that was previously accepted—anecdotes, case studies, vignettes, jargon-laced journalism, thinly disguised advocacy, and so on—is now held in low professional regard. The effects of IES's new standards are beginning to be felt in what increasingly is understood as the degree of rigor appropriate for education research.

One might wonder why this development came so late. Again, there is an answer. It was only near the end of the twentieth century, with the 1983 publication of *A Nation At Risk*, that all of U.S. public education became concerned with rigor.[24] For most of its four-hundred-year colonial and national history, the United States operated its military, government, commerce, and universities by using the talents of a small, educated elite. Before World War II most students did not attend high school. Still, there were relatively good jobs for those who were not well educated. Johnny could quit school, work on an assembly line, earn sufficiently, marry Mary, and pursue the American dream. But as Peter Drucker has shown, this happy blue-collar era is now over.[25]

This manufacturing-based economy worked well, or at least sufficiently, until the last quarter of the twentieth century, when microchip technology and rapid transportation flattened the world and rendered national boundaries of far less consequence for purposes of capital movement, commerce, and manufacturing. High-paying jobs for poorly educated workers still exist, but few are located in the Untied States. Now more than ever, the route to material—and possibly other forms of—fulfillment necessitates an individual's obtaining a good education.

Many U.S. households understand this fundamental economic transformation, and the broader political system has honored their preferences for a more rigorous education system. The 2002 enactment of the No Child Left Behind Act symbolized this new condition. It altered the centuries-long practice of judging schools by inputs, now rendering outcomes important. Because outcomes count, searching for a means of elevating outcomes becomes important. A demand has been constructed for rigorous research. This is what is new, but the process is only now getting started and the results are still meager.

LIVING WITH UNCERTAINTY

What can decision makers do when there are no scientific answers to important education policy questions? Elected officials cannot ignore education simply because they lack good evidence about an issue. They are responsible for coercive government actions on behalf of public education, including levying taxes and compelling student attendance at school, and so elected officials cannot simply ignore questions about how much money schools should get and how it should be used. Officials also are constantly bombarded by complaints and demands from parents, school employees, business leaders, and others, each group hoping to tilt policy in a direction favorable to itself.

Needing a basis on which to make policy, elected officials rely on the following five processes. They can lead to decisions, good or bad.

Political Bargaining

When in doubt regarding policy matters of substantial collective consequence, decision makers rely on political processes for determining direction. No one thinks that bargaining and arbitrage of interests can arrive at the most efficient solution to a problem. In fact, as Terry Moe has demonstrated, political settlements routinely are inefficient because they involve payoffs to the groups needed to form a coalition and because today's winners establish bureaucratic strongholds that allow them to retain advantages even when needs change and potentially more-effective uses of funds emerge.[26]

However, political settlements are by definition widely acceptable and satisfy officials' need to take action, even when those officials do not fully know what the practical consequences will be. Here is a line from the 1980s British TV series *Yes Minister* about the politician's syllogism that captures this predicament: "Something must be done; this is something; therefore this must be done. Yes. Let us do so."

Political settlements are appropriate when there are clashes of values. On what social ends and achievement purposes should schools be focused? What are the measures of school success (for example, attendance, test scores, aesthetic performances, athletic events, college admission, adult voting behavior)? To what degree should schools be instruments of broader social policy, such as income redistribution, racial or gender equality, or employment engines? Where geographically should schools be constructed, and to what degree should facilities be merely instructionally serviceable or more symbolic of a community's higher aspirations? Who should have access to schooling? Who should pay for schooling? Who, if anyone, should be excluded from schooling? Who gets to participate in decisions regarding schooling?

Questions such as these lend themselves less to empirical verification and more to popular legitimation. These questions, while having some empirical coloration, are rooted principally in matters of values and collective preferences. Under such circumstances, only the political system can create authoritative answers.

Judicial Processes

Starting in the mid-twentieth century, Americans increasingly relied on courts to decide difficult school-related issues. Courts can apply constitutional and common law principles and create solutions to problems that could not be arrived at through conventional electoral politics, such as ordering the white power structure of the old South to desegregate schools, an action that would not have been taken by white-dominated state governments. However, courts are not institutions for scientific or economic analysis. They can decide an issue if they can find a controlling principle. But they are not equipped to resolve technical uncertainties, and there is no reason to think that orders they issue will lead to efficient action toward a practical goal.

Courts are indispensable in deciding questions of whether governmental actions respect rights guaranteed by law. But they are vulnerable to litigants' actions. Litigants can stretch legal principles into new shapes to their own advantage, misrepresent facts, and make false claims about the efficacy of desired actions. The adversarial system allows opposing sides to rebut each other, but it does not guarantee that judges or juries will be sufficiently sophisticated to distinguish between well-grounded assertions and calculated nonsense.

Individuals will differ about whether constitutional equal protection guarantees have been distorted to cover issues that should not be adjudicated at all, but no one can say they have not been stretched. In education, litigation has led to expanded rights and entitlements for women as well as disabled, alien, non-English-speaking, and disadvantaged persons, and it also has become a vehicle for efforts to reallocate public funds and to compel higher levels of overall public spending, issues formerly resolved via direct political processes. Whatever their legitimacy, judicial actions to compel particular levels of spending on schools or to order redistribution of public budgets in particular ways are based essentially on advocates' claims and not on evidence linking actions to practical consequences.

Expert Processes

When no one knows for sure what will work, elected officials often refer questions to expert panels. By assembling individuals who know a lot about different parts of a problem, officials can obtain the best available options and can estimate consequences. This process can improve policy and prediction in the face of uncertainty, as Norman Dalkey and others demonstrated in their efforts on a specific expert process called Delphi.[27] Rigorously managed, pooled expertise can be better than individual expertise.

Pooled expertise, however, is far from perfect. Military planning, which almost always relies on expert processes, can place too much emphasis on lessons learned in the past war and pay too little attention to changes in alliances, power relations, military capabilities, and popular movements that will define the next war. In some circumstances, expert opinion might simply be the best of many bad sources of guidance.

Expert processes have played a part in education policy, particularly as judges and legislatures have sought guidance about how much to spend on public schools. Professional judgment panels, including educators and financial analysts, have been asked to estimate how much more must be spent to bring all public school students up to a set standard of achievement. Like expert groups convened in other fields, professional judgment panels in education have started with information about current spending and achievement levels and have tried to imagine a situation that does not exist. Also, like other groups, these education panels have been forced to assume a future world based on the current one and have prescribed marginal changes in spending based on instructional methods and technologies quite like those now in use. In other words, they have planned for the last war.

To date, there is no evidence that the spending levels prescribed by such panels lead to the outcomes sought.[28] Under the best of circumstances, like war planners, professional judgment panels may base their conclusions on careful reasoning, but they also are forced to make heroic assumptions about the behavior of regulators, administrators, teachers, students, and parents, none of which is likely to be borne out in practice. Under the worst conditions, professional judgment panels have been unprofessional, biased, filled with advocates, and tinged with greed.[29]

Performance Incentives

A common approach to uncertainty is to create strong incentives for improved performance, assuming that individuals and groups will therefore work harder and seek ways of becoming more effective. Performance incentives import one marketlike process into a system that is otherwise run bureaucratically.

Standards-based reforms enacted by most states, along with No Child Left Behind, try to create performance incentives. They threaten to close and replace low-performing schools and (vaguely) threaten the jobs of low-performing educators. Such incentives might lead to innovation and new evidence about what works and what it costs, but only if educators believe that the sanctions are real and unavoidable.

To date, accountability features of state standards-based reform laws have seldom been implemented, and interest groups are trying to pull the accountability teeth of No Child Left Behind. Whatever one thinks of such accountability provisions, it is clear that they do not create performance incentives as long as educators believe they are about to be neutralized or repealed.

Potential performance incentives are weak in the face of other incentives that are wired in to public education. For example, incentives that are now dominating public schools encourage classroom instructors to leave teaching and become specialists and administrators. Administrators themselves are encouraged to rise ever upward through the ranks until reaching posts where they seldom if ever see students. The current educational system provides higher pay, greater prestige, more discretion over one's time, and more interaction with adults the further one moves from day-to-day responsibilities for students and the harder it is to link an individual's work with student outcomes. Thus, like market processes, performance incentives have not yet proved to be sufficiently powerful to provide new information about effective methods or their cost.

Competition

When confronted with uncertainty, government often allows problems to be solved by individuals and groups acting in their own interest. The results might not conform to any particular set of values nor seek a particular end as effectively as possible. But they do avoid the costly side-payments characteristic of political decisions, and they do not create bureaucracies that subsequently make it difficult to reverse a particular distribution of benefits.

Americans differ in their views on the appropriate role of markets. Some argue that competition should resolve all issues except those that require authoritative action—for example, rationing the use of airwaves, creating the transportation infrastructure, and making foreign policy. Others argue that market-based decision making is appropriate only when the issues at stake are weighted toward individual significance but are of relatively minor collective consequence (such as a family's choice of a piano teacher or a soccer coach) or when issues are so freighted with conflict that no negotiated solution is possible (for example, whether a child attends a Catholic or Protestant school in the Netherlands).

Although U.S public education is governed through electoral politics and regulation, some education issues are left to private action. Parents can decide whether or not to buy piano or dance lessons or to pay extra to send children to private schools. Parents who are willing to pay can choose religious education. Teachers can decide whether they want to work in one school district or another.

These limited deferments to the market have not generated significant competitive pressure on schools, in part because public school districts have written off the groups that traditionally attend private school. Private schools, moreover, are content to serve niche markets and have no incentive to grow. Furthermore, families that choose private schools generally prefer traditional teaching methods and course materials, so private schools are seldom a source of innovative ideas.

HOW WE CAN KNOW MORE

If none of the mechanisms discussed so far is producing evidence about which methods are most effective and how much must be spent on public education, how can Americans reduce their uncertainty? We suggest two approaches that involve profound changes in decision making and use of resources. The first is rigorous research and development (R&D), and the second is more thoroughgoing use of marketlike mechanisms such as transparency, devolution of responsibility, performance incentives, and performance accountability.

Research and Development

The scientific way to reduce uncertainty is to study the process in question with an eye toward identifying and testing promising new models. At least in theory, R&D can provide evidence about what is possible and thus supports decisions on how much to spend and how to spend it.

At present there is fragmentary evidence about the characteristics of schools and instructional programs associated with higher performance.

Moreover, this evidence has limited applicability to spending decisions for three reasons. First, it is based on variations in current practice rather than an effort to formulate and test a wider set of possibilities. Second, the research often identifies the attributes of effective programs without showing how they can be reproduced where they do not now exist. Third, as a consequence of the limited scope of programs studied, the effects now documented appear too weak to achieve the goal of bringing all children up to high standards of achievement.

It is possible to imagine an R&D strategy sufficiently rigorous to identify ideas outside the range of current practice and to conduct rigorous testing of reproducible programs, but this strategy would need to be much more ambitious than any attempted to date.

If the United States is to know what it will cost to raise all students to high standards, it must at least have examples of schools and programs that attain these goals. In the absence of demonstrated exemplars, a serious R&D initiative is indispensable. The goal of such an initiative would be to create new methods for teaching and learning at the K–12 level that would dramatically accelerate learning, especially for low-income and minority students.

By methods we mean ways of presenting material and individualizing repetition and practice so that children do not develop large holes in their knowledge and skills. The methods sought would be much broader than a little module to teach one fact or concept: they would be entire systems for presenting a body of knowledge—for example, what one could normally consider a one-year course like third-grade reading or tenth-grade English, or even more broadly an approach to instruction that is consistent across a whole grade level or a whole school.[30]

Methods would combine material and skills to be learned, technologies for presenting them, and teacher actions to explain materials and guide student work. Again, a specific programmed learning module, lesson plan, or student assignment would all be elements of a method; a method would essentially be an architecture that combines material, technology, and teacher instruction. It also might combine these instructional elements with efforts to create a specific motivational and supportive climate for students and with social and health services.

An R&D initiative would focus on creating, testing, and disseminating evidence about whole new methods. It would make three kinds of related investments in (1) identifying component technologies, teaching techniques, and social interventions that might become integrated into broader systems; (2) assembling and testing combinations of such techniques into a broader method as defined earlier; and (3) demonstrating and disseminating evidence about promising methods so that they can be adopted by schools and districts.

Such an initiative could be designed in imitation of DARPA, the Defense Advanced Research Projects Agency. DARPA's goal is to create new weapons, sensors, and information management systems that will make the armed forces more effective. It makes investments at three levels: in technologies that might someday contribute to broader systems, in systems designs—that is, architectures that combine multiple technologies and affect human activities and performance; and in prototypes that the armed services can adopt with some confidence in their performance and cost.

DARPA invests in small technology innovations, but that's not all; it presses for the use of new ideas together to create entire new capabilities. It does not simply assemble off-the-shelf technologies; it also identifies holes that must be filled and invests in efforts to fill them. It is not driven only by technology; it also responds to the views of officials in the armed services about capacities they will need in the future.

DARPA bridges very different worlds. At one end it operates on the frontiers between science and technology, and at the other end it bridges systems integration with operational use. It is neither a purely scientific enterprise, which would support scholars to work on anything their theories suggested was interesting, nor purely a marketing organization, which would focus on producing things customers would buy now. Rather, it is an innovation-creating organization whose core skill is recognizing the systems implications of potential technologies.

To produce dramatically more effective methods of teaching and learning, an education R&D initiative would have to imitate DARPA in several ways. At a minimum, it would need the following:

- Strong management that can understand the whole field from promising technologies through systems to school operations
- A substantial amount of money to invest at all levels (technologies, systems development, testing, dissemination)
- Freedom to try out ideas that cost more than is now normally spent on schools but might produce significantly better results, and also to try out less expensive methods
- Independence to allow risk taking and pursuit of ideas that school administrators, teacher unions, and education schools might oppose because they trade technology for personnel

- A long time horizon to allow development of methods that incorporate entirely new technologies
- Accountability based only on the performance of methods developed

An education R&D initiative would face one big challenge that DARPA does not: unlike the armed services, school districts and teacher unions seldom are committed to the use of technology. Most are wedded to the labor-intensive model of a teacher in a small classroom serving as the main medium of instruction. School districts and labor unions are well organized to control government and to claim that any change in method must come with new money. Consequently, an education R&D organization should not be part of government or subject to its control. Because charter, magnet, and independent schools might be the first users of its products, an education R&D initiative must not be constrained, as most federally funded labs and centers have been, to keep the public school establishment happy.

These caveats mean that the organization must be privately funded, at least in part, and managed by a new independent organization or housed in a university, think tank, or laboratory, and not in a governmental or inter-governmental organization.

Such an R&D initiative is certain to open up new possibilities and to develop programs that can be tested and reproduced. One hopes it also will produce systems designs that can make schools more productive, particularly for the low-income and minority students who are now farthest behind.

Will it identify instructional systems that fulfill all of society's aspirations for schools? In the short run, it may not. A serious R&D initiative might reveal that the best we can do, given our imagination about schooling and the intrinsic limitations of instructional processes, is still less than we need. It might lead us to experiment with much higher levels of spending and much greater integration of education with family services and antipoverty programs. These experiments themselves might or might not work, at least at first. But a rigorous R&D initiative will make it possible for decisions about spending and use of funds to be made on the basis of evidence and not ideologies or advocacy.

A Public Education System Optimized for Performance

No matter how rigorous it is, an R&D initiative can do only so much. New programs can make a difference only if they are used. This is impossible in a public education system in which money is obligated in long-term commitments to people and buildings and adults are insulated from performance pressure. A public education system that would be hungry for the results of R&D, and would put into practice any new program that promised higher performance, would be one that allowed money, adult human resources, and students to flow readily from lower- to higher-performing schools. It also would discipline spending so that there was just enough to provide the most effective known instructional program for a given set of students, and no more. Such a public education system would have the following five key attributes.

Providing Transparent Funding

Without public funding, decent education would be beyond the reach of millions of families. The commitment to public funding is based on the realization that all Americans, even those who can afford to pay for education on their own, benefit from having a literate electorate and a competent, mobile work force.

Although no one can say for sure how much money is required for governments to provide every child with an excellent education, it is obvious that very low or erratic funding levels can put the goal of general public education at risk. This is especially true when the least is spent on children who have the fewest family resources.

Unfortunately, disadvantaged children, and the neighborhoods in which they live, are usually the weakest competitors for centrally controlled resources. School districts, like other governmental agencies, allocate their funds and attention in response to political pressure. In school districts, this comes from articulate and engaged families seeking the best possible schooling for their children, along with senior teachers who expect their loyalty to be rewarded with assignments to the most attractive schools. Because money and experienced teachers are always in short supply, the most influential families and neighborhoods win in this competition for resources, and others lose.

The most direct response to politically driven spending distortions is to attach funds to individual pupils so that all students will have the same baseline amounts spent on them and so that these amounts can be transparent to all observers. Having all students in a district benefit from the same level of spending would improve on the current arrangements. However, the struggle to find effective schools for disadvantaged children almost certainly requires weighted student funding to ensure that the neediest students receive more resources.

The rationale for transparent public funding implies more than using tax dollars to build buildings, pay salaries, or offer only one form of instruction, even if it does not work for many students. It requires support for every child's education in a way that overcomes poor families' financial disadvantages. As the next section illustrates, current methods of supporting public education that attach money to buildings, teachers, transportation, and administrative functions are not traceable to students and do not meet the lofty goal that initially justified public funding.

Concentrating Resources Near the Student

If public education is to be adaptable to the distinctive needs of particular children and to promising new models of instruction, it needs flexible resources. It must be possible to spend money differently on different children and to reallocate spending in ways required by promising new methods of instruction. This implies that decisions about spending should be standardized as little as possible and should be controlled by people who know children and are responsible for their learning. It also implies that as little money as possible should be obligated in long-term commitments and fixed expenditures.

Unfortunately, public school systems in the United States are built on very different premises. Because of long-term commitments to buildings, tenured employees, and programs established by national and state legislatures, resources are anything but flexible. Money is allocated to programs—such as vocational education, tutoring, transportation, and in-service teacher training—and to salaries. Spending decisions are made by the state or by a school district central office on behalf of all schools. Schools do not receive cash other than small amounts (normally less than $50,000 per year) for supplies, copying, small purchases, and field trips. Schools often cannot choose their own teachers: the district central office assigns them.

Thus at state and federal levels the question is seldom, "How much should we allocate for the education of a student?" but rather, "How big an appropriation can the supporters of teachers, or vocational education, or computer literacy, swing for [name the interest group] this year?"

A public school system that continually sought to find and use the most effective method for every student would need a dramatically different approach to spending and decision making. To be capable of reallocating funds from less-productive to more-productive uses, the system would need to avoid linking funding to specific employees, equipment, or programs. To support adaptation to students' needs, money would have to be controlled in close proximity to the student, by those directly responsible for providing instruction and attaining results.

These requirements differ sharply from current practice, and meeting them would require changes at every level. States either would need to consolidate all K–12 appropriations into one per-student allocation or would need to allow districts to combine separate accounts. Districts also would need to consolidate many different accounts—some now mandated by the state and others created for their own purposes—and to distribute finances directly to schools.[31] To put as many consequential decisions as possible near the student, school districts also would need to reduce automatic spending on their central offices to a modest amount, only enough to pay for financial administration, school performance assessment, and investment in new schools. Districts also could provide optional services and charge fees.

Using Community Resources Strategically
Persons who have been involved intimately with schools serving the most disadvantaged youth know that these students require more time and money, and a more comprehensive commitment to youth development, than normally attaches to the concept of school. The division between education and social service institutions is yet another barrier that prevents communities from doing all they can to educate their children.

As discussed earlier, KIPP and similar schools might not be the final answer to improving student achievement in high-poverty neighborhoods. However, they make it clear that a public education system built to strive constantly for higher performance would not rule out expanding what schools do and how they structure a student's time. That broader role, however, raises the question of money. It costs a great deal more money to operate a school eight to twelve hours per day rather than six and to develop integrated, learning-focused approaches to instruction, recreation, and family services.

As in the case of KIPP and its close relatives operated by churches, these schools require private investment in design, and most now derive some of their operating funds from philanthropy. However, there are only a few such schools, and philanthropy can stretch only so far. Communities that want to offer such schools to all students who could benefit need to find ways of supporting them with public funds.

Student-based public funding, especially if weighted for student needs, can provide some of the extra operating support. If basic state and local support were allocated so that all funds followed children and every student brought exactly the same amount to the school she attended, then categorical program funds could provide extra amounts to support more-intense educational programs for disadvantaged students. The combination of federal Title I, state categorical programs, and funds for education of the disabled could support a substantial amount of extra student weighting.

This situation exists in theory but not in practice. As researcher Marguerite Roza has shown, school districts often underfund schools serving disadvantaged children and then barely bring those schools up to spending equality by adding on state and federal categorical funds.[32] Within districts, the amounts spent on pupils who share a particular characteristic—for example, low-income status—now vary tremendously depending on which school a child attends. Current practices that seem to violate the intent of Title I comparability and nonsupplanting requirements are nonetheless legal because of a loophole that allows districts to ignore differences in the higher average salaries paid to teachers serving advantaged pupils.

Localities might find that the extra weighting permitted under existing categorical programs is still insufficient. They will have to consider spending more, at least for the neediest pupils. In some circumstances, extra money also could come from funds normally used to support separate health and social service agencies, and from philanthropy.

Schools serving disadvantaged children might well be able to expand their hours and days of student contact if separate social service agencies' youth budgets were combined. This budget melding would require as wrenching a change in social services as in education, because it implies that agency funds would be used at the point of delivery by individuals responsible for children's overall development, rather than controlled centrally and used to pay salaries for a fixed set of providers. If this could be done, poverty-area schools might evolve into charter youth service agencies whose core task is instruction but whose resources also are flexible. Such schools would be more like parishes than government agencies, able to draw from a wider array of expertise, and to spend more money, than is available to support their purely instructional roles.

In the future, public agencies responsible for education must overcome the tendency to make sharp distinctions between their own funds and those received from other agencies and from philanthropy. This change would be a major leap for school boards and district central offices accustomed to drawing bright lines between "our" money and employees and "theirs."[33]

Despite the constant agitation about it, the question, "How much spending on public education is enough?" is difficult to answer in the absence of a public education system in which funds from all sources can be used flexibly, ineffective activities can be abandoned, and resources can flow to effective uses. It probably takes more money to educate some children than others. However, it also takes less money to run a highly efficient system, in which virtually all funds are applied directly to instruction and student services, than an inefficient one, in which spending is driven by political and bureaucratic considerations.

Rewarding Performance

If public education is constantly to seek more-effective methods of instruction and better matches between children and teaching methods, then everyone in the system must face strong performance incentives. Although teachers and administrators all hope their work will benefit children, they also have other concerns—for example, complying with rules, avoiding conflict with coworkers and superiors, working in ways that satisfy themselves, and preserving time and energy for private pursuits. Strong performance incentives do not eliminate other motives, but they can profoundly affect individuals' priorities.

Educators are neither more nor less dedicated to their work than doctors, lawyers, engineers, and other professionals. In those other professions, however, pay, job security, work satisfaction, and prestige are strongly linked to performance. The doctor who invents a successful new surgical procedure reaps huge rewards professionally and financially. Once a promising new method is developed, other doctors have strong incentives to learn and adopt it: early adopters also can reap financial rewards, and those who use outmoded methods risk malpractice claims. Concepts of best practice have genuine operational meaning in medicine, law, and other professions. Other professionals face similar performance contingencies: a lot to gain from innovation, and a lot to lose from failure to pursue the best.

In other professions, too, practitioners experience some stress and strain, and some competent people ultimately find they cannot make it. These negative results are not good in themselves, but they are necessary means to intellectually aggressive practice and high overall system performance.

Today in public education, professionals are insulated from strong performance contingencies. Teachers are tenured, often so early in their careers that their full performance potential has not been developed or demonstrated. Pay is contingent on seniority and completion of coursework that might or might not enhance classroom performance. Choice of workplaces and other privileges also are based on seniority, and tenured teachers regardless of their pay level can be terminated only for egregious performance or outrageous behavior. On the other hand, ambitious young people cannot advance ahead of the seniority scale no matter how hard or brilliantly they work or how scarce their skills. Consequently, concepts of best practice have no operational meaning in education, are hard to pin down, and, even when discussed, receive little more than lip service.

Above all, even the least productive public schools can count on student enrollment. Free movement of children in search of programs that work for them could create strong performance pressures for schools. Choice also could allow educators with strong ideas about how to meet the needs of a given group of students—particularly at the secondary level, where student motivations and needs become diverse—to compete for students and the funding they bring.

School districts traditionally operate a fixed set of schools, a set that changes only when student populations grow or decline dramatically. Even in localities with extremely low-performing schools, districts invest new money and reshuffle staffs to strengthen existing schools rather than close weak schools and start new ones.

No Child Left Behind is pressing districts to think differently about the status of schools, making any school's existence and right to admit students contingent on performance. However, with few exceptions (for example, Chicago), districts are more inclined to fight No Child Left Behind provisions than to change their relationships with schools. As University of California, Berkeley, education professor Bruce Fuller noted, opponents who want to reject No Child Left Behind out of hand can characterize it, with some justification, as a punitive policy based on exhaustive testing of students. However, leaders who want to use NCLB as an asset for local school improvement also can characterize it as the first program that requires the creation of new options for children in unproductive schools.[34]

A public education system designed for constant improvement would make all commitments to individuals and organizations contingent on performance. At a minimum, it would leave room in employment relationships to reward spectacular performers and to develop alternatives to its lowest-performing schools. A school district bent on the highest possible performance would not guarantee anyone a permanent job nor hold students in a bad school. It would terminate any arrangement for which there was a higher-performing option clearly available. On the other hand, it would be constantly open to new options, whether initiated by teachers, principals, or independent groups.[35]

These requirements differ sharply from current practice and would imply profound changes in school district missions and capacities. Instead of making permanent commitments to people and institutions, a district would make contingent commitments, limited in time and renewable only after review. Instead of limiting their own options, such districts would constantly expand them, looking for a better instructional model for a given group of students, a better school leader or contract provider, and a better source of teachers.

As in other fields, this focus on performance would not come at the expense of incumbent teachers and school leaders. Many would stand out and would be able to claim better professional opportunities and more pay. Most could adapt to higher expectations, although, as in the case of physicians learning new procedures, it might require an investment of personal time and even money.

Without such an evidence-based orientation, no one in public education, from the school board member to the teachers in the classroom, can say with confidence that he has done the best possible job for the children in his charge.

Opening Education to New Ideas and People

If it were clear how to provide effective schools for all disadvantaged children, a public education system would have the simple challenge of administering proven models. However, in the face of profound uncertainty, public education needs to be open to many possibilities. Although the teachers and administrators employed by a big-city public school represent a significant share of the community's relevant expertise, they do not have all of it. Private schools, museums, youth service centers, arts and music organizations, churches, colleges and universities, and companies that invest heavily in training all have significant expertise and ideas. Surely all these will not be different from or better than those available within the traditional school system. But as public education strives to identify and implement new ideas for solving pressing problems, it cannot afford to ignore alternative sources of ideas.

The same is true for teachers and school leaders. In most big cities there are as many trained principals and teachers not working in the public school system as working in it. There are, moreover, people who have rare skills in the career teaching force, with expertise in physics, laboratory science, higher mathematics, music, dance, and visual arts. Individuals experienced in managing day care centers, private schools, museum educational programs, and other training programs know a good deal about managing instruction and creating a positive environment for students.

Professors and management consultants know things about turning around troubled organizations and surviving in a performance-pressured climate that public school employees have had little occasion to learn. A former head of Brooks Brothers, hired amid budget chaos in St. Louis, Missouri, took only eighteen months to reduce the overall work force from seven thousand to five thousand before leaving with the comment that schools are about students and learning, not adults and employment.[36]

Any combination of these skills might produce a school that is excellent for one purpose or another or create capacities to provide great instruction in particular areas. Public education needs to be open to such people, organizations, and ideas. It can apply the same expectations about performance and respect for public values to such outsiders as to school district careerists, but it would be self-defeating to impose arbitrary limits on what they attempt.

Although it is true that not just anyone can teach or lead a school well, it is also true that current entry requirements for those positions are not guarantees of competence. These requirements often develop capable people, but they also certify people who cannot perform the job while screening out many who could. Current state teacher and principal licensing requirements protect incumbents and establish education schools as gatekeepers, but they do not contribute much to improve school performance.[37]

A performance-driven public education system would need the freedom to provide schools by any means necessary and to create circumstances conducive to all schools' success. Even the best charter school laws fall short of this requirement, in part because of caps and in part because charter schools usually receive considerably less money per pupil and fewer in-kind donations from government, such as free facilities or state-supported teacher pensions, than do traditional public schools. In effect, charter school operators are told to take it or leave it. A public education system cannot create good options if it is forced to deal only with providers that are compelled to accept a bad deal.[38]

Some districts committed to aggressive experimentation and problem solving have found their state's charter school laws useful but not sufficient. They are supporting new start-ups via their inherent powers to contract instructional services.[39] Although districts have limited their use of the contracting power in the past—buying a tutoring program here and an enrichment program there—the broader power to contract for whole schools is there for the using.

CONCLUSION

Americans are now a very long way from being able to answer the questions policy makers repeatedly ask. They cannot say how much public education should cost, because public school systems have been constructed to privilege certain methods and rule out other, possibly more effective, ones. No amount of smart analysis of current data can overcome the narrowness of this experience with alternative instructional methods, and no amount of clever accounting can compensate for the fact that the real uses of funds and the costs of particular services have been carefully hidden.

Bad methods provide bad answers. Shortcuts to answers—studies that use rules of thumb to inflate current spending levels or that estimate spending needs by calculating the added cost of marginally more effective programs—can only mislead and disillusion policy makers and ultimately waste money.

Even with the best evidence, policy makers might get unwelcome answers. It might cost a lot more than policy makers are prepared to spend to bring all children's learning up to high standards. It might also require dramatic changes in how money is used—and therefore who gets paid from public funds—than policy makers are politically free to make.

But education policy is about meeting the needs of the young and not about comforting the old. Policy makers need valid answers, no matter how hard they are to get. Policy makers—and the public that pays taxes and ultimately decides how public funds are spent—need valid answers much more than they need quick or simple ones. Analysts who want to speak truth to power, and to their friends and neighbors, must be candid about which questions cannot be answered now and about how the nation can know more tomorrow than today.

8

Considering Outside-the-Box Changes in Education Funding

David H. Monk

This chapter explores several departures from conventional thinking about how states handle their responsibility for educating the nation's youth. It focuses primarily on the finance of K–12 educational systems. It also acknowledges that the boundaries of these systems are in flux, with increasing attention being given to the infusion of multiple service delivery systems into schools (for example, health and social services) and with efforts to expand services to preschool and to older learners in P–16 systems. Nevertheless, it is the extant K–12 educational system that has immense scale along with a fiscal and administrative history that can inhibit new thinking about how the structure is organized and financed. It is a worthy focus for this exercise.

Although it is easy to observe discontent with the current methods of financing and organizing schools, Americans also have become accustomed to the existing system, faults and all. Sizable bureaucracies have developed at local, state, and national levels to administer the system. These administrative structures have grown incrementally and have become adept at protecting themselves. The fact that the stakes are high—cultivating the minds of the next generation—adds to the gravitas associated with existing structures and their resistance to change.

It is easy to dismiss new ways of thinking because they introduce elements of the unknown and carry their own administrative burdens. It can be easy to turn away from new ideas on these grounds, even new ideas that may have considerable merit. So this chapter begins with a request for readers to remain open to new approaches even though there remain unanswered questions. Skepticism is important, but one needs to guard against getting too caught up too quickly in all the reasons something new will not work.

The following pages introduce five ideas that, if taken seriously, would have significant implications for how governments organize and finance U.S. schools. For each, I provide a sketch, anticipate some issues, and assess implications for school finance. I close with an effort to imagine what a system would look like if all five ideas were adopted simultaneously.

DIFFERENTIAL ADD-ONS AND VARIABLE PRICING

The central idea is to move away from the conventional all-or-nothing conception of the public school and introduce elements of differential user charges to the funding of public education. This idea is based on a school of thought within public finance that can be linked to the work of Knut Wicksell, who wrote at the turn of the twentieth century.[1] Wicksell took issue with the common practice in public finance of divorcing decisions about expenditures from decisions about revenues.

Governments are accustomed to this sharp division, almost to the point that it is hard to imagine otherwise. Indeed, in education finance it is common to first figure out the expenditure side of the budget and then impose the necessary broad-based taxes to raise the needed sums. Wicksell's insight was that significant gains can be made in satisfaction with the public sector if the imposition of tax (that is, the burden) is brought more directly into line with the receipt of benefits.

States do this to a degree through decentralized units of local government. Through their decisions about where to live, citizens thus have some choice about the level and mix of services they receive and the attendant costs.[2] But Wicksell would push the practice further and open the door on differing levels and mixes of services within public governing units along with corresponding taxes or fees.

There are existing and emerging mechanisms that promote this kind of agenda. For example, vouchers are designed to achieve better matches between parent and student preferences for education and, in at least some versions, allow for financial add-ons from participants to cover the costs of the extra services they seek. Thus, voucher programs can be thought of as a mix of a common base level of support with differential add-ons that correspond to elected services. But vouchers tip heavily toward involving the private sector and thereby miss the public dimension that is an important part of Wicksell's idea.

There are efforts within conventional public schools to promote choice, and there is an extensive history of entities, such as magnet schools, that are organized around themes. Although a case can be made in favor of the broadened range of choice afforded by magnet schools and other forms of public schools of choice, these efforts miss the central point of Wicksell's argument. Why? It's because there is no corresponding adjustment on the revenue or tax side. Students typically enroll in magnet schools with no adjustment for whatever differences there might be in the cost of their program relative to others. In fact, prevailing practices with respect to public schools of choice fit with the Wicksell idea only to the degree that all the options have the same cost, an unlikely result. Wicksell would worry about a possibly widening gap between the costs imposed and the benefits received as a consequence of school choice plans.

Charter schools constitute an interesting, more mixed approach. If they are structured so that participants can supplement the base allocation to cover the costs of their preferences, a key part of Wicksell's idea would be in place. However, if they are set up as separate entities so that public oversight is minimal, they would be functioning more like publicly subsidized private entities and thus would miss an important dimension of what Wicksell had in mind: publicly operated endeavors with variable levels of add-on services and corresponding pricing. In the following, the term *hybrid services* refers to these differentially priced add-on services that remain directly under the control of the public authority.

Operations

For Wicksell's idea to be viable, three preconditions must be met. First, there needs to be a defensible way to link differences in program benefits to differences in cost; second, governance authorities need to differentiate between services that constitute a base program that needs to be available to all and extensions on which it is appropriate to impose restrictions on access; and third, there needs to be a collective resolve to administer the program and enforce the rules.

Links Between Programs and Costs

Consider the case of an instrumental music program in an elementary school. Current practice provides the program, if at all, uniformly and typically at a low level. The costs are imposed on all taxpayers, and the program is vulnerable to budget-cutting pressures because of its uncertain place in the school's mission. Supporters of the program are in the awkward position of trying to persuade others, including taxpayers having no children in the school, to support an endeavor whose benefits are arguably far removed.

An alternative approach would entail conducting a cost analysis of the program and making participation conditional on a willingness to bear a portion of the estimated cost as a surcharge on the tax bill. Those parents seeing the value of the program could elect to participate. That program operating in public space would set an example, perhaps inspiring others to participate. Parents would elect to have their children participate or not based on their judgment about the match between cost and benefits. The school district would be responsible for conducting the cost analysis and establishing the surcharge; parents would make judgments about whether the anticipated and perceived benefits are worth the additional cost.

Defining the Base Program

Local authorities, presumably elected school boards, would need to draw lines among (a) what counts as the base educational program that will be available to all, (b) add-on programs delivered by the school board for an extra fee (which could be subsidized), and (c) other programs considered beyond the purview of the public school. School boards are accustomed to drawing only one line: between what is within and outside the purview of the school. Here a school board would be expected to draw two lines. Continuing with the instrumental music program, a school board needs to assign it to one of the three categories: (a) part of the base and available to all, (b) part of the school offering but available on a fee-for-service basis, or (c) not part of the school and available only, if at all, through the private sector.

The definition of the base program will go beyond a simple listing of discrete programs that are in and out of the three categories. In particular, important decisions need to be made about the quality of programs, and these decisions also will be made by public authorities at both local and state levels. A local school board, for example, might decide to offer a high-quality academic program to all students in the school. Alternatively, a school board might decide to define a lower level as the base and to offer an enrichment program as something parents and students could enroll in on a fee-for-service basis. In keeping with existing governance structures, these local decisions would not be made in a vacuum because the state would continue to provide oversight.

Enforcement

The addition of public school services that are available only on a fee-for-service basis adds a new enforcement challenge, because students will be denied access unless an additional payment has been made. A new boundary exists that will need to be respected in order for the system to work.

Consider the case of a group of parents who value the benefits of sending their children to a small elementary school that the school board feels is too costly to include in the base program. With the new system in place, parents could agree to cover the extra costs themselves, thereby improving their satisfaction with the school district without making anyone else overtly worse off.[3] However, given the place-bound nature of schools, one can imagine age-eligible children living in the neighborhood who will not be welcome in the school because of their parents' unwillingness or inability to pay the extra fee. Thus, there is the unpleasant prospect of students being denied entry to their neighborhood school for economic reasons. However, for the system to work, these students and their parents will need to accept going to the more distant school. Notice that in the absence of the new system, the small school would not be available in any case, because the school board decided it could not justify imposing the extra costs on all taxpayers in the district.

Implications for Equity, Efficiency, and Choice

The most obvious gains of the new system accrue in the freedom of choice category. Under reasonable assumptions, the new system broadens choice and achieves a better match between preferences and options.

On the efficiency side, there also may be gains, in terms of both exchange and production efficiency. The exchange gains derive from the better match between voter preferences and the mix and level of services being delivered. The production efficiency gains are less obvious but may accrue, thanks to the elements of market discipline that the new system introduces into the public sector.

For example, in the case of the small-school offering, the only reason parents would be willing to pay the extra tariff is that the school delivers whatever advantages those parents believe are attached to the school's small scale. If the school fails to deliver, the parents are free to vote with their feet, and the school will be forced to shape up or close for want of students.

The discipline of the market becomes a feature for any of the hybrid services that are offered. If parents can obtain a more cost-effective option elsewhere (for example, in the private sector), they will have the option of withdrawing their participation. The exit option introduces a desirable pressure on school personnel to deliver effective hybrid services and to get the pricing right. There is an appealing self-regulating dimension to the new system.

The most obvious area for worry is in the matter of equity or fairness. This concern arose earlier in reference to the fact that the parents of a student living near the small school might not be able to pay the extra cost of attending the small neighborhood school. How can it be desirable to tantalize students with publicly provided hybrid services that they are barred from receiving because of cost? Of course, this happens all the time, given the decentralized and highly unequal way in which governments currently fund public schools, but in the example here the denials are a bit more in your face because it all happens in one's home neighborhood and school district.

To address the difficulty, one can draw upon well-established principles in public finance that also can be found in education finance. For example, guaranteed tax base programs tie spending levels to tax burdens but adjust the magnitude of the burdens so that they are more equal. Similar adjustments could be built into the pricing mechanism so that families with less ability to pay for services would face more modest, but presumably not zero, costs. In principle, equity could be preserved through the use of differential pricing for the elective services.

Critique

Wicksell's ideas have been a part of the public finance literature for many years and are generally viewed as interesting but largely impractical given the complexities and realities of the modern public sector. Following are specific concerns raised in the critique.

Limitations of the Benefit Standard, Free Riders, and
"Jointness" in Production Problems

Much of the difficulty stems from the limited applicability of the benefit standard as the basis for apportioning tax burdens. The idea that tax burdens should be linked to benefits is fine as far as it goes. The difficulty is that it does not go very far in terms of the kinds of services provided by the public sector. Indeed, an important reason for the public sector is the existence of important services for which the benefit standard is ill suited. The private sector is most comfortable with the benefit standard, but it is folly to act as if the benefit standard is available to handle matters in the public sector when the public sector exists, in part, to deliver the kinds of services that do not lend themselves to the neat accounting presupposed by the benefit standard.

There are free rider problems to consider as well, but within educational contexts these seem less serious because well-established exclusionary devices are available. For example, tuition is commonly used as an exclusionary device for schools.

Inefficiencies also can enter because of the joint nature of production. In education, the fact that one student benefits from a teacher does not in itself impede another student from benefiting simultaneously from the same teacher. Under this assertion, the presence of empty seats in classrooms can be viewed as an inefficiency, because more students could benefit at no additional cost. However, one sees this kind of inefficiency routinely (witness the empty seats in theaters presenting popular productions).

Cost Estimation Problems

Significant challenges surround serious efforts to estimate the costs of add-on programs, in part because it can be difficult to disentangle the add-on portion from the base portion. Moreover, there is a dynamic dimension that adds complexity. Returning to the small-school example, the costs of operating the small school vary depending on its size, and efforts to be responsive to parent enrollment desires could generate fluctuating enrollments, thereby making it difficult to estimate costs. Moreover, what happens if the school is very popular and attracts more and more students so that it no longer offers the advantages of being small? Parents seeking the benefits of a small school then will have an incentive to withdraw their children and perhaps make efforts to start a new small school, again adding to the complexity of the cost analysis.

Although there is no denying how complex the cost analysis could become, it is important to keep in mind that precision is not necessary. Generating first approximations of the costs will be much easier and may be sufficient, particularly if periodic adjustments can be made over time as local authorities gain experience. Education finance is no stranger to reliance on first approximations, and one of the best examples is the use of transaction samples as the basis of equalization rates in the administration of the real property tax.

Problems in Defining the Base Program

It is easy to assert that the state will retain oversight regarding local authorities' decisions about how to define the base program, but in practice how would it work? Moreover, on what basis would the state intervene and second-guess a decision by one local authority to impose fees for, say, instrumental music lessons while another builds an instrumental program into the base offering? If the state is going to opine on how the lines should be drawn between the three categories implicit in the new system, why go through the charade of having local authorities make the initial decisions? The new system, despite its pro-local-choice garb, actually may sow the seeds for a far greater state role in calling the shots with respect to the public's responsibility for educating the next generation—a remarkably ironic turn of events.

In response, why not think of the state's job as defining a minimum base program, thereby opening the door for local authorities to build in enhancements that would enjoy partial public support? A key question for the state is whether it is willing to help fund the hybrid offerings as determined by the local authority. In this regard, one might think of the state as having a responsibility for lowering the surcharges to individuals who have lesser ability to pay.

Logistical Problems

If the surcharges take the form of increases in real property tax rates (to take advantage of the existing link between this tax and taxpayers' ability to pay as measured by their holdings of real property), numerous thorny logistical problems surface. For example, how would such a surcharge be imposed on renters or on taxpayers living in subsidized public housing?

It is better to think of the surcharge as something separate from the property tax rate. Each taxpayer would be categorized in terms of the number, and perhaps the level, of supplemental services chosen. Each service level would have an attached per-pupil cost, and the taxpayer would receive an invoice for the hybrid services. The charge could be adjusted according to an independently determined ability to pay, perhaps along the lines of how free and reduced-price lunch costs are determined. Again, these amounts need not be precisely determined. Reasonably accurate first approximations should be sufficient to launch and sustain the hybrid programs.

An Additional Observation

The reform envisioned here has the potential to be far-reaching, with effects that are difficult to predict. On one hand, by infusing differential add-ons and variable pricing into public schools, one could significantly strengthen public education by achieving an unprecedented match between the citizenry's will to provide resources and the extent and nature of schooling services available to all. Senior citizens, for example, might rally to the cause of public schools because it would be possible to tie their taxes directly to the kinds of essential educational services they have an interest in supporting, in contrast to add-ons whose benefits are more narrowly circumscribed. School boards might rise to the occasion and make good and principled decisions about what to offer within the base program and which hybrid services to offer.

On the other hand, the market forces unleashed by such a reform could undermine the very idea of the public school by making it possible for the affluent to drive down the base program to dysfunctional levels. Moreover, states could bobble the ball in their responsibility for tying surcharges to ability to pay, thereby further eroding equity in the system.

This combination of the uncertain and far-reaching nature of the results can undermine the case for implementing such a reform, particularly if the reform has an all-or-nothing, no-going-back character. If the existing system were functioning well, it would be even harder to justify moving into uncertain waters. But the status quo has serious deficiencies, and, as the final section suggests, it is both possible and desirable to take modest steps in the direction of implementing differential add-ons and variable pricing that include careful assessments of impact.

TECHNOLOGY AND INPUT SUBSTITUTION

Technology initiatives are widespread within education and are being fueled simultaneously by remarkable technological advances (in telecommunications and computing), nontrivial profit-making opportunities for vendors, and the promise of significant short- and long-term performance gains for students. Legislators and governors are eager to embrace success stories that combine the glamour of technology, quick results, and photo opportunities that play well in the media.

Modern initiatives, many of which involve putting laptop computers into the hands of students and teachers, seem at least nominally to reflect the importance of professional development and careful thinking about the proper role of technology in instruction, but still it is easier to buy equipment, deliver it to schools, and hope for the best than to work through the design of the deep kinds of reforms made possible by technology. The history of technological innovations in the schools is replete with story after story of new equipment that fits poorly and ends up being stored in closets or underused in other, less dramatic ways. One can hope that current initiatives will not repeat the mistakes of the past.

An entire subfield known variously as instructional design or instructional systems has grown up within education, a subfield in which research is being conducted on the properties of the interface between human learning and technology. These scholars are asking questions such as, If students have access to laptop technology with certain specifications and capabilities, what are the consequences in learning gains? Although important, this question misses an important idea that is vital to the way public agencies finance schools.

Implicit in the posed question is the idea that technology is an addition to an existing and otherwise unchanged instructional setting. The idea being missed is that it is common for inputs to productive endeavors to substitute for one another; as a result, decision makers do not need to think about technology only in terms of an add-on to existing practice. Indeed, arguably the power of technology to transform education will come only to the degree that technologies begin to substitute for resources, some of them quite costly, that already are in place in schools.

The idea that technology can substitute for important and costly resources such as teachers without adversely affecting outcomes raises any number of sensitive and politically volatile concerns. For example, there are long-standing worries about technologies taking jobs away from teachers, along with horrific images of young minds being shaped by soulless machines.

Reluctance to entertain input substitution possibilities is deeply seated in the field and may even be shaping the nature of the technologies that are being developed. Vendors may reason that they will enjoy greater success selling their innovations if those innovations are conceived solely as add-ons to the store of supplemental resources teachers draw on as they work with students.

It may be that decision makers are hobbling the development of technology because of this reluctance to think about input substitution possibilities. Why make instructional innovations the slave of prevailing practice to the point where educators are interested in innovation only to the degree that it "fits" with prevailing practice?

It is remarkable how hard "innovators" work at using technology, particularly telecommunications technology, to emulate traditional classroom instruction. For example, in efforts to meet the needs of schools in rural or isolated areas, educators use electronics to make it seem as much as possible as if the students and teacher are in the same classroom, what might in fact be a very conventional classroom. Success is measured by how quick and clear the images are and how easy it is for students at the remote location to do things such as write on a simulated blackboard. It is as if the conventional classroom constitutes the gold standard for education and is worthy of electronic emulation, although in other contexts that same conventional classroom is the target of much criticism. Why not see telecommunications and computing technology as a way to break loose from the conventional classroom structure, as is the case in some of the more innovative distance education applications?

The worries about job security for teachers may be overblown. First, no one knows much about the extent to which embodied human resources, in the form of software and communication technologies, can substitute for proximate human resources, such as the teacher in the classroom. This is largely an empirical question that can be answered after the research is conducted, and it may turn out that the substitution possibilities are limited. There is the old saying, "Any teacher who can be replaced by a technology should be," and it may be that some teachers are not easily substituted for, although this likely will vary with the levels of teachers' skills. Indeed, truly excellent teachers may not be substitutable, and substitution possibilities may be greater for more typical teachers.

Second, substitutability is a matter of degree and is not an all-or-nothing proposition. It is possible to demonize technology as being soulless, but this misses an important point. Technology, in fact, has an important human face to it and is better thought of as an embodied human resource than as something inhuman. It is useful to draw a distinction between proximate human resources such as classroom teachers and embodied human resources such as the subject matter expertise that is available online. Modern technological developments are part of long-standing efforts to embody human resources. Early technologies like the printing press made it possible for proximate human resources to make use of more distant, embodied human resources (that is, the authors of texts) and arguably enhanced rather than diminished the human elements of teaching and learning.

Third, if it turns out that there are considerable substitution possibilities between proximate teachers and technology, one could be looking at dramatic changes in the nature of teachers' work and reductions in the number of teachers needed relative to the number of students being educated. But those teachers who are engaged will work with larger numbers of students, though with responsibility for diagnosing and matching learners' needs by applying a wide and growing range of powerful interventions. Teaching could emerge with the professional respect that has been so elusive for so long.

Implications for Equity, Efficiency, and Choice

The hoped-for gains accrue largely in the efficiency—or, more precisely, the productivity—category. Benefits might take the form of enhanced learning outcomes for the same investment of resources, or as a reduction in the cost of achieving the existing mix and level of outcomes. Some combination of the two results is probably the most likely, and so there would be gains both in terms of students learning more and taxpayers realizing some savings, an attractive outcome to be sure and perhaps too good to be true.

Moreover, there are longer-term gains to consider. The Internet has ushered in an era of explosive growth in information, accurate as well as inaccurate, that is available at the touch of a button. Learners of all ages need skills to navigate and make sense of these data points, and success by schools in developing the ability to become less dependent on proximate teachers and more self-reliant in this environment will pay handsome dividends over time.

Equity concerns have surrounded technology from day one, but these are not much changed by a shift to substitutable rather than add-on technology. There are long-standing concerns about the so-called digital divide that separates young learners who are comfortable with technology from those who have missed opportunities to have contact with technology. These inequities stem from differences in the fiscal abilities and perhaps inclinations of schools to offer state-of-the-art curricula. If the hoped-for benefits of treating technology as a substitutable input are real, then the equity concerns could be exacerbated because the impact of technology will be enhanced, making a denial of opportunity more serious.

The new approach to technology also could enhance choice opportunities, because technology plays a key role in providing access to information and points of view. However, there is no guarantee here, and one needs to continue to be on guard for inappropriate restrictions on the ability of teachers and students to make inquiry. Moreover, if it is true that technology development to date has been hobbled by the prior expectation that it can serve only as an add-on, then a shift in the new direction should stimulate a richer research and development enterprise, with a resulting gain in the future power of instructional technologies.

Next Steps

Given the abundant ignorance about the input substitution possibilities surrounding resources such as teachers and instructional technology, research needs to be conducted that will give us a better sense of the actual possibilities. With this knowledge in hand, steps could be taken to encourage the kinds of substitutions that look promising. Reforms along these lines should be popular because they promise benefits for student learning and taxpayer savings.

Job security concerns for existing teachers, along with professional development needs, also need to be addressed. Presumably, some kind of protection for teachers already in place combined with opportunities to develop new skills would significantly reduce anxiety. It is important to stay focused on the longer-term gains and not to be stymied by short-term and transitory costs.

An Additional Observation

The properties of teaching and learning are themselves the result of how families rear children and how schools structure learning experiences. In other words, learners learn how to learn, and it may be that steps could be taken to make it easier for students to learn how to use instructional technologies rather than proximate human resources like teachers. Thus, even if governments or philanthropies support the research envisioned earlier and find that substitution possibilities for teachers are modest, this need not be viewed as an immutable result. One might take the view that it is hardly surprising to find that proximate teachers are essential, because schools have taught students to be dependent on them. A conscious effort to make the next generation of learners less dependent on proximate teaching resources could yield different results, and one needs to keep in mind that families and schools have considerable control over how they shape the ability of students to learn. Here is another instance where care should be taken not to be blinded by the properties of the status quo.

SUPPLEMENTAL RESOURCES AS RESPONSES TO UNCERTAINTY

There are useful lessons to learn from comparisons between education and meteorology as fields of study and endeavor. Both fields deal with complex phenomena and uncertainty is widespread. And yet the fields respond to complexity and uncertainty in quite different and instructive ways.

Forecasting weather remains a significant challenge despite remarkable scientific advances, largely because of the massive scale of the system and remaining ignorance about the determinants of weather. A similar situation affects those who are trying to understand schooling and human learning. One can point to scientific progress, but there remains extensive ignorance, with the consequence that considerable uncertainty surrounds efforts to anticipate, much less forecast, results.

In schooling, arguably the challenge is even greater because at issue is more than forecasts, and the parties are increasingly being held accountable for outcomes. The public does not typically hold the parties engaged in meteorology responsible for the weather, although it increasingly expects accurate forecasts. Indeed, there are growing economic consequences attached to forecasting errors, and commercial forecasters can lose business if their track record is weaker than their competitors'. Of course, everyone takes some pleasure in complaining about the perceived inaccuracy of weather forecasts, even as the actual quality has increased. Nevertheless, errors continue; it is clear that uncertainty continues to be a significant factor within meteorology as a field.

To continue with the comparison: think of classrooms as complex weather systems. Researchers and educators know some things about the properties of teaching and learning, but what they know is dwarfed by what they still do not understand. Furthermore, think of a troublesome student or group of students in a classroom as being like the arrival of a hurricane. And suppose further that forecasters are about as good at predicting the arrival and impact of these student-related disturbances in learning environments as they are at predicting the arrival and impact of actual hurricanes.

States do not respond to the threat of hurricanes by fortifying every city and locality equally. Rather, decision makers assess probabilities and store up resources, and then they deploy them differentially once they have better knowledge of where the actual hurricanes are heading and will make landfall. This practice does not always work well—the Katrina debacle providing a disturbing example of how the approach can fail—but still the approach makes conceptual sense in light of the uncertainties, and it is rather different from the way school leaders approach the unanticipated difficulties they ask teachers to handle as decisions are made about which students to assign to which classrooms.

The more typical approach within education is to ask teachers (and the other students in the class) to bear up as best they can under the assault of the disruptive students. School systems almost seem to take the position that these hurricanes are part of the cost of doing business and that everyone must put up with his fair share of the destruction. Moreover, school systems also seem to compound the problem by doing things such as knowingly assembling classes that are likely to be problematic and assigning these classes to novice teachers, perhaps on the grounds that getting through hurricanes like these is part of making one's bones as a teacher.

This behavior is costly given the predictable negative effects on novice teachers' willingness to persist—some of them presumably would have developed into talented teachers—not to mention the lost learning opportunities for students. Would it not make more sense to create a supplemental resource board, or a similar entity, that could deliver needed reinforcing resources to meet the extraordinary needs that emerge and could not be anticipated until after the school year was under way and there was an opportunity to assess the actual demands that arise from groupings of students in various classrooms—that is, as the "hurricanes" made landfall?

This supplemental resource board might exist at the local or, perhaps more logically, at regional or state levels. Site visits could be conducted as the year gets under way, and supplemental resources could be deployed on a temporary or long-term basis, depending on circumstances. The key would be to make quick assessments of need and to respond accordingly. It would be important for the interventions to be widespread enough so that being on the receiving end is not viewed as a stigma.

Progress would be monitored and adjustments in supply could be made periodically over the course of the year. Governance questions would need to be sorted out because multiple authorities might be involved, and it should be clear that the allocations are temporary and pinpointed, lasting no more than a full academic year. At the end of each year, the allocations would be gathered up and a reallocation would take place early in the next year.

Implications for Equity, Efficiency, and Choice

An intervention designed along these lines would have benefits in both equity and efficiency. Equity would be advanced to the degree that students are protected from capricious exposure to the adverse effects of dysfunctional groupings of students that create hurricanes in their instructional space. Current practice passes an equity test, in a strange sort of way, to the degree that students are equally exposed to these disruptions. Thus, only in the unlikely case that the disruptions are evenly distributed are students "fairly" disadvantaged. More realistically, the burdens are unequally distributed, and one suspects students coming from lower-income families and attending schools with less fiscal capacity are more likely to encounter these disruptions. Interventions that are designed to contain and offset the effects of these discrete instances of dysfunction could have salutary equity effects.

Efficiency benefits also can be discerned because students will be making better use of their time. Expenditures and the supply of resources may increase, but there should be corresponding gains in pupil performance. Moreover, teachers may feel better supported, and effective teachers will be more likely to remain in the teaching force, thereby relieving the system of costs associated with teacher turnover.

There does not seem to be much impact on freedom of choice except to reduce incentives to exit dysfunctional instructional settings, assuming the interventions being contemplated turn out to be effective in containing the damage.

An Additional Observation

The scope of this argument is relatively narrow, because it presumes that the broader system is basically functional and that the difficulties occur when unfortunate student combinations create problems that are hard to anticipate. As such, the argument sidesteps the perhaps more serious problem wherein the system is so overwhelmed that the weather, so to speak, is consistently horrible and only getting worse and the difficulty cannot be reduced to a definable single storm or series of storms—hurricanes or otherwise.

Moreover, the argument may overstate the case because there are occasions when schools provide differential staffing in response to unexpected difficulties in particular classrooms. However, the practice does not appear to be common, and given conventional thinking there may be a tendency to see the need for additional resources as a negative reflection on the teacher, along with an expectation for the teacher to "pay back" the extra help in some way in the future.

Even in the face of these caveats, the argument calls attention to the role of an important feature of educational systems—namely, the uncertain nature of the underlying teaching and learning technology—and it identifies a fresh way of thinking. Rather than being held hostage to unrealistic and even foolhardy efforts to nail down everything in teaching and learning with scientific precision, the new thinking involves accepting the reality of uncertainty and working to become as nimble as possible in responding appropriately to the hot spots that inevitably will develop. The new approach gets rid of the pernicious idea that hard classes and disruptive students are simply something teachers and students must endure.

DIFFERENTIATED STAFFING AND THE DYSFUNCTIONAL PURSUIT OF EXCELLENCE

It is customary in education to assign a high priority to the pursuit of excellence. The term itself is widespread, and one of the difficulties is that it is used so frequently that it can become hackneyed and even a caricature of itself. But rhetorical excess is really the least of the problems. More disturbing is a failure to recognize how problematic the unbridled pursuit of excellence actually can be. The downside of the unbridled pursuit of excellence can be seen by realizing that excellence comes at some cost and that these costs are likely to escalate as increasingly higher levels of excellence are reached.

The costs of excellence tend to be shrouded for several reasons. In the case of prominent athletes and performers, the time and effort required to reach stratospheric heights of accomplishment either are not talked about or are described in gauzy and highly romantic terms. Moreover, one of the features of persons who perform at extraordinarily high levels is a tendency to make the accomplishment look effortless. This characteristic also applies to the great teachers of the world, who routinely mislead aspiring teachers into thinking that excellent teaching is actually not very hard.

The tendency to make extraordinary accomplishment look easy helps to fuel the view that excellence is not so much a matter of hard work as a matter of being gifted and floating above the others. Even if excellence is more a matter of being chosen than the result of hard work in combination with talent, there remains a cost dimension. The truly chosen are in very short supply and will be able to command a price in the market.

The idea that everyone can be excellent is mischievous and misleading. The whole point of being excellent is that the individual's performance towers over the performance of others.

Moreover, something like excellence in teaching is much less well defined than the frequent use of the term would suggest. Teaching is complex, and any serious effort to compare the performance of one teacher to that of another involves assessments along any number of dimensions. Imagine a teacher whose performance along one dimension truly is off the chart but whose performance along other dimensions is more in the middle range. How should one compare this teacher with a colleague who lacks the off-the-chart performance along one dimension but whose scores taken collectively are superior to those of the first teacher?

And how does one account for the fact that teaching effectiveness is highly dependent on interactions with students, with the likely consequence that some teachers will be more effective with some students than with others? Should truly excellent teachers be only those who are consistently off the chart on all identifiable dimensions and consistently effective with every possible student and group of students they encounter? This would indeed be a small, elite group, perhaps even a null set.

It is clear that excellence is a murkier concept than commonly supposed and that its pursuit is not without costs. With this insight as a starting point, there are several pitfalls one should be sensitive to as part of any effort to place serious emphasis on promoting excellence in teaching.

Supply and Demand Issues

Excellence by its nature is in short supply, and excellent teachers are likely to have numerous options in other fields that offer more-attractive compensation. As long as school systems remain wedded to teacher compensation practices that fail to differentiate pay on the basis of performance, it will be difficult if not impossible to attract and retain significant numbers of truly excellent teachers.

Moreover, even if school systems could make changes in compensation to offer competitive wages for the excellent teachers, does it follow that this is the best use of their considerable talents, particularly if officials persist in assigning teachers to discrete classes where they work with relatively small numbers of students? Can one assume that the gains for this finite number of students are sufficient to justify this as the best use of the excellent teachers' talents? Would it not be better to find ways to share the benefits of excellence more broadly? Thus, one of the structural problems in schools in their current form is the circumscribed nature of the excellent teachers' zones of impact.

And if compensation systems change to attract and retain excellent teachers, there will be upward pressure on costs. Trade-offs will ensue, either within the education sector or elsewhere within the society. Would school systems be comfortable in increasing average class size, for example, as a way to finance the premiums that would have to be paid to attract and retain the excellent teachers?

Returning to the input substitution argument, recall the point that any teacher who can be replaced by technology should be. It may be that there are extraordinary teachers who cannot be replaced by any known technology. But suppose substitution possibilities do surround less extraordinary teachers. If so, why not take advantage of the substitution possibilities where they exist, particularly if some savings can be realized? Why not view these substitution possibilities as a means of enhancing the effectiveness of the vast majority of teachers who are engaged in the endeavor? Why let the capabilities of highly atypical individuals—the excellent teachers—inhibit the effective use of what technology has to offer the field of education?

Production Issues

There are many unanswered questions surrounding the preparation of teachers. Teacher educators labor mightily in their efforts to prepare the next generation of teachers, with limited guidance from the research literature. The problem becomes even more difficult if one draws a distinction between what it takes to prepare a good teacher in contrast to an excellent teacher. What can the truly excellent teacher do that a merely good teacher cannot do? Is excellence the same at the primary grade levels as at the secondary and post-secondary levels? Is it the same across content areas?

Suffice it to say that these questions are disputed terrain within the field of education and that the resulting uncertainties make it problematic to pursue aggressively a teacher excellence agenda.

Teacher Mediocrity

What about the other extreme in the teacher quality distribution? Teacher mediocrity warrants attention and faces its own definitional issues. One can distinguish between true disasters in the classroom and those teachers who are more functionally mediocre.

The existing system is actually fairly good at cleansing itself of the true disasters. Considerable filtering goes on in pre-service teacher preparation programs so that the schools are spared these disasters. Moreover, when disasters are hired into the schools, the schools themselves are quick to cut them loose, sometimes with remarkable speed. Often the separations are mutually agreed to because it can be personal, public, and daily torture for the teacher whose performance is a disaster.

The functionally mediocre teachers are more problematic for schools and students. These are the teachers who perform at relatively low levels but who have learned to get by. Their classes are reasonably orderly. Not much may be happening in terms of student learning, but the system runs and the time passes. These are the teachers who may exist in large numbers and who warrant more attention in terms of stimulating professional growth and improved performance.

An Alternative Strategy

The point is not that excellence in teaching is bad and something to be eschewed, but rather that school systems need to be attentive to the outliers in the right (that is, excellent) tail of the teacher quality distribution as well as those who are found elsewhere in the distribution. Systemwide improvement will not come only from taking the elite and moving them further to the right in the distribution of teaching talent, and yet this seems to be the focus, at least of contemporary rhetoric regarding a reverence for excellence in teaching.

It makes more sense to pursue strategies that address the full range of teaching talent. In particular, efforts can and should be made to provide a better definition of teachers' workloads so that teachers, the excellent as well as the not so excellent, are able to specialize in areas where they have expertise.

For those who are excellent, why not take steps to bring them into contact with larger numbers of students than would normally be the case? Why not let the class sizes of the excellent teachers grow larger, to the point that the marginal benefit of being in the excellent teacher's class is equal to the marginal benefit of being in the smaller class of the less excellent teacher? In such a world, the "unfairness" attached to some students' being assigned to the excellent teacher versus other students' being assigned to the less excellent teacher would be substantially reduced. One could imagine parents, for example, being indifferent to having their child assigned to an excellent teacher's class of sixty versus a less excellent teacher's class of fifteen. In such a world, the excellent teacher handling sixty students logically would be entitled to more generous compensation than would the less excellent teacher handling fifteen students.

And for those who are not excellent, why not work with them to define and develop more narrowly drawn areas of expertise than is normally the case? Rather than try to improve performance in multiple areas simultaneously, narrow the focus and set more realistic, attainable, and measurable goals. This narrowing of focus could fit logically with parallel efforts to promote substitution possibilities with technology. There could emerge a much more differentiated set of roles for professionals in instructional settings that complement various kinds and uses of technology. Medicine has made significant progress in achieving greater role differentiation, including the creation of physician assistants and nurse practitioners, who now handle numerous duties that previously were assigned only to physicians. Teaching appears to have reached a stage wherein greater role definition could be advantageous.

Implications for Equity, Efficiency, and Choice

A shift in emphasis away from the unbridled pursuit of excellence to a more balanced focus on all sections of the teacher quality distribution has the potential to generate significant benefits in both equity and efficiency. Of course, much depends on how the improved performance levels of teachers in the middle of the distribution are distributed across the system. Programs such as those operated by the National Science Foundation to improve the skill sets of science teachers tend to attract participants who already appear to be located in the upper parts of the teacher quality distribution. Efforts to engage teachers in the lower sections of the distribution fit logically with this effort to shift away from the unbridled pursuit of excellence, but care would need to be exercised in how such programs are described so that they are not off-putting. There is not much point in advertising a professional development program for weak teachers.

VITALIZED R&D FOR INTERESTING AND HARD PROBLEMS

In medicine, the well-established institutions of teaching hospitals, often located in urban areas, serve patients from highly varied economic circumstances. These teaching hospitals are connected directly to professional preparation programs in medical colleges. Teaching hospitals attract top researchers in the field whose work is considered instructive for neophytes. Medical colleges find ways to tap in to this expertise, seeing it as an important part of the preparation they offer students. Moreover, the medical services they provide are broadly available and reach disadvantaged individuals, because the cases under study are broadly distributed across income categories. The approach is appealing on numerous grounds, the fiscal crisis of many teaching hospitals notwithstanding.

In education, the interface between research and practice is more troubled. There is, for example, a history of laboratory schools in which the rhetoric is similar to descriptions of teaching hospitals, but many laboratory schools have evolved into elite private schools serving universities' felt need to provide schooling services for the children of faculty members. More recently, professional development schools have emerged that are intended to strengthen links between colleges of education and public schools, but these professional development schools vary widely and only occasionally involve a serious research component.

There is a pervasive and sharp divide between the research-oriented faculty in colleges of education and those who prepare the next generation of teachers. This occurs in part because the research-oriented faculty are small in number and often are based in fields like educational psychology that are connected only indirectly to teacher preparation. And it occurs in part because it has become possible and even fashionable to conduct research in ways that are disconnected from schools.

One of the keys to the success of the urban teaching hospital that serves the health needs of patients from highly varied economic circumstances is its ability to deal with problems that are interesting for the field. It is those interesting medical problems that attract the attention of top researchers, and it is those same interesting medical problems that arguably have pedagogical value for students of medicine. One reason the public sees nothing similar to urban teaching hospitals serving a diverse clientele in the field of education is that researchers and educators have not succeeded in making problems in the education field interesting.

What does it take to make a problem interesting? Several attributes come to mind. First, the problem needs to be tractable: there needs to be a feeling that progress can be made if the requisite effort is made. In other words, lost causes, or causes that are perceived to be lost, are not very interesting.

Second—and this is a variation on the first attribute—there needs to be an understanding of the kind of expertise that is needed to deal with various aspects of the problem. In other words, the problem needs to be divisible in the sense that persons with relevant expertise can make progress, even if other aspects of the problem remain intractable.

Third, for a problem to be interesting, its solution needs to have a significant impact. The expected impact might be narrow or broad, but there needs to be a reason for believing that it is real and that something real hangs in the balance.

Fourth, the necessary work needs to be reasonably convenient and not disagreeable. A problem could be otherwise interesting and engaging, but barriers will inhibit participation. Steps can be taken to reduce the barriers, or, alternatively, compensation can be offered to increase one's willingness to put up with the inconvenience.

With this as an initial means for assessing the interest level of problems, how do medical and education problems compare? With respect to whether a solution is significant, there are no inherent differences. Problems with education are certainly important and the stakes are high; the same can be said of medical problems. Some medical problems may be more narrowly focused, but this does not mean they are unimportant.

There are differences, however, in the tractability of problems. Medicine has enjoyed greater success at breaking problems into manageable pieces, developing responses and interventions, keeping track of the results so that the evidence is cumulative, and disseminating findings. It is not that medicine is without its difficulties, but education as a field has lagged in its ability to progress in these ways.

In terms of the convenience of the work, in medicine there is a level of mobility that can make things more convenient for the top talent. The patient with an interesting medical problem can sometimes do the traveling and come to a center where the relevant expertise is concentrated. However, this is not always the case, and sometimes medically interesting problems are place-bound and related to things like climate and cultural practice. In these cases, the medical expertise may face the inconvenience of needing to travel long distances.

Education tends to be place-bound, and the relevant expertise may need to travel to the site. Education's collective nature also makes relocation for the convenience of those having the relevant expertise less viable.

Thus, the significant difference between the fields lies in the comparatively intractable nature of the problems being faced by education. If the problems are intractable, they are less interesting and it follows that it will be more difficult to attract the talents of the researchers who are best equipped to provide answers to the underlying questions.

What is making the problems in education so intractable and therefore uninteresting? In part it is the limited progress that has been made, but this is not unique to education. All fields start with relatively little knowledge in hand. Just because education's present knowledge base is limited, that neither makes the problems uninteresting nor precludes future growth.

Part of the explanation can be found in the small number of truly talented individuals who have the ability and interests to do the relevant research. The field is still relatively new, and not many people have been engaged. This shortage is being recognized, and welcome new resources are being made available to expand the number of future researchers who have good skills for conducting powerful studies. The argument is actually circular, because the current shortage of skilled researchers with interests in education is related to the paucity of interesting problems in the field.

Another part of the explanation can be found in the nature of current practice, where problems are so overwhelming that it becomes difficult to establish an analytical foothold. Researchers have responded by developing ingenious designs for studies to overcome the quirks of practice that make conducting the research difficult. It would be better to shift the burden away from researchers and toward the world of practice; in that way, there would be greater willingness to adjust practice so that investigators can get definitive answers to important questions.

This plea for adjusting practice so that it is more amenable to study and richer in the supply of interesting problems has the potential to be far reaching. When schools become highly dysfunctional due to concatenations of far-reaching and interconnected problems, it is hard to imagine how the phenomenon can lend itself to fruitful study.

If educators and researchers are serious about making educational practice more amenable to study, would they know how to proceed? The answer is yes, and it would involve disentangling practices so that cleaner differences can be monitored and assessed. The more difficult question is whether there is a political willingness to disturb the operating, but at times quite dysfunctional, status quo.

Although this strategy is compatible with the growing emphasis on research with experimental designs, it adds an important extra expectation for educational practice. In other words, the burden is not solely on the researcher, but there emerges instead a shared responsibility to generate interesting problems that will attract the interest of relevant parties.

Crossing from Interesting to Hard

What happens when interesting problems become hard or otherwise intractable? The hardness of a problem will at some point undermine how interesting it is, and there are interesting (and hard) empirical questions to ask about the trade-offs between hardness and levels of interest. Indeed, some minimal level of difficulty is probably necessary for a problem to be interesting. If all the problems in a field were easy, it would not be much of a field.

Finding the proper balance between hard and interesting is the key for attracting and retaining the efforts of the research community. It is this balance that moves a field forward, and it is this balance that has proved to be elusive for education. In short, problems in education have been made too hard.

This need not be the case. One can take advantage of existing controls over educational practice to make changes that will make practice more amenable to study. If the problem thereby becomes less hard and more interesting, the talent will arrive and the stage will be set for further improvement as the field gains more knowledge.

TOWARD SYNTHESIS

Imagine a world replete with a public educational system enjoying unprecedented popular support because of its success in precisely linking benefits received with costs imposed, thanks to the advent of differential add-ons and variable pricing. Such a system will start off impressively and only get better as parents gain experience with matching services to their children's needs. Aspirations for pupils are likely to increase over time as parents having modest economic means come to realize that the subsidized costs they are asked to bear for additional services represent good value.

Local school board members will rise to the occasion and make principled decisions about what to include and exclude from the basic program. The state will step in and ensure equity in the availability of the basic program and whatever add-ons are chosen by parents. The measured introduction of such market pressures will add a refreshing level of self-regulating discipline.

Also, imagine a world where school systems succeed in shifting away from the current heavy reliance on costly proximate teacher resources in favor of embodied human resources, a trade-off made possible by the creative use of modern computing and telecommunications technologies. As teachers take on these new roles, their impact and level of professionalism will increase, with concomitant increases in social status and economic standing.

Classrooms will have a very different look and feel in this scenario, and students can look forward to much more individually tailored and effective learning experiences. Longer-term benefits also will arise to the degree that students become skilled in taking advantage of electronically conveyed information. The exponential growth in the availability of information is making it increasingly incumbent upon the schools to equip students with the skills to take charge of their own learning.

Build into this world a capacity to respond quickly and effectively when things are not going well in school settings because of unexpected problems that can be traced to a limited understanding of teaching and learning phenomena. A regional supplemental resource board will be equipped to make emergency allocations of resources to instructional settings where demonstrable problems exist. Data systems will be in place to pinpoint these locations, and action will be taken before students lose the ground that can be so difficult to regain.

Add to this world a differentiated staffing structure that makes better use of excellent teachers and helps other educational professionals develop particular areas of expertise. There are significant implications here for teacher roles and for professional development and pre-service preparation, and many of these changes can and should be made in tandem with shifts in the use of computing and telecommunications technologies.

Finally, imagine a world with a vitalized educational research and development effort that attracts top intellectual talent because the hard problems have now become interesting, thanks to improved partnerships between education practitioners and researchers. Current professional development schools are early steps in the right direction toward strengthening these partnerships, but much more needs to be done.

This is an attractive world. Is it an achievable world? The answer must be a qualified yes. Resources should not be a barrier. Significant savings should be forthcoming, thanks to a successful substitution away from the use of proximate and toward the use of embodied human resources. Moreover, differential add-ons have the potential to tap in to people's fundamental willingness to support education along with their willingness to make sacrifices for their children. One could imagine a significant increase in the size of the education sector of the economy as a consequence of achieving a better match between people's preferences and the costs they are expected to bear, thanks to the differential add-on and variable pricing mechanism.

Several of the other ideas would require funding, but the magnitudes should be manageable, particularly in light of the potential for savings. One could begin experimentally with the supplemental resource board and adjust the scale as experience warrants. The differentiated staffing idea carries costs, but these also could be covered by pulling back from the existing investments in professional development that are widely perceived to be ineffective.

The chief reason for the qualified nature of the yes lies in the political power of the vested interests that will be made nervous by the far-reaching and transformative nature of these reforms, not to mention the numerous logistical matters that need to be resolved. It is not unreasonable to be made nervous by these ideas. They are far reaching and it is hard to predict their effects, particularly for the differential add-on and variable pricing idea. The key will be to find ways to experiment incrementally with the approach and in ways that permit returning to the earlier state of affairs if the reform proves to be faulty.

For the moment, a good outcome will be that this argument stimulates further thought in these directions, particularly in terms of implementation and ways to test the ideas experimentally. Public agencies face an important series of crossroads in education funding, and there is merit in trying to think out of the box and in terms of fundamental change.

9

Linking Education Funding with Standards-Based Reform and Community-Based Resources

Michael W. Kirst and Lori Rhodes

There are many conceptual frameworks for financing U.S. education, including equity, adequacy, and parental choice.[1] Although these frameworks have reshaped how education finance is conceptualized, they fail to sufficiently incorporate two potentially important strategies for improving student performance. The first, systemic standards-based reform (SSBR), represents an attempt to align the school-based elements of learning—curriculum, testing, and the like—with ambitious learning goals. Codified in the federal No Child Left Behind Act (NCLB), the national movement for SSBR assumes that improvements in school systems alone are necessary and sufficient for all pupils to reach academic proficiency.[2]

In contrast, an out-of-school interventions strategy reaches beyond school-level technologies to addresses the economic and social conditions of school communities. Out-of-school interventions acknowledge the importance of child poverty, malnutrition, inadequate health care, and other negative influences on student learning and attempt to mitigate their effects.

SSBR and out-of-school interventions operate under different paradigms, but the two approaches are complementary (see table 9-1). This chapter examines their potential benefits. It focuses on the strategies' underlying theories, key concepts, and important operational and policy alignment issues. It identifies ways in which education finance systems must change to support their implementation. In the final section, we conclude that even though it is not clear whether either of these strategies alone can improve student learning or eliminate achievement gaps as envisioned by NCLB, exploration of

TABLE 9-1   Comparison of SSBR with school-linked services and community
school strategies

Strategy element	Systemic standards-based reform	School-linked services and community schools
Assumptions	Assumes accountability in the form of formal assessments are necessary to gauge student performance and improve achievement.	Assumes greater acknowledgment of outside factors and inclusion of community will increase student achievement.
Implementation	Coherent and comprehensive state policy design is needed to accomplish these local effects.	Needed are integrated focus on academics, youth development, family support, health and social services, and community development.
Problem it solves	Students not meeting standards, schools not meeting goals.	Disconnect between community and schools, high dropout and truancy rates, poor student achievement. Consolidates services for students and families.
Policy theory	Aligned policies lead to improved student performance.	More-coordinated and in-house service delivery to parents and children lead to improved student performance.
Target of action	Accountability through K–12 assessment.	High-quality education, positive youth development, family support, family and community engagement in decision making, and community development.
Scope of effort	Starts at federal level, states set standards (NCLB guidelines); relies on explicit aligned standards-based textbooks and instructional materials; initial teacher preparation; professional development; and state, district, and school formative and summative assessment.	Federal and state programs, community organizations (public and private), families, schools, local leaders and community members, universities and colleges.
Expected benefits	All students reach proficient levels.	Real-world learning through community problem solving and service. Development of a specific action agenda in response to ongoing assessments of the strengths and needs of the school system and community service agencies.

continued on next page

Strategy element	Systemic standards-based reform	School-linked services and community schools
Financial support	Federal and state funding.	Jointly operated and financed through a partnership between school systems and one or more community agencies (public and private). Requires start-up capital for planning joint finance arrangements and glue money to continue collaboration among agencies. Fiscal strategy is to divert these funding and program streams to one location at or near schools.
Complications	Concept of "proficient" means different things in different states. Test scores must be directly linked to economic costs. Need for better classroom formative and diagnostic assessment. Finance gap between SSBR's aims, current policy instruments, and school capabilities.	Difficult to create partnerships, coordinate financing, and hire personnel. Less-effective school-linked services overrely on referral to scattered agencies and then leave it to parents to find transportation. Some parents and youth have negative experiences and impressions of schools, and many school personnel are not familiar with local families, gangs, or neighborhoods. Not a systemic change and thus has limited impact. Expansion of social service functions engenders fear that schools will deemphasize their traditional academic priorities.
Support	Must be supported by elected officials, the public, business, and professional organizations.	National Association of Social Workers to unify and advocate for school social workers to take a lead role. Families, young people, principals, teachers, youth workers, neighborhood residents, college faculty members, college students, and businesspeople all work together to design and implement a plan for transforming the school into a child-centered institution. Partnership is one of the most important principles of effective community schools.
Role of the teacher	Teachers must be capable and willing to change their teaching practice. Teachers must integrate and coordinate their teaching content in a more uniform manner, horizontally across grade levels and vertically up and down the grades.	Schools need to connect social services and parent involvement with instructional programs so that teachers can know how family needs affect class performance. Unless teachers are invested with ownership in changes to school-linked services system, the changes become only a grafted-on project to the academic program.

a combined approach, working inside and outside schools simultaneously, seems warranted and may enrich public and professional debates regarding ways to achieve the nation's ambitious learning goals.

SYSTEMIC STANDARDS-BASED REFORM

Systemic standards-based reform began in the 1980s and spread across the United States as the dominant conceptual framework for improving K–12 education.[3] SSBR is now embedded in federal policy, a process that started with the Improving America's Schools Act of 1994 and continued through passage of NCLB in 2002.[4]

Theory of Standards-Based Reform

The theory of SSBR requires states to establish challenging content and performance standards for all students and to align key state policies affecting teaching and learning with these standards, including curriculum and curriculum materials, pre-service and in-service teacher training, and formative and summative assessments. States then grant schools and districts greater flexibility to design appropriate instructional programs but also hold them accountable for student performance. SSBR's many moving and interacting parts (see figure 9-1) must be supported by elected officials, the public, business, and professional organizations.

SSBR encourages teachers to develop high expectations for students and to coordinate teaching in a uniform manner, collaborating horizontally across grade levels and vertically up and down the grades.[5] It is not sufficient for teachers to know their pupils' learning strengths and weaknesses; teachers also must be able to change their practices to overcome those weaknesses. In this regard, periodic diagnostic tests are crucial to teachers' understanding of and response to particular student needs. The SSBR model also anticipates that teachers will internalize state accountability expectations as their own school's standards of performance.[6]

SSBR is not merely an add-on reform like kindergarten or vocational education. Rather, it penetrates the English, math, and science classrooms that have been the core of academic learning. In essence, SSBR is a policy theory for classroom instructional improvement and improved pupil performance.

Aligning State Policy with SSBR Elements

In an SSBR context, coherent and comprehensive state policies are needed to motivate local actors, in part through rewards and sanctions, and to improve local capacity. Figure 9-2 displays the policy components that ulti-

FIGURE 9-1   Systemic standards-based reform framework

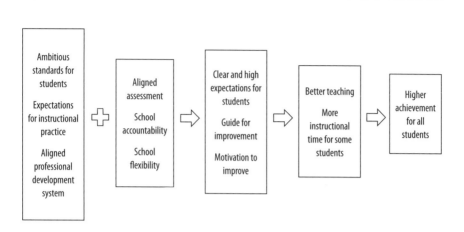

Source: National Research Council, Committee on Understanding the Influence of Standards in K–12 Science, Mathematics, and Technology Education, *Investigating the Influence of Standards: A Framework for Research in Mathematics, Science, and Technology Education,* eds. Iris R. Weiss, Michael S. Knapp, Karen S. Hollweg, and Gail Burrill (Washington, DC: National Academy Press, 2001).

mately must work together to improve instructional practice and student learning.[7]

Student academic content standards sit at the center of the wheel. States need to formulate, specify, and align other policies with these standards. In practice, however, frequent misalignments arise between content standards and other policy elements, illustrated in figure 9-2 as spokes of the wheel.[8] For example, a major inconsistency in some state SSBR policies is the failure to connect K–12 standards, especially performance standards, with the performance standards used by businesses to hire high school graduates.

Linking Education Finance with SSBR Elements

No education finance system has been founded on the concepts and specific policy requirements of SSBR. The adequacy movement that emerged in the late 1980s prompted a closer alignment of SSBR concepts and resource calculations, but with mixed success.[9] Although analysts have made progress drawing these connections, results on the policy and practice fronts have been limited. Several states now fund remedial programs that assist students who fail to pass high school exit exams and end-of-grade tests, but these programs are token efforts compared to overall spending.[10] Most states

FIGURE 9-2 Policy alignment required by systemic standards-based reform

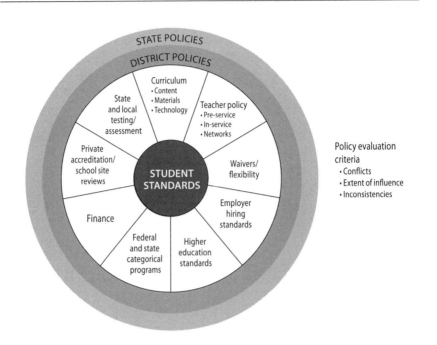

have never attempted to align their academic goals with education finance mechanisms or, having attempted it, fail to make the connection.[11] In fact, some finance mechanisms even work against this alignment. California, for example, operates more than sixty categorical funding programs. Although some of these programs address state standards, most impede the development of coherent, standards-based instructional programs in schools and districts.

Linking education finance with SSBR elements requires adherence to a conceptual and analytical framework that explicitly addresses program resources, academic time, teacher attributes, assessment and remediation, and student needs, all of which have cost implications. These elements are described in detail next, with examples and cost factors provided from California.

Incorporating Program Resources

Researchers William Koski and Hillary Weiss began to make the connection between education finance and state academic standards by identifying specific educational resources that teachers and students need if they are to implement and learn California's content standards.[12] The authors identified each resource that the standards explicitly required or implicitly assumed to be available, excluding costs associated with infrastructure, support staff, and specialized programs. Their evaluation was not a costing out exercise; it sought only to identify the resources that the state anticipates will be available to all children.

For instance, California has explicit content standards and an end-of-course exam for high school biology. Koski and Weiss identified the laboratory materials needed to conduct standards-based experiments, including measuring instruments and scientific calculators. Similarly, the researchers also identified the computer technology, Internet access, and library and media resources implied in the state's English language arts and history standards.

Koski and Weiss found many resource requirements embedded in the standards but not available in California school districts. To fully determine the costs of SSRB resources nationwide, this type of analysis needs to be extended deeper into classroom instruction and the reteaching cycles needed for continuous improvement in pupil outcomes.[13]

Incorporating Academic Time

SSBR also requires sufficient instructional time to teach a state's academic standards. California describes the time needed for a basic program in reading language arts, but then it lists instructional elements that reinforce and extend the basic program:

- Thirty minutes of extra support for English language learners in K–8
- Thirty minutes of extra support for struggling readers in K–8
- Fifteen to twenty minutes of intensive vocabulary instructional support in K–3
- A minimum of ninety lessons, each one lasting fifteen minutes, for each of the five sets of technical skills in a primary classroom reading intervention kit for grades 1–3[14]

Instructional time allocations have direct cost implications, especially when stipulated on such a granular level.

Incorporating Teacher Attributes

Research on standards-based reform demonstrates how changes in classroom teaching depend on the intellectual ability, knowledge, and skills of teachers and other staff; the quality and quantity of instructional materials and resources; and the social organization of instruction (for example, teacher collaboration that enhances coherent instruction within and across grades).[15]

Building this kind of capacity has direct cost implications, primarily through funding professional development. However, education finance systems do not always cover these costs. California eliminated most of its state-funded professional development, relying at one point primarily on federal Reading First funds, which covered only 3 percent of the state's elementary teachers. In addition, the state developed SSBR-aligned standards for initial pre-service teacher preparation, but it has no system to reimburse state universities for their costs in meeting these new standards.

Incorporating Assessment and Remediation Costs

Improved classroom formative and diagnostic assessments constitute an essential element of SSBR theory. The resulting data can identify needs for professional development and student intervention, thus improving teaching and learning. Diagnostic assessments are different from annual state accountability tests. Though a core component of SSBR, accountability tests can neither cover the large number of state standards—or even the subset of so-called power standards some states recognize—nor help teachers spot learning deficiencies in a timely manner.

Although diagnostic assessments are necessary if school systems are to improve instruction and learning, developing and implementing them can be costly. Purchasing them represents a significant expense. Alternatively, developing diagnostic tests requires substantial teacher time—the same time that is necessary for teacher preparation, collaboration, and professional development.

Addressing the identified instructional or learning needs can be costly, too. Coaches may be helpful in improving instruction, but they represent an added expense. Low-performing schools may need resource-intensive assistance through instructional support teams and mentoring for teachers. And low-performing students may require additional resources and time for remediation.[16]

Incorporating Student Needs

SSBR also requires attention to individual student needs. English language learners, for example, often require more instructional time to enhance their English skills and to keep current on subject matter. They may need more tutoring or special instructional materials to enhance their regular curriculum program. Secondary schools may need additional course offerings to enable ELL students to master English or to prepare for post-secondary education. And teacher preparation may need to be enhanced.[17]

Aligning education finance with SSBR means linking resources with the program components, academic time, teacher attributes, assessment and remediation, and student needs that support better student learning. Yet most states have not taken this step. At a practical level, states need new knowledge to better understand the policy and practice barriers to SSBR implementation and to fill the gap between SSBR's aims, current policy instruments, and school capabilities. A research strategy is needed, including randomized trials, to help elected officials, educators, and others understand and manage the complex linkages within SSBR.

OUT-OF-SCHOOL INTERVENTIONS

Although funding systemic standards-based reform may improve student learning to a degree, critics contend that out-of-school interventions, services, and support are necessary if states are to close achievement gaps between white students and students of color.[18] Education historian Patricia Graham argued the case this way.

> Educational problems are most acute among children from low-income families, particularly minority families, whose schools are much weaker and whose homes and communities are less likely to provide resources such as museums, libraries, books, healthy recreational activities, and a culture of success based on educational achievement. Many reforms adopted in the post-Risk era [that is, *A Nation At Risk*], such as graduation exams that determine whether students can receive diplomas, tend to punish these students, since they are unlikely to receive, either at home or in school, the instruction that would allow them to score well. Their teachers and parents often did not receive such instruction, and they find themselves unable to teach children what they themselves do not know, however much they may want to do so.[19]

Graham's comments support the idea that concentrated poverty contains pathologies—including poor health, crime, high unemployment, bad housing, and drugs—that undermine good outcomes for children. Others have made similar arguments. Joy Dryfoos, for example, concluded that "American schools are failing because they cannot meet the complex needs of today's students. Teachers cannot teach hungry children or cope with young people who are too distraught to learn."[20] And Isadora Hare described the scale of the problem, noting that 40 percent of children are at risk of educational failure because of complex social, economic, and emotional problems.[21]

This broader context raises the question of whether education reform—including finance reform—that accomplishes ambitious student learning goals might depend on a combination of inside- and outside-school approaches, encompassing economic policies that have a direct impact on children, families, and schools, and not only changes aimed solely at classrooms.[22] As researcher Jean Anyon noted, "Macroeconomic policies like those regulating the minimum wage, job availability, tax rates, federal transportation, and affordable housing create conditions in cities that no existing educational policy or urban school reform can transcend."[23]

To address these outside-school conditions, Randi Weingarten, president of the American Federation of Teachers, supported the concept of community service schools when she suggested that teachers, policy makers, parents, and community leaders "imagine a Federal law that promoted community schools—schools that serve the neediest children by bringing together under one roof all the services and activities they and their families need . . . schools that are open all day and offer after-school and evening recreational activities and homework assistance . . . child care and dental, medical and counseling clinics, or other services the community needs."[24]

President Obama appeared to support this broader notion of education reform when he proposed extensive modeling of the Harlem Children's Zone, "a nonprofit community agency that runs a broad-based program to meet the educational, health, and social-service needs of residents in a 97-block area of New York."[25] In fact, federal support for community service schools started in 2008, when the Department of Education instituted a Full-Service Community Schools grants program that generated more than nine hundred letters of intent and more than five hundred grant proposals, all for an appropriation of only $5 million.[26]

Policy Frameworks

Several policy frameworks inform out-of-school interventions. The broadest framework focuses on enhancing the jobs and income of parents.[27] This framework asserts that higher parental economic and work status will lead to increased school achievement by their children. Policy interventions aligned with this framework include the negative income tax, job placement and training, and revamped welfare policies. And indeed, some studies of family income maintenance demonstrate a positive impact on school achievement.[28]

Another policy framework focuses on community development and links to schools.[29] This framework suggests that low-income, racially segregated ghettos with high unemployment rates need new industries and economic development strategies and that parents who are working will enhance their children's education. The Johnson administration's 1966 Model Cities program was based on this theory. Under that program, new government money was targeted at sections of cities having few businesses. Schools were one of several local agencies that designed integrated approaches to economic growth, new business creation, and comprehensive public services.

A third policy framework promotes school–community links and starts with schools as the hub of numerous parent and child services. Known as school-linked services, this approach places fragmented city and county agencies at or near schools for coordinated and accessible delivery of services to parents and their children. School-linked services provide direct services to children and families; connect children and families with community services; coordinate services within schools; and facilitate communication among teachers, children, and families.[30] The school-linked services idea is that provision of social services supports student learning. For example, health-care services or health referrals often are provided because illnesses and their related school absences can lower student achievement. Over time, this school-linked services approach has developed into the broader community school vision.

The Community School Vision

A community school is both a place and a set of partnerships. It has an integrated focus on academics, youth development, family support, health and social services, and community development. Its curriculum emphasizes real-world learning through community problem solving and service. By extending the school day and week, it reaches families and community residents.

Community schools enhance the academic, social, emotional, and physical development of students. They also support the families and communities that surround schools. Sitting at the center of communities, these schools help children and give adults a network.

According to researcher Jane Quinn, community schools are most successful when they are grounded in the following research-based premises.

- All young people need ongoing support and opportunities on the road to successful adulthood.
- Children do better in school when their parents regularly support, monitor, and advocate for their education.

- Constructive learning activities during nonschool hours are essential to children's school success.
- Children's participation in high-quality afterschool programs results in a variety of important learning and developmental outcomes.
- Community-based youth development programs promote positive academic and social outcomes among teenagers.
- Consistent adult guidance and support promote positive youth development.
- Positive youth outcomes are enhanced when key developmental influences work together.
- Fragmentation among educational and social services hinders effectiveness.
- Community schools show great promise as the best way to promote children's learning and development.

In this vein, Quinn cited several successful examples of community schools, such as Beacons, Bridges to Success, Children's Aid Society community schools, Communities in Schools, Healthy Start, Schools of the 21st Century, and Arne Duncan's Chicago initiative to make over some of Chicago's public schools as community schools.[31]

As noted, one component of community schools involves the integration of school-linked services, even though schools do not fund or operate these diverse services.[32] A school with many services, alternatively referred to as a full-service school, provides an "innovative system of delivering services in which community agencies and schools collaborate to provide a variety of health and social services to children and their families at or near school sites."[33] Dryfoos described a full-service community school's multiple features this way.

> A community school, operating in a public school building is open to students, families, and the community before, during, and after school, seven days a week, all year long. It is jointly operated and financed through a partnership between the school system and one or more community agencies. Families, young people, principals, teachers, youth workers, neighborhood residents, college faculty members, college students, and businesspeople all work together to design and implement a plan for transforming the school into a child-centered institution.[34]

Full-service community schools encourage student learning through community service alone or through service learning, which combines classroom instruction with service roles in communities, thus expanding students' vision beyond classroom walls. Community schools also include a family support center, which helps with child rearing, employment, housing, medical and mental health services, and the like. Ultimately, according to the vision of the Coalition for Community Schools, full-service community schools link "high quality education, positive youth development, family support, family and community engagement in decision making, and community development."[35]

Community schools tailor their resources to the needs of students, families, schools, and communities, with school and community groups together setting priorities for action.[36] For instance, some community schools emphasize particular age groups, such as adolescents, teens, or preschoolers. For students between the ages of eleven and twenty-one, interventions may include residential schools, internships, mentors, sports, gang prevention, Job Corps in rural areas, mental health services, and youth empowerment services, where dropouts can reconnect to school.[37] Health clinics based in secondary schools strive for better health outcomes by focusing on birth control and family counseling as well as treating disease.

According to Dryfoos, primary responsibility for high-quality education in full-service community schools rests with school authorities, and the primary responsibility for "everything else" rests with outside agencies.[38] In other words, school systems continue to pay for education, and other services are supported by an array of nonschool funding sources. These outside services can be related to health, mental health, and social services as well as tutoring, case management, and adult education programs. In this holistic and inclusive approach to education—an approach that includes students, parents, teachers, and the community—programs ultimately are aimed at improving academic achievement in classrooms.

In short, community schools offer advantages that traditional schools acting alone do not. Community schools bring human and financial resources into schools so that teachers and students can focus on learning. They engage and motivate students by fostering social, emotional, and physical growth as well as academic skills. And they build social capital for schools as well as students. In the end, "community schools build young people's social capital by connecting them to resources and relationships that can help solve problems and open the doors to opportunity. The same advantages apply to school districts. Communitywide partnerships give school districts a voice and a forum in which to bring school needs and perspectives to a wide audience."[39]

Hugh Price summarized the effect of these schools as galvanizing communities to create a pervasive culture of achievement that celebrates and provides protective cover to achievers and that neutralizes negative peer pressures.[40]

Key Components and Operational Considerations

The community schools concept is broad, and specific finance designs for school-linked services nest within it.[41] Although researchers and advocates have identified important components of community schools, there is insufficient policy theory or experience to verify their assertions. Consequently, the following list of desirable community school components reflects only best thinking at this time.[42] Additional experimentation is needed to verify, refine, or expand this list. With this caveat as context, desirable components of community schools include the following:

- A wide range of services provided by public and private agencies
- Parent education, adult education, and afterschool recreation programs funded by various city governments and community colleges
- Health services, including a nurse practitioner, who, unlike school nurses, can administer medications and treat specific health problems
- Emergency services provided by private or public agencies
- Provision of food, clothing, emergency funds, transportation, and child care
- Mental health services, including counseling
- On-site assistance from social welfare offices for family problems
- Preschool and child care programs

All these components benefit from community engagement and support, and particular attention should be paid to linking afterschool programs, sports teams, and resources such as museums and parks to child protection, job training, and other social services.[43]

In addition to these desirable components, the following operational considerations are important to the success of community schools.

Partnerships with Other Agencies

Partnership is one of the most important principles of effective community schools. No single entity can provide all the needed services, so community schools must build partnerships between schools and other organizations and institutions, private as well as public.[44] Often, a lead organization coordinates the relationship, bringing new expertise to schools and reducing burdens on school staff. The lead organization can be a community-based organization, a public agency, or the school itself.

Terry Saunders Lane looked at partnerships between universities and public schools and identified five factors that contributed to their success: development of a specific action agenda in response to ongoing assessments of school and community agency strengths and needs; availability of skilled, ethnically diverse social services personnel, who provide consistent leadership and clinical services throughout the project; availability of new funding and contributed resources; understanding of the political context of school-linked services; and long-term school and university commitment to implementation of school-linked services.[45]

Efficiencies and Effectiveness of Co-Location

Co-locating services at the same site creates considerable access efficiencies for consumers, in the same way that it is easier to shop at Wal-Mart than to drive or take a bus to six specialized stores. Consequently, service co-location can improve service availability even if there is minimal collaboration among the service providers. In this regard, the more services at any one site, the better. Less-effective school-linked services overrely on referrals to scattered agencies and then leave it to parents to find transportation.

Although co-locating has advantages, there should be no dogmatic preference for schools as the location of school-linked services. The key concept is linkage, not location. In fact, some parents and youth have negative experiences with and impressions of schools, and many school personnel are not familiar with families, gangs, or neighborhoods. Consequently, the co-located services could be initiated by a medical center, a community family center, or another local organization.

Integration with School Restructuring

Schools need to connect social services and parent involvement with instructional programs so that teachers know how family needs affect class performance. Unless teachers are invested in school-linked services, the services offered will become only another grafted-on component to academic programs, one whose benefits are not likely to be realized.

Development of Comprehensive Family Services

Importantly, community schools meet parents' needs, too, including emergency child care, food, clothing, and other services that many public or private programs do not provide. Accordingly, service centers could include parent outreach and parent staffing at the neighborhood level, develop a family focus that adapts to various cultural needs, and expand child care by preparing neighborhood parents to become licensed child care providers.

Services Through Local Youth Organizations

Finally, community schools can involve or provide services or activities through local youth organizations, which can speak for adolescents rather than label and treat them as problems. In part as a result of fragmentation and in part as a result of an embedded paternalistic approach toward children and youth, these populations have not been asked to participate in identifying the problems and alternative solutions that affect them.

What's more, when different needs are served by isolated agencies, young people find it difficult to coordinate their wants or needs. Few teachers, physicians, juvenile court staff, social workers, or others focus on the interactive or interdependent nature of their contribution to the experience of the youth they serve. Instead, these professionals look only at their own performance as members of particular agencies. If no one is looking at all the elements of young persons' lives, considering how they fit together, the cumulative effect of the help they receive cannot be known. After all, the entire environment creates the conditions that dictate whether young persons will lead productive and satisfied lives. Youth organizations may be able to play this coordinating role.

Cost Factors, Funding Strategies, and Alignment Issues

School-linked services require planning funds, glue money to continue collaboration among agencies, and capital funds to support facility costs.[46] As detailed later, officials can finance some services by diverting existing streams of children's services funding to a location at or near school sites. Richard Rothstein defined the reach of out-of-school services to include stable housing, summer programs, and school–community health clinics, which exceed the scope of current children's funding, arguing as follows.

> A school-community clinic should include services that middle-class families take for granted and that ensure children can thrive in school. Clinics associated with schools in lower-class communities should include: obstetric and gynecological services for pregnant and post-partum women; pediatric services for children through their high-school years; physicians to serve parents of school-age children; nurses to support these medical services; dentists and hygienists to see both parents and children semiannually; optometrists and vision therapists to serve those who require

treatment for their sight; social workers to refer families to other services; community health educators to instruct young women in proper health habits during pregnancy, or to organize smoking reduction campaigns; and psychologists or therapists to assist families and children who are experiencing excessive stress.[47]

In addition, Rothstein stressed that the achievement gap grows during the summer when middle-class children read books, visit museums, and travel, activities that reinforce their school-year learning. There are scant studies of the costs of summer programs for lower-income children that provide similar support. Because the typical black child now attends a school that is more segregated than in the 1960s, financial analysis also is required to determine the cost of improved housing to create racially mixed neighborhoods.[48]

Implementing School-Linked Services

What would implementation of a school-linked services approach look like? A fiscal strategy would first use existing financing to fund programs in health, social services, juvenile justice, and so on, rather than add social workers and nurses to school payrolls. It would divert these funding and program streams, aiming them all at one location at or near schools.

Schools would stay open from six o'clock in the morning until six in the evening, providing city-funded day care, recreation, and adult education. School health clinics would operate as subsidiaries of a local hospital, which would provide the necessary medical licenses, eligibility to receive Medicaid funds, and liability insurance. That same hospital also would handle billing for health services and employ health workers at the school site.

Federal services for abused children would provide funds for children's protective services, and the federal maternal and child health grant would be used for mental health counseling. Federal or state categorical funds for children's services (for example, drug abuse prevention) would provide resources for planning and administration.

The United Way would fill cracks where no federal or state categorical programs provided coverage, including emergency needs such as clothing and rent payment. City funds would be used for afterschool recreation and beforeschool child care, and community colleges would provide programs to help parents become wage earners and improve their parenting skills.

A first principle in this strategy is that school-linked services primarily use funds that are already being spent on children's services. The redirection of money from several physical locations to one, such as a school, is another crucial theme, with funds often shifting from more-restrictive to more-inclusive school-linked services. For example, specialized funds to combat drugs and smoking could be combined into a broader children's health prevention approach.

In addition, changes to state and federal funding mechanisms may be necessary to create better alignment and to support efficient and effective school-linked services. If collaboration among agencies is more effective than the current fragmentation, then funding mechanisms could create incentives for collaboration. If flexibility between frontline service providers across agencies (teachers, social workers, public health nurses, and the like) achieves better outcomes, then financing formulas could provide such flexibility. If service interventions are more effective early on or at an early age, then financing mechanisms could be redirected to front-end prevention priorities instead of back-end treatments. Finally, federal and state funding sources could be redesigned to meld multiple funding sources and to cut across historically separate children's services domains.

By themselves, however, school-linked financing strategies are not likely to change service systems enough to create significantly better children's outcomes. Finance changes must be accompanied by related transformations in the governance, technology, attitudes, and capacities of children's service employees up and down the system.

Typically, implementation of school-linked services engenders information exchange among service providers and joint projects. However, it does not include changes to categorical program rules or regulations, nor does it change systems to facilitate multiple agency intake and assessment, confidentiality waivers, common staff development for numerous child and family professionals and aides, integrated case management, or agreement on common outcomes that would be used for accountability. School-linked services employees stationed at schools from child protective services, for example, may still get promoted based on criteria in their home agency rather than their collaborative performance. System alignment across such elements could significantly improve the effectiveness of school-liked services over time.

Evaluation Findings and Practical Concerns

Research on the efficacy of school-linked services and full-service community schools is limited, but success stories are emerging. One example involves a community school in Evansville, Indiana, that used site-based decision making to identify student needs and to mobilize school and community resources to meet them. Throughout that school, standardized test scores increased, as did student attendance, mobility, and discipline.

According to Martin Blank and Dan Caddy, the Indiana work affirms what the Coalition for Community Schools found in its review of twenty major community school evaluations.[49] The review found that community schools show significant and widely evident gains in academic achievement and essential areas of nonacademic development, increased family stability and more involvement with schools, increased teacher satisfaction and more positive school environments, and better use of school buildings and increased security and pride in neighborhoods.[50]

Similarly, the Coalition for Community Schools found that thirty-six of forty-nine programs with any form of documentation reported academic gains, such as improved reading and math test scores. They also reported improvements in attendance, fewer suspensions, lower dropout rates, reduced high-risk behaviors (substance abuse, teen pregnancy), improved access to services, and higher rates of parental involvement.[51]

These success stories notwithstanding, educators nationwide are struggling to understand why many students still perform below grade level, failing to graduate from high school college-ready—or graduate from high school at all—despite implementation of numerous academic support strategies. A growing body of research indicates that in addition to academic support, students need social support to "address the health, developmental, and other noncognitive barriers to learning."[52]

For more than thirty years, Communities In Schools, Inc. (CIS), the nation's largest dropout prevention organization, has coordinated community-based services and provided direct services to more than 1.2 million students at 3,250 schools in twenty-seven states.[53] The CIS model highlights the importance of identifying, delivering, and integrating a combination of social and academic support services for students most at risk.

A longitudinal evaluation was conducted of more than 1,700 CIS schools.[54] The evaluation indicated that the most effective strategy for improving students' academic outcomes combined an on-site coordinator who oversees the integration and delivery of social support programs, school-level and student-level needs assessments to identify the most appropriate prevention and intervention services, community partners, a range of services to support the whole school and targeting strategies for individual students most at risk, evaluation data, and annual planning with modifications as needed.[55] The social support provided with the most frequency in CIS schools (between 75 and 90 percent of school sites) included mentoring; tutoring, academic support, and homework assistance; dropout prevention; personal, social, and life skills development; and speakers, workshops, events, and clubs.[56]

Although these studies indicate the potential of school-linked services and community schools, they may not reduce practitioners' concerns about implementing such a strategy. And they do not conclusively demonstrate that widespread application of this strategy will reduce or eliminate the achievement gap.

There is a long history of providing health and social services in schools, with a period of major initiatives at the turn of the twenty-first century. School leaders now, however, are wary of taking on new responsibilities without adequate and stable funding, and they are even more wary of launching projects funded by soft money. In hard times, health and social services often are the first items to be eliminated as school system leaders attempt to make budget cuts as far from classrooms as possible.

In addition, community schools are another "reform" in a long wave of changes in school roles, and they remain an uncertain, and thus risky, venture. The expansion of social service functions also engenders fear that schools will deemphasize their traditional academic priorities. Critics argue that schools have enough trouble teaching complex concepts and skills without taking on the rest of children's services. Moreover, conservative critics believe that providing school-linked services such as child care will encourage more women to work, with the subsequent loss of "high quality" child rearing done by "homemakers."[57]

CONCLUDING THOUGHTS

For the past two decades, systemic standards-based reform has been at the forefront of education reform in the United States. In theory, this reform improves classroom instruction through implementation of aligned standards, textbooks, and instructional materials; standards-inclusive initial teacher preparation and professional development; and state, district, and school formative and summative assessments operating within a coherent intergovernmental policy system, including education finance.

Unfortunately, instead of being guided by the key elements of standards-based reform, education finance systems represent a historical aggregation of programs, policies, and spending restrictions that are not aligned with the resource needs posed by standards-based reform. To realize the promise of SSBR, education finance policies and practices must accurately reflect SSBR's components and costs and must effectively support the changes in teaching and learning embodied in this framework.

However, even though finance policies aligned with SSBR may improve student performance, they may not be sufficient to bring all students to standards or to eliminate the achievement gap. Achieving these goals may require an intervention strategy that acknowledges and addresses the out-of-school factors that influence student learning. School-linked services and the more extensive full-service community schools provide a wide range of services to students and their families through partnerships with local organizations, all of which attempt to mitigate the social pathologies that undermine good outcomes for poor and minority children. These services—which include parent education, afterschool programs, health services, mental health services, preschool, and on-site assistance from social welfare services—can be funded by reallocating resources from various child and family programs.

Given the in-school and out-of-school influences on student learning, and the parallel but incomplete development and implementation of SSBR and out-of-school intervention strategies, a further exploration of these strategies seems warranted, asking particularly whether the combination of two approaches—(1) fully funded SSBR and (2) school-linked services or community schools—could improve student learning and reduce the achievement gap to a greater extent than either of these strategies alone might accomplish.

At this point, the field knows little about the potential of either of these strategies to influence student achievement, and even less about the potential effect of implementing these strategies in concert. The research literature does not provide clear and linked theories of action that explain how out-of-school interventions alone, or in various combinations, would improve student outcomes. Therefore, additional work is necessary if states are to develop policy theories that combine the two strategies, validate these theories, and determine the optimal allocation of resources between in-school standards-based reform and out-of-school interventions.

PART V

Building a Smart-Money Educational Resource System

10

Creating the Political Conditions for Education Finance Policy Change

Lorraine M. McDonnell

In the 1990s and the first decade of the 2000s, one question in particular continued to intrigue policy analysts: under what conditions are policy regimes likely to remain stable, and under what conditions are they altered in fundamental ways? This focus originated in attempts to explain how issues are placed on decision makers' agendas. It was later expanded to consider the broader puzzle of why, in a system wherein most policy making is incremental, large and profound changes sometimes occur, even to the point of reversing well-established policies. The theories that have guided exploration of this question provide a useful way to identify the political conditions under which significant changes in school funding arrangements are possible.

This chapter first outlines two theories of policy change derived from the conceptual building blocks that have come to encapsulate the primary determinants of public policy: ideas, institutions, and interests. In the second main section, I discuss the implications of these theories for placing recommendations for change on policy agendas, and in the third section, I examine the implications of several recent cases of major changes in education policies.

THEORIES OF POLICY CHANGE

Two models of agenda setting and policy change have withstood numerous empirical tests in a variety of policy domains, and they now dominate the literature of political science and policy analysis research.

The Kingdon Model

The first model, proposed by John Kingdon and based on research he conducted in the late 1970s, explains the process by which a proposal reaches the governmental agenda and is considered by policy makers, though not necessarily enacted into law.[1]

Kingdon hypothesized that policy emerges from the joining of three independent process streams: problems, policy proposals, and politics. "They are largely independent of one another, and each develops according to its own dynamics and rules," he wrote. "But at some critical junctures the three streams are joined, and the greatest policy changes grow out of that coupling of problems, policy proposals, and politics . . . A problem is recognized, a solution is developed and available to the policy community, a political change makes it the right time for policy change, and potential constraints are not severe."[2]

Policy entrepreneurs often are critical to the process of bringing the three streams together; in effect, they open a policy window. They are willing to invest their resources in calling attention to problems and mobilizing support for pet proposals in the hope of obtaining future policies they favor.

The Baumgartner and Jones Model

Kingdon's model is designed to explain the agenda-setting process for most social policies, whether they involve major changes or only incremental ones. In contrast, the second model focuses on policy enactment as well as on agenda setting, and it seeks to explain cycles of policy stability and change.

In their research, subsequently replicated in other studies, Baumgartner and Jones set out to explain a persistent condition in U.S. public policy: the fact that most policy making is incremental, but dramatic and deep changes in policy do occur.[3] Borrowing from the natural sciences, Baumgartner and Jones called this condition punctuated equilibrium: long periods of stability interrupted by major alterations to the system. Stability is maintained by the creation of policy monopolies, which are structural arrangements supported by powerful policy ideas. These ideas or policy images are generally connected to core political values, combine empirical information and emotive appeals, can be easily understood, and are communicated directly and simply through images and rhetoric.

However, policy monopolies and the interests they represent can be disrupted, resulting in major policy changes. A primary reason for such changes is that those opposed to or excluded from the policy monopoly constitute slack resources that policy entrepreneurs can mobilize. They do so through a redefinition of the dominant policy image using ideas that challenge it and capture the imagination of the media, policy makers, and the public.

Policy entrepreneurs provide new understandings of policy problems and new ways of conceptualizing solutions. These ideas can fuel powerful changes as they are communicated through a variety of rhetorical mechanisms, including stories about decline or negative consequences resulting from the current policy monopoly and stories of hope about what can be accomplished with a new framing of the policy problem and solution.[4] Yet according to Baumgartner and Jones, new ideas "are not controlled or created by any single group or individual, but are the result of multiple interactions among groups seeking to propose new understandings of issues, political leaders seeking new issues on which to make their name, agencies seeking to expand their jurisdictions, and voters reacting to the whole spectacle."[5]

Although the fragmentation of the U.S. policy system often makes it difficult to construct a coherent policy, its multiple arenas give policy entrepreneurs seeking change alternative points of entry into the system as they move among institutions at the same and at different governmental levels. In their empirical work, Baumgartner and Jones showed the progression of alternative policy images as they are reflected in media accounts, interest group activity, congressional hearings, executive agency outputs, budgetary allocations, and public opinion. Even when new ideas lead to policy changes, however, the old policy monopoly often continues until the institutional structures and norms through which new policies are implemented also are transformed.[6]

In a 2006 analysis of the origins of No Child Left Behind (NCLB), Manna supplemented Baumgartner and Jones's theory, focusing on policy change in a federalist system. Manna introduced the concept of borrowing strength, which "occurs when policy entrepreneurs at one level of government attempt to push their agendas by leveraging the justification and capabilities that other governments elsewhere in the federal system possess."[7] For example, those policy entrepreneurs promoting NCLB could mobilize around the license or arguments states had made to justify the involvement of higher levels of government in classroom processes and outcomes, and around the capacity or resources and administrative structures that state reforms had created.

Manna noted that although federal officials were able to borrow strength from the states in the case of NCLB, the process also can work in the other direction. For example, state officials may take advantage of the license provided by a president using the bully pulpit to advance particular reform arguments as a point of leverage in promoting their own policy agenda.[8]

These theories of policy change are intended primarily to be ex post—explaining cycles of stability and change after they occur—rather than predictive of future shifts. However, these theories can provide a basis for what might be called grounded speculation about the political conditions likely to facilitate major alterations in the design of education finance policies.

POLITICAL CONDITIONS FOR POLICY CHANGE: IMPLICATIONS FROM THEORY

This section examines three factors common to theories of agenda setting and policy change as they apply to policies linking the allocation of educational resources and student learning. The three factors are as follows:

- The content and appeal of an alternative policy image
- The structural arrangements undergirding the current policy monopoly and the constraints and opportunities they pose for attempts at change
- The array of interests supporting the status quo as compared with those that are potential sources of mobilization for change

Central to this latter category is the availability of skilled policy entrepreneurs.

Alternative Policy Images

Proposals to link education finance systems with student learning connect (and possibly alter) two existing policy monopolies: education finance reform and standards-based accountability. For the past thirty years, most education finance policies have been grounded in state constitutional principles, with courts and legislatures as the primary policy arenas, and political debates have centered on competing definitions of equity and their redistributional and cost implications. Aggrieved parties in this policy domain typically have used the courts as the initial venue in seeking redress, and since the U.S. Supreme Court's 1973 decision in Rodriguez, the politics of education finance have been confined to state policy arenas, although variants of the basic policy ideas have spread across the states.[9]

In contrast, policies focused on student learning and school performance have been premised on the need for externally imposed accountability on schools as public institutions, and typically such policies have originated in the executive and legislative branches as part of what has come to be known as the standards and accountability movement. These policies originally relied on hortatory strategies, motivating action through the promulgation of test-based information and a call to shared curricular values, but subsequently they relied on the imposition of rewards and sanctions based on test results.

Political debates focused initially on what should be taught and tested, and later on how performance is measured and test results used. Unlike education finance, wherein policies have been confined to state–local relationships, those focused on student learning and school performance include all three governmental levels, with the federal government's involvement based largely on license and capacity borrowed from the states.

Policy Survivability Criteria

Kingdon posited that for ideas to survive political scrutiny and remain on policy agendas, they need to meet criteria of technical feasibility, value acceptability, and tolerable cost. In education policy, technical feasibility includes such factors as the level of expertise required given practitioner capacity, the ease of administration and oversight, and, above all, whether there is sufficient evidence that a policy proposal can achieve its instrumental goals. These criteria often are related directly or indirectly to improved student learning, and information about them is typically the most problematic. Research and experimental evidence is often incomplete, context dependent, difficult to interpret, and even contentious. As a result, interpretations of data on what works, how it works, and how well it works often become political claims that spill over into issues of value acceptability.

Education finance reform and standards, along with accountability, have posed significant challenges for their supporters on all three dimensions, but they have been a more serious difficulty for education finance. Among the most visible technical challenges has been defining what constitutes an adequacy standard and then calculating the cost of meeting that standard for different types of students at different grade levels. Depending on which method is used, the per-pupil cost of meeting a state-specific adequacy standard can vary by more than 30 percent.[10]

Value acceptability has posed an even greater barrier to education finance reform. Beginning with its original justification in the notion of fiscal neutrality, finance reform has been grounded in a few generative concepts.[11] Fiscal neutrality derived its power from "conceptions of educational rights grounded not only in equal protection of individuals, but also in universal guarantees to maintain adequate provision of services for all citizens under compulsory education laws."[12] Yet over time, the equity-based concepts underlying finance reform have become symbolic representations in policy discourse, with multiple meanings that depend on how people use, interpret, and respond to these concepts.[13]

So, for example, on several occasions since 1991, 80 percent or more of those responding to the Gallup Poll of the Public's Attitudes Toward the Public Schools have said that the amount of money allocated to education in their state should be the same for all students "whether or not they live in wealthy or poor districts."[14] Within roughly the same period, however, Reed found in his analysis of public opinion data from Connecticut, Kentucky, New Jersey, and Tennessee that when respondents perceived finance reforms as a threat to local control of their districts, they typically reacted negatively and opposed them.[15] In these instances, the more powerful concept of local control clashed with notions of equity.

Value acceptability also has been problematic when education finance reform has been perceived as redistribution from wealthier districts and students to poorer ones, and when the question of tolerable cost has become an issue, especially when states have little or no fiscal slack.[16]

Technical feasibility has been a continuing challenge for the standards and accountability movement—particularly as it relates to the question of appropriate test use—and the challenge has grown with NCLB and the spread of high-stakes tests.[17] In its early days, opposition to the curricular values embodied in the standards and assessments of several states weakened the value acceptability of the movement.[18]

However, this reform strategy subsequently enjoyed broad support across the ideological spectrum, although the basis for such support varied. One reason state policy makers favor standards and accountability strategies is their seemingly low cost, especially as compared with education finance reforms. Even when these policies are accompanied by funding for student remediation or the professional preparation of teachers, they appear to be low cost because they are one of the most effective strategies available to policy makers to influence what happens in individual schools and classrooms.[19] Moreover, much of their cost is either hidden or shifted to the lowest levels of the system. Certainly, a major point of contention over NCLB has been calculating the true costs of meeting its requirements and identifying who should bear those costs. Yet tolerable cost issues have not been a major obstacle to advancing standards and accountability goals in the way they have for finance reform.

With regard to the survivability of educational performance as a policy focus, concerns about student learning and school performance have evolved into what has become known as test-based accountability, with the main tool for measuring performance a standardized test administered by states. Those tests are now more or less aligned with state curriculum and performance standards, and they serve as the sole or primary determinant of school quality.

Although some psychometricians and educational practitioners have been highly critical of the system and have proposed alternatives, the consensus seems to be that test-based accountability will continue to be the core idea defining policies related to student learning and school performance.[20] If that continues to be the case, it may limit strategies for connecting education finance schemes to performance criteria, because the link will have to be based primarily on standardized test results.

Alternative policy images will be constrained by the technical and political baggage associated with the two core policy ideas, but establishing a link between them also will generate its own set of feasibility issues. For example, central to the idea of adequacy is the notion that finance levels should be related to the costs associated with giving students sufficient opportunity to meet state standards. As a result, education finance and standards have been linked rhetorically. However, even in Kentucky, where new education finance and accountability systems were implemented simultaneously, the two were not directly linked, because accountability rewards and sanctions were allocated independently of the finance system.

The lack of working models makes feasibility issues especially salient, but it also may raise concerns about value acceptability. For example, linking finance and student learning creates dual policy targets: schools that are held accountable and students, who are the ultimate recipients of learning resources. Consequently, if the idea is to gain broad acceptance, proponents will need to demonstrate that there are feasible and effective strategies for sanctioning schools for nonperformance that do not also harm students. Imposing sanctions on schools has always raised the concern that in trying to motivate them to improve their performance, sanctions may cause students to suffer. The more that decision makers integrate rewards and punishments into the basic finance system, the greater the apprehension may be.

A major criterion for judging the technical feasibility and value acceptability of alternative policy images is the extent to which they provide a new understanding of policy problems and new ways of conceptualizing solutions. Inefficient resource use, chronic underachievement by U.S. public school students, and limited progress in breaking the nexus between student background characteristics and achievement are the major problems for which the proposed solution is to link finance systems and student learning. Proponents frame these problems as caused by multiple, interrelated causes:

- An intergovernmental patchwork of funds, programs, and allocation formulas
- Incomplete information about the actual costs of various educational interventions in various places and for various kinds of students
- A lack of political and administrative mechanisms that directly link authority for resource allocation and accountability for results
- Overregulation of educational processes, with little sensitivity to varying needs and circumstances across school contexts
- An absence of effective incentives for educators to improve student learning

Neither this problem definition nor the proposed solution is new. Reports by the National Research Council (NRC) and the Committee for Economic Development (CED) proposed an analogous change to the current education finance regime based on a similar analysis of problems.[21] Although it is difficult to discern exactly why these prior efforts have had a limited impact in shaping the policy agenda, there are several likely explanations.

The first is simply that it often takes time to challenge and replace a long-standing policy monopoly. New policy images gain traction as they are picked up by the media, become part of the discourse among relevant issue networks, serve as a basis for mobilizing individuals and groups discontented with the status quo, and ultimately lead to concrete proposals that reach various decision-making agendas. This process, especially in a fragmented policy system, can take a decade or more.[22]

It can take even longer for policy ideas that are operationally and ideologically complex, and that may be the second reason education finance directly linked to student learning has stalled as a policy alternative. In the NRC and CED reports it is clear that the proposed strategy is complex, because it touches on many complicated and controversial aspects of education policy and practice.

For example, to address problems of overregulation, it is proposed that greater decentralization occur in allocation and expenditure decisions that take into consideration individual student needs and ways to meet them in various local contexts. This solution raises the value-based question of how authority over publicly financed schooling should be allocated among governmental levels and between the public and private sectors, as well as the technical issue of how to hold schools accountable for educational outcomes without, in the process of measuring those outcomes, unduly constraining how they operate.

Similarly, both reports presented performance-based compensation for teachers as a mechanism for remedying the lack of effective incentives to improve performance. Although the CED report strongly endorsed this strategy, it and the NRC report, like reports by other commentators, acknowledged the checkered history of alternatives to the single salary schedule.[23] Some of the reasons for that history stem from design problems: inadequate and unstable funding, an inability to develop and administer valid performance evaluations, and compensation plans at odds with school cultures.[24]

State and local teacher union affiliates have varied in their support for and opposition to teacher salary plans that include pay-for-performance components or are linked to the acquisition of knowledge and skill. A few, such as the Denver Classroom Teachers Association, have been notable for their active support of an incentive-based compensation plan.[25] Nevertheless, even as the architects of recent plans have tried to address the shortcomings of earlier ones and the idea has gained greater currency, it remains technically challenging and politically controversial. The court challenge by the Florida Education Association to the Florida pay-for-performance program is only one instance.[26] Teacher incentive programs also are examples of a policy proposal having ambiguous evidence linking it to improved student learning; thus, much of the rationale for it is based on analogies from private sector and higher-education experience.

Linking education finance and student learning also is likely to raise the complex issue of how such policies should be funded. Theoretically, allocation and expenditure arrangements could be considered independently of the way revenue is raised, but they rarely are. So placing education finance policies on state agendas always runs the risk of reopening questions about how high tax burdens should be and who should bear them.

As discussed later in this chapter, if taxation issues become attached to proposals for new finance arrangements, a different set of interests will be mobilized than if the proposal is confined to educational and expenditure decisions. Because the current patchwork of programs has been identified as part of the problem, a comprehensive plan substantially replacing existing finance and accountability systems—or at least better integrating their components—would seem to be the preferred strategy. However, a desire to avoid the incrementalism or geological layers that have hindered past education reforms may need to be balanced against the dangers of overloading. As Kingdon noted, overloading a proposal can jeopardize enactment of those constituent items for which it would be reasonable to expect action if a more sequential or incremental agenda were used.[27]

Yet overloading might be inherent in a comprehensive plan that would necessarily touch on key aspects of education policy and practice. Furthermore, opponents can use overloading strategically to frustrate action by highlighting the complexity of a proposal, adding even more provisions in the hopes it will collapse of its own weight, or by using elements of the proposal to mobilize a range of groups to wage political battles on multiple fronts.

Strategic Calculations

However, strategic is the operative term, because none of these constraints is immutable. They can be overcome, or at least reduced, depending on how skillfully one frames and communicates policy problems and proposals. Each phase of promoting an alternative policy in various political arenas involves strategic calculations. As Stone argued, problem definition is more than the statement of a goal and the observed discrepancy between it and the status quo. "It is rather the strategic representation of situations . . . Dissatisfactions are not registered as degrees of change on some universal thermometer, but as claims in a political process. Representations of a problem are therefore constructed to win the most people to one's side and the most leverage over one's opponents."[28]

Problem definition is important strategically not only as a persuasive tool but also because the way a policy problem is defined shapes the proposed solution. Effective problem definitions use a variety of rhetorical tools, including symbols, numbers, metaphors, and stories.[29] They identify causes that not only point toward particular solutions and away from others but also assign responsibility (or blame) to specific individuals and institutions. An apt example is *A Nation At Risk*'s "rising tide of mediocrity," a metaphor that defined the diminished economic competitiveness of the United States as a problem of inadequate educational performance rather than flawed corporate investment policies or ineffective management strategies.[30]

Technical feasibility and value acceptability are criteria by which policy solutions are judged, but as with the problem definitions to which they are linked, it is essential to communicate their value along these dimensions. Rhetorical framing cannot replace the substance of a policy proposal or evidence about its potential effectiveness, but new policy ideas must combine empirical information with emotional appeals if they are to engage policy makers and the public. Education researchers often are uncomfortable with reducing sophisticated policy proposals to slogans, but experience has shown that strategy to be successful.

Examples include "equal funding for equal tax effort," "all children can learn to high standards," and "parental choice." These examples have four characteristics in common: (1) they embody a theory that assumes a positive relationship between a particular policy intervention and improved educational outcomes; (2) they are grounded in an evidentiary base, although not necessarily a strong or unambiguous one; (3) even though they may have redistributional implications, the frame is universal and inclusive of all students and communities; and (4) they use simple, everyday language.

The power of an alternative policy idea to engage policy makers and their constituents is key to fundamental change.[31] It is difficult to judge the receptivity of current political conditions to the linking of education finance systems with student learning and school performance, because the answer depends on the content of specific proposals. Nevertheless, theories of policy change and the course of past education reforms suggest that research-based evidence about likely effectiveness and technical feasibility is a necessary, but not sufficient, condition for placement of the issue on national and state policy agendas. The sufficient conditions are the extent to which the policy problem and its proposed solution resonate with widely accepted values, are framed so as to mobilize supporters and minimize opposition, and can be communicated simply and concretely.

Institutions and Policy Change

A major reason policy ideas can endure, become monopolies, and are resistant to change is that they are embedded in institutional arrangements that may persist even after new ideas emerge and formal policies change. The political science research literature offers two complementary, though somewhat different, explanations for this condition—one adapted from historical analysis, and one from economics.

Historical institutionalists have used the concept of path dependence to explain how and why social policies can become entrenched and difficult to alter. In its simplest form, path dependence refers to the process by which policy choices create institutional arrangements that make it costly to reverse or change them.[32] Large consequences may result from relatively small or contingent events, but after particular courses of action are introduced, it may be virtually impossible to reverse them.[33] Those who examine policy stability and change from this perspective also stress the importance of timing and sequence, and they distinguish formative moments in policy development from periods that reinforce the status quo.

The economics-based explanation is derived from Moe's theory of the politics of structural choice.[34] Moe's initial premise is that in a democracy all interests must cope with political uncertainty: they will not always be in the political majority, and when other interests come to dominate, opponents may significantly change or reverse their policies.

One way for current majorities to lock in their legislative victories and protect them from future tampering is through the structures by which policies are implemented and administered. Consequently, the dominant coalition attempts to ensure that those structures embody a set of rules governing institutional behavior—decision-making criteria, allocation rules, personnel evaluation standards—that insulates the agency from legislative oversight and alteration of its policies (for example, by placing a greater emphasis on professionalism than is technically justified because professionals resist political interference). However, to the extent that a dominant coalition must engage in political compromise with its opponents, the resulting administrative structure also may include elements that will make those structures vulnerable when majorities change.

These two theories are consistent with each other, and they provide an elaboration of Baumgartner and Jones's analysis of policy monopolies. In the case of merging education finance and student learning, they point to the importance of determining the degree to which the current policy monopoly of education finance systems unconnected to education accountability arrangements is institutionalized. However, there is a prior, related question that should be considered: how is the broader institutional context of education policy making likely to affect change efforts? Two aspects are especially relevant: the general fragmentation of education policy in the United States, and the tension between state authority and localism that has shaped education finance policy since 1980.

Education policy analysts have long noted that the most distinctive institutional characteristic of U.S. public education is its fragmentation. Not only do multiple levels of government share authority over public education and responsibility for its funding, but also power is fragmented among institutions within each level. This fragmentation has resulted in less-coherent policy, but it also has increased access to the policy process, giving interests multiple entry points and the ability to shop for the venue likely to give them the greatest advantage.

Advocates for education finance reform, along with those pursuing desegregation and the education of students with disabilities, have been the most successful in using the courts as an initial point of access into the policy system. Evans and his colleagues identified the pivotal role of the courts in their analysis of school district revenues, expenditures, and enrollments using Census of Government School System Finance data between 1972 and 1992.[35] They found that court-ordered reforms had led to an increase in the states' share of education revenues and a significant redistribution of resources to the poorest districts, but in states where reform was attempted without successful litigation, neither the overall level of education revenues nor their distribution changed. Clearly, reliance on the courts can be a long, contentious process, as the New Jersey and Texas education finance cases illustrate.

Having to pursue policy change through several venues also may affect the choice of policy ideas and the ways they are framed as images. As Baumgartner and Jones noted, "Some types of images may be well accepted in one venue, but considered inappropriate when raised in another institutional arena. Norms of compromise, fair shares, and reciprocity common in the legislative arena have little legitimacy in the courts, for example."[36]

However, tension between state authority and institutional norms of localism may make reliance on the courts inevitable if education finance reform involves redistribution. Reed addressed the question of why the egalitarian assumptions underlying decisions in education finance lawsuits are often diminished when state legislatures fashion remedies in response to judicial mandates. He identified the institutional configuration "by which resources are delivered to children according to a regime of property taxes, home values, and local control of revenues" as the source of an explanation.[37]

Based on his analysis of public opinion data from four states, Reed concluded that even though there has been a trend away from local control, its persistence as a defining characteristic of the U.S. educational system shapes public attitudes toward educational opportunity, particularly opposition to education finance reform viewed as a threat to localism. In emphasizing the institutional design of public education, Reed detailed how the local governance of municipalities and school districts and local control of property tax receipts "implicitly structure our beliefs about the proper way to organize education, and indirectly, they inform a good deal of our democratic politics surrounding education."[38]

Reed's analysis also indicated that the link between the primacy of local control and public attitudes influences the behavior of state legislatures. These political arenas have traditionally reinforced geographical inequalities by preserving local control over a significant proportion of education funding. However, in their education finance rulings, state supreme courts threaten to disrupt this equilibrium by requiring redistributive remedies.

It is this constellation of rules, norms, and structures that explains why the legislative crafting of education finance remedies is often prolonged, and why the primacy of local control over local resources persists even as state courts have moved to change distributional rules and make them more equitable. Basically, Reed wrote, "the geographic nature of property taxes and home rule intersects with the geographic nature of state electoral representation, yielding a political logic that can produce intense opposition to court decisions that seek the reform of school financing."[39]

If theory and experience are reliable guides, then the policy system's fragmentation, by affording multiple points of access and leverage, presents opportunities for those who advance new approaches to education finance. However, localistic norms and interests work against strategies involving redistribution. For education finance policy, localism is the institutional characteristic that most approximates Moe's politics of structural choice: communities advantaged under the status quo typically seek to maintain the norms and allocation rules that preserve their advantage even in the face of policies challenging it. Consequently, if redistribution is an actual, or even a perceived, component of proposed alternatives, the courts are likely to be a necessary venue for policy making.

Barring an unforeseeable change at the federal level, alternatives to current finance systems also will have to be pursued on a state-by-state basis. However, given rapid diffusion rates of educational innovations across states over the past two decades, this feature of the federalist system is no longer the obstacle it once was.

Because proposals that would merge education finance and student learning connect two existing policy monopolies, each needs to be considered separately when one assesses the degree of institutionalization. Because of differences in education finance arrangements across states, the extent of institutionalization varies. However, several characteristics apply to a majority of states, though not all, and they seem to be well institutionalized: a mix of state and local funding, including some categorical or targeted state funding; a portion of the funding weighted for student groups judged more expensive to educate; allocation formulas not directly linked to either actual costs or school performance; and grounding in state constitutional principles.[40] But as Education Week reported in 2005, "Public school finance systems are in flux."[41]

That fluctuation is caused in part by the fact that more than 70 percent of the states have faced court challenges to their finance systems since 2000 or are currently facing one.[42] Equally important, however, is a shift in the basis on which plaintiffs are challenging these systems, relying more on state constitutions' education clauses than on pure equal protection arguments.[43] These lawsuits have served as focusing events, keeping education finance on state policy agendas and creating the potential that the path dependence developed over the past three decades can be diverted in a different direction. As a result, the shift from equity to adequacy criteria has begun to weaken the institutional norms and rules that have defined education finance systems, rendering the policy monopoly vulnerable to change.

Systems to promote accountability for student learning have some elements that are well institutionalized and would be difficult to change, whereas other, less entrenched elements likely could be modified. The core policy idea of accountability through the use of an externally imposed assessment has been in place at the state level since the 1980s. As a result, some elements are well institutionalized: the regular administration of standardized tests in several subjects and grade levels, the public reporting of test scores, and, more recently, the alignment of those tests with state-defined academic content standards.

Even the notion of standards and accountability at the federal level has had wide currency since the 1990s and has been integrated into federal categorical programs, giving federal policy greater coherence and making it more difficult to change than when there were more disparate, smaller programs.[44] On the other hand, elements of NCLB, such as Adequate Yearly Progress (AYP) and the required testing of all students every year, are not yet well institutionalized.[45]

At the classroom level, a variety of studies has found that teachers modify their instruction in response to state assessments.[46] However, the extent of change has been limited, typically involving shifts in classroom activities (for example, devoting more instructional time to tested subjects and aligning curricular content with state standards) rather than in ways students are taught conceptual understanding of subject matter.

With regard to the classroom, then, test-based accountability has led to significant changes and has produced a greater effect than top-down policy usually induces in education. Nevertheless, these changes are not yet deeply embedded in school and classroom practice. So within a system that measures performance in part or in whole by standardized tests, it would be relatively easy to make changes at the margin to influence, for example, how teachers spend their instructional time.

Once again, judgments about the likelihood that existing policy monopolies can be replaced depend on the nature of the alternative policy image. Whether it involves significant redistribution, whether the courts are involved, and how finance and performance would be linked—all are critical. Still, enough elements of current systems are either in flux or are not deeply embedded to suggest that in a number of states the institutional context offers, on balance, more opportunities than constraints. To take advantage of these opportunities, however, requires political skill in mobilizing those interests that are amenable to change and countering the array of interests supporting the status quo.

The Interests

In assessing the prospects for major policy change, one needs to identify groups dissatisfied with the status quo. These groups also must be open to persuasion that the benefits of a new approach to education finance are greater than those of the current system and outweigh the costs of change, and they must be able to be mobilized to support the alternative. As Baumgartner and Jones indicated, the process of mobilization—or in Kingdon's model, linking the problem, proposal, and politics streams to create an open policy window—typically requires the active involvement and skill of one or more policy entrepreneurs.[47]

Although mobilization of supporters is critical, equally important is the need to identify potential sources of opposition and define strategies for weakening or neutralizing their attempts at countermobilization. In some cases, that might mean offering concessions in exchange for either supporting or promising not to oppose the new initiative.

For example, in Kentucky, North Carolina, and several other states, the teacher unions agreed not to oppose new accountability measures in the early 1990s as a quid pro quo for the state making more money available for teacher salaries. In other instances, supporters have used resources such as leverage provided by a favorable judicial decision, public opinion, or the ability to link a proposal for change in one state to a national movement; in effect, these supporters borrow strength or legitimacy from other jurisdictions.

Four factors are immediately obvious in assessing the interest environment for proposals to link finance and student learning.

A Crowded Environment

The first factor is that the interest environment is dense, consisting of a wide range of individuals and groups. If one includes all those who have a stake in a state's education finance or accountability systems, the list is long: the governor, state legislators, teacher unions, business organizations, plaintiffs' groups and other organizations representing students having inadequate opportunities to learn, taxpayer organizations, local school board and administrator associations, parent groups, publishers of tests and instructional materials, private sector providers of supplemental services, and, in some states, national or grassroots organizations representing cultural conservatives.

Variation in Stakeholder Views

Second, the position taken by a particular type of group and the extent to which it is mobilized can vary from state to state, depending on the nature of the proposal and state-specific historical and political factors. For example, Carr and Fuhrman contrasted the outcome of attempts at finance and broader school reform in Kentucky and Alabama, states located in the same region faced with similar judicial decisions during roughly the same time period.[48] The Kentucky Education Association (KEA) was not an active participant in supporting the Kentucky Education Reform Act (KERA), but it accepted KERA, with its strict accountability provisions, in exchange for the new resources it would pump into the system. Culturally conservative groups such as the Eagle Forum never opposed the finance provisions related to KERA and expressed opposition only to its curricular standards and accountability provisions several years into KERA's implementation.[49]

In contrast, the Alabama Education Association (AEA) opposed the Alabama First initiative, largely because AEA's candidate for governor needed to distance himself from the reform proposal of his opponent, the sitting governor. Conservative groups, such as the Eagle Forum and the Christian Coalition, framed Alabama First as social engineering and opposed it and its financing early on.[50] The timing of the conservative groups' opposition in the two states may have differed because Alabama First was under consideration in 1994, four years after KERA, at the height of the cultural conservative movement's nationwide focus on schools.

Different Policy Arenas

A third factor is that the types of groups participating in education finance court cases often differ from those that become engaged after the issue moves into the legislative arena. The primary reason is institutional, with the two arenas having different norms and rules of decision making. Plaintiffs' groups representing low-wealth districts or low-income students can prevail in court because their cases are grounded in constitutional principles, and decisions typically lack allocation rules detailed enough to make clear either the cost or the extent of redistribution. However, once the issue is in the legislative arena, broad-based coalitions are needed to demonstrate to policy makers that influential interests and their constituents will not punish them if they make significant changes in the way schools are financed.

When they are effective, groups composed of policy elites and representatives of major interest groups, such as the Prichard Committee in Kentucky, can act as policy entrepreneurs, proposing alternative policy visions and building support coalitions.[51] Although one or more groups with broad-based membership may be needed for reforms to be enacted, they do not necessarily ensure success if opposition groups are strong and represent diverse interests and ideology. This situation characterized the effort in Alabama, where the A+ Coalition for Better Education, a group similar to the Prichard Committee, could not overcome a formidable array of opponents, including the AEA, culturally conservative and antitax groups, and suburbanites afraid that their schools would suffer under the reform plan.[52]

Another factor related to moving from judicial to legislative venues is public opinion. As Reed demonstrated, it can serve as a brake on what legislators are willing to enact in response to court rulings.[53] Like the behavior of interest groups, public opinion needs to be examined within the context of individual states and specific proposals. However, national data provide clues about the public's attitudes that groups advocating for change can consider in developing strategies. One national survey conducted in 2004 found that fewer than half the respondents reported understanding very or fairly well how schools are funded and the roles various levels of government play in funding.[54] Nevertheless, 42 percent of those in the same sample believed that a great deal or quite a bit of money is wasted in education, and an additional 34 percent said that a fair amount is wasted.

According to the 2001 Phi Delta Kappa/Gallup Poll, a majority of those with no school-aged children (59 percent) and a greater proportion of public school parents (65 percent) believed the quality of education provided by the public schools in their state differed a great deal or quite a lot from district to district.[55] A bare majority of parents and the public (52 percent) in the 2003 PDK/Gallup Poll supported their state providing equal funding per student, as compared with 45 percent who thought that the amount of funding should be varied to meet each student's educational needs.[56]

Hart and Teeter asked several questions that explicitly attempted to tap public attitudes about equity versus adequacy funding models and the extent of the state role.[57] Fewer than half (40 percent) of respondents in the sample felt that the state should "equalize the amount of money spent per student so schools in poorer areas have as many resources as wealthy ones," and 37 percent (within the margin of error) believed that the state should "direct money where it is needed most, so students with special needs or in poorly performing schools get adequate attention." Some 20 percent of the sample felt that the "state shouldn't make efforts to direct school funding, and [should] leave these decisions to local districts."

Although whites and African Americans were evenly divided, Hispanics overwhelmingly (65 percent) preferred a system in which funding is directed where it is needed most over one that guarantees equal funding. Democrats disproportionately (55 percent) preferred the adequacy model, and the same proportion of Republicans preferred the equity model. Hart and Teeter also found almost even divisions in their sample between those who preferred increased state funding of schools (50 percent) as compared with those who preferred that schools be funded with local taxes (44 percent).[58]

These data suggest that fiscal accountability is a concern and that even though the public recognizes quality differences between districts, it is divided about moving away from an allocation system based on equal shares. In their report, Hart and Teeter argued that the public's closely divided opinions mean they provide little guidance to decision makers about policy direction. That very well may be the case and may make it difficult to move on finance-related issues, because policy makers fear that, in choosing one alternative over another, they will incur the disapproval of a large segment of the public.

However, closely divided opinion might make it easier for interest groups to influence a majority of the public in support of their position, because they need change the minds of only a small segment. Furthermore, self-reports of low knowledge levels among the public suggest that informational campaigns could be effective in reshaping public opinion, particularly if the alternative policy image were framed as a way to combat perceived wasteful spending.

Because the alternative policy image under consideration involves linking finance systems to student learning, public opinion data on attitudes toward test-based accountability also are relevant. A variety of poll data indicated strong support for standardized testing and its high-stakes uses, with the public also seeming to acknowledge its shortcomings and potential consequences.[59]

The shape of public opinion has changed somewhat since the advent of NCLB. The overwhelming majority (69 percent) of those questioned in the 2006 PDK/Gallup survey believed that the performance of students on a single statewide test does not provide a fair picture of whether or not the school needs improvement.[60] However, despite an acknowledgement of the limits of standardized testing, the majority of parents of public school students indicated that the emphasis on achievement testing in their community was either about right (37 percent) or not enough (17 percent).[61] In addition, more than 60 percent of parents and those without school-age children favored requiring that all students pass an exam to graduate from high school, and support for that particular use of high-stakes tests has been stable for almost thirty years.[62] Although the question was not asked in 2006, in the 2005 PDK/Gallup poll, half of those surveyed supported having one measurement of a teacher's and a principal's quality be their students' performance on standardized tests.[63]

As with education funding, a significant proportion of the public reported that it knows little about specific accountability policies. For example, even four years after NCLB's enactment, less than half of public school parents (49 percent) and only 42 percent of those without children in school reported in the 2006 PDK/Gallup Poll that they know a great deal or a fair amount about NCLB.[64] The public also showed ambivalence about tests as instruments of accountability, but it still supported their use even for purposes whose validity and fairness have been called into serious question— for example, the continuing support for high school exit exams. As they do for education finance, survey items related to effective use of resources and accountability for results seem to elicit strong and stable response patterns over time on various surveys. Consequently, these concerns may provide yet another basis for influencing public opinion in support of strategies linking resources and student learning.

Importance of National Organizations
A fourth factor defining the interest environment is the continued prominence of national organizations. Since the 1980s, they have functioned as transmission mechanisms for disseminating new ideas to their state and local affiliates and communicating information about operational models. These groups include interest-based ones such as those in the intergovernmental lobby (for example, the National Governors Association, the National Conference of State Legislatures, and the Council of Chief State School Officers), the National Business Roundtable, the American Federation of Teachers (AFT), and the National Education Association (NEA), as well as ideological groups such as the Eagle Forum and the American Civil Liberties Union.

Most of these organizations operate as loose confederations. Consequently, as evidenced by the varying positions of AFT and NEA state affiliates, their state and local counterparts may ignore or reject policy ideas promoted by the national organizations. Nevertheless, as the rapid spread of ideas about how to design standards and accountability, school choice, finance, and teacher policies has demonstrated, these organizations have become critical conduits for new ideas and for the political rationales and operational details that facilitate placement on state policy agendas.

The Interest Environment and Policy Change

What does the interest environment suggest about the possibility of change? Are there interests outside the current policy monopoly that appear open to mobilization to support new conceptions of education finance and student learning? Unfortunately, the answer is less straightforward than if the alternative were a completely different policy image rather than a reconfiguration and linking of two existing ones.

Perhaps the best way to answer the question is to consider the possibility of policy entrepreneurs persuading various interests that a new configuration will either reinforce those policies they most care about or will mitigate the negative effects of policies to which they are opposed. So, for example, plaintiffs' groups were effective in the judicial arena with early adequacy-based arguments. Other groups that are focused on the educational needs of low-income students, such as the Education Trust, have emphasized accountability policies. These two types of groups work on behalf of constituents who have not been well served by the dominant policy monopoly, but each has tended to emphasize only one policy instrument. Yet, depending on the details of specific policies, they might be persuaded that a strategy linking finance and student learning would give them additional tools and greater leverage to accomplish their existing goals more effectively.[65]

In contrast, because classroom teachers are bearing most of the burden of NCLB, organizations representing them might be convinced that a linked system would mitigate the effects of the current accountability regime. Certainly the prospect of pay for performance could be a major, though not insurmountable, obstacle to obtaining their active support. However, teachers might see the idea of funding tied to the actual costs of educating different types of students and resources targeted directly to instructional needs as a way to make the current system more professionally enabling and less burdensome.

Similar arguments could be made for local school boards and school administrators, who often feel frustrated and marginalized under the current system. For business groups, the framing of an alternative policy image would be a way to reinforce and refine the accountability and instructional support strategies many of them support as a means to ensure a high-quality workforce and continued economic competitiveness. But, again, the success of that framing would depend on the details of specific proposals and their implications for who pays and in what form.

Theories of policy change have proved useful in identifying the major determinants of change and the process by which fundamental policy shifts occur. However, because policies depend on context, change models are limited in their generalizability. They can highlight categories of variables and processes that are significant, identify a few patterns that are broadly applicable across policy domains and contexts, and provide a systematic approach for analyzing emerging policy issues. The discussion thus far has drawn on those theories as a way to categorize and assess the political and ideational factors likely to constitute opportunities and constraints in efforts to link education finance systems with student learning.

In the following section, two empirical cases are examined to augment this grounded speculation based on theories of policy change. Like the theory-based analysis, these cases suggest broad implications, but their applicability to other situations is limited by the specific nature of the policies, the time period, and the political culture of the institutional venues in which they were enacted.

POLITICAL CONDITIONS FOR POLICY CHANGE: IMPLICATIONS FROM PAST CASES

The first case, the comprehensive education reform legislation enacted in Kentucky in 1990, has assumed almost iconic status because of its scope. Yet now, twenty years after the process began, it is clear that Kentucky's experience is an anomaly unmatched in any other state. Nevertheless, outliers often can illustrate more starkly than modal cases the factors that best explain policy success or failure, and the Kentucky case comes closest in substantive policy details to what might be involved in linking finance and accountability strategies. In this case, extant research has sought to explain success in policy enactment and the ease with which the issue moved from the legislative to the judicial arena.

The second case comes from research on how another major education reform—school choice—has been placed successfully on state policy agendas. This research is included because it highlights the central role of policy entrepreneurs.

Education Reform in Kentucky

The enactment of KERA is consistent with Kingdon's model. A policy window opened when a solution was linked to a set of problems and both were joined to favorable political conditions.[66] Three related factors dominated the problem stream in Kentucky: the state's chronically low educational achievement, its persistent regional inequities, and the need for greater economic development.

The state's problem stream even included a focusing event: the 1987 opening of a Toyota manufacturing plant in Georgetown, Kentucky. The plant's arrival signaled the state's success in attracting new industries, but the high proportion of job applicants who were not high school graduates and were otherwise unqualified focused a spotlight on the state's educational shortcomings. It also revealed the connection between low levels of educational attainment and the need for greater economic development.

Those filling the proposal stream in Kentucky borrowed ideas and models from the national standards movement. In 1988, Governor Wallace Wilkinson sought to address the state's persistently low educational achievement by proposing a series of reforms based on a set of student standards, an alternative assessment to measure progress on those standards, cash awards for teachers and schools that showed improvement on test scores and attendance, and expanded instructional autonomy for individual schools. However, legislators balked at the $75 million annual price tag; and, based on the state's recent unsuccessful experience with standardized testing, they also questioned whether an appropriate test could be developed to measure student performance. Consequently, Wilkinson's proposals stalled in the legislature.

During the 1988 legislative session, the governor's initiative was passed by the state senate, but the legislation never got out of committee in the House. The governor then created a twelve-member Council on School Performance Standards to determine which skills and knowledge Kentucky students were to master and how best to measure that learning. The council had completed about two-thirds of its work, and Wilkinson was hoping to call the legislature into a special session in August to try again to deal with education reform, when a major state supreme court decision was announced in June 1989.

This decision provided an opportunity that significantly changed the nature of the political stream and necessitated an even broader reform than Wilkinson had proposed. In *Rose v. Council for Better Education*, the Kentucky Supreme Court directly addressed the major educational problems facing the state.[67] It agreed with the trial court that each child in the state was entitled to an education that provided seven specific types of skills and knowledge, including oral and written communication skills; knowledge of economic, social, and political systems; grounding in the arts; and sufficient levels of academic or vocational skills "to compete favorably with their counterparts in surrounding states, in academics or the job market."[68]

The court also ruled that the maintenance and funding of common schools in Kentucky are the sole responsibility of the General Assembly (the state legislature), that common schools should be available and free to all Kentucky children, that they should be substantially uniform throughout the state, and that common schools should "provide equal educational opportunity to all Kentucky children, regardless of place of residence or economic circumstance."[69]

The governor and his staff had expected the supreme court decision "to be purely fiscal." But its broader scope gave Wilkinson "an unexpected vehicle." According to one of the governor's aides, "The court decision came down, and we had just come out with our six goals. The decision had seven—it was made for us! The Court said that the constitutional solution had to be performance-based. So the court order broke the deadlock with the General Assembly."[70]

In the case of Kentucky, then, reform legislation was the result of a confluence of clearly articulated problems, the expansion of an existing policy proposal, and a unique set of political circumstances that provided the opportunity for a marked departure from past policies. Nevertheless, despite its uniqueness, the Kentucky case suggests three major implications that can inform other attempts at fundamental change in state education policy.[71]

First, observers often comment on the speed with which Kentucky moved from the supreme court decision in 1989 to the legislative enactment of KERA in April 1990. But this observation misses the critical point that there had been a softening up of the agenda for six years prior to KERA; during that time, policy entrepreneurs had defined the problem, had refined the content of the proposal stream, and had built public support.

For example, during the 1980s, the Prichard Committee, acting as a policy entrepreneur, conducted an extensive public information campaign to create strong grassroots support for reform and for the tax increases necessary to fund it. Its efforts included an electronic forum that drew some twenty thousand participants across the state and, through group study and deliberation, the publication of a report articulating a vision of schooling and outlining proposals to advance that vision—a report that foreshadowed the KERA reforms.[72]

Consequently, the public had been primed to understand the causal connection between better public education and the economic development needed to stem out-migration and continued rural poverty.[73] Policy elites, such as those in the legislature and governor's office, also had time to draw on in-state and expert resources outside Kentucky and to create a proposal for which they could claim ownership.[74]

A second implication from the Kentucky case relates to the nature of the decision in Rose and the distinct advantage of a strong link between judicial and political mobilization. Although the state supreme court's decision articulated a clear vision of common schooling and specified the elements of a constitutionally adequate education, it did not micromanage the remedy stage, as courts in other states such as Texas have done.[75] The Kentucky court mandated that the General Assembly design a new system and then removed itself from the process.

A major reason there was no need to micromanage is that in the Kentucky case, "legal and political mobilization were mutually reinforcing, converging toward a particular vision of educational reforms."[76] That vision was the nineteenth-century common school philosophy reflected in Rose and updated to the late twentieth century in KERA.

This consistency between the two bases of mobilization is explained in part by Kentucky's populist political culture. But the more instrumental reason is that the two primary policy entrepreneurs—the Council for Better Education and the Prichard Committee—although working separately in different arenas, shared a philosophy of schooling. As the group representing the plaintiffs, the Council for Better Education reinforced its common school ideology by making clear from the beginning that it was "anti-Robin Hood," meaning that given the state's low spending for education, council members felt it would be morally wrong to take resources away from districts. Consequently, they advocated an infusion of new funding and leveling-up, and not redistribution of existing resources. Council members approached wealthier districts to reassure them of their intentions, and this ethical stance had the strategic benefit of avoiding much of the localism that has plagued reformers in other states.[77]

The third implication of the Kentucky case is by now quite obvious: the critical role of policy entrepreneurs. The Prichard Committee's work was crucial to all three streams, and the Council for Better Education's lawsuit led to Rose, the focusing event that upset the existing policy monopoly and broke the legislative stalemate. These in-state entrepreneurs were assisted by academics and reformers outside Kentucky, who offered new ideas about curriculum, testing, teaching, and school governance policies that had been incorporated into the systemic reform and standards and accountability movements.

Elected officials in Kentucky also acted as policy entrepreneurs. They were in the best position to shape the political conditions for KERA's passage, but in developing the legislation they relied on others for feasible and potentially effective policy solutions.

Policy Entrepreneurs and School Choice

In promoting policy innovations, policy entrepreneurs typically tap in to issue networks that allow them to communicate their ideas to those with shared interests and to be linked by formal and informal contacts.[78] A good example of this process is the role of policy entrepreneurs and issue networks in the diffusion of ideas about school choice. Drawing on a survey of state education policy experts, Mintrom found that policy entrepreneurs were identified as advocates of school choice in twenty-six states.[79] Then, using event history analysis models of the diffusion of school choice ideas across the United States, Mintrom and Vergari found that greater involvement in policy networks significantly increased the likelihood that policy entrepreneurs achieved their legislative goals.[80]

However, the explanatory variables for getting the school choice issue on a state's legislative agenda differed from those explaining whether or not a choice policy was subsequently enacted. The researchers found that in getting the choice issue on the agenda, policy entrepreneurs used both interstate (or external) policy networks and internal, in-state networks consisting of individuals with ties to members of the local policy making community. The external networks served as sources for new ideas, and the internal networks provided relevant contacts and a source of information about how best to present proposals to garner serious attention. However, once the issue was on the agenda, the factors that predicted legislative approval were different. At the approval stage, not only was the presence of an internal network significant, but also approval was more likely if the teacher union did not strongly oppose the policy and student test scores had declined, signaling a need for policy change.

This example illustrates the critical role of policy entrepreneurs and issue networks in spreading new ideas and in altering established policy monopolies, but it also shows how ideas and interests intersect. In this case, the strength of union opposition had no effect on the likelihood of legislative consideration of school choice, but such opposition reduced the chances for legislative approval. In essence, the influence of a critical group whose interests could be threatened by school choice was not a significant factor in determining whether this new idea was seriously considered, but the group's position did make a difference in whether it was transformed into policy.

Drawing on case studies of policy entrepreneurs as well as his quantitative data, Mintrom also identified six "keys to policy entrepreneurship."[81]

- Creativity and insight: Policy entrepreneurs should be able to recognize how proposing particular policy innovations can alter the nature of policy debates. In the case of school choice, they took the idea of breaking the relationship between family residential location and the schools to which they can send their children, transforming it into a compelling policy proposal. However, because their proposal would likely put them at odds with those who benefit from the status quo, creativity was also needed in framing the proposal so that it appeared to be an appropriate solution to a current problem.
- Social perceptiveness: Framing a policy proposal so that it appeals to others requires understanding how they view certain social conditions and then anticipating how they are likely to react to proposals for change. Mintrom argued, "Probably the only sound way to develop social perceptiveness is to actually spend a lot of time talking with and listening to people from a range of backgrounds."[82]
- Social and political dexterity: Policy entrepreneurs were able to interact in a variety of social and political settings. According to Mintrom, they were "inveterate networkers."[83] They were in constant contact with their counterparts in other states to learn what the latter had done to introduce choice, but they also were actively involved in a variety of in-state networks. Those activities were aimed not only at networking among natural allies but also at gaining a sense of opponents' views. Understanding opponents' arguments and learning effective ways to counter them required social perceptiveness, because entrepreneurs had to listen carefully to criticisms of their proposals and to understand the opposing views well enough to use them in modifying and strengthening the formulations of their ideas.
- Persuasiveness: Policy entrepreneurs should be able to argue persuasively, and often that means using different arguments for different groups while keeping their basic idea and overall story consistent.
- Strategic sense: Policy entrepreneurs are essentially building coalitions in favor of their policy idea, and in doing so they need to discern what type of coalition will best support their pursuit of policy change. Often these decisions require judging the advantages of coalitions composed primarily of political and economic elites as compared with ones that also include or are essentially grassroots mobilizations. A related decision involves a strategic calculation about how large and broad-based the

coalition must be to succeed, because that assessment has implications for the concessions that are required to get a proposal enacted.

- Leadership by example: Mintrom found in the case of school choice that it was important that policy entrepreneurs translate their ideas into action. They needed to demonstrate that their visions of the future were believable and feasible and that they had a strong personal commitment to the idea. In some cases, such commitment meant establishing a private voucher program or starting a charter school.[84]

Mintrom concluded, "Other things being equal, policy entrepreneurs who exhibit the qualities discussed here are more likely to achieve success than those who do not."[85] But he noted that policy entrepreneurs are embedded in particular social contexts. Consequently, to understand why some succeed and others fail, "we need to look both at the broader conditions they faced and the individual actions that they engaged in."[86]

This in-depth analysis of policy entrepreneurs is consistent with the general theories of Kingdon and of Baumgartner and Jones, but it provides a much richer sense of the type of human agency required for major policy change, particularly in the face of well-entrenched institutional norms and rules. For example, in applying Kingdon's metaphor of the policy window, Mintrom found that policy entrepreneurs must do more than merely be prepared to move quickly when a window opens or an opportunity for action becomes available; they must be able to open windows and to create opportunities.

Mintrom's analysis also demonstrated the importance of Baumgartner and Jones's concept of venue shopping and the diffusion of policy ideas across arenas. In the case of school choice, entrepreneurs whose proposals were stalled or thwarted in the legislative arena could move (or threaten to move) to the ballot initiative arena. Because school choice is the other major new education policy idea, in addition to standards and accountability, that has emerged on state policy agendas over the past two decades, the experience of its policy entrepreneurs seems especially relevant to attempts to alter education finance systems.

CONCLUSIONS

To some extent, the political conditions for major policy change are straightforward: an engaging and feasible idea framed as a solution to a pressing problem, skilled policy entrepreneurs willing to invest resources in advancing that idea, interests dissatisfied with the status quo and able to be mobilized, weak or neutralized opposition, multiple points of access into decision-making arenas, administrative institutions vulnerable to change, and sufficient time for agenda-setting and change processes to work.

Both theory and numerous empirical analyses suggest that although these factors are not always sufficient for change to occur, they are usually necessary. Because they have been found to be broadly applicable to a range of policy domains over time, they provide a valid framework for systematically assessing the likelihood of successful agenda setting and enactment of a given policy proposal.

But these generic conditions and the relationships among them as specified in models of policy change are only a starting point for such analyses. They identify categories of significant variables, but assessing the status of each factor requires in-depth, context-specific information. For example, an idea's feasibility can be judged only in terms of the resources available in a particular jurisdiction. Whether it is framed as a solution to a pressing problem will depend on how it is perceived by key audiences in that jurisdiction.

Consequently, this chapter provides only a starting point for assessing how amenable current conditions are to new education finance arrangements. Not only does that judgment depend on specific proposals for linking funding and student learning, but it also requires detailed knowledge of current political conditions in states where those proposals would be advanced, because any change will depend on interactions between policy proposals and politics. So at this point, all would-be reformers have is a good sense of the factors that are likely to be important, along with some clues about points of leverage for altering the status quo. Although those points of leverage—whether judicial decisions or trends in public opinion—are only possibilities, they suggest that if used skillfully, they hold significant opportunities for change.

11

Choosing the Smart-Money Path to Education Finance Innovation

Jacob E. Adams, Jr.

At one point in the 1995 Ron Howard movie Apollo 13, Jim Lovell (Tom Hanks), soon-to-be commander of that ill-fated yet epic voyage, turns to his wife, Marilyn (Kathleen Quinlin), and says, "From now on we live in a world where man has walked on the moon. It's not a miracle; we just decided to go."[1] History affirms both the drama of that decision and the enormous technical, economic, and political accomplishments that transformed it into footprints on the lunar surface.[2] According to President Kennedy, that success would serve the nation's ambitions in science and industry, peace and security, and its obligations to "ourselves and others."[3]

But those successes lay ahead. Even as the president announced the choice to go to the moon, he acknowledged, "This is in some measure an act of faith and vision." And indeed, as he spoke those words, the knowledge, techniques, and tools that would get a crew safely to the moon and back had not been invented, the investment costs were unknown, and the individuals who would make it all happen could only guess at the skills they might need. Yet the context made the effort worthy, and the nation succeeded.

Fast-forward forty years, when U.S. officials set the nation on another "untried mission": to educate all students to meet standards. The No Child Left Behind Act of 2001 codified this ambition.[4] That act of public policy making, controversies notwithstanding, committed the United States to a goal and backed it with the authority of the state.[5] Moreover, it created an expectation that the advantages inherent in this standard of public accomplishment would accrue to all students and, by extension, to the communities in which they live and work. Unlike the space race, however, this endeavor has yet to see elected officials make the investments, develop the technologies, or organize the capacities needed to accomplish this goal, and the nation has not succeeded.

Smart Money makes the case that this failure does not stem from a lack of effort; the United States has seen seemingly constant and varied education policy making for nearly thirty years.[6] Rather, the cause of this failure is the inability of conventional structures, tools, and practices to get the job done. Policy responses to date have been too small, their ideas too flawed, and their designs too dependent on conventional means. Professional responses have been hampered by policy artifacts built for other purposes and keyed to other values, policy artifacts that miss the connection between resources and student learning.

Accomplishing ambitious learning goals requires more. Above all, it requires an education system that retools these connections, integrating its parts so that all students can move toward the proficiencies the public now expects. That movement, however, awaits another set of choices, ones that back the nation's education ambition with the means to succeed.

SMART-MONEY CHOICES

Granted, those choices are tough. The smart-money approach to education resources and ambitious learning goals requires educators to adopt continuous improvement as the core resource strategy for schools and districts and to move resources from less-effective to more-effective uses.[7] Inside schools and classrooms, these choices imply more collaboration, data analysis, adaptation, skill development, and shared expertise. Outside classrooms, they require knowledge and strategies that link resources to learning, and the discretion and fortitude to fund that learning before any regard for competing claims. These choices need not diminish the human connections that inspire and animate teaching and learning, but they do organize the enterprise around a shared conception of success and practices that move teachers and students toward that goal.

Smart-money choices are tough, again, for elected officials and policy-level administrators, who must reconfigure resource systems to support continuous improvement. Only they can deliver resources transparently and flexibly, focus and enable educators' work, expand knowledge about resources, experiment with new methods, and redesign resource accounting and accountability. These policy choices introduce new structures, tools, and practices (see table 11-1) that enable educators to find the particular

TABLE 11-1 Policy structures, tools, and practices that support continuous improvement

Structures	Tools	Practices
• Student-based funding • School-linked accounts • Reform-oriented collective bargaining • Strengthened charters or similar experimental settings • School–community resource partnerships	• Performance incentives for adults and students • Data systems that link student learning, resources, and human resource information • Research and development • Investments in educators' capacities to align and adapt resource use • Revised accounting and financial reporting standards that reflect outcome principles and measures • Contingencies on jobs, schools, and funding	• Using student learning as the touchstone for resource decisions, top to bottom • Making resource decisions strategically and explicitly with reference to student learning • Evaluating resource decisions by their effects on instruction, instructional materials, and student outcomes • Defining and integrating the resource roles of policy and practice • Revised accounting and reporting practices

resource configurations and instructional approaches that work best in their classrooms, schools, and districts.

For legislators, chief state school officers, and other policy leaders, these choices affirm their roles in setting goals, providing resources, structuring accountability, removing impediments, and otherwise creating system conditions that enable students to succeed. At the same time, these choices imply substantially less policy focus on mandating or constraining the means that educators bring to their work and less focus on addressing issues centrally that would impose one-size-fits-all requirements on schools and classrooms.

Thus, the politics of educating all students to meet standards blends new opportunities for public accomplishment with the need to better integrate the respective resource roles of policy and practice, and then managing the changes this implies for education governance. In this context, smart-money choices would better align the goals of policy and practice; allow sound theory and instructional technology to emerge from continuous improvement or research and development; directly address issues of administrator, teacher, and student motivation and capacity; and integrate finance system components to best promote student learning. In other words, these choices offer new traction on the knotty problems of policy and implementation that have hampered success thus far.[8]

This potential could better serve U.S. ambitions in education, economy, and civic society and its obligations to students, families, and communities. However, that same potential depends on the choice by elected officials, educators, and others to do this work, to manage this transition, and to search for better measures of resource fairness, productivity, and accountability.

DIFFERENT ROLES, DIFFERENT NEEDS

Using educational resources to accomplish ambitious learning goals involves much more than applying a reform model wholesale to U.S. schools, nor would any model be self-executing. Lessons from policy implementation indicate that any substantial change in structures and methods, any meaningful improvement in student learning, must emerge from the steady work of policy, administration, and practice.[9] The kinds of changes envisioned in this book also encompass the work of researchers and evaluators, systems analysts, communities—and students, the often overlooked factor in educational improvement. After all, students, however supported, must do the work that lifts their learning over any performance bar. To treat them as something other than partners in this enterprise is to invite failure.

No matter one's role, change requires individuals to think or act differently from the way they do now. As a result, change introduces uncertainty into the work of elected officials, administrators, and teachers—uncertainty regarding the benefits, costs, and unintended consequences of new resource expectations and practices. In such a context, individuals must develop their own sense of meaning regarding new expectations and practices, and legislators, superintendents, principals, and teachers throughout the system will develop those meanings as they navigate the complex challenges, uncertain consequences, and personal adaptations that change implies.[10] They will do this through the lens of their evolving motivation and capacity, and thus their needs, traditions, and practices will establish general conditions for innovation.[11]

From the vantage of legislators, views from the states regarding general conditions for innovation are remarkably similar.[12] Regardless of the particular policy or educational challenges that shape legislators' experiences, the pressures and conditions of innovation are consistent across those experiences. For instance, innovation requires an external stimulus, such as an economic or education crisis, or litigation that requires a legislative response. In short, the equilibrium of policy decisions, budgetary commitments, and interest group politics is sufficiently powerful that only unusual circumstances allow legislators to substantially alter these arrangements.

Innovation also requires legislative focus, encompassing the organization of legislative structure, members, capacity, and political will. Marshaling these resources means working through the budget process and working with legislative champions who have the technical and political know-how to get results (something that is not easy in term-limited settings). It also means working in concert with the handful of members who control or substantially influence education policy, including "the guy with the gavel," and working with sufficient information to make a compelling case for change.

Innovation requires an external coalition. In some contexts, gubernatorial leadership is key. In all contexts, innovation is facilitated by consensus among administrators, school board members, and teacher unions. If taxes are on the table, then business representatives must be included in the consensus. All told, policy innovation is as much about creating the opportunity for change through coalition building as it is about generating specific reform proposals.

Finally, innovation requires attention to the realpolitik of legislative change. Because the public interest in improved educational results sometimes conflicts with the narrower interests of constituents or organized groups, the calculation of winners and losers becomes a key nuts-and-bolts concern for legislators, who want to maximize the former while minimizing the latter. Compromise is part of that process, although it alters the shape of innovations. And change frequently must be phased in, again altering the practical effect of what is accomplished. Such day-to-day legislative realities affect the timing and extent of what is possible and require a match between legislative strategy and context. Amid these dynamics, altering finance systems, as smart-money innovation would do, creates new legislative opportunities; at the same time, there are few rewards for elected officials to take on entrenched systems.

From an administrative vantage, educational leaders need to align policy initiatives with local improvement efforts so that policy creates a supportive context for accomplishing student learning goals. As it is, policy presents substantial impediments to success. In this regard, innovation requires coordinated state and local attention to effective resource use. Local leaders say they spend too much time and effort complying with state mandates and not enough time thinking creatively about big-picture improvements. In other words, a compliance orientation drives out strategic thinking.

Innovation requires improved administrator knowledge and skill regarding resource use. One superintendent recounted that the alignment of resources with student learning is now a mantra and then lamented that principals do not know how to do it. The resource choices and trade-offs that underlie improved performance depend on improved capacity to make these judgments.

Innovation requires new policy tools that simultaneously serve fiduciary and student learning goals. Examples include flexibility in categorical funding and restructured collective bargaining that would allow resources to be allocated according to student need.[13] Other tools include new metrics that link resource use with student outcomes, budgeting systems that make it possible to see what is spent on professional development and similar strategic choices, and new accounting and auditing systems that stress student learning rather than fidelity to spending rules.

In sum, even though the perspectives of state legislators differ significantly from those of school district leaders—grappling with coalitions and policy opportunities on one hand, with teacher recruitment, curriculum, reporting requirements, and the like on the other—together they highlight a need for better state–local relations. A closer relationship could mean informed policy making and sustained attention to the local adaptations and practical consequences of policy in practice.

Teachers bring yet another set of concerns to the table. Teachers are focused on materials, lessons, and students—particularly their students, the ones whose abilities and challenges immediately shape teachers' goals, decisions, and actions. The dynamics of change hit these educators hardest, because teachers are the primary actors who transform innovations into practical effects for students and schools. Their street-level decisions define the innovations that students experience. In other words, innovations substantially derive their practical effect from teachers' routines and discretion; the choices they make about adopting change, in whole or part; the way they distribute benefits and sanctions or deal with pressure; the trade-offs they make; the degree to which they understand and use performance information; whether they come together to work on issues of practice or deal with them individually, and the like.[14] Even so, there is nothing automatic about teachers' embrace of policy innovations.[15] The atmosphere that innovations introduce—too many changes on too short a schedule—can leave veteran teachers feeling like rookies and state leaders wishing they had never cast change in terms of "reform."[16] At base, teachers need innovations that enable effective practice.[17] Policy theories, designs, and resources matter as starting points, but their practical consequences are determined day to day as teachers work with students.

In turn, student motivation and engagement are fundamental to learning.[18] In fact, by some reckonings, student motivation constitutes one of the most important challenges confronting public education.[19] The salience of these issues places the fate of ambitious learning goals smack in the middle of students' physical, psychological, task, social, and cultural contexts.[20] Furthermore, it burdens teachers and teaching with understanding the things individual students know and care about and then using this knowledge as a starting point for meaningful, enticing, and customized lesson plans.[21] In sum, productive innovations engage students in the work, motivate them to ambitious levels of performance, and build their capacities to get the job done.

As it happens, the smart-money choices that support the U.S. ambition to educate all students to meet standards must be made by elected officials but also by educational leaders, teachers, and students. Thus, as an overarching innovation, these choices end up being mediated in the spheres of policy, administration, and practice, and the consequences of using education resources to accomplish ambitious learning goals will take on meanings and motivations appropriate to each sphere.

Choosing to do this work becomes a matter of fit among, first, the impediments recognized in these spheres; second, the smart-money solutions to these impediments; and, third, perceptions of feasibility, and hence the willingness of policy entrepreneurs and other change agents to embrace both the greater potential and the greater uncertainties of change in education finance at this scale.

In chapter 10 of this volume, Lorraine McDonnell uses a political lens to discuss conditions that open policy windows, creating opportunities for education finance innovation.[22] Political perspectives and policy windows are central concerns in a smart-money context, because the ability to use resources productively at scale begins with policy changes that allow practitioners to think and act differently. Over time, though, it will be a range of perspectives and needs that adapt both policy and practice into better tools for problem solving, service delivery, and the accomplishment of public goals. Because the settings of policy, administration, and practice lend themselves to different perceptions of problems and solutions, impediments and possibilities, time horizons and key constituents, and because all play equally important roles in accomplishing ambitious learning goals, the challenge for policy entrepreneurs and others who would champion these ideas is one of aligning opportunities for innovation across these domains.

NEXT STEPS

Steady work is one thing, but continuing that work in a more enabling context promises greater accomplishments. To the extent that smart-money perspectives and innovations represent new possibilities to accomplish ambitious learning goals, the transition from constraining to enabling resource contexts becomes a matter of making smart-money choices into feasible choices, creating means and circumstances that permit this work to move forward.

Acknowledging the Context

Feasibility begins with the acknowledgment of a larger public context that supports the kinds of choices and innovations at issue here. For instance, ambitious learning goals represent a persistent value in U.S. public policy, one that has driven education discussions since 1980. Federal and state governments have promoted this value variously in terms of performing at the boundary of individual ability, all students at standards, all students achieving proficiently, America 2000, Goals 2000, NCLB, and the like.

Regardless of the language, the underlying commitment to greater student learning has remained. It has survived presidential, gubernatorial, and legislative electoral cycles; changes in political party; and leadership transitions in education agencies. It has motivated state accountability structures—in red and blue states—and has supported reauthorizations of the federal Elementary and Secondary Education Act.[23] And it has focused legislative and judicial decision making. These attributes place smart-money choices and innovations in the mainstream of public interests, signaling the value acceptability of their fundamental purpose.

Ambitious learning goals also represent a persistent need. Public debates regarding the emerging economy, civic society, social diversity, or equal opportunity center largely on the need for greater accomplishments in public education. The global economy particularly dominates governmental and academic discussions.[24] However, the public now emphasizes education's role in producing literate citizens who can participate in civic life (26 percent) and preparing young persons to make the transition from high school to college or technical school (25 percent). These two educational purposes were the most frequently cited among six options in a 2004 survey examining attitudes toward public education funding.[25] In contrast, 10 percent of respondents identified preparing good workers to succeed in the modern economy as education's main purpose.

Given governmental and public preferences for greater student learning, it is not surprising that 74 percent of respondents in that same poll reported that the quality of public schools is a concern, with 55 percent of them viewing the nation's schools as a major concern. At the same time, nearly half (45 percent) reported that schools need either major changes (30 percent) or a complete overhaul (15 percent). Only 14 percent believed that schools were working well, and 60 percent viewed low-income schools as inadequate or in crisis. These attributes place smart-money choices and innovations in the mainstream of public assessments regarding education's central contribution and need for better performance.

Ambitious learning goals further represent a persistent effort in education policy and practice. Ever since *A Nation At Risk* set the states on a path to greater student learning, that goal has dominated national and state commissions, professional conferences, think tank reports, judicial opinions, and legislative or gubernatorial initiatives.[26]

At this writing, the federal Race to the Top Fund, a multibillion-dollar competitive grant program, is promoting standards and accountability, effective teachers and principals, data systems, and turnaround efforts for low-performing schools as strategies to boost student learning.[27] In a nutshell, this initiative symbolizes the nation's learning ambition and continuing efforts to achieve it.

The public backs continued reform efforts, too. Depending on the initiative, 68 to 87 percent of respondents in the 2004 poll cited earlier even agreed to spend more money if spending was tied to school improvement, although 76 percent believed that money dedicated to education is wasted a great deal (24 percent), quite a bit (18 percent), or a fair amount (34 percent). These attributes place smart-money choices and innovations in the mainstream of the nation's attention to meaningful change and to issues of productivity in the process.

Finally, public education itself enjoys persistent public support. According to the nonpartisan organization Public Agenda, schools remain one of the public's top concerns, and most Americans want decisive action to improve the nation's schools.[28] This context places smart-money choices and innovations in the mainstream of issues the public deems most important. Together, persistent policy values, educational needs, improvement efforts, and public support constitute a congenial context for the smart-money agenda.

Managing the Change

Even within a broadly supportive context, smart-money perspectives and innovations challenge resource conventions in policy and practice. In managing a transition from conventions to innovations, two questions stand out: what is possible given the means at hand and circumstances as they are? And what can be done to change those means and circumstances to create additional opportunities?

When assessing immediate opportunities for innovation, advocates should remember that public policies and new practices represent solutions to problems. Elected officials and practitioners search for or accept new perspectives and ways of doing business when conventional methods come up short. Either goals, expectations, values, demands, or conditions change, creating problems that garner attention, or new technologies arise that promise improvements in an agency's fairness, productivity, or accountability. Either way, these disturbances rattle the equilibrium that policy and practice are accustomed to and thus encourage consideration of new options.[29]

The lesson here for innovators is to be opportunistic in the selection of initial reform sites—seeking places where elected officials or practitioners are searching for solutions and fitting smart-money perspectives and innovations to those needs. States might welcome overtures, but school districts and charter schools offer smaller-scale and more-varied options.

Such opportunism situates innovators at the confluence of problems, solutions, and the political forces that open policy windows, although this approach applies equally in policy and practice settings.[30] For instance, the introduction of student-based funding would require elected officials to alter funding formulas and hence alter established policies, but the adoption of continuous improvement or of strategic approaches to school or district resource decision making does not require such changes, at least to a degree. In the latter cases, practitioners often can find room within statutory or regulatory boundaries to instill new practices, even if policy changes would enable them to accomplish much more. They may also have access to waivers, a policy tool that exempts schools or districts from education code requirements, usually for a specific purpose and period. In short, fitting smart-money solutions to existing perceptions of need and using available tools to gain flexibility can enhance the feasibility of innovation.

In assessing immediate opportunities for innovation, policy entrepreneurs and others also can build on experience. Continuous improvement, strategic resource trade-offs, student-based funding, and reform-oriented collective bargaining are not new to education. Neither are charter schools as places of experimentation, school–community resource partnerships, performance incentives, performance-oriented data systems, research and development, and capacity-building investments, although the application and development of these innovations in the smart-money context is original. Preceding chapters highlight instances of such activities.

Ongoing experiments present opportunities but merit caution. They may jump-start the further development and testing of structures, tools, and practices that productively connect resources to student learning. At the same time, these experiments have been operating without benefit of other system support that smart money deems essential to their success. Hence, observers cannot judge their utility or potential as smart-money components based on their performance in isolation. Nevertheless, to the extent that such experiments have identified and addressed technical, economic, or political challenges related to innovation's design and implementation, they enhance the prospects of adopting similar initiatives in more-coherent contexts.

With innovations of this magnitude, however, opportunities are limited to attach new perspectives and means to existing problems or to build on isolated experiences. The question then becomes how to create new opportunities to explore the potential of smart-money ideas. Here again, the perspectives of legislators and local leaders point the way. For instance, the similarity of their views regarding conditions that support innovation creates a remarkable opportunity to learn and apply lessons across states.

The key is to invest in a knowledge infrastructure that can cull and disseminate these lessons. No state, and certainly not the nation, will ever get finance reform to scale, will ever find a greater measure of resource fairness, productivity, and accountability, if each school or district is left alone to develop its own innovations and integrate them productively. Change on this scale requires a mechanism that supports demonstrations, identifies proof points, and shares lessons across school, district, and state boundaries—lessons that can speed the process and enhance the feasibility of innovation's design and implementation.

Similarly, the novelty of ambitious learning goals, the scale of the performance challenge, and the need to redesign finance systems heighten the demand for research and development on new resource structures, tools, and practices. Policy makers and educational practitioners operate in demanding environments that are geared more to enacting and implementing innovative ideas than generating them. Whether innovations come from research or practice, the field needs immediate attention to their generic development and subsequent attention to their local adaptation. The potential of smart-money innovations—such as student-based funding, performance incentives that make sense in K–12 settings, new labor–management relations, and revised accounting and financial reporting standards and practices—all await such development.

Whether developers work at design tables, in charter schools, or in traditional settings, their purpose is to test the integrity and utility of new resource mechanisms, just as test pilots find errors in airplane design. Using resources to accomplish ambitious learning goals depends ultimately on continuing efforts to learn what works, where, under what conditions, and at what cost.

Furthermore, because innovations must be available when circumstances change, innovators need to pursue development work on resource structures, tools, and practices regardless of the short-term prospects for change. Advancing the redesign of resource systems now through research and development sets up states and school districts to take advantage of strategic or crisis-based opportunities when they arise.

Realistically, smart-money perspectives and innovations introduce problems of scale for elected officials and practitioners alike—the too-much-at-once issue. The solution lies in sequencing innovations so as to match the long-term utility of system redesign with the shorter-term realities of technologies, budgets, and coalitions. The most feasible sequence would first move forward the least novel, least technically difficult, least costly, least problematic components, followed by their more challenging counterparts. The exact sequence will depend on the particulars of the state and local settings where opportunities arise. Schools that are already experimenting with continuous improvement or with development activities regarding performance-oriented educational data systems illustrate instances where innovators might align smart-money perspectives and innovations with ongoing national, state, or local activities.[31]

Whatever the order, breaking a coherent resource system into smaller, more manageable components challenges innovators not only to match new or retooled system components with policy and practice needs and opportunities, but also to promote logical system connections even as components appear stepwise in practice. For instance, providing school principals with greater resource discretion without also investing in their capacity to make strategic decisions or the system's ability to track them invites missteps or malfeasance. Adopting student-based funding without resource reporting by school, strategy, and results conveys nothing about the resource uses and instructional practices that matter most to student learning. Instituting contingencies on jobs, schools, or funding without also deploying account-ability mechanisms that can fairly parse the accountable individuals' con-tributions to the results invites resistance. In short, even though sequencing innovations enhances feasibility, it risks obscuring the system as a whole, the potential of system components, or lessons that recommend innovation in other locations.

BEYOND CONVENTION

Drawing on available support, opportunistically selecting reform sites, building on experience, investing in a knowledge infrastructure, and devel-oping and sequencing the components of innovation can enhance the fea-sibility of smart-money perspectives and innovations, but these practices cannot diminish the scale of the challenge represented in educating all stu-dents to meet standards. The United States has been "reforming" its elemen-tary and secondary schools for nearly thirty years, but the results still do not match public expectations, nor do they reflect the measure of work contrib-uted by many people.

In this regard, public education is not alone. The day President Ken-nedy committed the United States to send a man to the moon and back, he acknowledged that "we have had our failures . . . we are behind . . . but we do not intend to stay behind."[32] He then committed the nation to making the investments, developing the technologies, and organizing the capacities that the moon project required.

Smart Money's authors make the case that conventional resource struc-tures, tools, and practices miss the connection between resources and student learning. Their analyses can help elected officials and educators recognize impediments, integrate resources with student learning, expand resource knowledge, experiment with new ideas, and start to build a resource system that secures the connection between resources and student learning.

The authors' analyses occur in the context of making smart-money invest-ments in U.S. schools. That metaphor—smart money—keeps the resource focus on using educational resources to accomplish ambitious learning goals. Its intent is to enable, to discipline, both policy and practice to use learning goals as the touchstone for resource decisions and to make those decisions strategically and explicitly in regard to learning. That discipline extends to evaluating resource decisions in terms of their effect on instruction, instruc-tional materials, and student learning, and it defines and integrates respec-tive resource roles for policy and practice. From this basis, smart money supports policy entrepreneurs and others who would acknowledge the magnitude of the nation's challenge regarding student performance and who would craft policy and professional responses on this scale.

Accomplishing ambitious learning goals demands new knowledge and corresponding structures, tools, and practices that put it to work. In other words, accomplishing those goals means working beyond the boundaries of resource convention. That work begins with an affirmation that the goal is meaningful, the potential is worth the effort, and the challenges can be overcome. It gains new possibilities through the perspectives and actions recommended in this book. It will take these things, at least, for America's schools to accomplish the results the public now expects.

Ideas that prove their efficacy create new opportunities for public accomplishment. But ideas alone change little. Their practical effect is forged in the steady work of elected officials and educators, students and communities, researchers and philanthropists, labor and management.

In transmitting the report of the National Commission on Excellence in Education to the secretary of education, the commission's chair, David Pierpont Gardner, wrote, "The Commission deeply believes that the problems we have discerned in American education can be both understood and corrected if the people of our country, together with those who have public responsibility in the matter, care enough and are courageous enough to do what is required."[33] The starting point for smart-money investments in U.S. schools in 2010 is no different from what it was in 1983. Elected officials, educators, and others must choose to do the work, to manage the transition, and to search for improved measures of resource fairness, productivity, and accountability. Without that assent, nothing ambitious can be accomplished.

Notes

Introduction: Smart Money and America's Schools

1. For all references to NAEP data in this section, see National Center for Education Statistics, Reading 2007: National Assessment of Educational Progress at Grades 4 and 8, NCES 2007-496 (Washington, DC: U.S. Department of Education, Institute of Education Sciences, 2007); National Center for Education Statistics, Mathematics 2009, NCES 2010-451 (Washington, DC: U.S. Department of Education, Institute of Education Sciences, 2009); and National Center for Education Statistics, 12th-Grade Reading and Mathematics 2005, NCES 2007-468 (Washington, DC: U.S. Department of Education, Institute of Education Sciences, 2007).

2. Because of changes in the twelfth grade mathematics test, the 2005 results cannot be compared to earlier tests.

3. Chester E. Finn, Jr., and Michael J. Petrilli, foreword to *The Proficiency Illusion* (Washington, DC: Thomas B. Fordham Institute and Northwest Education Association, 2007). See also Chester E. Finn, Jr., Liam Julian, and Michael J. Petrilli, *The State of State Standards 2006* (Washington, DC: Thomas B. Fordham Foundation, 2006).

4. Finn and Petrilli, foreword, 2.

5. Victor Bandeira de Mello, Charles Blankenship, and Don McLaughlin, Mapping State Proficiency Standards Onto NAEP Scales: 2005–2007, NCES 2010-456 (Washington, DC: U.S. Department of Education, Institute for Education Sciences, National Center for Education Statistics, 2009).

6. See, for example, Allan R. Odden and Sarah J. Archibald, *Doubling Student Performance . . . and Finding the Resources to Do It* (Thousand Oaks, CA: Corwin Press, 2009); and the Knowledge Is Power Program, KIPP, at http://www.kipp.org.

7. Signposts in this regard were the 1982 election of Bill Honig, a reform-minded California superintendent of public instruction, and passage of the Hughes-Hart Educational Reform Act of 1983 (Senate Bill 813); National Commission on Excellence in Education, *A Nation At Risk: The Imperative for Educational Reform* (Washington, DC: U.S. Government Printing Office, 1983).

8. Examples are The Accelerated Schools Project, America's Choice, and Success for All. Comprehensive school reforms were promoted initially by the New American School Development Corporation, then by the Comprehensive School Reform Demonstration Act, and finally by the No Child Left Behind Act. See Brian Rowan, Richard Correnti, Robert J. Miller, and Eric M. Camburn, *School Improvement by Design: Lessons from a Study of Comprehensive School Reform Programs* (Philadelphia: University of Pennsylvania, Consortium for Policy Research in Education, 2009).

9. To explore these reform topics further, on intensification, see Joseph Murphy, ed., *The Educational Reform Movement of the 1980s: Perspectives and Cases* (Berkeley, CA: McCutchan, 1990); on restructuring, see Joseph Murphy, *Restructuring Schools: Capturing and Assessing the Phenomenon* (New York: Teachers College Press, 1991);

on privatization, see John E. Chubb and Terry M. Moe, *Politics, Markets, and America's Schools* (Washington, DC: Brookings Institution, 1990); on contracting, see Paul T. Hill, Lawrence C. Pierce, and James W. Guthrie, *Reinventing Public Education: How Contracting Can Transform America's Schools* (Chicago: The University of Chicago Press, 1997); on charter schools, see Joseph Murphy and Catherine Dunn Shiffman, *Understanding and Assessing the Charter School Movement* (New York: Teachers College Press, 2002); on finance litigation, see Eric A. Hanushek and Alfred A. Lindseth, *Schoolhouses, Courthouses, and Statehouses: Solving the Funding Puzzle in America's Public Schools* (Princeton, NJ: Princeton University Press, 2009).

10. For an overview of reform strategies, see Jacob E. Adams, Jr., "Education Reform: Overview," in *Encyclopedia of Education*, 2d ed., vol. 2, ed. James W. Guthrie (New York: Macmillan Reference USA, 2003), 689–695.

11. On class size reduction, see http://www.cde.ca.gov/LS/cs/. On Kentucky's education reform, see Kentucky General Assembly, House Bill 940, Regular Session 1990, March 24, 1990.

12. Adams, "Education Reform."

13. Michael W. Kirst, "Organizations in Shock and Overload," Thrust for Educational Leadership 8, no. 5 (1979): 9–11.

14. Larry Cuban, "Reforming Again, Again, and Again," *Educational Researcher* 19, no. 1 (1990): 3–13.

15. On Kentucky's reform experience, see Kentucky Institute for Education Research, "All Children Can Learn," VHS, produced by Diana J. Taylor (Lexington, KY: Moran Video Production, 2000); and Roger S. Pankratz and Joseph M. Petrosko, eds., *All Children Can Learn: Lessons from the Kentucky Reform Experience* (San Francisco: Jossey-Bass, 2000).

16. No Child Left Behind Act of 2001, Public Law 107-110, 115 Stat. 1425, January 8, 2002.

17. On the connection among legislators, their work, and reelection, see David R. Mayhew, *Congress: The Electoral Connection* (New Haven, CT: Yale University Press, 1974).

18. National Commission on Excellence in Education, *A Nation At Risk*, 12.

19. John F. Kennedy, "We Choose to Go to the Moon" (speech, Rice University, Houston, Texas, September 12, 1962), http://www.historyplace.com/speeches/jfk-space.htm.

20. On institutional change in education, see, for example, Charles Taylor Kerchner, David J. Menefee-Libey, Laura Steen Mulfinger, and Stephanie E. Clayton, *Learning from L.A.: Institutional Change in American Public Education* (Cambridge, MA: Harvard Education Press, 2008).

21. Thomas L. Friedman, *Hot, Flat, and Crowded: Why We Need a Green Revolution—and How It Can Renew America* (New York: Farrar, Straus and Giroux, 2008).

22. Jonathan Alter, "Teddy's Rightful Heir: Alan Khazei Should Get His Seat," *Newsweek*, November 9, 2009, 22.

23. See, for example, Richard J. Murnane and Frank Levy, *Teaching the New Basic Skills: Principles for Educating Children to Thrive in a Changing Economy* (New York: Free Press, 1996); Lisa Stuart, *21st Century Skills for 21st Century Jobs*, ED 445 249 (Washington, DC: U.S. Department of Commerce, U.S. Department of Education, U.S. Department of Labor, National Institute for Literacy, and Small Business Administration, 1999).

24. Public Policy Institute of California, *California 2025: Planning for a Better Future* (San Francisco: PPIC, 2009).

25. These ends have been seen as core purposes of public education. See Center on Education Policy, *Why We Still Need Public Schools: Public Schools or the Common Good* (Washington, DC: CEP, n.d.).

26. *Rose v. Council for Better Education, Inc.*, 790 S.W. 2d 186 (Ky. 1989) at 212.

27. Campaign for Fiscal Equity v. State of New York, 86 N.Y.2d 307 (N.Y., 1995) at 316.
28. For examples of eighteenth-century thinking, see Center on Education Policy, *Why We Still Need Public Schools*.
29. See, for example, California's content standards at http://www.cde.ca.gov/be/st/ss/ or Massachusetts's standards at http://www.doe.mass.edu/frameworks/current.html. On variation in state standards, see Finn, Julian, and Petrilli, The State of State Standards 2006, and Bandeira de Mello, Blankenship, and McLaughlin, Mapping State Proficiency Standards Onto NAEP Scales: 2005–2007.
30. No Child Left Behind Act of 2001, Public Law 107-110, 115 Stat. 1425, January 8, 2002, "An Act . . . "
31. http://www.corestandards.org, focusing on English language arts and mathematics.
32. For a fuller discussion of these dynamics, see Jacob E. Adams, Jr., and Robert F. Sexton, "Reform and the Dynamics of Governance: Why Improving America's Schools Requires More Than Changing Who's In Charge," *Education Week,* December 5, 2007, 24–25.
33. Thomas D. Snyder, Sally A. Dillow, and Charlene M. Hoffman, *Digest of Education Statistics 2008,* NCES 2009-020 (Washington, DC: U.S. Department of Education, Institute for Education Sciences, National Center for Education Statistics, 2009), table 25.
34. For an eloquent description of that "most important function," see Brown v. Board of Education, 347 U.S. 483 at 493, 1954.
35. Snyder, Dillow, and Hoffman, *Digest of Education Statistics,* tables 26 and 32.
36. Campaign for Fiscal Equity v. State of New York, 86 N.Y.2d at 317, 1995.
37. See, for example, Shelley De Wys, Melissa Bowen, Allison Demeritt, and Jacob E. Adams, Jr., *Performance Pressure and Resource Allocation in Washington* (Seattle: University of Washington, Center on Reinventing Public Education, School Finance Redesign Project, 2008).
38. On policy instruments, see Lorraine McDonnell and Richard F. Elmore, "Getting the Job Done: Alternative Policy Instruments," *Educational Evaluation and Policy Analysis* 9, no. 2 (1987): 133–152; Lester M. Salamon, ed., *The Tools of Government: A Guide to the New Governance* (New York: Oxford University Press, 2002).
39. On motivation as the direction, persistence, and vigor of human effort, see Martin E. Ford, *Motivating Humans: Goals, Emotions, and Personal Agency Beliefs* (Newbury Park, CA: Sage, 1992).
40. On the importance of sound policy theory, see Daniel A. Mazmanian and Paul A. Sabatier, *Implementation and Public Policy* (New York: Scott Foresman, 1983; repr., Lanham, MD: University Press of America, 1989).
41. The Hughes-Hart Educational Reform Act of 1983 (Senate Bill 813).
42. David Tyack and Larry Cuban, *Tinkering Toward Utopia: A Century of Educational Reform* (Cambridge, MA: Harvard University Press, 1995).
43. For a classic statement on the importance of motivation and capacity, see Milbrey W. McLaughlin, "Learning from Experience: Lessons from Policy Implementation," *Educational Evaluation and Policy Analysis* 9, no. 2 (1987): 171–178. Regarding implementers' "levels of use" of innovations, see Gene E. Hall and Shirley M. Hord, *Change in Schools: Facilitating the Process* (Albany: State University of New York Press, 1987).
44. In the absence of certain technology, even proposed methods that plausibly link resource decisions with student learning may represent an improvement over current practice when that practice is driven by considerations other than student learning.
45. Nothing in this conception of a tightly integrated, mutually reinforcing educational system is meant to imply a regimented, centrally determined set of educational strategies or practices across states, school districts, or schools. On the contrary, the smart-money perspective anticipates an education system of shared central and local responsibilities that promotes the continuous improvement of instruction and student learning, supported

by research and development. Chapters 1 and 4, particularly, address the need for local adaptations and the rational coexistence of (some) centralized and (some) locally determined system components.

46. For a summary of governmental finance issues and actions, see Hanushek and Lindseth, *Schoolhouses, Courthouses, and Statehouses.*

47. Washington Legislature, House K–12 Finance Work Group, *Position Paper: Is Our K–12 Finance Structure Consistent with Our Standards-Based Education Policies?* (Olympia: Washington Legislature, n.d.); Washington Learns Steering Committee, *Washington Learns: World-Class, Learner-Focused, Seamless Education* (Olympia: Washington Learns Steering Committee, 2006).

48. De Wys et al., *Performance Pressure and Resource Allocation.*

49. Members of the National Working Group on Funding Student Learning and their affiliations during the group's tenure included Jacob E. Adams, Jr., chair, professor, Claremont Graduate University; Christopher T. Cross, chairman, Cross & Joftus, LLC; Christopher Edley, Jr., dean and professor, Boalt Hall School of Law, University of California, Berkeley; James W. Gurthrie, professor, Peabody College, Vanderbilt University; Paul T. Hill, John and Marguerite Corbally professor and director, Center on Reinventing Public Education, University of Washington; Michael W. Kirst, professor emeritus, Stanford University; Goodwin Liu, associate dean and professor, Boalt Hall School of Law, University of California, Berkeley; Susanna Loeb, associate professor, Stanford University; David H. Monk, dean and professor, Pennsylvania State University; Allan R. Odden, professor and co-director, Consortium for Policy Research in Education, University of Wisconsin, Madison; and Joanne Weiss, partner and chief operating officer, New Schools Venture Fund.

50. National Working Group on Funding Student Learning, *Funding Student Learning: How to Align Education Resources with Student Learning Goals* (Seattle: University of Washington, Center on Reinventing Public Education, School Finance Redesign Project, 2008), www.crpe.org/cs/crpe/view/csr_pubs/247.

51. SFRP's body of work can be found at www.crpe.org/cs/view/projects/3.

Chapter 1: Ambitious Learning Goals Require a New Approach to Educational Resources

1. No Child Left Behind Act of 2001, Public Law 107-110, 115 Stat. 1425, January 8, 2002.

2. For a popular perspective, see Jonathan Alter, "Teddy's Rightful Heir: Alan Khazei Should Get His Seat," *Newsweek,* November 9, 2009.

3. Education clauses in thirty-two states require school systems characterized by qualities such as "thorough and efficient," "ample," or "adequate." Five states require only that school systems be uniform, and fourteen require only free schools open to all. Courts have found adequacy obligations in all three types of clauses.

4. For a prototypical example, see Rose v. Council for Better Education, Inc., 790 S.W. 2d 186, Ky. 1989.

5. Opinion of Justices, Alabama Coalition for Equity v. Hunt, 624 So.2d 107, Ala., 1993.

6. For an illustration of these judicial perspectives, see the introduction to this volume.

7. For an example of how equity adjustments work in practice, see Jacob E. Adams, Jr., and William H. White, "The Equity Consequence of School Finance Reform in Kentucky," *Educational Evaluation and Policy Analysis* 19, no. 2 (1997): 165–184.

8. For a wider discussion of equity and adequacy, see Bruce D. Baker and Preston C. Green, "Conceptions of Equity and Adequacy in School Finance," in *Handbook of Research in Education Finance and Policy,* eds. Helen F. Ladd and Edward B. Fiske (New York: Routledge, 2008), 203–221; and National Research Council, Committee on Education Finance,

Equity and Adequacy in Education Finance: Issues and Perspectives (Washington, DC: National Academy Press, 1999). For opposing viewpoints on the efficacy of adequacy to improve student results, see Eric A. Hanushek, ed., *Courting Failure: How School Finance Lawsuits Exploit Judges' Good Intentions and Harm Our Children* (Stanford, CA: Education Next Books, 2006) and Michael A. Rebell, *Courts and Kids: Pursuing Educational Equity Through the State Courts* (Chicago: University of Chicago Press, 2009).

9. Government Performance and Results Act of 1993, Public Law 103-62, 107 Stat. 285, August 3, 1993.

10. The Council for Excellence in Government, *Linking Resources to Results*, September 19, 2002, http://www.excelgov.org/index.php?keyword=a432fbadc917c3&PHPSESSID=4b2 48c1cffe690e239d7f17d801ccc.

11. Governor Chris Gregoire, "Gov. Gregoire Kicks Off Quest to Improve Washington Education," *U.S. State News,* June 3, 2005.

12. Washington Learns Steering Committee, *Washington Learns: World-Class, Learner-Focused, Seamless Education* (Olympia: WLSC, 2006).

13. California Legislature, Assembly Bill No. 25. 2007-08 Regular Session, Assembly Member Brownley, December 4, 2006, 3.

14. On the means and reliability of adequacy estimates, see Thomas A. Downes and Leanna Stiefel, "Measuring Equity and Adequacy in School Finance," in *Handbook of Research in Education Finance and Policy,* eds. Ladd and Fiske, 222—237; and Susanna Loeb, *Difficulties of Estimating the Cost of Achieving Education Standards* (Seattle: University of Washington, Center on Reinventing Public Education, School Finance Redesign Project, 2007).

15. Thomas D. Snyder, Sally A. Dillow, and Charlene M. Hoffman, *Digest of Education Statistics* 2008, NCES 2009-020 (Washington, DC: U.S. Department of Education, Institute for Education Sciences, National Center for Education Statistics, 2009); and Allan R. Odden and Lawrence O. Picus, *School Finance: A Policy Perspective,* 4th ed. (Boston: McGraw-Hill, 2008).

16. National Research Council, Committee on Education Finance, *Making Money Matter: Financing America's Schools* (Washington, DC: National Academy Press, 1999); Marguerite Roza, Kacey Guin, and Tricia Davis, *What Is the Sum of the Parts? How Federal, State, and District Funding Streams Confound Efforts to Address Different Student Types* (Seattle: University of Washington, Center on Reinventing Public Education, School Finance Redesign Project, 2007).

17. Susanna Loeb, *Difficulties of Estimating the Cost of Achieving Education Standards* (Seattle: University of Washington, Center on Reinventing Public Education, School Finance Redesign Project, 2007).

18. Hanushek, ed., *Courting Failure.*

19. Shelley De Wys, Melissa Bowen, Allison Demeritt, and Jacob E. Adams, Jr., *Performance Pressure and Resource Allocation in Washington* (Seattle: University of Washington, Center on Reinventing Public Education, School Finance Redesign Project, 2008).

20. Paul A. Minorini and Stephen Sugarman, "School Finance Litigation in the Name of Educational Equity: Its Evolution, Impact, and Future," in *Equity and Adequacy in Education Finance: Issues and Perspectives,* eds. Helen F. Ladd, Rosemary Chalk, and Janet H. Hansen (Washington, DC: National Academy Press, 1999), 34–71.

21. Marguerite Roza, *Many a Slip 'tween Cup and Lip: District Fiscal Practices and Their Effect on School Spending* (Seattle: University of Washington, Center on Reinventing Public Education, 2005).

22. See Goodwin Liu, "Interstate Inequity in Educational Opportunity," *New York University Law Review* 81 (December 2006): 2044–2128.

23. See Christopher T. Cross and Marguerite Roza, "How Federal Categorical Funding Prevents the Effective Use of Resources," this volume, and Goodwin Liu, *Improving Title I Equity Across States, Districts, and Schools* (Seattle: University of Washington, Center on Reinventing Public Education, School Finance Redesign Project, 2007).

24. Roza, Guin, and Davis, *What Is the Sum of the Parts?*

25. Marguerite Roza, *Allocation Anatomy: How District Policies That Deploy Resources Can Support (or Undermine) District Reform Strategies* (Seattle: University of Washington, Center on Reinventing Public Education, School Finance Redesign Project, 2007).

26. Eric A. Hanushek, *Incentive Based Financing of Schools* (Seattle: University of Washington, Center on Reinventing Public Education, School Finance Redesign Project, 2007).

27. Regarding the disconnect between compensation and results, see Hanushek, *Incentive Based Financing of Schools*. For broader perspectives on teacher compensation, see Dan Goldhaber, Michael DeArmond, Albert Liu, and Dan Player, *Returns to Skill and Teacher Wage Premiums: What Can We Learn by Comparing the Teacher and Private Sector Labor Markets?* (Seattle: University of Washington, Center on Reinventing Public Education, School Finance Redesign Project, 2007), and Anthony T. Milanowski, Hope Longwell-Grice, Felicia Saffold, Janice Jones, Allan Odden, and Kristen Schomisch, *Recruiting New Teachers to Urban School Districts: What Incentives Will Work* (Seattle: University of Washington, Center on Reinventing Public Education, School Finance Redesign Project, 2007). Regarding resistance by school systems to institute incentives for student performance, see De Wys et al., *Performance Pressure and Resource Allocation in Washington.*

28. De Wys et al., *Performance Pressure and Resource Allocation in Washington.*

29. See Cross and Roza, "How Federal Categorical Funding Prevents the Effective Use of Resources," this volume.

30. De Wys et al., *Performance Pressure and Resource Allocation in Washington.*

31. Stephen Frank and Karen Hawley Miles, *District Resource Allocation Modeler (DREAM): A Web-Based Tool Supporting the Strategic Use of Educational Resources* (Seattle: University of Washington, Center on Reinventing Public Education, School Finance Redesign Project, 2007). Saying that administrators lack the capacity to use resources productively is a recognition that the leadership expectation regarding resource management has changed. These same administrators are highly skilled in managing resources in terms of compliance and accounting regulations. Change the expectation, and new capacities will develop.

32. Jacob E. Adams, Jr., and Michael A. Copland, "Principal Licensing and Leadership for Learning: The Need for Coherent Policy," *Leadership and Policy in Schools* 6 (2007): 153–195.

33. Frank and Miles, *District Resource Allocation Modeler (DREAM).*

34. Roza, *Allocation Anatomy.*

35. Frank and Miles, *District Resource Allocation Modeler (DREAM).*

36. See Tomas B. Timar, *Categorical School Finance: Who Gains, Who Loses?* (Berkeley: University of California, Policy Analysis for California Education, 2004).

37. See Cross and Roza, "How Federal Categorical Funding Prevents the Effective Use of Resources," this volume.

38. Roza, *Allocation Anatomy.*

39. Ibid.

40. The term "zones of wishful thinking" refers to conditions that are needed for a school reform model to be successful but are not created by the reform itself. For instance, charter school success depends on the availability of large numbers of competent school providers, but charter school legislation does not create these providers. It creates only a mechanism to accommodate them if they come forward. Thus, reformers are left hoping that (compe-

tent) providers will appear. See Paul T. Hill and Mary Beth Celio, *Fixing Urban Schools* (Washington, DC: Brookings Institution, 1998).

41. On gaining efficiencies that free up resources, see Jason Willis, Robert Durante, and Paul Gazzerro, *Toward Effective Resource Use: Assessing How Education Dollars Are Spent* (Seattle: University of Washington, Center on Reinventing Public Education, School Finance Redesign Project, 2007).

42. On strategic spending, see Karen Hawley Miles and Stephen Frank, *The Strategic School: Making the Most of People, Time, and Money* (Thousand Oaks, CA: Corwin Press, 2008); and Allan R. Odden and Sarah J. Archibald, *Doubling Student Performance . . . and Finding the Resources to Do It* (Thousand Oaks, CA: Corwin Press, 2009).

43. Education Trust, *Dispelling the Myth: High Poverty Schools Exceeding Expectations,* 1999, http://www.seisummit.org/Downloads/aspd/EdTrustdispell.pdf; Willis D. Hawley, *The Keys to Effective Schools* (Thousand Oaks, CA: Corwin Press, 2002); Miles and Frank, *The Strategic School;* Robert J. Marzano, *What Works in Schools: Translating Research into Action* (Alexandria, VA: Association for Supervision and Curriculum Development, 2003); Odden and Archibald, *Doubling Student Performance.*

44. Martin E. Ford, *Motivating Humans: Goals, Emotions, and Personal Agency Beliefs* (Newbury Park, CA: Sage, 1992); Martin E. Ford and Donald H. Ford, *Humans as Self-Constructing Human Systems: Putting the Framework to Work* (Hillsdale, NJ: Lawrence Erlbaum Associates, 1987).

45. Milbrey Wallin McLaughlin, "Learning from Experience: Lessons from Implementation Research," *Educational Evaluation and Policy Analysis* 9, no. 2 (1987): 171–178.

46. David K. Cohen and Heather C. Hill, *Learning Policy: When State Education Reform Works* (New Haven, CT: Yale University Press, 2001).

47. Diana Sharp and John Bransford, *Learning Science Meets School Finance: The How People Learn Framework as a Tool for Resource Decisions* (Seattle: University of Washington, Center on Reinventing Public Education, School Finance Redesign Project, 2007).

48. National Research Council, Committee on a Feasibility Study for a Strategic Education Research Program, *Improving Student Learning: A Strategic Plan for Education Research and Its Utilization* (Washington, DC: National Academy Press, 1999).

49. National Research Council, Committee on Education Finance, *Making Money Matter.*

50. This discussion is based on Ford, *Motivating Humans.*

51. Milbrey W. McLaughlin, "The Rand Change Agent Study Revisited: Macro Perspectives and Micro Realities," *Educational Researcher* 19, no. 9 (1990): 11–16.

52. Laurence Steinberg with B. Bradford Brown and Sanford M. Dornbusch, *Beyond the Classroom: Why School Reform Has Failed and What Parents Need to Do* (New York: Simon & Schuster, 1996).

53. De Wys et al., *Performance Pressure and Resource Allocation in Washington.*

54. National Working Group on Funding Student Learning, *Funding Student Learning: How to Align Education Resources with Student Learning Goals* (Seattle: University of Washington, Center on Reinventing Public Education, School Finance Redesign Project, 2008).

55. Jacob E. Adams, Jr., foreword to ibid.

56. National Working Group on Funding Student Learning, *Funding Student Learning,* 13.

57. Ibid., 16.

58. Ibid., 18.

59. Ibid.

60. Ibid., 22–23.

61. Ibid., 26.

62. Ibid., 29.

Chapter 2: How Federal Categorical Funding Prevents the Effective Use of Resources

1. Elementary and Secondary Education Act of 1965, Public Law 89-10, 79 Stat. 27, April 11, 1965.
2. U.S. Department of Education, "Impact Aid Section 8002: Payments For Federal Property," http://www.ed.gov/programs/8002/index.html.
3. General Accounting Office, Report to the Congress: The Federal Program of Aid to Educationally Deprived Children in Illinois Can Be Strengthened (Washington, DC: Comptroller of the United States, 1972), http://archive.gao.gov/f0202/094049.pdf.
4. General Accounting Office, Report to Congress: Opportunities for Improving Administration of Federal Program of Aid to Educationally Deprived Children in West Virginia (Washington, DC: Comptroller of the United States, 1970a), http://archive.gao.gov/f0202/092570.pdf.
5. General Accounting Office, Report to the Congress: Improvement Needed in Administration of the Federal Program of Aid to Educationally Deprived Children in Ohio (Washington, DC: Comptroller General of the United States, 1970b), http://archive.gao.gov/f0202/093775.pdf.
6. No Child Left Behind Act of 2001, Public Law 107-110, 115 Stat. 1425, January 8, 2002, section 1120 (a).
7. Andrew Brownstein and Charles Edwards, "ED, Advocates Seek to Beef Up Comparability," *Title I Monitor*, March 7, 2006.
8. Funds indicate resources for general or restricted purposes; functions indicate broad classifications of school district activity, such as instruction, administration, or transportation; and objects are commodities that support broader activities, such as salaries, books, or buses.
9. Goodwin Liu, "How the Federal Government Makes Rich States Richer," in *Funding Gaps 2006* (Washington, DC: Education Trust, 2006), 2–4.
10. Office of Management and Budget, Catalog of Federal Domestic Assistance (Washington, DC: U.S. General Services Administration, 2006), http://12.46.245.173/cfda/cfda.html.
11. Jackie Kimbrough and Paul T. Hill, *The Aggregate Effects of Federal Education Programs* (Santa Monica, CA: The RAND Corporation, 1981), vi–vii.
12. Education Consolidation and Improvement Act of 1981, part of (Omnibus Budget Reconciliation Act of 1981) Public Law 97-35, 95 Stat. 483, August 13, 1981.
13. U.S. Department of Education employee, personal communication, 2006.
14. Consortium for Policy Research in Education, *Sources and Levels of Education Revenues and Changes Over Time* (Madison: University of Wisconsin, 2007), http://www.wcer.wisc.edu/CPRE/finance/revenue.php.
15. Ibid.
16. Bryan C. Hassel and Marguerite Roza, *Funding the Child: Getting Results in South Carolina Through Weighted Student Funding* (Columbia: The South Carolina Policy Council in Cooperation with the Thomas B. Fordham Institute, 2007).
17. Thomas B. Timar, *Categorical School Finance: Who Gains, Who Loses?* (Berkeley: University of California, Policy Analysis for California Education, 2004).
18. Larry McCarthy, "California's Structural Budget Deficit: Eliminate Massive Fraud and Waste," Cal-Tax Commentary, 2006, http://www.caltax.org/Digest/2006/mar06_mccarthy_california_structural_budget_deficit.html.
19. Timar, *Categorical School Finance*.
20. Ibid., 1.
21. Cathy S. Krop, *The Finances of Education Governance Reforms in California* (Santa Monica, CA: The RAND Corporation, 1996), 81.

22. Little Hoover Commission, *Dollars and Sense: A Simple Approach to School Finance* (1997), 48, http://www.lhc.ca.gov/lhcdir/143/TC143.html.

23. Ibid.

24. Interview with school district leader, October 2006.

25. Linda Jacobson, "Graduation Coaches Pursue One Goal," *Education Week,* November 15, 2006, http://www.edweek.org/ew/articles/2006/11/15/12gradspecialist.h26.html.

26. Hassel and Roza, *Funding the Child.*

27. Interview with vice principal for academic affairs, December 2006.

28. Goals 2000: Educate America Act, Public Law 103-227, 108 Stat. 125, March 31, 1994.

29. Improving America's Schools Act of 1994, Public Law 103-382, 108 Stat. 3518, January 25, 1994.

30. Travis Hicks, "Ed-Flex Hasn't Spurred Innovation," *Title I Online,* 2007, http://www.thompson.com/libraries/titleionline/news_desk/tio070117b.html.

31. Office of the Inspector General, *Combining Funds in Schoolwide Programs: Final Audit Report* (Atlanta: U.S. Department of Education, 2000).

32. Section 1903 (a) (1) (c).

33. Office of Elementary and Secondary Education, "Notice Authorizing Schoolwide Programs to Consolidate Federal Education Funds and Exempting Them From Complying With Statutory or Regulatory Provisions of Those Programs," *Federal Register* 69 (Washington, DC: U.S. Department of Education, 2004), 127.

34. Office of the Inspector General, The Illinois State Board of Education's Administration of Provisions Relating to Consolidating Funds in Schoolwide Programs (Washington, DC: U.S. Department of Education, 2005).

35. Heather Rose, Jon Sonstelie, and Ray Reinhard, *School Resources and Academic Standards in California: Lessons from the Schoolhouse* (San Francisco: Public Policy Institute of California, 2006).

36. Ibid., 71.

37. Marguerite Roza and Claudine Swartz, "School Spending Profiles: A Framework to Enlighten Resource Allocation Decisions," *Public Budgeting & Finance* 27, no. 1 (2007): 69–85.

38. Of course, the trade-off here was that Title I students no longer would miss regular classes for a pullout program and that services and record keeping would be simplified.

39. Hicks, "Ed-Flex Hasn't Spurred Innovation."

40. Hassel and Roza, *Funding the Child.*

41. For more on IDEA, see http://idea.ed.gov; for the loss of revenue, see Jay P. Greene and Greg Forster, *Effects of Funding Incentives on Special Education Enrollment* (New York: Manhattan Institute, Center for Civic Innovation, 2002).

Chapter 3: Allocating Resources Through Traditional Versus Reform-Oriented Collective Bargaining Agreements

1. No Child Left Behind Act of 2001, Public Law 107-110, 115 Stat. 1425, January 8, 2002.

2. The Education Partnership, *Teacher Contracts: Restoring the Balance* (Providence, RI: The Education Partnership, 2005), http://www.ecs.org/html/Document_noID.asp?CHouseID=6012; Frederick Hess and Martin R. West, *A Better Bargain: Overhauling Teacher Collective Bargaining for the 21st Century* (Washington, DC: Harvard University Program on Education Policy and Governance, 2006), www.ksg.harvard.edu/pepg/PDF/Papers/BetterBargain.pdf; Jessica Levine, Jennifer Mulhern, and Joan Schunck, *Unintended Consequences: The Case for Reforming the Staffing Rules in Urban Teachers' Contracts* (New York: The New Teacher Project, 2006), http://www.tntp.org/ourresearch/unintendedconsequences.html.

3. School Finance Redesign Project, interview with district administrator, November 2005.

4. One example is civil service provisions, which preceded collective bargaining laws, occupational heath and safety laws, and special education rules and regulations.

5. The remaining states, many of them in the South, do not permit teacher bargaining.

6. For more information regarding the selection of these school districts, see Shelley De Wys, Melissa Bowen, Allison Demeritt, and Jacob E. Adams, Jr., *Performance Pressure and Resource Allocation in Washington* (Seattle: University of Washington, Center on Reinventing Public Education, School Finance Redesign Project, 2008).

7. Agreement and partnership between School District No. 1 in the City and County of Denver, State of Colorado and Denver Classroom Teachers Association, September 1, 2005–August 31, 2008; Agreement between Minneapolis Public Schools and the Minneapolis Federation of Teachers, 2003–2005; Agreement between Montgomery County Education Association and Board of Education of Montgomery County, 2005–2007; Agreement between the Rochester City School District and the Rochester Teachers Association, 2004–2006; Agreement between the Toledo Board of Education and the Toledo Federation of Teachers, 2001–2004; Contract between the Columbus Board of Education and the Columbus Education Association, 2000–2003 (plus addendum, 2003–2004). All contract language quoted from the named districts is taken from these documents. Contracts in the numbered districts remain unnamed to protect the anonymity required by the Institutional Review Board process of the University of Washington.

8. Enacted in 1935, the National Labor Relations Act is the nation's principal (private sector) labor law. National Labor Relations Act, Public Law 74-198, 49 Stat. 449, July 5, 1935.

9. Julia E. Koppich, "The As-Yet-Unfulfilled Promise of Reform Bargaining: Forging a Better Match Between the Labor Relations System We Have and the Education System We Want," in *Collective Bargaining in Education: Negotiating Change in Today's Schools,* eds. Jane Hannaway and Andrew J. Rotherham (Cambridge: Harvard Education Press, 2006), 203–227.

10. Charles T. Kerchner and Julia E. Koppich, *A Union of Professionals: Labor Relations and Educational Reform* (New York: Teachers College Press, 1993).

11. Robert Fisher and William Ury, *Getting to Yes: Negotiating Agreement Without Giving In* (New York: Penguin Books, 1984).

12. Martin Malin and Charles T. Kerchner, "Charter Schools and Collective Bargaining: Compatible Marriage or Illegitimate Relationship" (presented paper, Claremont Graduate University, 2006).

13. Ibid.

14. NLRB v. Yeshiva University, 444 U.S. 672, 1980.

15. Kerchner and Koppich, *A Union of Professionals;* Charles T. Kerchner, Julia E. Koppich, and Joseph G. Weeres, *United Mind Workers: Unions and Teaching in the Knowledge Society* (San Francisco: Jossey-Bass Publishers, 1997).

16. Koppich, "The As-Yet-Unfulfilled Promise of Reform Bargaining."

17. National Labor Relations Act.

18. Ibid., section 7.

19. Charles T. Kerchner and Douglas E. Mitchell, *The Changing Idea of a Teachers' Union* (New York: Falmer Press, 1988).

20. Ibid.

21. Ibid.

22. Richard Kahlenberg, "The History of Collective Bargaining Among Teachers," in *Collective Bargaining in Education: Negotiating Change in Today's Schools,* eds. Hannaway and Rotherham, 7–25.

23. Koppich, "The As-Yet-Unfulfilled Promise of Reform Bargaining."

24. Kerchner and Mitchell, *Changing Idea of a Teachers Union*; Kahlenberg, "The History of Collective Bargaining Among Teachers"; Koppich, "The As-Yet-Unfulfilled Promise of Reform Bargaining."
25. Collective bargaining for public employees, including teachers, is authorized by state, and not federal, statute.
26. The NEA, whose membership included college presidents, professors, and school administrators, opposed collective bargaining for teachers until the late 1960s. At that point, the NEA eliminated college and school administrators from its ranks and embraced collective bargaining for teachers.
27. Kahlenberg, "The History of Collective Bargaining Among Teachers."
28. This number includes teachers who belong to the NEA or AFT in states that have no collective bargaining.
29. Susan Moore Johnson and Morgaen Donaldson, "The Effects of Collective Bargaining on Teacher Quality," in *Collective Bargaining in Education: Negotiating Change in Today's Schools,* eds. Hannaway and Rotherham, 111–140.
30. Although negotiated agreements are often referred to as "teacher contracts," in fact they are bilateral agreements between school districts and unions. Contracts are neither legal nor legally binding unless they carry the signatures of union officials as well as school board members (or the superintendent acting as the board's designee).
31. Kerchner, Koppich, and Weeres, *United Mind Workers.*
32. Ibid.
33. The National Commission on Excellence in Education, *A Nation At Risk: The Imperative for Educational Reform* (Washington, DC: U.S. Department of Education, 1983).
34. Albert Shanker, "A Nation at Risk," in *The Power of His Ideas: Al in His Own Words* (AFT convention proceedings, Washington, DC: American Federation of Teachers, 1983).
35. Robert Chase, "It's Not Your Mother's NEA" (speech, National Press Club, Washington, DC, February 5, 1997).
36. Teachers are members of state-specific retirement programs; the amount contributed by the district and each employee is often a negotiated matter.
37. Contracts also limit secondary teachers' preparations (the number of different classes they can be required to teach in a single semester) and the number of classes to which they are assigned each day (most commonly five), and they indicate whether elementary teachers have salaried preparation time. Also included are the numbers of meetings teachers can be required to attend each month (for example, faculty meetings and parent–teacher meetings).
38. Teachers are credited with a negotiated number of sick days per year (usually ten to twelve). Unused sick leave can be accumulated year to year. Some jurisdictions allow some portion of unused sick leave to be cashed in at retirement.
39. District 5's contract provides for unpaid study leaves.
40. Tenure provides that teachers who have successfully passed a probationary period are entitled to due process before being dismissed. Layoff results when a circumstance (for example, reduced funding) requires the district to reduce the number of staff members.
41. Not all states have a tenure law per se. In fact, tenure is more common in higher education. Some states use the notion of a "continuing contract" for K–12 teachers.
42. The term *single salary schedule* refers to a uniform salary structure that promotes equity in teacher compensation, based on objective, measurable criteria that are not subject to administrator discretion. See Consortium for Policy Research in Education, Single Salary Schedule (Madison, WI: University of Wisconsin, Wisconsin Center for Education Research, 2007), http://cpre.wceruw.org/tcomp/general/singlesalary.php.
43. Many states provide state-paid bonuses for teachers who earn board certification. But many districts top off these bonuses with additional salary.

44. The contract states that a joint union–management committee has responsibility for approving eligible teachers, but it does not describe the duties attached to this designation.

45. Toledo Review and Alternative Compensation System for Instructional Leadership (Toledo, OH: Toledo Federation of Teachers and Toledo Public Schools, February 2003).

46. In interviews, principals in District 5 complained that seniority governs all transfers, but the language of the contract does not indicate this to be the case.

47. Extracontract agreements typically are in the form of memoranda of understanding or trust agreements, which sit outside the collectively bargained contract.

48. Often, the teacher can grieve whether or not the procedure was followed but not the outcome.

49. Thomas McGreal, *Successful Teacher Evaluation* (Alexandria, VA: Association for Curriculum and Development, 1983); Donald M. Medley and Homer Coker, "The Accuracy of Principals' Judgments of Teacher Performance," *Journal of Educational Research* 80, no. 4 (1987): 242–247.

50. See, for example, Julia E. Koppich, "Toward Improving Teacher Quality: An Evaluation of Peer Assistance and Review in Montgomery County Public School" (presentation, Montgomery County Public Schools, Montgomery County, Maryland, 2004).

51. Dan Lortie, *Schoolteacher* (Chicago: University of Chicago Press, 1975).

52. See, for example, Dan Goldhaber, "The Mystery of Good Teaching," *Education Next* 2, no. 1 (2002): 50–55; Goldhaber, "Teachers Matter, But Effective Teacher Quality Policies Are Elusive," in *Handbook of Research in Education Finance and Policy*, eds. Helen F. Ladd and Edward B. Fiske (New York: Routledge, Taylor and Francis Group, 2008), 146–165; Kati Haycock, "Good Teaching Matters . . . a Lot," *Thinking K–16* 3, no. 2 (1998): 3–14.

53. There may be additional committees that operate but are not named in the contract. For example, in Montgomery County the union is directly involved with the school district in developing the budget, but the contract lists no budget committee per se.

54. Here, again, "all" refers to all contracts in this sample but could be applied more broadly to the range of contracts in districts across the country.

55. This provision may require fair share, meaning that all members of the bargaining unit either be members of the union or pay a fee to cover the cost of negotiations and administration of the agreement.

56. In these districts there often is a right-to-work teachers' organization that opposes collective bargaining.

57. A grievance in this context is defined as a violation of local policy or state law. See also Mitch Price, "Memorandum #3: Legal Research Regarding the Collective Bargaining Paper" (Seattle: University of Washington, Center on Reinventing Public Education, 2006).

58. Teachers' levels of pay are calibrated to student test scores, calculated on a value-added basis in which students' annual growth is measured.

59. Price, "Memorandum #3."

60. The Education Partnership, *Teacher Contracts: Restoring the Balance.*

61. Koppich, "The As-Yet-Unfulfilled Promise of Reform Bargaining."

62. Kerchner, Koppich, and Weeres, *United Mind Workers.*

63. Koppich, "The As-Yet-Unfulfilled Promise of Reform Bargaining."

64. Julia E. Koppich, "Addressing Teacher Quality Through Induction, Professional Compensation and Evaluation: The Effects on Labor-Management Relations," in *Education Policy*, eds. Lora Cohen-Vogel and Carolyn Herrington (Thousand Oaks, CA: Corwin Press, 2005), 90–111.

65. Susan Moore Johnson, "Teaching's Next Generation: Who Are They? What Will Keep Them in the Classroom?" *Education Week,* June 7, 2000, 33, 48.

66. Kerchner, Koppich, and Weeres, *United Mind Workers*; Charles T. Kerchner and Julia E. Koppich, "Negotiating What Matters Most: Student Achievement" (presented paper, Claremont Graduate University, Claremont, California, March 17, 2006).

Chapter 4: Organizing School Systems for Continuous Improvement

1. Elementary and Secondary Education Act of 1965, Public Law 89-10, 79 Stat. 27, April 11, 1965.

2. No Child Left Behind Act of 2001, Public Law 107-110, 115 Stat. 1425, January 8, 2002.

3. The quality of standards varies greatly from state to state. Weak standards states, such as Alaska, Montana, and Wyoming, do not offer in their standards enough rigor or depth to ensure that students have the skills they need to succeed upon graduation. Strong standards states, such as California, Massachusetts, and Indiana, provide high-quality models for setting academic expectations. See Chester E. Finn, Jr., Michael J. Petrilli, and Liam Julian, *The State of State Standards 2006* (Washington, DC: Thomas B. Fordham Foundation, 2006), http://www.edexcellence.net/foundation/publication/publication.cfm?id=358.

4. These policies are made more complex by the fact that each state defines its own standards, develops its own test of these standards, and sets its own benchmarks for adequate yearly progress. Aligning each state's accountability system with the federal requirements of NCLB is often a difficult task that is not always done with care and expertise, resulting in sometimes misaligned accountability metrics and systems riddled with gaps and disconnects, all of which makes the jobs of educators in those states much more difficult.

5. See, for example, Paul Black and Dylan Wiliam, "Inside the Black Box: Raising Standards Through Classroom Assessment," *Phi Delta Kappan* 80, no. 2 (1998): 139–148; Amanda Datnow, Vicki Park, and Priscilla Wohlstetter, *Achieving with Data: How High-Performing School Systems Use Data to Improve Instruction for Elementary Students* (Los Angeles: University of Southern California, Center on Educational Governance, 2007), http://www.newschools.org/viewpoints/AchievingWithData.pdf; EdSource, *Similar Students, Different Results: Why Do Some Schools Do Better?* (Mountain View, CA: EdSource, 2006), http://www.edsource.org/pub_SimStu6-06_SummaryReport.html; Kim Marshall, *Interim Assessments: Keys to Successful Implementation* (New York: New Leaders for New Schools, 2006), http://www.marshallmemo.com/articles/Interim%20Assmt%20Report%20Apr.%2012,%2006.pdf; Ida Oberman, *Challenged Schools, Remarkable Results: Three Lessons from California's Highest Achieving High Schools* (San Francisco: Springboard Schools [now Pivit Learning Partners], 2006), http://www.springboardschools.org/research/other_research.html; Scott Thompson, "Creating a High-Performance School System," *Phi Delta Kappan* 84, no. 7 (2003): 488–496; Mary Jo Waits, Heather E. Campbell, Rebecca Gau, Ellen Jacobs, Tom Rex, and Robert K. Hess, *Why Some Schools with Latino Children Beat the Odds . . . and Others Don't* (Tempe: Arizona State University, Morrison Institute for Public Policy and Center for the Future of Arizona, 2006), http://www.asu.edu/copp/morrison/LatinEd.pdf; Kiley Walsh, *After the Test: How Schools Are Using Data to Close the Achievement Gap* (San Francisco: Learning Point Associates and Bay Area School Reform Collaborative, 2003), http://www.springboardschools.org/research/other_research.html.

6. This definition is provided by the Center for Continuous Instructional Improvement, part of the Consortium for Policy Research in Education at the University of Pennsylvania's Graduate School of Education.

7. Datnow, Park, and Wohlstetter, *Achieving with Data,* 18.

8. Siobhan Leahy, Christine Lyon, Mamie Thompson, and Dylan Wiliam, "Classroom Assessment—Minute by Minute, Day by Day," *Educational Leadership* 63, no. 3 (2005): 18–24.

9. Marshall, *Interim Assessments.*

10. Anthony Bryk, personal communication, 2006.

11. Datnow, Park, and Wohlstetter, *Achieving with Data; Oberman, Challenged Schools, Remarkable Results;* Waits et al., *Why Some Schools with Latino Children Beat the Odds . . . and Others Don't;* Walsh, *After the Test.*

Chapter 5: Making Strategic Resource Decisions

1. No Child Left Behind Act of 2001, Public Law 107-110, 115 Stat. 1425, January 8, 2002.

2. Eric A. Hanushek, "Assessing the Effects of School Resources on Student Performance: An Update," *Educational Evaluation and Policy Analysis* 19, no. 2 (1997): 141–164.

3. See, for example, Allan R. Odden and Sarah J. Archibald, *Doubling Student Performance . . . and Finding the Resources to Do It* (Thousand Oaks, CA: Corwin Press, 2009).

4. David Tyack and William Tobin, "The 'Grammar' of Schooling: Why Has It Been So Hard to Change?" *American Educational Research Journal* 31, no. 3 (1994): 453–479; Allan Odden, David Monk, Yassaer Nakib, and Lawrence Picus, "The Story of the Education Dollar: No Academy Awards and No Fiscal Smoking Guns," *Phi Delta Kappan* 77, no. 2 (1995): 161–168; Stephen Frank and Randi Feinberg, *District Spending on Small and Large High Schools: Lessons from Baltimore City, Boston, and Chicago* (Watertown, MA: Education Resource Strategies, 2009).

5. Karen Hawley Miles and Stephen Frank, *The Strategic School: Making the Most of People, Time, and Money* (Thousand Oaks, CA: Corwin Press, 2008); Linda Darling-Hammond, *The Right to Learn: A Blueprint for Creating Schools That Work* (San Francisco: Jossey-Bass, 1997).

6. See, for example, Richard J. Murnane and Frank Levy, *Teaching the New Basic Skills: Principles for Educating Children to Thrive in a Changing Economy* (New York: Free Press, 1996).

7. National Research Council, Committee on Developments in the Science of Learning, *How People Learn: Brain, Mind, Experience, and School,* eds. John D. Bransford, Ann L. Brown, and Rodney R. Cocking (Washington DC: National Academy Press, 1999).

8. Linda Darling-Hammond and Gary Sykes, eds., *Teaching as the Learning Profession* (San Francisco: Jossey-Bass, 2003); Milbrey W. McLaughlin and Joan Talbert, *Developing the Teaching Profession: Learning to Improve Student Achievement* (New York: Teachers College Press, 2005).

9. Education Resource Strategies is a nonprofit organization dedicated to supporting school system leaders in transforming student performance through strategic use of resources. See http://www.ers.org. Miles and Frank, *The Strategic School;* Regis Anne Shields and Karen Hawley Miles, *Strategic Designs: Lessons from Leading Edge Small Urban High Schools* (Watertown, MA: Education Resource Strategies, 2008).

10. To learn more about University Park and resource use in other high-performing schools, see http://www.educationresourcestrategies.org/small_schools.htm.

11. Shields and Miles, *Strategic Designs.*

12. See, for example, Dan Goldhaber, "The Mystery of Good Teaching," *Education Next* 2, no. 1 (2002): 50–55; Dan Goldhaber, "Teachers Matter, But Effective Teacher Quality Policies Are Elusive," in *Handbook of Research in Education Finance and Policy,* eds. Helen F. Ladd and Edward B. Fiske (New York: Routledge, Taylor and Francis Group, 2008), 146–165; Kati Haycock, "Good Teaching Matters . . . a Lot," *Thinking K–16* 3, no. 2 (1998): 3–14.

13. Allan Odden, Lawrence O. Picus, Michael Goetz, Michelle Mangan, and Mark Fermanich, *An Evidence-Based Approach to School Finance Adequacy in Washington* (North Hollywood, CA: Lawrence O. Picus and Associates, 2006).

14. Steven G. Rivkin, Eric A. Hanushek, and John F. Kain, "Teachers, Schools and Academic Achievement," *Econometrica* 73, no. 2 (2005): 417–458.

15. Regis Anne Shields and Karen Hawley Miles, "Strategic Professional Development Review," in *A Grand Bargain for Education Reform: New Rewards and Supports for New Accountability,* eds. Theodore Hershberg and Claire Robertson-Kraft (Cambridge, MA: Harvard Education Press, 2009).

16. Elena Silva, *On the Clock: Rethinking the Way Schools Use Time* (Washington, DC: Education Sector Reports, January 22, 2007), http://www.educationsector.org/research/research_show.htm?doc_id=442238.

17. Malcolm Gladwell, *Outliers: The Story of Success* (New York: Little, Brown & Co, 2008). For instance, in his discussion of the success of Knowledge Is Power Program (KIPP) students, Gladwell notes that, like students in Asian countries, KIPP students spend about 60 percent more time on task than most U.S. students, with much of this time focused on core academic subjects.

18. Margurite Roza and Karen Hawley Miles, *Taking Stock of the Fiscal Costs of Expanded Learning Time* (Washington, DC: Center for American Progress, 2008); Silva, *On the Clock.*

19. David Farbman and Claire Kaplan, *Time for a Change: The Promise of Extended-Time Schools for Promoting Student Achievement* (Boston: Massachusetts 2020, 2005), http://www.mass2020.org/files/file/Time-for-a-change(1).pdf.

20. Roza and Miles, *Taking Stock of the Fiscal Costs of Expanded Learning Time.*

21. Miles and Frank, *The Strategic School.*

22. Ibid.

23. Marguerite Roza, *Frozen Assets: How Rethinking Teacher Contracts Could Free Billions for School Reform* (Washington, DC: Education Sector Reports, 2007). To explore the resources freed by making targeted changes to class size by grade or subject or in other areas, explore the Web-based District Resource Allocation Modeler (DREAM) at http://www.educationresourcestrategies.org.

24. Odden et al., *An Evidence-Based Approach to School Finance Adequacy in Washington.*

25. Ibid.

26. Barbara A. Wasik and Robert E. Slavin, "Preventing Early Reading Failure with One-to-One Tutoring," *Reading Research Quarterly* 28, no. 1 (1993): 178–200.

27. For simple ways of calculating these costs, please see the District Resource Allocation Modeler (DREAM) tool.

28. Russell Gersten and Joseph A. Dimino, "RTI (Response to Intervention): Rethinking Special Education for Students with Reading Difficulties (Yet Again)," *Reading Research Quarterly* 41, no. 1 (2006): 99–108; Nate Levenson, "A Win-Win Approach to Reducing Special Education Costs," *District Management Journal* (Spring 2009): 20–27; Jay G. Chambers, Tom B. Parrish, and Jenifer J. Harr, *What Are We Spending on Special Education Services in the United States, 1999–2000?* (Washington, DC: American Institutes for Research, Center for Special Education Finance, updated June 2004); Stetson and Associates, Inc., "Inclusive Education for All of Our Students: A Special Session for Duval County Public School Parents" (presentation, spring 2007), http://www.duvalschools.org/static/parents/getinvolved/ese/downloads/dcps%20parent%20presentation%2003%2021%2007%20revised.pdf.

29. Roza, *Frozen Assets;* Shields and Miles, *Strategic Designs.*

30. Barnett Berry, Diana Montgomery, Rachel Curtis, Mindy Hernandez, Judy Wurtzel, and Jon Snyder, *Creating and Sustaining Urban Teacher Residencies: A New Way to Recruit,*

Prepare, and Retain Effective Teachers in High-Needs Districts, ED 502406 (The Aspen Institute and The Center for Teaching Quality, 2008), http://www.eric.ed.gov:80/ERIC-Docs/data/ericdocs2sql/content_storage_01/0000019b/80/3e/b8/0e.pdf

31. See District Resource Allocation Modeler (DREAM).
32. Roza and Miles, *Taking Stock of the Fiscal Costs of Expanded Learning Time.*

Chapter 6: Merging Costs with Effective Resource Strategies

1. An earlier version of this chapter appeared as "Using Available Evidence to Estimate the Cost of Educational Adequacy," *Education Finance and Policy* 3, no. 3 (2008): 374-397.
2. Allan Odden and Lawrence O. Picus, *School Finance: A Policy Perspective,* 4th ed. (New York: McGraw Hill, 2007).
3. Eric A. Hanushek, ed., *Courting Failure: How School Finance Lawsuits Exploit Judges' Good Intentions and Harm Our Children* (Stanford, CA: Education Next Books, 2006).
4. No Child Left Behind Act of 2001, Public Law 107-110, 115 Stat. 1425, January 8, 2002.
5. Paul A. Minorini and Stephen D. Sugarman, "Educational Adequacy and the Courts: The Promise and Problems of Moving to a New Paradigm," in *Equity and Adequacy in Education Finance: Issues and Perspectives,* eds. Helen F. Ladd, Rosemary Chalk, and Janet S. Hansen (Washington, DC: National Academy Press, 1999), 175–208.
6. James W. Guthrie and Richard Rothstein, "Enabling 'Adequacy' to Achieve Reality: Translating Adequacy into State School Finance Distribution Arrangements," in ibid., 209–259; Allan Odden, "Equity and Adequacy of School Finance Today," *Phi Delta Kappan* 85, no. 2 (2003): 120–125; Odden and Picus, *School Finance: A Policy Perspective.*
7. Hanushek, *Courting Failure.*
8. Odden and Picus, *School Finance: A Policy Perspective.*
9. For the cost function approach, see William Duncombe, John Ruggiero, and John Yinger, "Alternative Approaches to Measuring the Cost of Education," in *Holding Schools Accountable: Performance-Based Reform in Education,* ed. Helen F. Ladd (Washington, DC: Brookings Institution, 1996), 327–356; Jennifer Imazeki and Andrew Reschovsky, "Assessing the Use of Econometric Analysis in Estimating the Costs of Meeting State Education Accountability Standards: Lessons from Texas," *Peabody Journal of Education* 80, no. 3 (2005): 96–125; Andrew Reschovsky and Jennifer Imazeki, "The Development of School Finance Formulas to Guarantee the Provision of Adequate Education to Low-Income Students," in *Developments in School Finance 1997* (NCES 98-212), ed. William J. Fowler, Jr. (Washington, DC: U.S. Department of Education, National Center for Education Statistics, 1998), http://nces.ed.gov/pubs98/dev97/index.asp; Andrew Reschovsky and Jennifer Imazeki, "Reforming State Aid to Achieve Educational Adequacy: Lessons from Texas and Wisconsin" (presented paper, Tennessee State University, Nashville, April 26, 1999); Andrew Reschovsky and Jennifer Imazeki, "Achieving Educational Adequacy Through School Finance Reform," *Journal of Education Finance* 26, no. 4 (2001): 373–396. For the professional judgment approach, see John Augenblick, John Myers, Justin Silverstein, and Anne Barkis, "Calculation of the Cost of a Suitable Education in Kansas in 2000–2001 Using Two Different Analytic Approaches" (report prepared for the Kansas Legislative Coordinating Council, 2002), http://www.jlmyersgroup.com/KansasAdequacyStudy2002summary.pdf; James Guthrie, Gerald C. Hayward, James R. Smith, Richard Rothstein, Ronald W. Bennett, Julia E. Koppich, Ellis Bowman, Lynn DeLapp, Barbara Brandes, and Sandra Clark, *A Proposed Cost-Based Block Grant Model for Wyoming School Finance* (Davis, CA: Management Analysis and Planning Associates, LLC, 1997), http://legisweb.state.wy.us/schoolx/cost/final/final. htm. For the successful schools or districts approach, see John Augenblick, *Calculation of the Cost of an Adequate Education in Maryland in 1999–2000 Using Two Different*

Analytic Approaches (Denver: Augenblick and Meyers, 2001); Augenblick et al., "Calculation of the Cost of a Suitable Education in Kansas"; Mark Fermanich, Michelle Turner Mangan, Allan Odden, Lawrence O. Picus, Bethany Gross, and Zena Rudo, *Washington Learns: Successful District Study* (North Hollywood, CA: Lawrence O. Picus and Associates, 2006); Allen Dupree, John Augenblick, and Justin Silverstein, *Report on the Cost of Education* (Trenton: New Jersey Department of Education, Division of Finance, Office of School Funding, 2006). For the evidence-based approach, see Allan Odden, Lawrence O. Picus, and Mark Fermanich, *An Evidence-Based Approach to School Finance Adequacy in Arkansas* (North Hollywood, CA: Lawrence O. Picus and Associates, 2003); Allan R. Odden, Lawrence O. Picus, and Michael Goetz, *Recalibrating the Arkansas School Funding Structure* (North Hollywood, CA: Lawrence O. Picus & Associates, 2006); Allan R. Odden, Lawrence O. Picus, Mark Fermanich, and Michael Goetz, *An Evidence-Based Approach to School Finance Adequacy in Arizona* (Phoenix: Rodel Charitable Foundation of Arizona, 2004); Allan Odden, Mark Fermanich, and Lawrence O. Picus, *A State-of-the-Art Approach to School Finance Adequacy in Kentucky* (North Hollywood, CA: Lawrence O. Picus and Associates, 2003); Allan R. Odden, Lawrence O. Picus, Michael Goetz, Mark Fermanich, and Michelle Turner Mangan, *An Evidence-Based Approach to School Finance Adequacy in Washington* (North Hollywood, CA: Lawrence O. Picus & Associates, 2006); Allan R. Odden, Lawrence O. Picus, Sarah Archibald, Michael Goetz, Michelle Turner Mangan, and Anabel Aportela, *Moving from Good to Great in Wisconsin: Funding Schools Adequately and Doubling Student Performance* (Madison: University of Wisconsin, Wisconsin Center for Education Research, Consortium for Policy Research in Education, 2007); Allan R. Odden, Lawrence O. Picus, Michael Goetz, Mark Fermanich, Rich Seder, William Glenn, and Rob Nelli, *An Evidence-Based Approach to Recalibrating Wyoming's Block Grant School Funding Formula* (North Hollywood, CA: Lawrence O. Picus & Associates, 2005).

10. Lori L. Taylor, Bruce D. Baker, and Arnold Vedlitz, *Measuring Educational Adequacy in Public Schools,* Bush School Working Paper No. 580 (College Station: Texas A&M, Bush School of Government & Public Service, 2005), http://bush.tamu.edu/research/working-papers/ltaylor/measuring_edu_adequacy_in_public_schools.pdf; Guthrie and Rothstein, "Enabling 'Adequacy' to Achieve Reality"; and Odden, "Equity and Adequacy of School Finance Today."

11. Odden et al., *An Evidence-Based Approach to School Finance Adequacy in Arkansas;* Odden et al., *Recalibrating the Arkansas School Funding Structure;* Odden et al., *An Evidence-Based Approach to School Finance Adequacy in Arizona;* Odden, Fermanich, and Picus, *A State-of-the Art Approach to School Finance Adequacy in Kentucky;* Odden et al., *An Evidence-Based Approach to School Finance Adequacy in Washington;* Odden et al., *Moving from Good to Great in Wisconsin;* Odden et al., *An Evidence-Based Approach to Recalibrating Wyoming's Block Grant School Funding Formula.*

12. See, for example, Samuel Stringfield, Steven Ross, and Lana Smith, *Bold Plans for School Restructuring: The New American Schools Designs* (Mahwah, NJ: Lawrence Erlbaum, 1996).

13. For evidence supporting each of these recommendations, see the earlier Odden et al. citations as well as Odden and Picus, *School Finance: A Policy Perspective*, chapter 4.

14. At-risk students are generally those students eligible for the federal free and reduced-price lunch program, often with adjustments for high school students, where lunch eligibility is typically underreported.

15. For an example, see Jennifer Imazeki, *Regional Cost Adjustments for Washington State* (report prepared for the K–12 Advisory Committee of Washington Learns, 2006).

16. Jacob E. Adams, Jr., "Ambitious Learning Goals Require a New Approach to Educational Resources," this volume; Diana Sharp and John Bransford, *Learning Science Meets School*

Finance: The How-People-Learn Framework as a Tool for Resource Decisions (Seattle: University of Washington, Center on Reinventing Public Education, School Finance Redesign Project, 2007); Joanne Weiss, "Organizing School Systems for Continuous Improvement," this volume.

17. Compare, for example, Hanushek, *Courting Failure,* with Allan R. Odden and Sarah J. Archibald, *Doubling Student Performance . . . and Finding the Resources to Do It* (Thousand Oaks, CA: Corwin Press, 2009).

18. For example, see Odden et al., *An Evidence-Based Approach to School Finance Adequacy in Washington; Odden et al., Moving from Good to Great in Wisconsin.*

19. For studies of the efficacy of these approaches in the private sector, see John Kotter, *Leading Change* (Boston: Harvard Business School Press, 1996); Kotter, *The Heart of Change* (Boston: Harvard Business School Press, 2002). For studies on the efficacy of these approaches in education, see Daniel Duke, "What We Know and Don't Know About Improving Low Performing Schools," *Phi Delta Kappan* 87, no. 10 (2006): 728–734; Michael Fullan, *The New Meaning of Educational Change* (New York: Teachers College Press, 2002).

20. The prototypical district could include any number of students or schools; the numbers used here are used merely to produce an average per-pupil cost for the various recommendations. Once that per-pupil figure is reached, it could be used as the expenditure per-pupil figure in a foundation program, which then would provide a greater total amount of money to larger districts and a lesser total amount of money to smaller districts; actual amounts would depend on the exact numbers of students in the district. Further, districts with higher numbers of ELLs or students eligible for free and reduced-price lunch would also be eligible for larger amounts of money.

21. For numbers of ELLs, see National Center for Education Statistics, *Digest of Educational Statistics* (Washington, DC: U.S. Department of Education, National Center for Education Statistics, 2006). For special education students, see Lee Hoffman and Jennifer Sable, *Public Elementary Students, Staff, Schools, and School Districts: School Year 2003–04* (NCES 2006-307) (Washington, DC: U.S. Department of Education, National Center for Education Statistics, 2006), http://nces.ed.gov/pubsearch/pubsinfo.asp?pubid=2006307.

22. Although several evidence-based studies included minimum staff to deal with the increased cost of small schools and districts, this per-pupil figure is a simple proration, up and down, of the costs of the model. In analyses of the statewide differences in per-pupil costs between models that include minimum staff positions and those that use simple proration, minimal cost differences exist.

23. A census approach bases special education funding on the number of all school-aged children rather than the count of children receiving special education services, essentially capping the number of eligible children at a percentage of the total student population.

24. This estimate is based on a high-cost student with disabilities requiring $50,000 above regular-pupil costs. For every 1,000 students, assuming that 13.7 percent have disabilities and assuming that 2 percent of those students are high cost, then 2.74 will be high-cost students. The total cost for these students would be 2.74 × $50,000, or $137,000, or $137 per regular student, and $50,000 per high-cost special education student.

25. Odden et al., *Moving from Good to Great in Wisconsin.*

26. National Center for Education Statistics, *Digest of Education Statistics,* 2005, NCES 2006-030 (Washington, DC: U.S. Department of Education, 2006).

27. See Odden et al., *An Evidence-Based Approach to School Finance Adequacy in Washington.*

28. See Lori Taylor and William J. Fowler, *A Comparative Wage Approach to Geographic Cost Adjustment* (Washington, DC: National Center for Statistics, 2006).

29. National Education Association, *Rankings and Estimates: Rankings of the States 2005 and Estimates of School Statistics 2006* (Washington, DC: National Education Association Research, 2006).

30. Adams, "Ambitious Learning Goals Require a New Approach to Educational Resources."

Chapter 7: Making Resource Decisions amid Technical Uncertainty

1. Thomas D. Snyder, Sally A. Dillow, and Charlene M. Hoffman, *Digest of Education Statistics 2008* (Washington, DC: U.S. Department of Education, Institute of Education Sciences, National Center on Education Statistics, 2009), tables 3, 179, and 185.

2. New Jersey's so-called Abbot districts at one point received more than $20,000 annually per pupil. Student achievement proficiency remained at half the state average. Kentucky has been the site of increased school spending since 1990, and its National Assessment of Educational Progress scores in reading, mathematics, science, and writing have remained stagnant. See Melissa A. Clark, *Education Reform, Redistribution, and Student Achievement: Evidence from Kentucky Education Reform Act* (Princeton, NJ: Mathematica Policy Research, Inc., 2003). For evidence regarding Kansas City and the absence of achievement gains despite the spending of billions in added resources, see Paul Ciotti, "Money and School Performance: Lessons from the Kansas City Desegregation Experiment," *Cato Policy Analysis* 298 (March 16, 1998).

3. George W. Bohrnstedt and Brian M. Stecher, eds., *What We Have Learned About Class Size Reduction in California* (Sacramento: California Department of Education, 2002).

4. See www.kipp.org.

5. See www.successforall.net.

6. Melissa Roderick, Mimi Engel, Jenny Nagaoka with Brian A. Jacob, Sophie Degener, Alex Orfei, Susan Stone, and Jen Bacon, *Ending Social Promotion: Results from SummerBridge* (Chicago: University of Chicago, Consortium on Chicago School Research, 2003).

7. Minority student achievement in Texas as measured by state and national examinations is an example of sustained academic improvement. However, the Texas improvements pursue precisely the model this chapter advocates. The state in a sustained manner has tried new strategies, evaluated outcomes, reinforced effective practices, and moved forward with new ideas when old ones proved ineffective. It is noteworthy that Texas does not spend much money on a per-pupil basis.

8. See, for example, Richard Rothstein, *Class and Schools: Using Social, Economic, and Educational Reform to Close the Black–White Achievement Gap* (New York: Teachers College Press, 2004).

9. See, for example, William G. Howell and Paul E. Peterson, *The Education Gap: Vouchers and Urban Schools*, revised ed. (Washington, DC: Brookings Institution, 2006).

10. State programs and local district efforts make episodic attempts to operate so-called gifted and talented programs. However, these programs seldom receive serious attention in policy or funding.

11. Others in the same localities—the school a few blocks away, the teacher in the next classroom, the school board—have few if any incentives to explore and imitate what is effective. Teacher union leader Roger Erskine labeled this process "random acts of innovation." See Roger Erskine, "Beyond Random Acts of Innovation," *Education Week*, September 27, 1995, www.edweek.org/ew/articles/1995/09/27/04erskin.h15.html?r=575835170. Former Xerox CEO David Kearns asserted the same argument when he founded the New American Schools Development Corporation, a $150 million nonprofit initiative to develop new designs for urban schools. He later discovered that innovative ideas were not sufficient: existing public education structures and practices can bend with new school designs, adopting their innocuous parts, rejecting the rest, and returning to the status quo ante.

12. No Child Left Behind Act of 2001, Public Law 107-110, 115 Statutes 1425, January 8, 2002.

13. Marguerite Roza, "Rethinking Data Capacity," in *Making School Reform Work: New Partnerships for Real Change,* eds. Paul T. Hill and James Harvey (Washington, DC: Brookings, 2004), 83–97.

14. See Julia E. Koppich, "Allocating Resources Through Traditional Versus Reform-Oriented Collective Bargaining Agreements," this volume.

15. David B. Tyack, *The One Best System: A History of American Urban Education* (Cambridge: Harvard University Press, 1974); David B. Tyack and Larry Cuban, *Tinkering Toward Utopia: A Century of Public School Reform* (Cambridge: Harvard University Press, 1995); Raymond E. Callahan, *Education and the Cult of Efficiency* (Chicago: University of Chicago Press, 1962).

16. For a general discussion of mayoral control, see Michael D. Usdan, Michael W. Kirst, Fritz Edelstein, Kenneth K. Wong, Paul T. Hill, Warren Simmons, Ellen Foley, and Marla Ucelli, "Mayoral Leadership in Education: Current Trends and Future Directions," *Harvard Educational Review* 76, no. 2 (Summer 2006): 147–152.

17. James B. Conant, *The American High School Today* (New York: McGraw-Hill, 1959).

18. See, for example, Alfie Kohn, *The Homework Myth: Why Our Kids Get Too Much of a Bad Thing* (Philadelphia: Da Capo Press, 2006).

19. Sara Bennett and Nancy Kalish, *The Case Against Homework: How Homework Is Hurting Our Children and What We Can Do About It* (New York: Crown, 2006).

20. Clinical trials—which in medicine both provide evidence of the efficacy of well-defined therapies and allow physicians in practice to balance scientific findings and patient uniqueness—have not been accepted in education.

21. This ethical position seems to assume that there is no risk of harm or failure in whatever treatments children would get absent a clinical trial.

22. Abraham Flexner, *Medical Education in the United States and Canada, Bulletin Number 4* (New York: Carnegie Foundation for the Advancement of Teaching, 1910).

23. Education Sciences Reform Act of 2002, Public Law 107-279, 116 Stat. 1940, November 5, 2002.

24. National Commission on Excellence in Education, *A Nation At Risk: The Imperative for Educational Reform* (Washington, DC: U.S. Government Printing Office, 1983).

25. Peter F. Drucker, "The Age of Social Transformation," *Atlantic Monthly,* November 1994, 53–80.

26. Terry M. Moe, "The Politics of the Status Quo," in *Our Schools & Our Future: Are We Still at Risk?* ed. Paul Peterson (Stanford, CA: Hoover Press, 2003).

27. Norman R. Dalkey, *The Delphi Method: An Experimental Study of Group Opinion* (Santa Monica, CA: The RAND Corporation, 1969).

28. See, for example, Eric A. Hanushek and Alfred A. Lindseth, *Schoolhouses, Courthouses, and Statehouses: Solving the Funding-Achievement Puzzle in America's Public Schools* (Princeton, NJ: Princeton University Press, 2009).

29. James W. Guthrie and Matthew G. Springer, "Courtroom Alchemy: Adequacy Advocates Turn Guesstimates into Gold," *Education Next* 7, no. 1 (2007): 20–27.

30. Some readers will recognize the similarity between this and the original goal of the New American Schools initiative. However, the selection process for New American Schools design teams was dominated by conventional public educators who rejected ideas that would substitute technology for teacher labor, saying (1) the unions would not stand for it and (2) we all know the mark of a good school is a spirit of collaboration of adults and not the methods used. Accordingly, New American Schools designs focused more on ways to foster good adult relationships than on new methods of instruction.

31. One middle-sized urban district studied by the Center on Reinventing Public Education maintains two hundred thousand separate financial accounts.
32. Marguerite Roza and Paul T. Hill, "How Teacher Salary Averaging Helps Some Schools to Fail," draft conference paper for Brookings Conference, The Teachers We Need (Seattle: University of Washington, Center on Reinventing Public Education, 2004).
33. Paul T. Hill and James Harvey, *Making School Reform Work* (Washington, DC: Brookings Institute, 2004).
34. Bruce Fuller, "Children Are the Losers in Polarized Debate over 'No Child Left Behind' Program," *Washington Post,* February 1, 2004.
35. Ted Kolderie, "Teacher Ownership as Entrepreneurship in Public Education," in *Social Entrepreneurship,* ed. Marilyn Kourilsky (Toronto: Senate Hall Press, 2003).
36. John Merrow, "Can D.C.'s Search Make the Grade?" *Washington Post,* August 8, 2004.
37. Bradley Portin, Paul Schneider, Michael DeArmond, and Lauren Gundlach, *Making Sense of Leading Schools: A Study of the School Principalship* (Seattle: University of Washington, Center on Reinventing Public Education, 2003); Paul T. Decker, Daniel P. Mayer, and Steve Galzerman, *The Effects of Teach for America on Students* (Princeton, NJ: Mathematica Policy Research, Inc., 2004).
38. National Working Commission on Choice in K–12 Education, *School Choice: Doing It the Right Way Makes a Difference* (Washington, DC: Brookings, 2003).
39. Ana Beatriz Cholo and Tracy Dell'Angela, "100 New Schools to Be Created," *Chicago Tribune,* June 23, 2004.

Chapter 8: Considering Outside-the-Box Changes in Education Funding

1. Knut Wicksell, "A New Principle of Just Taxation," in *Classics in the Theory of Public Finance,* eds. Richard A. Musgrave and Alan T. Peacock (London: MacMillan, 1958), 72–118.
2. Charles M. Tiebout, "A Pure Theory of Local Expenditures," *Journal of Political Economy* 64, no. 5 (1956): 416–424.
3. However, if affluent parents use the new system to enhance opportunities for their children, the children of the less affluent could be worse off in a relative sense.

Chapter 9: Linking Education Funding with Standards-Based Reform and Community-Based Resources

1. James W. Guthrie, Matthew G. Springer, R. Anthony Rolle, and Eric A. Houk, *Modern Education Finance and Policy* (Boston: Allyn and Bacon, 2007).
2. No Child Left Behind Act of 2001, Public Law 107-110, 115 Stat. 1425, January 8, 2002; and Patrick J. McGuinn, *No Child Left Behind and the Transformation of Federal Education Policy, 1965–2005* (Lawrence: University Press of Kansas, 2006).
3. For an early state-based perspective, see Bill Honig, *Last Chance for Our Children: How You Can Help Save Our Schools* (Reading, MA: Addison-Wesley, 1985). For a theoretical overview, see Marshall S. Smith and Jennifer O'Day, "Systemic School Reform," in *The Politics of Curriculum and Testing,* eds. Susan H. Fuhrman and Betty Malen (New York: Falmer Press, 1991), 233–267.
4. Improving America's Schools Act of 1994, Public Law 103-382, 108 Stat. 3518, October 20, 1994.
5. EdSource, *Similar Students, Dissimilar Results: Why Do Some Schools Do Better?* (Mountain View, CA: EdSource, 2006), www.edsource.org/pub_SimStu6-06_Summary Report.html.
6. Richard Elmore, "Accountability and Capacity," in *The New Accountability: High Schools and High-Stakes Testing,* eds. Martin Carnoy, Richard Elmore, and Leslie Santee Siskin (New York: Routledge Falmer, 2003), 188–198.

7. Ibid.

8. Guthrie et al., *Modern Education Finance and Policy*, 50–58; Michael W. Kirst and Andrea Venezia, *From High School to College: Improving Opportunities for Success in Postsecondary Education* (San Francisco: Jossey Bass, 2004).

9. For progress at the analytic level, see, for example, Allan R. Odden, Michael E. Goetz, and Lawrence O. Picus, "Merging Costs with Effective Resource Strategies," this volume; Jon Sonstelie, *Aligning School Finance with Academic Standards: A Weighted-Student Formula Based on a Survey of Practitioners* (San Francisco: Public Policy Institute of California, 2007). For examples of adequacy analyses by analytic method, see chapter 6, notes 8–10, this volume. Note, though, that the science of all costing-out methods has come under attack. See, for example, Eric A. Hanushek, "Science Violated: Spending Projections and the 'Costing Out' of an Adequate Education," in *Courting Failure: How School Finance Lawsuits Exploit Judges' Good Intentions and Harm Our Children*, ed. Erik A. Hanushek (Stanford, CA: Education Next Books, 2006), 257–312.

10. Paul Minorini and Stephen Sugarman, "Educational Adequacy and the Courts: The Promise and Problems of Moving to a New Paradigm," in *Equity and Adequacy in Education Finance: Issues and Perspectives*, eds. Helen Ladd, Rosemary Chalk, and Janet Hansen (Washington, DC: National Academy Press, 1999), 175–208.

11. See, for example, National Working Group on Funding Student Learning, *Funding Student Learning: How to Align Education Resources with Student Learning Goals* (Seattle: University of Washington, Center on Reinventing Public Education, School Finance Redesign Project, 2008), 5.

12. William S. Koski and Hillary Anne Weiss, "What Educational Resources Do Students Need to Meet California's Educational Content Standards? A Textual Analysis of California's Education Content Standards and Their Implications for Basic Educational Conditions and Resources," *Teachers College Record* 106, no. 10 (2004): 1907–1935.

13. See Joanne Weiss, "Organizing School Systems for Continuous Improvement," this volume.

14. California Reading First, *Assurances for the Sake of Our Students: Improving Student Achievement in Reading and Language Arts!* second revision (Sacramento: Sacramento County Office of Education, California Technical Assistance Center, 2008).

15. Susan H. Fuhrman, ed., *Designing Coherent Education Policy: Improving the System* (San Francisco: Jossey-Bass, 1993).

16. Betheny Gross and Margaret E. Goertz, eds., *Holding High Hopes: How High Schools Respond to State Accountability Policies* (CRPE research report series, University of Pennsylvania, Consortium for Policy Research in Education, 2005), ED 493112.

17. See Russell W. Rumberger and Patricia Gandara, "Seeking Equity in the Education of California's English Learners," *Teachers College Record* 106, no. 10 (2004): 2032–2056, including the notion that the resource needs of English learners often are insufficiently specified.

18. For example, 39 percent of white eighth graders met the National Assessment of Educational Progress proficiency level in reading, but only 15 percent of low-income students and 13 percent of black students reached this level. See Thomas B. Fordham Institute, *How Well Are States Educating Our Neediest Children? The Fordham Report 2006* (Washington, DC: Thomas B. Fordham Institute, 2006).

19. Patricia Albjerg Graham, "The Long Haul," *Education Next* 3, no. 2 (2003): 21.

20. Joy Dryfoos, *Full-Service Schools* (San Francisco: Jossey-Bass, 1994), xv.

21. Isadora R. Hare, "School Social Work in Transition," *Social Work in Education* 16, no. 1 (1994): 64–68.

22. Jean Anyon, *Radical Possibilities: Public Policy, Urban Education, and a New Social Movement* (New York: Routledge, 2005); Jean Anyon and William Julius Wilson, A

Ghetto Schooling: Political Economy of Urban Educational Reform (New York: Teachers College Press, 1997); Laura R. Bronstein and Timothy B. Kelly, "A Multidimensional Approach to Evaluating School-Linked Services: A School of Social Work and County Public School Partnership," *Social Work in Education* 20, no. 3 (1998): 152–164; Rothstein, *Class and Schools*; William Julius Wilson, *The Truly Disadvantaged: The Inner City, the Underclass, and Public Policy* (Chicago: University of Chicago Press, 1990); William Julius Wilson, *When Work Disappears: The World of the New Urban Poor* (New York: Alfred A. Knopf, 1996).

23. Anyon, *Radical Possibilities,* 2.

24. Jane Quinn, *Community Schools: The Intersection of Research and Common Sense,* October 16, 2008, http://www.tcrecord.org/Content.asp?ContentId=15416.

25. Dakarai I. Aarons, "President Envisions Anti-Poverty Efforts Like Harlem's 'Zone,'" *Education Week,* March 11, 2009, 6.

26. Quinn, *Community Schools.*

27. Daniel P. Moynihan, *On Understanding Poverty* (New York: Basic Books, 1969).

28. Pamela Morris, Greg J. Duncan, and Christopher Rodrigues, *Does Money Really Matter? Estimating the Impacts of Family Income on Children's Achievement with Data from Random-Assignment Experiments* (paper, MDRC, February 12, 2004), www.gse.uci.edu/person/duncan_g/docs/1doesmoneymatter.pdf.

29. Wilson, *When Work Disappears.*

30. Paula Allen-Meares, "Social Work Services in Schools: A Look at Yesteryear and the Future," *Social Work in Education* 18, no. 4 (1996): 202–209; Paula Allen-Meares, *Social Work Services in Schools,* 5th ed. (Boston: Allyn & Bacon, 2006); James P. Comer, *School Power: Implications of an Intervention Project* (New York: Free Press, 1980); Janet. E. Levy and William Shepardson, "A Look at Current School-Linked Service Efforts," *Future of Children* 2, no. 1 (1992): 44–55.

31. Quinn, *Community Schools.*

32. Hare, "School Social Work in Transition."

33. Isadora R. Hare, "School-Linked Services," in *Encyclopedia of Social Work,* 19th ed., vol. 3, ed. Richard L. Edwards (Washington, DC: National Association of Social Workers, 1995), 68.

34. Joy Dryfoos, "Full-Service Community Schools: Creating New Institutions," *Phi Delta Kappan* 83, no. 5 (2002): 394.

35. Ibid.

36. The military has success with these same low-achieving students by stressing values such as belonging, teamwork, self-discipline, and structure. See Hugh B. Price, *Demilitarizing What the Pentagon Knows About Developing Young People: A New Paradigm for Educating Students Who Are Struggling in School and in Life* (Washington, DC: Brookings Institution, Center on Children and Families, 2007).

37. Milbrey W. McLaughlin, Merita A. Irby, and Juliet Langman, *Urban Sanctuaries: Neighborhood Organizations in the Lives and Futures of Inner-City Youth* (San Francisco: Jossey Bass, 2001).

38. Dryfoos, "Full-Service Community Schools."

39. Martin J. Blank and Dan Cady, "System Change Through Community Schools," *School Administrator* 61, no. 1 (2004): 27.

40. Hugh B. Price, *Mobilizing the Community to Help Students Succeed* (Alexandria, VA: Association of Supervision and Curriculum Development, 2008).

41. Joy G. Dryfoos, Jane Quinn, and Carol Barkin, *Community Schools in Action: Lessons from a Decade of Practice* (New York: Oxford University Press, 2005).

42. Martin J. Blank, "How Community Schools Make a Difference: Research and Practice in Community Schools," *Educational Leadership* 61, no. 8 (2004): 62–65.

43. McLaughlin, Irby, and Langmann, *Urban Sanctuaries.*

44. Dryfoos, Quinn, and Barkin, *Community Schools in Action.*

45. Terry Saunders Lane, "School-Linked Services in Action: Results of an Implementation Project," *Social Work in Education* 20, no. 1 (1998): 37–47.

46. Michael Kirst, "Supporting School-Linked Children's Services," in *Rethinking School Finance: An Agenda for the 1990s,* ed. Allan Odden (San Francisco: Jossey Bass, 1992), 298–321.

47. Rothstein, *Class and Schools,* 64.

48. Orlando Patterson, "The Last Race Problem," *New York Times,* December 28, 2006.

49. Blank and Cady, "System Change Through Community Schools."

50. Martin J. Blank, Atelia Melaville, and Bela P. Shah, *Making the Difference: Research and Practice in Community Schools* (Washington, DC: Institute for Educational Leadership, Coalition for Community Schools, 2003), www.communityschools.org/CCSFullReport. pdf.

51. Dryfoos, "Full-Service Community Schools."

52. California Educational Supports Project, "Addressing the Need to Improve Academic Achievement Among California Students Through Learning Supports" (unpublished brief, WestEd, University of California, San Francisco, Philip R. Lee Institute for Health Policy Students).

53. http://www.cisnet.org.

54. Preliminary results from an independent third-party evaluation by ICF International, including an in-depth analysis of 1,766 CIS schools and comparative analysis of outcomes for approximately 1,200 CIS (implementing the model with low fidelity) and non-CIS comparative schools.

55. CIS, Inc., *Communities in Schools and the Model of Integrated Student Services: A Proven Solution to America's Drop-Out Epidemic,* 2008, http://www.cisnet.org/about/National-Evaluation/Normal.asp?Segment=2.1.

56. *2006–2007 Results from the CIS Network,* http://www.cisnet.org/media/pubs.asp.

57. Bruce Fuller, *Standardized Childhood: The Political and Cultural Struggle Over Early Education* (Stanford, CA: Stanford University Press, 2007).

Chapter 10: Creating the Political Conditions for Education Finance Policy Change

1. John W. Kingdon, *Agendas, Alternatives, and Public Policies,* 2nd ed. (New York: Harper Collins, 1995).

2. Ibid., 19, 165.

3. Frank R. Baumgartner and Bryan D. Jones, *Agendas and Instability in American Politics* (Chicago: University of Chicago Press, 1993); Baumgartner and Jones, *Policy Dynamics* (Chicago: University of Chicago Press, 2002).

4. Deborah Stone, *Policy Paradox: The Art of Political Decision-Making,* rev. ed. (New York: W.W. Norton, 2002), 138.

5. Baumgartner and Jones, *Agendas and Instability in American Politics,* 237.

6. An alternative conceptualization similar to a policy monopoly is the notion of *policy regime,* which refers to a set of ideas, interests, institutions, and the interactions among them that structures governmental activity in a specific policy domain and that tends to be stable over time. Some analysts have argued that policy regimes are less stable than is implied by the notion of policy monopoly but slower to change than assumed in a theory of punctuated equilibrium. See, for example, Patrick J. McGuinn, *No Child Left Behind and the Transformation of Federal Education Policy, 1965–2005* (Lawrence: University Press of Kansas, 2006). However, this distinction seems more semantic than empirical in that both theories assume interaction among ideas, institutions, and interests; both find

that policy ideas are more likely to persist if they are embedded in institutional arrangements; and even in the case of a punctuated equilibrium, the route to change can occur over several decades as alternative policy images gain currency among interest groups, the media, policy makers, and the general public. Consequently, the terms *policy regime* and *policy monopoly* are used interchangeably in this chapter.

7. Paul Manna, *School's In: Federalism and the National Education Agenda* (Washington, DC: Georgetown University Press, 2006), 5.

8. Ibid., 15.

9. *San Antonio Independent School District v. Rodriguez*, 411 U.S. 1, 1973.

10. David J. Hoff, "The Bottom Line," *Education Week, Quality Counts*, January 5, 2005, 29–36.

11. A *generative concept* can be viewed as a type of policy idea. It not only captures the normative assumptions embodied in a particular policy goal but also synthesizes empirical data so as to identify strategies for achieving the goal and perhaps even to provide criteria for measuring progress toward it. James listed individual differences, differentiated curricula, and fiscal neutrality as examples of generative concepts that have animated major changes in U.S. education. He views them as "implicit normative structures" that help "to organize new policy systems." See Thomas James, "State Authority and the Politics of Educational Change," *Review of Research in Education* 17 (1991): 202.

12. Ibid., 204.

13. Stone, *Policy Paradox*.

14. Lowell C. Rose and Alec M. Gallup, "The 34th Annual Phi Delta Kappa/Gallup Poll of the Public's Attitudes Toward the Public Schools," *Phi Delta Kappan* 84, no. 1 (2002): 44.

15. Douglas S. Reed, *On Equal Terms: The Constitutional Politics of Educational Opportunity* (Princeton, NJ: Princeton University Press, 2001).

16. Melissa C. Carr and Susan H. Fuhrman, "The Politics of School Finance in the 1990s," in *Equity and Adequacy in Education Finance: Issues and Perspectives*, eds. Helen F. Ladd, Rosemary Chalk, and Janet S. Hansen (Washington, DC: National Academy Press, 1999), 136–174.

17. National Research Council, Committee on Appropriate Test Use, *High Stakes: Testing for Tracking, Promotion, and Graduation,* eds. Jay P. Heubert and Robert M. Hauser (Washington, DC: National Academy Press, 1999); Robert L. Linn, Eva L. Baker, and Damian W. Betebenner, "Accountability Systems: Implications of Requirements of the No Child Left Behind Act of 2001," *Educational Researcher* 31, no. 6 (2002): 3–16; Daniel Koretz, "Alignment, High Stakes, and the Inflation of Test Scores," in *Uses and Misuses of Data for Educational Accountability and Improvement,* eds. Joan L. Herman and Edward H. Haertel (Malden, MA: Blackwell, 2005), 99–118.

18. Lorraine M. McDonnell, *Politics, Persuasion, and Educational Testing* (Cambridge, MA: Harvard University Press, 2004).

19. Although the impact of such assessments varies—depending on the type of test, the grade levels being tested, students' socioeconomic status, and the uses to which the tests are put—a growing body of research indicates that school and classroom practices do change in response to these tests. See, for example, David K. Cohen and Heather C. Hill, *Learning Policy* (New Haven, CT: Yale University Press, 2001); William A. Firestone, David Mayrowetz, and Janet Fairman, "Performance-Based Assessment and Instructional Change: The Effects of Testing in Maine and Maryland," *Educational Evaluation and Policy Analysis* 20, no. 2 (1998): 95–113; McDonnell, *Politics, Persuasion, and Educational Testing;* William A. Mehrens, "Consequences of Assessment: What Is the Evidence?" *Education Policy Analysis Archives* 6, no. 13 (1998), http//ericae.net/ericdc/EJ582965.htm; Brian M. Stecher, Sheila Barron, Tessa Kaganoff, and Joy Goodwin, *The Effects of Standards-Based Assessment on Classroom Practices: Results of the 1996–97 RAND*

Survey of Kentucky Teachers of Mathematics and Writing, CSE Technical Report 482 (Los Angeles: University of California, Center for the Study of Evaluation, 1998); Shelby A. Wolf, Hilda Borko, Rebekah L. Elliott, and Monette C. McIver, "That Dog Won't Hunt! Exemplary School Change Efforts Within the Kentucky Reform," *American Educational Research Journal* 37, no. 2 (2000): 349–393. Clearly, the effects of mandated assessments have not always been beneficial for students and not what policy makers intended. Nevertheless, given the limited array of strategies available to them, politicians have viewed standardized testing as too powerful a lever not to use it. From their perspective, assessment policies also produce results quickly because test scores typically rise during the first few years after a new test is introduced. The validity of such gains has long been questioned by researchers; see Daniel M. Koretz, Daniel F. McCaffrey, and Laura S. Hamilton, "Toward a Framework for Validating Gains Under High-Stakes Conditions" (paper presented at the annual meeting of the National Council on Measurement in Education, Seattle, April 11, 2001); Robert L. Linn, "Assessments and Accountability," *Educational Researcher* 29, no. 2 (2000): 4–16. But most policy makers remain convinced that something real occurs, if only because the tests shine a public spotlight on educators, who must then respond.

20. Lynn Olson, "School Accountability Systems Seen As Unlikely to Face Major Overhaul," *Education Week,* January 31, 2007, 11.

21. National Research Council, Committee on Education Finance, *Making Money Matter: Financing America's Schools,* eds. Helen F. Ladd and Janet S. Hansen (Washington, DC: National Academy Press, 1999); Committee for Economic Development, *Investing in Learning: School Funding Policies to Foster High Performance* (Washington, DC: CED, 2004).

22. Part of the time spent challenging an existing policy monopoly is often used by policy entrepreneurs in softening up the agenda. "These entrepreneurs attempt to 'soften up' both policy communities, which tend to be inertia-bound and resistant to major changes, and larger publics, getting them used to new ideas and building acceptance for their proposals. Then when a short-run opportunity to push their proposals comes, the way has been paved, the important people softened up. Without this preliminary work, a proposal sprung even at a propitious time is likely to fall on deaf ears" (Kingdon, *Agendas, Alternatives, and Public Policies,* 128).

23. See, for example, James W. Guthrie and Matthew G. Springer, "Teacher Pay for Performance: Another Fad or a Sound and Lasting Policy?" *Education Week,* April 6, 2006, 42, 52.

24. National Research Council, *Making Money Matter.*

25. Bess Keller, "Denver Voters Pave Way for Incentive Pay," *Education Week,* November 9, 2005, 3, 18.

26. Jessica L. Tonn, "Fla. Districts Seek Teacher Performance Pay Funds," *Education Week,* January 10, 2007, 14, 18.

27. Kingdon, *Agendas, Alternatives, and Public Policies,* 185.

28. Stone, *Policy Paradox,* 133.

29. Stone, *Policy Paradox.*

30. National Commission on Excellence in Education, *A Nation At Risk: The Imperative for Educational Reform* (Washington, DC: U.S. Government Printing Office, 1983).

31. Policy makers, their constituents, and the public more generally have been referred to as a single entity. However, the terms of discourse may need to be unique for each group. One question that policy entrepreneurs must typically consider is who the target of their advocacy is, and at what point they should move their efforts from policy elites to the public and vice versa. The framing of the problem and their preferred solution may need to be different for the two groups, especially if courts, as nonmajoritarian institutions,

are involved. Similarly, policy entrepreneurs must consider the extent to which policy proposals are broadly applicable or must be tailored to particular jurisdictions.

32. Historical institutionalists have borrowed the concept of *increasing returns* from economists as a precise way to examine the extent of path dependence and the possibilities for institutional change. Increasing returns processes pinpoint how the costs of switching from one alternative to another will, in certain social contexts, increase significantly over time. The reasons are varied but include large set-up or fixed costs, learning effects that lead to the continued use of familiar institutional arrangements and processes, and coordination effects, with the benefits to one individual or jurisdiction increasing as others adopt similar policies and procedures. See Paul Pierson, "Increasing Returns, Path Dependence, and the Study of Politics," *American Political Science Review* 94, no. 2 (2000): 251–267.

33. Pierson, ibid.

34. Terry M. Moe, "Political Institutions: The Neglected Side of the Story," *Journal of Law, Economics, and Organization* 6 (1990): 213–254.

35. William N. Evans, Sheila E. Murray, and Robert M. Schwab, "Schoolhouses, Courthouses, and Statehouses After Serrano," *Journal of Policy Analysis and Management* 16, no. 1 (1997): 10–31.

36. Baumgartner and Jones, *Agendas and Instability in American Politics,* 32.

37. Reed, *On Equal Terms,* 128.

38. Ibid., 132.

39. Ibid., 135.

40. As discussed in the preceding section, the single salary schedule is one of the most well institutionalized policies related to school finance.

41. *Education Week, Quality Counts,* January 6, 2005.

42. Lynn Olson, "Financial Evolution," *Education Week, Quality Counts,* January 6, 2005, 8, 14.

43. Carr and Fuhrman, "The Politics of School Finance in the 1990s"; Peter Schrag, *Final Test* (New York: Free Press, 2003).

44. Manna, *School's In.*

45. By the time NCLB was enacted, the overwhelming majority of states had experience with some form of statewide standardized testing of elementary and secondary students. However, only six states used standards-based assessments to test students in all the subjects and grade levels required by NCLB, although twenty were testing students in English language arts and mathematics in grades 3 through 8 and once in grade 10, 11, or 12. See Center for Education Policy, *From the Capital to the Classroom: State and Federal Efforts to Implement the No Child Left Behind Act* (Washington, DC: CEP, 2003). Not only was the expanded scope of standardized testing new to most states with the enactment of NCLB, but also only about half had assessment systems aligned with specific content and performance standards, and about the same number had linked positive or negative incentives to schools' test scores by 2001. See Council of Chief State School Officers, *State Student Assessment Programs: Annual Survey: Summary Report* (Washington, DC: CCSSO, 2001); Frederick M. Hess, "Refining or Retreating: High-Stakes Accountability in the States," in *No Child Left Behind? The Politics and Practice of School Accountability,* eds. Martin R. West and Paul E. Peterson (Washington, DC: Brookings Institution Press, 2003).

46. For a review of these studies, see McDonnell, *Politics, Persuasion, and Educational Testing.*

47. Baumgartner and Jones, *Agendas and Instability in American Politics.*

48. Carr and Fuhrman, "The Politics of School Finance in the 1990s."

49. McDonnell, *Politics, Persuasion, and Educational Testing.*

50. Carr and Fuhrman, "The Politics of School Finance in the 1990s"; Schrag, *Final Test.*

51. A noteworthy coalition is the Delaware Public Education Partnership. It is an organization established by a coalition of groups—including the Delaware Business Roundtable, the Delaware Education Association, the Metropolitan Urban League of Wilmington, the Delaware School Boards Association, and the Delaware Chamber of Commerce—to promote a broad school reform plan. Funding tied to student need, along with teacher salaries based on skill and performance, was part of the coalition's Vision 2015 proposal. See Jeff Archer, "Coalition Calls for Overhaul of Del. Education System," *Education Week*, October 25, 2006, 26; *Vision 2015, Executive Summary,* February 22, 2007, www.vision2015delaware.org.

52. Schrag, *Final Test.*

53. Reed, *On Equal Terms.*

54. Peter D. Hart and Robert M. Teeter, *Equity and Adequacy: Americans Speak on Public School Funding: A National Public Opinion Survey Conducted for the Educational Testing Service,* August 24, 2004, http://www.tc.columbia.edu/Hechinger.

55. Lowell C. Rose and Alec M. Gallup, "The 33rd Annual Phi Delta Kappa/Gallup Poll of the Public's Attitudes Toward the Public Schools," *Phi Delta Kappan* 83, no. 1 (2001): 41–58.

56. Lowell C. Rose and Alec M. Gallup, "The 35th Annual Phi Delta Kappa/Gallup Poll of the Public's Attitudes Toward the Public Schools," *Phi Delta Kappan* 85, no. 1 (2003): 41–56.

57. Hart and Teeter, *Equity and Adequacy: Americans Speak on Public School Funding.*

58. Because the Hart and Teeter survey seems to have used a double-barreled question to measure the state versus local dimension, preferences for one level over another also were tapping attitudes about higher taxes, waste, and local control. A more pointed question about redistribution was asked of California residents by the Public Policy Institute of California (PPIC) in its 2006 survey: "Should schools in lower-income areas get more funding from the state to pay for teachers and classroom materials, even if it means less funding for other schools?" Among all respondents, the division was almost even, with 49 percent saying yes and 44 percent no. But there were significant differences between the two parties, with a majority of Democrats (54 percent) favoring the idea and a majority of Republicans (57 percent) opposing it. Whites were divided, with 45 percent supporting and 49 percent opposing it, whereas in other racial and ethnic groups the majority supported it. See Public Policy Institute of California, *PPIC Statewide Survey: Special Survey on Education,* January 16, 2007, www.ppic.org/content/pubs/survey/s_406mbs.pdf.

59. For a review, see Lorraine M. McDonnell, "Assessment and Accountability from the Policymaker's Perspective," in *Uses and Misuses of Data for Educational Accountability and Improvement,* The 104th Yearbook of the National Society for the Study of Education, Part 2, eds. Joan L. Herman and Edward H. Haertel (Malden, MA: Blackwell Publishing, 2005), 35–54.

60. Lowell C. Rose and Alec M. Gallup, "The 38th Annual Phi Delta Kappa/Gallup Poll of the Public's Attitudes Toward the Public Schools," *Phi Delta Kappan* 88, no. 1 (2006): 41–53.

61. Ibid.

62. Jennifer Hochschild and Bridgett Scott, "Trends: Governance and Reform of Public Education in the United States," *Public Opinion Quarterly* 62, no. 1 (1998): 79–120.

63. Lowell Rose and Alec M. Gallup, "The 37th Annual Phi Delta Kappa/Gallup Poll of the Public's Attitudes Toward the Public Schools," *Phi Delta Kappan* 87, no. 1 (2005): 41–63.

64. Rose and Gallup, "The 38th Annual Phi Delta Kappa/Gallup Poll of the Public's Attitudes Toward the Public Schools."

65. Just as the allocation rules for school funding would be critical to these groups' decision to support a new strategy, so would the details of how performance would be measured and the information used, because groups have split on these issues. For example, some civil rights organizations, such as the National Association for the Advancement of Colored People (NAACP) and the Mexican American Legal Defense and Educational Fund, have strongly opposed the high-stakes use of standardized tests, especially when they are the sole criterion for making decisions about students' promotion and graduation. In contrast, the Education Trust, an organization that promotes high standards for disadvantaged students, supports increased testing as part of a strategy to close the achievement gap between affluent and low-income students and between white students and students of color. See McDonnell, "Assessment and Accountability from the Policymaker's Perspective." For the Education Trust and similar groups, the required reporting of subgroup test scores under NCLB has been a major point of leverage to make the education system more responsive to the needs of the groups' constituents.

66. McDonnell, *Politics, Persuasion, and Educational Testing.*

67. *Rose v. Council for Better Education, Inc.,* 790 S.W.2d 186 (Ky. 1989).

68. *Rose* at 212.

69. Ibid.

70. McDonnell, *Politics, Persuasion, and Educational Testing,* 53.

71. However, on one important dimension Kentucky differed from other states facing court-ordered finance reform. Kentucky's demographics removed racial politics from the agenda, whereas in other states it became a major factor. As Carr and Fuhrman, "The Politics of School Finance in the 1990s," indicated, the politics of race have significantly affected finance reform in Alabama, New Jersey, and Texas, because in each state the benefits were perceived as accruing mostly or even exclusively to racial minorities, and the white majority opposed tax increases or the redistribution of resources. In contrast, because racial minorities are a smaller proportion of the population in Kentucky and are concentrated in wealthier districts, racial politics were not salient.

72. Michael Paris, "Legal Mobilization and the Politics of Reform: Lessons from School Finance Litigation in Kentucky, 1984–1995," *Law and Social Inquiry* 26, no. 3 (2001): 631–684.

73. For example, in his analysis of KERA's enactment, Paris, "Legal Mobilization and the Politics of Reform," cited state poll data from 1989 in which 67 percent of those surveyed said they would be willing "to pay higher taxes if they were convinced the money would be used to improve schools." In addition, the period between mid-1989 and mid-1990 is the only time in recent history when Kentucky poll respondents ranked education above unemployment, jobs, and the economy as the most serious problem facing the state (fn. 44).

74. This sense among legislative leaders that KERA was their creation became especially important to its survival when the testing provisions came under attack several years later. One of the elected officials most involved in KERA's passage noted that the development process "gave members of the legislature pride of ownership" and motivated them to defend it even at considerable political cost. See McDonnell, *Politics, Persuasion, and Educational Testing,* 90.

75. Reed, *On Equal Terms.*

76. Ibid., 669.

77. Paris, "Legal Mobilization and the Politics of Reform"; Reed, *On Equal Terms.*

78. Kingdon, *Agendas, Alternatives, and Public Policies;* Fred M. Wirt and Michael W Kirst, *The Political Dynamics of American Education,* 3rd ed. (Richmond, CA: McCutchan, 2005).

79. Michael Mintrom, "Policy Entrepreneurs and the Diffusion of Innovation," *American Journal of Political Science* 41, no. 3 (1997): 738–770.

80. Michael Mintrom and Sandra Vergari, "Policy Networks and Innovation Diffusion: The Case of State Education Reforms," *Journal of Politics* 60, no. 1 (1998): 126–148.

81. Michael Mintrom, *Policy Entrepreneurs and School Choice* (Washington, DC: Georgetown University Press, 2000.)

82. Ibid., 271.

83. Ibid., 272.

84. Paris made a similar point about the Prichard Committee and the KERA reforms: "When Prichard Committee members did the hard work of organizing town forums, developing a network of supporters in local school districts across the state, and arriving at their reform program through long hours of study and debate, they made their vision more real by practicing precisely what they were preaching about 'education'" ("Legal Mobilization and the Politics of Reform," 673).

85. Mintrom, *Policy Entrepreneurs and School Choice*, 275.

86. Ibid.

Chapter 11: Choosing the Smart-Money Path to Education Finance Innovation

1. *Apollo 13*, VHS, directed by Ron Howard (1995; Universal City, CA: Universal Home Video, 1997).

2. See, for example, Alan Shepherd and Deke Slayton with Jay Barbree and Howard Benedict, *Moon Shot: The Inside Story of America's Race to the Moon* (Atlanta: Turner Publishing, Inc., 1994).

3. All three quotations in this section are taken from John F. Kennedy, "We Choose to Go to the Moon" (speech, Rice University, Houston, Texas, September 12, 1962), http://www.historyplace.com/speeches/jfk-space.htm.

4. *No Child Left Behind Act of 2001*, Public Law 107-110, 115 Stat. 1425, January 8, 2002.

5. On politics and policy making as the "authoritative allocation of values," see David Easton, *The Political System: An Inquiry into the State of Political Science* (New York: Alfred A. Knopf, 1953).

6. For a fuller discussion of this policy history, see Jacob E. Adams, Jr., "Ambitious Learning Goals Require a New Approach to Educational Resources," this volume.

7. These recommendations and those in the next paragraph are discussed in ibid. and developed by the National Working Group on Funding Student Learning. See National Working Group on Funding Student Learning, *Funding Student Learning: How to Align Education Resources with Student Learning Goals* (Seattle: University of Washington, Center on Reinventing Public Education, School Finance Redesign Project, 2008), www.crpe.org/cs/crpe/view/csr_pubs/247.

8. Adams, "Ambitious Learning Goals Require a New Approach to Educational Resources," provides a full discussion of these recommendations for elected officials and educators.

9. Richard F. Elmore and Milbrey Wallin McLaughlin, *Steady Work: Policy, Practice, and the Reform of American Education* (Santa Monica, CA: The RAND Corporation, 1988).

10. Michael G. Fullan with Suzanne Stiegelbauer, *The New Meaning of Educational Change*, 2nd ed. (New York: Teachers College Press, 1991).

11. On the role of individual-level motivation and capacity in implementation, see Milbrey W. McLaughlin, "The Rand Change Agent Study Revisited: Macro Perspectives and Micro Realities," *Educational Researcher* 19, no. 9 (1990): 11–16.

12. The following discussion of the perspectives of legislators and school district leaders is based on focus groups conducted in winter and spring 2009 by Claremont Graduate University (Jacob E. Adams, Jr., principal investigator) with the cooperation of the National Conference of State Legislators (Julie Bell) and Arizona Business and Educa-

tion Coalition (Susan Carlson), and with support from The Spencer Foundation, Grant No. 200900171. Legislative participants included current and former state legislators and legislative staff from Arkansas, California, Colorado, Georgia, Hawaii, Minnesota, North Carolina, Ohio, Pennsylvania, and Texas. They included Democrats and Republicans, senators, and house or assembly members. Administrative participants included superintendents, associate superintendents, budget directors, and a superintendent's chief aide who oversees district innovation efforts. These education leaders represented school districts in Arizona, California, Kentucky, Illinois, Maryland, and Washington.

13. For a discussion of these issues, see Christopher T. Cross and Marguerite Roza, "How Federal Categorical Funding Prevents the Effective Use of Resources," and Julia E. Koppich, "Allocating Resources Through Traditional Versus Reform-Oriented Collective Bargaining Agreements," both in this volume.

14. Michael Lipsky, *Street-Level Bureaucracy: Dilemmas of the Individual in Public Services* (New York: Russell Sage Foundation, 1980).

15. On a teacher's transformation from policy disregard to careful use, see Holly Holland, "A Teacher's Viewpoint," in Roger S. Pankratz and Joseph M. Petrosko, eds., *All Students Can Learn: Lessons from the Kentucky Reform Experience* (San Francisco: Jossey-Bass, 2000), 195–199.

16. Kentucky Institute for Education Research, "All Children Can Learn," VHS, produced by Diana J. Taylor (Lexington, KY: Moran Video Production, 2000). See the comments particularly of Helen Mountjoy, chair, state board of education, and veteran teacher Linda Edin. Mountjoy's problem with the word *reform* was that it made teachers feel as if their hard work before had been wasted.

17. McLaughlin, "The Rand Change Agent Study Revisited."

18. David A. Goslin, *Engaging Minds: Motivation and Learning in America's Schools* (Lanham, MD: Scarecrow Press, 2003); National Research Council, Committee on Increasing High School Students' Engagement and Motivation to Learn, *Engaging Schools: Fostering High School Students' Motivation to Learn* (Washington, DC: National Academies Press, 2004).

19. National Research Council, Committee on a Feasibility Study for a Strategic Education Research Program, *Improving Student Learning: A Strategic Plan for Education Research and Its Utilization* (Washington, DC: National Academies Press, 1999).

20. These contexts compose Goslin's conceptual framework. See Goslin, *Engaging Minds*.

21. Diana Sharp and John Bransford, *Learning Science Meets School Finance: The How People Learn Framework as a Tool for Resource Decisions* (Seattle: University of Washington, Center on Reinventing Public Education, School Finance Redesign Project, 2007).

22. Lorraine McDonnell, "Creating the Political Conditions for Change in Education Finance Policy," this volume. On the concept of policy windows, see John W. Kingdon, *Agendas, Alternatives, and Public Policies* (Boston: Little, Brown & Company, 1984).

23. "Quality Counts 2001, A Better Balance: Standards, Tests, and the Tools to Succeed," *Education Week,* January 11, 2001; *Elementary and Secondary Education Act of 1965,* Public Law 89-10, 79 Stat. 27, April 11, 1965, the latest iteration being NCLB.

24. See, for example, National Center on Education and the Economy, *Tough Choices or Tough Times: The Report of the New Commission on the Skills of the American Workforce* (San Francisco: Jossey-Bass, 2007).

25. Educational Testing Service, *Equity and Adequacy: Americans Speak on Public School Funding,* public opinion research conducted by Peter D. Hart and Robert M. Teeter (Princeton, NJ: ETS, 2004).

26. National Commission on Excellence in Education, *A Nation At Risk: The Imperative for Educational Reform* (Washington, DC: U.S. Government Printing Office, 1983). See the

introduction in this volume for further analysis of education policy changes during the 1980–2010 period.

27. http://www.ed.gov/programs/racetothetop/index.html.
28. http://www.publicagenda.org/citizen/issueguides/education/overview.
29. On system disturbances, see David Easton, *A Systems Analysis of Political Life* (New York: John Wiley & Sons, Inc., 1965).
30. Kingdon, *Agendas, Alternatives, and Public Policies.*
31. See chapter 4 in this volume and the Data Quality Campaign, at http://www.dataquality-tycampaign.org.
32. Kennedy, "We Choose to Go to the Moon."
33. National Commission on Excellence in Education, *A Nation At Risk,* iii.

About the Editor

Jacob E. Adams, Jr. is professor of education at Claremont Graduate University. His work focuses on the policy context of K–12 education, with particular attention to ways in which governance and finance policies and implementation practices influence school capacity. He directed the School Finance Redesign Project, examining how K–12 finance can be redesigned to better support student performance, and he chaired the National Working Group on Funding Student Learning. Prior to his academic career, Adams served in government positions at federal, state, and local levels, including the campaign and administrative staffs of California's former state superintendent, Bill Honig. He received his PhD in education from Stanford University.

About the Contributors

Christopher T. Cross is chairman of Cross & Joftus, LLC, an education consulting firm. From 1994 to 2002 he served as president and chief executive officer of the Council for Basic Education (CBE). Before joining CBE, Cross served as director of the Education Initiative of The Business Roundtable and as assistant secretary for educational research and improvement for the U.S. Department of Education. From 1994 to 1997, he served as president of the Maryland State Board of Education. He is the author of *Political Education: National Policy Comes of Age* (Teachers College Press, 2003). Cross holds a master's degree in government from California State University, Los Angeles.

Michael E. Goetz is assistant professor of educational leadership at the University of Cincinnati. Previously he worked with the Consortium for Policy Research in Education (CPRE). Before joining CPRE, Goetz managed K–8 educational centers for Score Learning, Inc., in New York and taught middle school math and science in Kansas City. He has worked on school finance adequacy studies in Arizona, Arkansas, North Dakota, Washington, Wisconsin, and Wyoming, and recently won the American Education Finance Association New Scholar Award. He is completing his PhD in educational leadership and policy analysis at the University of Wisconsin, Madison.

James W. Guthrie is the Patricia and Rodes Hart Professor of Educational Leadership and Policy and director of the Peabody Center for Education Policy at Vanderbilt University. Guthrie is founder and chairman of the board of Management Analysis and Planning, Inc. (MAP), a private sector management consulting firm specializing in public finance, organizational studies, and litigation support. He is the author or coauthor of fourteen books and more than two hundred professional and scholarly articles. He is a past president of the American Education Finance Association and former vice president of the American Education Research Association. He also served as editor-in-chief of the *Encyclopedia of American Education* (Macmillan Reference, 2003). Guthrie is principal investigator for the National Center on Performance Incentives at Vanderbilt University. Previously a professor at the University of California, Berkeley, for twenty-seven years, he holds a PhD in education from Stanford University.

Paul T. Hill is the John and Marguerite Corbally Professor at the University of Washington, Bothell, and director of the Center on Reinventing Public Education. He is a non-resident senior fellow at both the Brookings Institute and Hoover Institution, and directed the National Working Commission on Choice in K–12 Education. Dr. Hill chairs the National Charter School Research Project and leads its Charter School Achievement Consensus Panel. His current work focuses on school choice, finance, accountability, and charter schools. His books include *Charter Schools Against the Odds* (Hoover Institution Press, 2006) and *Fixing Urban Schools* (Brookings Institution Press, 1998, with Mary Beth Celio). He was the lead author (with Lawrence Pierce and James Guthrie) of *Reinventing Public Education: How Contracting Can Transform America's Schools* (University of Chicago Press, 1997). Hill holds a PhD in political science from The Ohio State University.

Michael W. Kirst is professor emeritus of education and business administration at Stanford University. Before joining the Stanford faculty, Kirst held positions with the federal government, including staff director of the U.S. Senate Subcommittee on Manpower, Employment and Poverty, and director of program planning for Elementary and Secondary Education in the U.S. Office of Education. He is a former president of the California State Board of Education. He is the author of *The Political Dynamics of American Education,* 4th edition, (McCutchan, 2009, with Fred Wirt) and *From High School to College* (Jossey Bass, 2004, with Andrea Venezia). Kirst received his PhD in political economy and government from Harvard University.

Julia E. Koppich is president of Koppich & Associates, an education consulting firm. Her areas of specialization include education policy and public sector labor relations. She has served as a consultant to the U.S. Department of Education, National Commission on Teaching and America's Future, National Governors' Association, National Board for Professional Teaching Standards, National Alliance of Business, American Federation of Teachers, and the National Education Association. She is the author of *A Union of Professionals* (Jossey Bass, 1993, with Charles Kerchner) and *United Mind Workers: Unions and Teaching in the Knowledge Society* (Jossey Bass, 1997, with Charles Kerchner and Joseph Weeres). Koppich currently provides technical assistance for the federal Teacher Incentive Fund and is a senior researcher on the national Strategic Management of Human Capital Project. She holds a PhD in educational policy analysis from the University of California, Berkeley.

Lorraine M. McDonnell is professor of political science at the University of California, Santa Barbara. Prior to coming to UCSB, she was a senior political scientist at RAND. Her research has focused on the design and implementation of K–12 education policies and their effects on school practice. In recent studies, she examined the politics of student testing, particularly the curricular and political values underlying state assessment policies. Her publications have focused on various aspects of education politics and policy, including teacher unions, the education of immigrant students, and the role of citizen deliberation. She served for seven years on the National Research Council's Board on Testing and Assessment, and is currently a member of the NRC's advisory committee for the Division of Behavioral and Social Sciences and

Education. She was the 2008–2009 president of the American Educational Research Association and is a member of the National Academy of Education.

Karen Hawley Miles is executive director and founder of Education Resource Strategies, a nonprofit organization in Boston, Massachusetts, that helps urban school leaders use resources strategically to improve student learning. Dr. Miles has worked intensively with urban districts to improve their funding systems, including Atlanta, Boston, Charlotte, Los Angeles, Chicago, Baltimore, New York, Providence, Rochester, and Cincinnati. She is the author of *The Strategic School: Making the Most of People, Time and Money* (Corwin Press, 2009, with Stephen Frank). Prior to her work at ERS, she worked at Bain & Company as a strategy and management consultant for hospitals and corporations. She holds a PhD in education from Harvard University.

David H. Monk is professor of educational administration and dean of the College of Education at The Pennsylvania State University. Prior to becoming dean, he was a member of the Cornell University faculty for twenty years and also served as a third grade teacher. Monk is the author of *Educational Finance: An Economic Approach* (McGraw-Hill, 1990), in addition to numerous articles in scholarly journals. He was the inaugural co-editor of *Education Finance and Policy*, The Journal of the American Education Finance Association (MIT Press) and serves on the editorial boards of that journal and the *Journal of Education Finance*, *Educational Policy*, and the *Journal of Research in Rural Education*. He is a past president of the American Education Finance Association and holds a PhD from the University of Chicago.

Allan R. Odden is co-director of Strategic Management of Human Capital (SMHC), a project of the Consortium for Policy Research in Education (CPRE). The mission of SMHC is to improve student achievement and reduce achievement gaps by getting more powerful instructional practices into all classrooms through reform and restructuring of state and district human resource management systems. He also is professor of educational leadership and policy analysis at the University of Wisconsin, Madison, and codirector of the Consortium for Policy Research in Education (CPRE). His most recent book is *Doubling Student Performance . . . and Finding the Resources to Do It* (Corwin Press, 2009, with Sarah Archibald). He was professor of education policy and administration at the University of Southern California (1984-1993) and past president of the American Education Finance Association. Odden earned his PhD at Columbia University.

Lawrence O. Picus is professor of education at the University of Southern California. His current research interests focus on adequacy and equity in school finance as well as efficiency and productivity in the provision of educational programs for PreK–12 school children. His most recent book is *School Finance: A Policy Perspective,* 4th edition (McGraw Hill, 2008, with Allan Odden). Picus has consulted extensively on school finance issues in more than twenty states and conducted adequacy studies in Arkansas, Arizona, Kentucky, Wyoming, Wisconsin, North Dakota, and Washington. He is past president of the American Education Finance Association and holds a PhD from the RAND Graduate School.

Lori Rhodes is a doctoral student in the history of education program at Stanford University. Before beginning her studies at Stanford, Ms. Rhodes taught elementary school for nine years, primarily in bilingual classrooms in Los Angeles.

Marguerite Roza is research associate professor at the University of Washington's College of Education. Her research focuses on quantitative policy analysis, particularly in the area of education finance. Her recent research has investigated spending patterns among schools within urban districts and the relationship to state and federal education spending. Ongoing studies involve investigations of spending policies amidst the recession and in conjunction with recent federal stimulus funds. This work has appeared in *Phi Delta Kappan, Brookings Papers on Education Policy 2004*, the *Peabody Journal of Education, Education Next,* and NCES's *Developments in Education Finance.* Roza earned a PhD in education from the University of Washington. Prior to her academic career, she served as a lieutenant in the U.S. Navy, teaching thermodynamics at the Naval Nuclear Power School.

Joanne Weiss is senior advisor to the United States secretary of education and director of the Race to the Top Fund, leading the $4.35 billion flagship program designed to encourage and reward states that are making serious and comprehensive education reforms. Prior to joining the department, she was partner and chief operating officer at NewSchools Venture Fund, a venture philanthropy firm working to transform public education by supporting education entrepreneurs and connecting their work to systemic change. Weiss spent the prior twenty years in senior leadership roles at organizations that designed, developed, and marketed technology-based education products and services in K–12, higher education, and adult basic education. She holds a degree in biochemistry from Princeton University.

Index